Julian Roberts was educated at Cambridge. He has taught in London and Cambridge, and is now Deutsche Forschungsgemeinschaft Research Fellow in Philosophy at the University of Bayreuth. He has published *Walter Benjamin* (1982) and *German Philosophy. An Introduction* (1988).

The Logic of Reflection

The Logic of Reflection

GERMAN PHILOSOPHY IN THE
TWENTIETH CENTURY

Julian Roberts

Yale University Press
New Haven and London · 1992

Set in Garamond by SX Composing Limited, Essex
Printed and bound in Great Britain by St Edmundsbury Press

Library of Congress Cataloging-in-Publication Data

Roberts, Julian, 1950–
    The logic of reflection : German philosophy in the twentieth
century / by Julian Roberts.
        p.   cm.
    Includes bibliographical references and index.
    ISBN 0–300–05207–3 (alk. paper)
    1. Philosophy, German—20th century.   I. Title.
B3181.R63   1992
193—dc20   91–41729
                                                      CIP

A catalogue record for this book is available from the British Library.

Contents

boundaries 10. A space bounded from within 11. Reflexivity
12. Finitism 13. Cardinality 14. Induction; infinity 15.
Systems and language games 16. Rules 17. Irreflexivity of
systems 18. Translatability, theory, grounding 19.
Contradiction 20. Wittgenstein and Gödel 21. Logic and
ethics 22. 'Im Anfang war die Tat'

4. Subjectivity and 'Life-world': Husserl   155
1. Introduction 2. Biographical and preliminary 3.
Psychologism 4. Infinite regress 5. Circularity 6. Insight and
eidos 7. Communication and 'meaning' 8. The 'proper
kingdom' of logic 9. Experience and essence 10. Epoché 11.
'Acts' and the given 12. Real time 13. Truth and foundedness
14. Logical objects 15. Apophansis 16. Picture, name 17.
Semantic rules 18. Objects 19. Modification and reflection
20. Leibniz 21. Monadology 22. The elementary disjunction
of form and content 23. Immanence 24. Truly existent
objects 25. Perception 26. Orders of compossibility; the
horizon 27. Positionality 28. History 29. Induction 30.
Self-pondering 31. Subjectivity 32. 'Life-world' 33. Science –
the questionable tradition 34. Lost foundations

**5. Dialogue and History: Jürgen Habermas and the
Erlangen School**   218
1. Introduction 2. Positivism and Utopia 3. Circularity 4.
The Vienna Circle 5. Reflection 6. History 7. Normativity
8. Macro-subjects 9. *Ideologiekritik* 10. Quasi-
transcendentalism 11. Axiom and construction 12.
Intuitionism 13. Mathematics and pre-scientific practice 14.
Logic of dialogue 15. Formalist and naturalist foundations 16.
Rationalisation 17. Life-world 18. Reflection and language
19. Symmetry 20. Pathology and colonisation 21. History and
the metaphysics of unconstraint

6. Conclusion   281
1. The Good, the true and the beautiful 2. Reflection: the
pattern of argument 3. Reflection and its implications: *Logic:
beyond monologue; Ethics: beyond atomism; Aesthetics: beyond
beauty*

Bibliography   290

Index   300

Preface

... for the eye sees not itself
but by reflection, by some other things.

Julius Caesar I, ii

Can knowledge 'see', or have knowledge of, itself? Any such knowledge would certainly seem to be different from knowledge of 'other things'; and, centrally, it provokes questions about the bearer of knowledge – the 'subject'.

In structure, this book is a critical interpretation of major German-speaking philosophers of the last hundred years. The historical character of such an approach probably needs less justifying to 'continental' philosophers than it does to their 'analytical' colleagues – to judge, at all events, by the methodological speculations that preface a number of recent British commentaries. My own view, however, is that much analytical philosophy adopts a misconceived image of philosophical argument, believing it to be able to proceed, if necessary, in a solipsistic vacuum. On the analogy of the natural sciences, such an approach purports to *discover* the truth from a fixed universe of what is the case, and imagines that this discovery can as well be performed by one person as by many. Truth, in such a view, is truth whoever knows it, and even if nobody knows it: 'The truth of a sentence does not lie in its being thought,' as Frege put it in one of his ripostes to 'psychologism'. From this perspective, of course, commentary on particular œuvres does look like no more than a diversion into biography.

The contrary position, which is associated with the constructivism I have described below, is dialogical. The fundamental 'other' is not the fixity of an outside world waiting to be discovered; it is the dissentive complexity of *other knowledges* and, indeed, 'subjects'. To that extent Frege was wrong, and psychologism was right: philosophers as much as lay people inhabit a world constituted in interaction, where *all* truths emerge in a historical practice of dialogue and debate. In that respect, commentary is not merely interesting or educative, for it alone can lay bare the adversarial texture of the known. By that token, indeed, it has claims to be the instrument of philosophical enquiry *tout court*. The better image for philosophical enquiry is not discovery, but *forensic proof*.

This book could not have been written without a fellowship from the Alexander von Humboldt foundation. The help of colleagues at the University of Bayreuth was essential, especially those in the philosophy department – Ulli Metschl, Herbert Scheit, and Willi Vossenkuhl – whose expertise covers the topics of this book. Willi Vossenkuhl, in particular, was an unfailing source of inspiration, guidance and support. Charles Lewis yet again provided indispensable suggestions and criticisms, as did James Bradley, Andrew Bowie, Peter Dews, Raymond Geuss, Chris Lawn, and Michael Rosen, not to mention my students at the universities of Bayreuth and Cambridge, and at the Architectural Association School of Architecture. Throughout it all, the urbane efficiency of my publisher Robert Baldock greatly eased the discomforts of gestation.

Bayreuth, December 1991

Introduction

1. Critical transcendentalism

Metaphysics is the branch of philosophy concerned with what is self-evident, or, at least, with what is held to be the case but is incapable of further demonstration. Those who are hostile to metaphysics would probably take the view that if anything falls into this category, then infinitely many things do; the opposite point of view contends that not very much is self-evident, which make it important to decide what is. The first group could be described as *sceptical*; their opponents as *critical*.

The greatest critical programme in recent Western philosophy was Kantian transcendentalism, which (in its classic form) sought to derive the few inescapable conditions for truth, goodness and beauty. In the twentieth century, this programme has met with increasing hostility. Indeed, it was precisely the success of the critical project, in formal logic, that provoked disillusion and resistance. In Frege's attempt to out-transcendentalise Kant, success in critical technique (reduction of mathematics to bare formal elements) was countered by a dramatic collapse of the programme for a critical ontology (Russell's paradox). The apparent disparity between mathematical logic's dazzling achievements on the one hand and its failure to say anything significant, or indeed anything at all, about more intuitive philosophical concerns, has encouraged scepticism even among logicians.

This scepticism, however, has been more characteristic of philosophy in the Anglo-American realm and in France than it has of German thinking. Thinkers in Germany and Austria, where indeed modern mathematical logic largely originated (together with the Vienna Circle's highly influential nominalism), have remained far more optimistic about the chances for a generalised critical project. The most prominent *anti*-transcendentalist in Germany was, of course, Heidegger. But Heidegger is not particularly representative. In particular, a rigorous transcendentalism which embraces the challenge of mathematical logic has also produced crucial work. Husserl was the progenitor of this tradition (though 'phenomenology' as such was a failure, as we shall see); and its contemporary representatives are to be found, for example, in the so-called Erlangen school. Habermas, though better known than they, is in fact one of their major beneficiaries.

The central arguments of transcendentalism are, first, that we only make sense of the 'object' world on the assumption that our dealings with it are conditioned by something *non*-objectual. The 'non-objectual' can be regarded in various ways – as context, as modality, as spatio-temporality, for example. Since Kant, the term most commonly used to describe it has been *subject* (though this should not be understood as 'person' or 'natural individual'). Recovery of this 'subject' is achieved by what the same tradition terms *reflection*.

Critical transcendentalism's second basic argument is that 'reflection' on the 'subject' does not displace the logic of the object world: on the contrary, it extends it and, indeed, explains how it is possible. Irrationalistic interpretations of reflection (such as, notably, Heidegger's) depict a logicality lost in a cosmos governed by 'fate' and similar categories. Within the critical tradition, however, the 'understanding' of the object world is embedded within the wider realm of 'reason' (to use Kant's terms). That is why we can legitimately speak of a *logic of reflection*.

This book reconstructs the project of critical transcendentalism.

2. 'Continental' and 'analytical' philosophy, and history

A book with 'German philosophy' in the title is apt (in Britain, at least) to fall between two warring factions – the 'continental' camp, following Derrida, Heidegger, and others; and the 'analytical' camp who swear by Ayer and Ryle. Both, in different ways, proclaim the 'end of metaphysics'; and neither would have much sympathy for the sort of project attempted here.

In these terms, the dispute will not be a theme here (the extremer aspects of this doctrinaire entrenchment seem anyway to be confined to Britain). There is, however, one issue of substance that has emerged on the periphery of the stand-off between 'continentals' and 'analyticals', namely the question of the relationship between *systematic* philosophy and philosophy's *history*. In the past, it has been an article of faith among analytical philosophers that the history of philosophy is not philosophy. Most negatively, it is dismissed as merely ornamental 'history of ideas'. A little less drastically, it is regarded as something useful for beginners – an educative demonstration of what the past got wrong. But there is no real notion, in the analytical tradition, that the study of philosophy's history can be any more than propaedeutic.

On the continental side, notoriously, Hegel stands for the contention that the history of philosophy *is* systematic philosophy. This is what is popularly supposed (among analytical philosophers) to be the import of *Geist* and Hegel's disreputable metaphysics.

Such an opposition caricatures the issues. Encouragingly, however, recent discussion of the question has become increasingly fruitful, and the analytical tradition has started to make *itself* the object of historical enquiry.[1] This book, in any event, proceeds on the premise that there is no absolute distinction for philosophy as an activity, between the systematic and the historical. Grounds for affirming this will emerge in what follows, especially in the latter part of chapter one, and in chapter five.

Meanwhile, looking back on the exegetical part of my labours, I can only endorse Hegel's comment in the foreword to the *Phenomenology*:

> When one is faced with any substantial and well-wrought argument, the easiest thing is to *judge* it; more difficult is to *grasp* it; and the most difficult thing, which unites the first two, is to *produce an account of it.*

3. Scheme of contents

The book consists of five chapters. The first chapter is a reconstruction of transcendentalism, with reference also to contemporary American thinkers. Implicitly, the chapter echoes in modern terms the progress of classical transcendentalism from Leibniz to Hegel. The stages of the argument are (I believe) the same; it is mainly the vocabulary, and, of course, the degree of sophistication in mathematical logic that are different. (The classical argument is set out in the first three chapters of my *German Philosophy*.)

The titles of the remaining four chapters mention names of German-speaking thinkers. The selection is governed by the intention of the book as outlined above, and as expanded in chapter 1. That should explain why, for example, no chapter title mentions Heidegger (though I have used his work on the orientation problem in chapter 1). Similar considerations apply to my omission of names like Lukács, Adorno, Benjamin, and the neo-

---

1 See, most recently, Peter Hylton's book on Russell (1990), which has a long introduction on this question (though it is still oddly uncritical about the anathematisation of Hegel). The wider debate has, of course, been going on for some time in North America and at the margins of British philosophy departments. See, for example, Rorty, Schneewind & Skinner, 1984; the debate between Skinner and his critics in Tully & Skinner, 1988; and, for influential earlier work, Dunn, 1968. Rosen, 1990 has discussed the issue in terms close to many of the concerns of this book.

Kantians. For these writers, I have frequently referred to material already published elsewhere.

Chapters two to five can, to a degree, stand as independent exegesis and commentary on the philosophers named.

Formulaically, I would summarise their argument as follows. I have represented Frege as, from a Kantian perspective, a resolute anti-intuitionist comparable with Leibniz. At the same time, it is his apparent success in deriving mathematics from logic that sets *the* philosophical challenge for the twentieth century.

In the chapter that discusses Wittgenstein, I have argued that the *Tractatus* is the model for 'exorcising the subject', as this also came to dominate the post-Vienna Circle understanding of *practice*. Wittgenstein is (in my terms) a nominalist; and his later work shows the nominalist disappointment characteristic of metaphysics since Carnap (especially Quine or Davidson).

Husserl represents another side to the developments discussed in chapters two and three; but his early attempt to rationalise time and space is comparable, as I have argued in chapter four, with what Kant called Leibniz's 'intellectualising of appearances', and has the same weaknesses. The later Husserl (the Husserl of the 'life-world') overcompensated by lapsing into what is an almost relativist position, at least as it stands.

The most interesting continuation of the Husserlian project appears in the constructivism of the Erlangen school, and in Habermas's appropriation of related themes. The fifth chapter pursues attempts to rescue transcendentalist aspects of the Husserlian project, and also seeks to vindicate (against Habermas) the thought that although there may be aspects of human practice that are 'unprethinkable', intersubjectivity is, in the end, a rational tribunal.

Whereas Frege believed that particularity is bounded by reason, successors of Husserl have explored the notion that reason might be bounded by the particularity of historical human practice. Is this 'life-world' rationally recoverable? Is reason in history still reason? The Conclusion reiterates the view that it is, and, moreover, that previously marginalised areas of philosophy such as aesthetics hold the key to its investigation.

1

Reflection: The Subjective Conditions of Understanding

1. Introduction

A human being, we might say, is an animal that can know its own limitations. This is an asset: only those who know what they cannot do discover the conditions of what they can do. Limitations are deceptive things, however, and it is easy to imagine that by knowing them one has somehow crossed them. The result is bad metaphysics. Good metaphysics, we shall argue, consists of 'reflection', which might be described as observing limits, but dynamically.

In this chapter we will reconstruct the basic steps of an effective metaphysical position. It consists, roughly, of two parts: a 'negative' part, which shows (by examples from the philosophy of time and space, and from the antinomies of reasoning) the limits of conceptuality; and a 'positive' part, which argues that, in view of these limits, knowledge can only be accounted for as the *historical interaction of knowing subjects*. The discussion is a reconstructive anticipation of what I take to be the underlying discussion in German metaphysics during the last hundred years.

2. Transcendental reflection

'Reflection' is a term much used in current philosophical debate, and it is beset by vagueness. Our sense is Kant's: reflection is the act by which we discover the 'subjective conditions under which we arrive at concepts' (B 316).

'Reflection', under this definition, does *not* mean any of the following.

a. It does not mean, as in colloquial speech, to 'think hard about something'.

b. Although reflection (at least in this definition of Kant's) is directed towards something he terms 'subjective', it does not mean introspection, or being aware of one's empirical self ('subject'). I may be hot, happy, or puzzled; but such knowledge of my own state, or indeed of my own 'existence', does not constitute reflection for our purposes. Nor does perception of the operations of my mind, in a Lockean manner.[1] Reflection is not directed towards natural individuals.

c. It does not mean physical reflection (as in mirrors), nor any connotation derived from that.[2] The concept is puzzling, but it is not inherently paradoxical, and any association of reflection with, say, the infinite image you get by placing two mirrors opposite one another, or (more technologically) the feedback from a video camera filming its own monitor, is entertaining but misleading. In particular, the logical questions arising from self-reference are not usefully approached with this imagery.[3]

The basic distinction envisaged by Kant's definition is this. 'Concepts' are part of the 'objective' world, as distinct facts of some kind. The question is, though: where does this objectivity come from? Concepts are systematic and holistic. They lend themselves to calculation and, to a degree, a priori determination. Reality, on the other hand, is obviously only calculable to a limited extent. It is unpredictable: the 'future' is not part of our conceptual scheme. And it is displayed in a rather untidy way: space is not particularly logical.

We could say (and common sense possibly would) that our inadequate grasp of 'objectivity' results from the restricted capacity of our brains. The reason why we don't know things is that there are too many things out there for us to know all at once.

Or we could look at it another way. We could say that we only know, 'objectively', what we have worked our way through (by means of concepts and whatever else is in our cognitive equipment). We have applied ourselves to something, and there it is – as 'knowledge'. Clearly such activity will never exhaust the possibilities of knowing more. So in that sense there are always other things to know. But those 'things' are possibly better not thought of as out there, ready and waiting, but rather as some more or less undetermined future state of our own minds. We cannot predict it from within the conceptual scheme we have already (although that scheme arguably does contain within itself all sorts of *implicitly* 'known' things). It is, in that respect, and to that extent, entirely contingent and unformed.

1 See Reuter, 1989, 28ff on this.
2 Cf. Gasché, 1986. Also Hofstadter, 1979, for a popular application.
3 Self-reference, which assumed major prominence because of Russell's paradox, is only one aspect of the problem of *totality*. In any case, as Barwise and Etchemendy (1987) have shown, using the work of Peter Aczel, set-theoretic self-membership is not inherently paradoxical: the standard axiom system for set theory can be consistently altered to permit it.

And that contingency, unformedness, is what Kant means here by 'subjective'. It is, so to speak, where conceptualisable objectivity emerges from. It is the dark container of the future, the untidy display of space. It is limitless possibility, the raw material of the world we actually come to know. It precedes determination, and is in that sense 'free' (necessity is only attributable to things already bound within a determinate scheme).[4]

This dichotomy – between our conceptually constructed, already elaborated world ('objectivity'), and the contingency from which concepts extract it ('subjectivity') – underlies Kant's definition of reflection. In a sense, to reflect is to describe what is not, and to that degree it is metaphysical. But refusing to accommodate what is not describable (or 'provable') can lead to worse metaphysical confusion. In another sense, the notion of subjectivity associated with reflection, because of the dimension of 'indetermination', invites the importation of 'free' natural individuals. But this should be resisted: at the level of reflection, interpolating 'individuals' is no more justified than the opposition of freedom and necessity. All these concepts have first to be 'reconstructed'; the subjectivity of reflection is something purely formal, in the first instance.

At the same time, this 'formality' is not to be understood as itself conceptual or systemic. It is, as Kant indicates, a condition of conceptuality, not itself an element in it. This is what distinguishes reflection of this kind – let us call it *transcendental* reflection – from the introspective reflection of a Lockean variety. In Leibnizian terms, 'reflexive acts', by means of which we come to notions like 'me' or 'substance', are distinct from the 'principles of reasoning' (which are, for Leibniz, non-contradiction and sufficient reason; VI, 601, 612). In Kant, where these distinctions are thrown into sharper focus, we read, for example, that space is a 'condition' but is not a 'discursive' or 'general' concept (B 39).

This distinction between the conditions of a conceptual system and its principles is illustrated by two areas of discussion: computability and truth predicates. Computability is a concern of artificial intelligence. If we can show, as we can, that there are certain things machines will *never* be able to compute, then what kind of rationality is it that manages to 'know' those things? More precisely, there are situations in which a computer cannot reach a decision, either because it cannot settle for one of two equally compelling alternatives, or because it carries on 'thinking' indefinitely. In either case, the machine slides into an infinite computation, and thus becomes incapable of producing a result either on the current question or on any

4 'Subjective' has not always had its current rather trite meaning of 'pertaining to the individual ego'. See Heidegger's discussion of hypokeimenon (cf. *Introduction* pp. 260-1). For the scholastics, 'subject' meant, in particular, what was subject to change, and thus susceptive of contraries (see McKeon, 1930, vol. 2, 499).

other.[5] Even if you programmed the machine to stop itself after a certain amount of apparently fruitless calculation, so that it said to itself 'I'm going to abandon this line', you could still, in principle at least, get situations where the computer went into an infinite calculation over whether to apply its stopping routine. For a human being, though, these are unreal problems. The decision to stop a line of thought by settling on some answer anyway, or to move sideways, is always available. But what is the *rationality*, if any, of such decisions?

Another way of illustrating the problem is in terms of truth. This is rather like the child's game of 'who says?' Anything I say can be challenged by the question 'who says?' I 'win' as long as I can think of authorities for whatever it was I last said. But as soon as I am reduced to answering, '*I* say', I have lost, because that is a mere affirmation by me and not an authoritative ground.[6] Truth can only be expressed by recourse to 'meta-languages' (a higher calculus) outside the language of whatever is to be true. In Tarski's example, we need a formulation along the lines of ' "snow is white" is true if and only if snow is white', where the initial sentence is embedded in some meta-sentence, and where the grammar of the two is essentially different. (A more obvious way of illustrating this would be to express it as ' "Schnee ist weiß" is true if and only if snow is white'.) But the difficulty is that I either, as with 'who says?', end up with some sort of subjective affirmation ('because I can *see* it's white!'), or I carry on infinitely with ever new meta-languages to justify my last sentence. The former is the problem of any axiomatic method; the latter is the problem of infinite regress.

There seems, in other words, always to be a point where the buck stops. For all its sophistication, regular computation in the prescribed channels has limits. We can see those limits; the machine (or the immediate calculus) cannot. The limits (for example, points where we take a decision which is purely 'arbitrary' in terms of the calculation, or where we move into another calculus to talk *about* the one we started in) are, for a machine, confusing, if not fatal. For us, though, they are part of the natural world of reasoning. The two questions this raises are 1) can problems of 'computability' be solved by, for example, teaching 'machines' to reason more 'naturally' (or, equivalently, by devising less restrictive calculi)? And 2) if there really is an absolute limit on calculability (i.e. computation within *any* pre-set framework, however flexible), then what is the status of the decisions with which human beings implement their own calculations? Are they also 'rational', and, if so, in what sense?

---

5 The classic text is Boolos & Jeffrey, 1980 (now, as of 1990, in its third edition).
6 Am *I* allowed to 'say' of my *own* statements that they are true, in the 'who says?' game? Can a calculus for producing theorems contain its own truth-predicate? See Metschl, 1989a.

'Reflection', then, is the concern with what lies outside the regular (and, in principle, mechanically reproducible) use of reasoning. To set the question up a little more precisely, we shall look at three classic instances of 'reflection' in our sense: orientation, the transcendental subject, and self-reference. After that we shall reconstruct the main elements of what we could call a 'post-Kantian' rationality.

3. Orientation

Orientation concerns itself with spatial questions like 'direction' (right and left, up and down). By analogy, and with particular emphasis on the phenomenological work of thinkers like Heidegger, it is extended to problems of time. Space and time, Kant's 'forms of appearance' (B 34), are the most accessible area for 'reflection', and we shall therefore spend longest with them.

Traditionally, ontology deals with the *identity* of things. What makes a thing what it is and not something else? In particular, what makes something remain the same *across time*? For example, in what sense is an acorn 'the same' as the oak tree that grows from it? Am I 'the same person' as I was when I was five years old, or twelve weeks after conception? Am I 'the same' waking and sleeping, or healthy and in an incurable coma? I may be the same body, but am I the same 'person'?

There are, perhaps, two initial ways of approaching this question. The first says that there are basic subsistent identities of some kind, and that the conditions in which they find themselves at any particular moment are secondary to that basic identity. For example, we intuitively 'know' that people have identities; they bear proper names, and those proper names reliably and consistently identify their bearers through time, regardless of the contingencies of life. Analogously, 'things' bear names, and are also in some regard subsistent. In more technical terminology, this view argues for the existence of simple *substances*, and regards their situation at any given moment as *accidental*.[7]

The second view is more sceptical about the existence, or subsistence, of substances, and would argue that the being of any one thing is primarily determined by its position in the current order of the world. For example, we are interested more in the fully grown oak tree and its current market value than we are in the entirely abstract 'oakness' of an acorn. Or: we are more interested in saving a kidney patient for his family and colleagues

7 David Lewis (1973) distinguishes between *essence* and accident (p. 40); and this terminology is accepted by those who speculate about 'essentialism'. The problem is that 'essence' is useful as a pair to 'existence'; 'substance' is the more normal pair to 'accident'.

than we are in preserving the merely physical integrity of an incurably comatose potential donor. The 'identity', here, is given by actual context, not by underlying substance. The difference between a present actual identity and an abstract or merely possible one is, in this sense, more important than the 'substantial' identity between one basic thing and another.

Identity is a problem, it seems, because of time and space.[8] The obvious problem is time, as emerges from our examples. This arises not only in connection with topics like personal identity, but also in connection with questions like causation. Is there really a 'law' that leads from a cause to its 'effect', or is it simply chance, a merely apparent regularity?

Why are time and space a problem? One way of putting it might be as follows. 'Identification' seems to require a calculus of differentiation. For our usual conceptual processes to work, we must be able to say of things whether they do or do not have some property. For example, this is a book, it is not a cauliflower, it has a white cover, it is not by Kant, and so on. For each property I ask a question, 'is it such-and-such?', and I have a definite answer – yes or no. What is more, so long as the book exists at all, the answers to the questions are probably the same. I can, so to speak, write them down and carry them around with me without them losing their truth.

As soon as we introduce a temporal dimension into this, things start to be more complicated. What if I say, the book is 'new'? This would seem to be a conceptually satisfactory property to attribute to anything. But what about the 'writing down' test? If I attribute newness to the book I bought last week, what will the status of this attribution be in five years' time, when it is dog-eared and losing its pages?

Some properties, it seems, are sensitive to context. If I take the slice of time in which I first describe the book, it is 'new'. At a later slice of time, it is no longer new. At either slice, there is a context; and some of the book's properties – here, those relating to temporal matters – are only to be found within that particular context-slice.

This seems to suggest that in any situation beyond the most simple – in any situation involving 'reality', time and space, and so on – we need to take account of two levels of ordering: a simple calculus of properties, and an ordering of contexts.

This does not by any means throw us into uncertainty. The obvious intuitive way of dealing with the problem is to say that time contexts *are* ordered in a rationally recoverable way. Put simply, we can say that there is a good reason for everything being the way it is at a particular moment of time. The book is where it is because someone put it there; and it is no

8 The 'problem of trans-world identity' is, as Lewis puts it, something that afflicts only entities that have 'location in time and space' (*Counterfactuals*, 39).

longer new because it was subjected to a long series of events at the end of which it was dog-eared, and the date on the calendar was five years on. In Leibnizian terms, the book bears its properties at any given moment under guidance from the law of non-contradiction (it must not be *both* new and not new); and it acquires its attributes at distinct segments of time according to the principle of sufficient reason (it is thus and not otherwise because of some determinate cause).

With this account we may, if we wish, remain. It is true that notions of causation can be attacked (as they are, notably, in the Humean tradition). Certainly the regularity of causation seems to attribute things to 'reality' that are much less evident than a simple calculus of properties outside time. But it makes intuitive sense; and it is difficult to imagine how one could act intelligently in daily life without relying on causal regularities.

There is a lingering feeling, however, that such an acquiescence fails to investigate fundamental questions. Is the 'principle of sufficient reason' the same sort of thing, logically, as the law of non-contradiction? If not, why not?

4. Counterparts

We can approach this from a slightly different angle. The principle of sufficient reason, in whatever form, sounds like an extension of logic's aprioristic claims – arguably, to an uncomfortable degree. The law of non-contradiction seems to be absolute and inescapable; is the same to be true of causation?

Now, we can follow current usage and call particular contexts 'worlds'. An instantaneous time-slice, for example, is a 'world'. Within any world, the law of non-contradiction reigns supreme. The relations *between* worlds – say, between the world in which my book is new, and the world in which it is old and dog-eared – are governed (perhaps) by rules like the principle of sufficient reason. We shall suspend, for the moment, questions about the 'identity' between the book earlier and later (at world one and at world two), and shall call the two entities 'counterparts' of each other. It may be that we shall conclude that the new book and the old book are the same thing, identical in all but their accidents; but for the time being we shall just regard them as 'counterparts' – very similar but not necessarily identical.

Now, is there a 'logical' rule that justifies our calling the book in world one *the same as* the book in world two? That depends on our attitude to things like the principle of sufficient reason. If we were Leibniz, and felt that, for example, 'the present is pregnant with the future' in some strongly determinate, predictable way, then we might regard such an identity as supported by a 'logic' of some kind. If we were Hume, on the other hand, we might accept the identity as a pragmatic thing, but deny the aprioristic connotations of 'logic'.

In the end, though, it is hard to say what the difference between the two positions would be. Is the identity 'logical', or is it some looser pragmatic thing? It does not perhaps matter very much; it still seems to be an identity. So: from a purely intuitive point of view, counterparts across temporally distinct worlds are not very easy to differentiate with precision.

There is, however, a way of presenting counterparts which makes their difference more intuitive. That is to look at them separated by *spatial* worlds. This is what Kant used in his argument against Leibniz, and against what he regarded as his predecessor's excessive 'intellectualisation' of the universe (B 331).

Counterparts, in this argument, are to be understood as entities that are conceptually identical but situated in separate worlds. 'Conceptually identical', in Kant's argument, means indistinguishable according to Leibniz's law of the identity of indiscernibles.[9] Kant's reproach is that Leibniz thinks all things can be distinguished conceptually or 'internally', i.e. in terms of an abstract predicative calculus appropriate to pure operations of the understanding (cf. B 330). Illustrative evidence for Kant's understanding of Leibniz would be supplied by Leibniz's conjecture that, for example, any two leaves can always be distinguished 'internally', by means of their distinct properties of shape, colour, structure or whatever. Merely being in different places, which would be an 'external' difference, is ultimately always a redundant means of differentiation. In our terminology, then, and according to Kant's reproach, Leibniz would say that there never *are* counterparts distinguished only by world (or context); if that was indeed the only 'difference', then they would be identical.

Kant thinks, however, that he *can* produce counterparts that are conceptually identical but obviously, intuitively, distinct. He has various examples for this. They are all spatial, and are often termed 'incongruent' counterparts.[10] The most familiar one is that of the gloves. Consider a pair of gloves, identical in size, shape, material and in every respect except for the fact that one is made for a left hand, the other for a right hand. In describing these gloves – their weight, their dimensions, the angles that describe their three-dimensionality – we will use exactly the same prop-

---

9 'His principle of indiscernibility, which is only valid for concepts of things in general' (B328).
10 Strictly, what Kant is talking about is not *incongruent* counterparts, but counterparts that are congruent but differently oriented. See B320; *Prolegomena* §13; *Metaphysische Anfangsgründe der Naturwissenschaft*. For the term, see Walker, 1978.

erties for the one as for the other. There is only one difference, and for that (despite its very evident consequences) we have to look quite hard. It is here (very informally): if we describe the gloves according to three axes perpendicular to one another, then the only difference between the gloves will be that the values will run in different directions on the third axis. Once we have three dimensions – space – it makes an immediate intuitive difference whether our third axis goes into the paper, so to speak, or comes out of it. And *that*, at least in this understanding of incongruence, is something not definable 'conceptually', but only by some additional means.[11]

More precisely, we can say this. The general category is orientation. Generally speaking, geometrical entities can be oriented. A straight line can be given an orientation (the 'direction' it runs in); a surface can be oriented (its right- or left-handedness about some straight line: i.e. whether the surfaces to the left or the right of the line are to be deemed 'positive'); and, as we saw, so can a three-dimensional space. The point about all these orientations is, first, that they are *arbitrary* (which direction or handedness we decide on is, so to speak, up to us, and is not some intrinsic quality of the geometrical entity itself); and second, that this arbitrariness is the contribution of some kind of *observer* (orientational determinations such as direction or handedness quite literally 'depend on where I'm standing').[12]

Given congruence between figures, orientational diversity can (in conceptual principle) be overcome by regular manipulations of one kind or another. There is nothing intrinsically difficult, for example, about adjusting a right-handed space to fit a left-handed one. A graphics program on a computer will execute this operation with ease. But that, in a sense, is the whole point. The conceptual differences are so small, but the intuitive ones are fundamental: in actuality, a right glove cannot be 'converted' for a left hand.

5. Subjectivity

The phenomenon of orientation seems to offer a more direct route into diversities of 'world' and counterpart than do questions about time. Causation and the persistence of identity appear relatively straightforward to intuition, though the conceptual difficulties they raise may be puzzling. With orientation, on the other hand, there emerges a directly recognisable division between concept and intuition: each is quite unproblematic in its own terms, but they seem distinct from each other in what they do, though at

11 Kant's examples rely on right- and left-handedness in the description of spirals, or geographical orientation. But the principle is the same.
12 See Reinhardt & Soeder, 131, 147.

the same time entirely dependent on each other.

This division of labour, between the intuitive and the conceptual, is fundamental for various modern approaches to rationality. The most important discussion of this, from which others derive more or less directly, is Kant's. Kant starts from the assertion that there are two pernicious strands in philosophy: *dogmatism* and *superstition*.[13] Dogmatism, roughly, is the belief that the understanding can deal with supersensory things as well as it can with the objects of sense and experience. Kant associates it especially with Spinoza, though in terms of his wider argument the relation with Leibniz is more important (143). Superstition is 'the complete submission of reason to facts' (145). Both aberrations lead to *enthusiasm* (Schwärmerei), i.e. the making of extravagant, untestable and authoritarian claims about religious matters. In both cases, the philosophical error is fundamentally the same, namely, the failure to delimit correctly the limits of conceptuality (143n).

In Kant's view, orientation was a useful way of underlining the limits of the understanding.[14] His interpretation of orientation was that (a) it showed that intuition contained something 'that is not contained in the mere concept of a thing in general' (B 340); and (b) that orientation required 'the feeling of a difference in my own *subject*, namely that of the right and left hand' (134).

Kant inferred from this that conceptuality was limited by intuition; and that this limitation took the form of a *necessary involvement of the subject in any dealings with reality*. 'Objectivity', here, is what is dealt with by the understanding by means of knowledge; subjectivity is the precondition of any application of understanding to reality. This subjectivity was not non-rational; its sphere was determined precisely by the boundaries of conceptuality. Within that, it was entirely determinate (and thus not exposed to dangers of 'enthusiasm'). 'Orienting oneself in thought thus, in general, means that because of the inadequacy of the objective principles of reason one makes a determination according to a subjective principle of reason.' (136n)

This viewpoint has the following correlatives. First, the role of 'subjectivity' is exactly circumscribed by the inadequacies of the understanding, and only in terms of such precisely determined inadequacy does it have its own legitimation. In Kantian terms, the faculty proper to subjectivity is *feeling*. But, in the topology of the mind (B 324f), the 'space' for feeling is

---

13 I am here following 'Was heißt: sich im Denken orientieren?' (VIII 131-147). Page references to this text unless otherwise specified.
14 In 'Was heißt', Kant refers to the boundaries of reason (Vernunft). In the *Critique of Pure Reason*, however, Kant speaks specifically of 'die Grenzen des Verstandes', i.e. of understanding, and this is probably a better indication of his argument (B336).

determined by understanding, which itself operates through the faculty of knowledge (Wissen). So the feeling of subjectivity arises with the understanding's insight into its inadequacy ('Reason does not feel; it has insight into its own inadequacy and effects, through the drive for knowledge, a feeling of need', 139n). Feeling can only enter legitimately into the proceedings when the inadequacies of knowledge have been 'fully conceded' (140).

This determinate feeling is characterised by Kant as *reasonable belief* (Vernunftglaube). Reasonable belief defers unreservedly to reason as the arbiter of *truth*; but at the same time it is a necessary means of 'orientation' (in Kant's generalisation of the term) within the topology of the mind. In that respect, it has the same dignity as knowledge.

> Now, all belief is a determination [Fürwahrhalten] which is subjectively adequate, but *consciously* inadequate in an objective sense [mit Bewußtsein unzureichend]; in that respect it is counterposed to knowledge. (141)

The regularities of reasonable belief are expressed in terms of *maxims*. Maxims are rules which are self-imposed, and in that sense 'subjective', but imposed with a view to a *general* interest, and in that sense 'objective'. This is a mechanism familiar from the operations of practical reason, and the formulation 'I ought never to act except in such a way that I can also will that my maxim should become a universal law' (cf. *German Philosophy* 54). This same 'will for universality' applies also to the more purely intellectual topics explored in the orientation essay. The self-imposed maxim is formulated here as the demand 'always to think for oneself'; and what this means, at least in Kant's exposition, is that one should always ask oneself

> whether it could be appropriate to make the reason or rule for one's inferences into a general principle of one's use of reason (146n).

The point is, with the intellectual universe as with the moral one, that rationality *requires* a reconstitution of objectivity *by means of* 'subjectivity'. The human world is something made by human beings, not something found inert and neutral in a given universe. The discovery of that rational self-making is the aim of Kant's delimitation of the field of mere knowledge, and of his context-setting within a project of maxim-guided subjectivity.[15]

6. Time

The 'orientational' problems of *time* have been attended to more closely in the twentieth century, particularly by Heidegger. Heidegger's discussion,

15 See *German Philosophy* 54ff for a discussion of this in the specifically moral realm.

in part, takes the form of a critique of the view that what happens in time is a depiction of eternity.[16] In eternity, of course, nothing 'happens' – it is always already there, in glorious simultaneity. History, in this view, is merely the debased form in which eternal truths reach this mortal world. We cannot have insight all at once, otherwise there would be no difference between us and the angels. So we get it in instalments, as educative revelations.[17] But such 'history' is essentially imperfect; the temporal element in it reflects only our own inadequacy. Ideally, we would want to read the book itself, not the comic-strip version vouchsafed in 'history'.

This is the easiest way of looking at history, and it is very widespread. It is particularly attractive to those who believe in nineteenth-century paradigms of natural science – science 'discovers' things. Science is in a state of ignorance with respect to those things still awaiting discovery, and its whole concern should be to overcome this ignorance. Any attention paid to its 'history' – times when it was even more lamentably ignorant than now – is an embarrassment only justified, if at all, by the educational needs of the young.

From this point of view, history of any kind, and certainly that of philosophy, is difficult to justify. It may be a heuristic exercise for those who still need such things. In general, however, those with the ability to do so should be expanding the frontiers of knowledge, moving ever closer to the millennium where all will be revealed. As far as 'philosophy' is concerned, then, logic should be given pride of place, since logic may help us build better computers and make 'scientific discoveries'.[18]

In Heidegger's view, Hegel was guilty of precisely the 'flattening' (Nivellierung) of history represented by the project of Eternity. One does not have to read Heidegger's commentary to know that there is some intuitive justification for this. Hegel's well-known contention that 'Spirit realises itself in History' offers summary evidence for Heidegger's reproach. In this account, time does indeed appear to be no more than a receptacle for the altogether superior verities of Geist; and it is difficult to see why historical change as such, rather than its end-product, should be of any interest. Heidegger's account here is not adequate: Hegel's view of truth situates it in process, not in result.[19] But his own viewpoint is

16 'Abbild der Ewigkeit' – Heidegger on the Timaeus (SuZ, 423. In what follows, I am drawing mainly on Being and Time §§78-83. Page references are to this text.
17 E.g. Lessing, Die Erziehung des Menschengeschlechts. Lessing's overall position is not, of course, exhausted by this rather abrupt interpretation.
18 The fact that the founders of modern mathematical logic were all mathematicians, not philosophers, and the fact that computer scientists seem to be able to do their job without assistance from philosophers is, for this view, best passed over in silence!
19 The view that history merely fills up time with the 'results' (discoveries?) achieved by Spirit is arguably, in Hegel's terms, 'dogmatism'. 'Dogmatism . . . is the view that truth consists in a sentence that is a firm result or that is immediately known' (Phänomenologie, 41).

important.

Heidegger argues, roughly, that the 'eternity' view of history rests on an unacknowledged, and illegitimate, interpretation of the nature of time. For 'history' to work in the way contended for, time has to be considered as an infinite subset of space. It is, in that view, a set of points where events may situate themselves. These points, Heidegger suggests, would have to be considered as in some way subsistent in themselves. Or, they would be true values for x in the statement, 'x is a time-point'. Furthermore, these time-points would form a well-ordered and infinitely countable set.[20] Any sub-set of the set of time-points has a first member ('from this point on, etc.'). But it need have no last member, and the set generally need have no first member either. So time, while well ordered, is held to *be*, ontologically, infinite.[21]

Given this, Heidegger indicates, history could indeed be conceived as a mapping of 'discoveries' against the succession of time-points. Perhaps the discoveries would one day be exhausted; but more probably not, in which case the infinite sequence of nows will continue, infinitely, to situate them.

7. Datability

But, in Heidegger's view, this account of time is clearly absurd. In the first place time, like space, cannot be a subject of predication. There is no domain of true values for x in 'x is time'. The fundamental character of time is *orientation*; and orientation eludes the procedures of predication.[22] In time, orientation consists of *datability* (§79). Datability is the capacity to identify relations of 'earlier' and 'later'. It corresponds, in Heidegger's exposition, to orientations such as right and left. Just as there is no 'set' of 'lefts', or 'left-handedness', so too there is no 'set' of 'earliers'.

There may, of course, be earlier and later events, just as there are right-handed and left-handed spirals. One sunrise, for example, may be earlier or later than another (412). And it is this possibility – the possibility of asso-

---

20 Clock time, according to Heidegger, gives us a 'present to hand set of nows' (eine vorhandene Jetztmannigfaltigkeit) (*SuZ*, 417). The sequence of nows, furthermore, is 'continuous and without gaps' (*SuZ*, 423).

21 *SuZ*, 424. Heidegger is arguing, like Hilbert ('On the Infinite'), and also indeed like the constructivists, that the infinite is a construction of thought, and need not be attributed to reality. It is not entirely clear why the 'vulgar' interpretation of time should depend so strongly on a claim that time is infinite; but, as we shall see, Heidegger's own case *does* depend on showing that time is finite.

22 *SuZ*, 108. Heidegger's discussion is, loosely, a commentary on Kant, especially on the orientation arguments of 'Was heißt: sich im Denken orientieren?' (see above), and on the related passage in *Metaphysische Anfangsgründe der Naturwissenschaft* where Kant claims, notoriously, that orientation shows space to be 'merely subjective', and not a property of 'Things in Themselves' (*Gesammelte Schriften IV* 484).

ciating something essentially non-predicable with something that is predicable, and oriented – that makes possible conventional chronological
time. Time, which is orientable, but not identifiable (predicable) may be
envisaged by associating it with something identifiable. The essentially
changeable is brought into speech by associating it with something unchangeable, or recurrent. The sunrise, for example, is *the same thing, again*.
But, equally, it is oriented in time; each one is later or earlier than the
others; and as a result of this orientation we become aware of time.

This recurrence of the same yields something constant; and that constancy forms the basis for *measure* (417). The measure displayed on a
measuring rod is the same for all measuring rods. Its utility lies in the constancy that recurs in all rods. The constant recurrence of the 'same' sunrise
can perform a measuring function for time. It is not, of course, the same
sunrise, any more than the various measuring rods are the same. But the
degree of sameness that it does have allows us to pin down the changeabil-
ity of time; and thus we obtain a view of something evanescent through the
lens of something fixed.

Now the problem with this, in Heidegger's account, is that we can be
misled by our ability to apply measurement to time. In fact, Heidegger
argues, time *precedes* any of the things that happen 'in' it. It is, indeed, a
'possibility condition' for the emergence of a world at all (419). Without
orientation, there would be nothing to orient.

For Heidegger, what one might call the cosmogonic event is not an
(Aristotelian) coition of form and matter, but an *ecstasy*. Ecstasy is intended to be understood with all its connotations of pre-cognitive knowledge. It is a coming-about which *dispenses* with the understanding.[23] It
does, however, come equipped with time and space; and that is reflected in
the inescapably orientational character of everything, and in the fact that
this orientation is not reducible to the mechanisms of the understanding.
'Datability,' says Heidegger, 'is the reflection (Widerschein) of the ecstatic
constitution of temporality' (408).

Because of this, the precedence of temporality is absolute, and any view
of it in terms of sets of objects identifiable to the understanding (sunrises,
stages of a clock mechanism) is inevitably derivative. By such means, we reduce time to one of the things it makes possible; but we do not understand
time itself.

---

23 This raises more issues than I can deal with here. Very formulaically, though: for Heidegger, experience is not necessarily synthetic. It happens already within the purely aesthetic
realm of time and space. This basic metaphysical move reflects Heidegger's existentialism:
'there is always something, before we reach cognisable essences'. See my chapter on Schelling
in *German Philosophy*.

8. Significance and the 'moment'

Time, then, is not an aspect of the understanding. It comes earlier; it is associated with the first stirrings of Being. How, if not cognitively, do we apprehend these stirrings?

Heidegger again uses the notion of ecstasy and an associated complex of metaphors to explore this. Ecstasy means 'standing-out', or 'going out of oneself'. The ecstatic creates intelligibility not in speech and the regular processes of the understanding, but in spontaneous shapes and movements such as *dance*. Such creations are homogeneous, in some sense, and at the same time pure significant surface.[24] Ecstasy then, like, say, dance, is significant though non-cognitive, and it expresses itself in pure orientation. Dance is not communicative, nor ratiocinative, nor even expressive 'of' anything: it simply 'stands out' in irreducible significance.

Datability, for Heidegger, is the 'vocabulary', so to speak, of ecstasy in time (spatial orientation would be its vocabulary in space). But this vocabulary is, of course, non-conceptual; and in order for Being to 'be' prior to conceptuality it needs more than these quite abstract orientational phenomena. In particular, it needs significance (Bedeutsamkeit). And this significance arises in one of Heidegger's axiomatic notions, that of *whole* (Ganzheit).[25]

The whole structures pre-conceptual Being. It is, to continue that comparison, what makes the dance a dance, rather than merely a set of disjointed locations. Any particular existence, for Heidegger, is structured teleologically. It has a purpose. This is not mechanical purposiveness, directed towards some external end, but the purely internal purposiveness familiar, for example, from Kant's aesthetics. Heidegger characterises it as a structure of 'wherefore' ('Wozu'), but, more generally, as one of 'appropriateness' (Geeignetheit – 414). Significance arises in the arrangement of an existence towards some purpose appropriate to itself. Existence attends to, concerns itself with ('besorgt') its surroundings; and these surroundings then form a teleologically structured whole around it.

This ecstatic stretching-out in time and space, which I have compared with the dance, is the original entry of Being. To the extent that we understand our existence at all, that is what we understand. And, indeed, it is something we 'always already' (i.e. before we set to work on it conceptually) understand. 'Verstehen', which is part of the complex of

---

24 On these ideas see also Nietzsche, Rilke, Deleuze. More in my *German Philosophy*.
25 Heidegger's term 'Ganzheit' does not play a part in his discussion of the 'vulgar conception of time'. The argument, however, is congruent with those passages where he does use this term, e.g. §§46-53. In general, Heidegger associates 'besorgen' with the notion of a teleologically structured whole (see *SuZ*, 68).

'ecstasy' terms, indicates the immediacy of the passage from originatory 'standing-out' to interpretative 'under-standing'.

Now, the notion of time as a depiction of eternity lacks both these crucial ingredients – datability and significance (422). The more fundamental of these two is significance. Significance (Bedeutsamkeit) is what is 'besorgt'; it is what gives Dasein its wholeness, stretched out between the two bounds of decision (Entschlossenheit) and death. Within that extension, datability provides the orientation, and indeed the constant reminder that each existence only 'is' with respect to the two bounds before and after. The crucial terminus is death, the future. Existence towards the finitude of death constitutes wholeness, authenticity, and so on.

In other words, datability is, so to speak, a *memento mori*. In the inescapability of earlier and later lies also the inescapability of finitude. Each 'now' lives only from its embeddedness in a bounded whole.

Eternity's conversion of time into infinite measurability, on the other hand, eradicates this reference to boundedness. In eternity's view, time is a sequence of countable now-points. It is the recurrence of the same 'now here', 'now here' of the sunrise, or of the clock hand in a particular point, as Heidegger puts it (421).[26] That recurrence, though, is countably infinite. And it displaces any possible reference to what Heidegger calls the 'horizon' within which world, significance, or datability make themselves accessible (423).

'Now-time' then, the obsession with measure that underlies the 'vulgar interpretation of time', loses touch with the dimensions of datability, the 'earlier' and 'later', and thereby also loses touch even with what it imagines to be the present. The authentic present, according to Heidegger, is not the 'now', but the *moment* (338).

The moment is quite different from the 'now'. While the now serves as a measured location *within* a ready-established view of time as recurrent sameness, the moment surges outwards to the bounds of existence. In particular, it turns its face to the future (338).[27] The now measures the astronomic infinity of the cosmos; but the moment is *cosmogonic*.

---

26 Heidegger understands measurement also as an attempt to reduce time to space (418). He is thinking, *inter alia*, of Aristotle's account of time in terms of movement – measurable change of place. I am unsure how conclusive this is, given that space, in Heidegger's argument, is *also* orientational and pre-conceptual, and therefore cannot readily supply a 'bridge' into the conceptual world of measurable constancy.

27 The moment, Kierkegaard said, is the obverse of eternity. His terminology differs from that of Heidegger, but the argument is the same. The moment, as generally in the philosophical tradition since the *Parmenides* 156d (the *exaiphnes*), is the window of escape from the continuum. Heidegger's 'Now-time' is continuum time; the moment is its destruction in favour of an ecstatic boundedness. But this is an old theme. See my *German Philosophy*, passim.

9. History and repetition

Heidegger's vision of the moment ruptures the notion of a continuous history, 'internal to time' (426). Now-time sees time as an infinitely extended and regular container within which events order themselves. From that perspective, past and future are simply other locations in temporal space. Orientation – datability – gives way to measure and to tense, which counts the intervals between particular points in the temporal continuum (for example, by the historical chronologies of the *calendar* – 418). In vulgar history, the 'now' arrogantly measures the distance of other points in time from itself; in Leibniz's phrase, it 'goes pregnant with the not-yet-now'. In authentic history, by contrast, the present springs from the *future*, in the moment's ecstatic embrace of the whole (see 427).

For Heidegger, vulgar history is associated with the dealings of the 'public' world. For the idealists, the public was a court of appeal; the learned world, or the world of rationally acting ends-in-themselves, were communities into which the individual aspired to be accepted.[28] For Heidegger, however, this is a world of 'distance, mediocrity, levelling' (127); far from being an 'ascent' into 'concrete life', as Hegel might have contended, the individual's entry into this sphere constituted a 'fall' (178).

The public, with its measured levelling of all distances, seeks to create an infinite life for itself. Time becomes endless, and so does the '*man*' in its fantasy identity as a 'public'.[29] Now-time, public time, is a 'looking away from' the end of existence, i.e. from death. The '*man*' cannot die; and, as such, the '*man*' is irredeemably inauthentic. Everyone dies alone. But that is an existentially *positive* thing: death is the inalienable property of the individual as individual. To lose one's 'decisiveness to death' is to lose one's individuality. '"*Man*" never dies, because it *cannot* die, insofar as death is only every mine. . .' (424)

In Heidegger's account, 'authentic' history is not continuation, as it would be *sub specie aeternitatis*, but *repetition* ('Wiederholung', as opposed to 'Wiederkehr', recurrence). Authentic existence does not find a stretch of vacant now-points that it somehow has to fill up; it throws forth (entwirft) a life, entire in the moment of decision. That life emerges in the orientation of time; time is subordinate to the *Entwurf*. In searching for a life to 'throw forth', existence does not insert itself meekly into the dull progression of absolute time. Nor does it contribute to the meagre accumulations of the '*Man*'. Instead, it resumes the unfulfilled possibilities of the past. Living your life is, or should be, a heroic vindication of what

28 See *German Philosophy*, chapter 1, for a discussion of Kant's attitudes towards the public.
29 I.e. German '*man*' – the impersonal pronoun, translated as 'one', or, often, 'they'.

might have been.

> The authentic repetition of some past possibility of existence – that Dasein should choose its own hero – is founded existentially in forward-running decisiveness; for only at that point occurs the choice that frees for a heritage of struggle and for faith in the repeatable. (385)

10. Orientation and rationality

Heidegger is undoubtedly right in his attack on any notion that history fills up time from eternity. Eternity is empty; there is no book of nature waiting to be read.

However, Heidegger's apparent fear of the natural sciences, and his attempts to relativise them in terms of some 'fundamental ontology', are relics of bygone debates. It may be that the apparent triumphs of formal logic aroused defensive reactions among philosophers uncertain of their capabilities in those areas. Or, more probably, it may be that rationalistic or 'scientific' attempts to prescribe political reform, in the manner of the Young Hegelians, or Comte, or Mill, were increasingly unwelcome to the authorities in the years following the turn of the century. Whatever the reason, there was a stream of work from Dilthey and Rickert onwards stressing the separation between the natural and the human sciences, and the more 'fundamental' character of the latter. (In England, this was still being echoed half a century later, in the Snow-Leavis debate!) In this context, philosophy became a means of disparaging the claims of natural science – a project which Heidegger readily joined, but which we may view with more detachment.

The point is perhaps this. Any attempt to transfer 'positivist' methods from the natural sciences to the human sciences, let alone an attempt to instal them as a general ontology, is obviously uninteresting. But the fear that the natural sciences will somehow colonise the whole of knowledge, in the manner announced by Engels, is equally unreal.

Tightly formalised systems of investigation, and particularly those of 'logic', are important aids to understanding what claims about truth and knowledge might be; and as such, they *do* lay the foundations for socially valuable contributions of philosophy to, say, ethics and politics.[30] This view, now almost universally dismissed, is worth taking seriously. In particular, the fear that 'logic' is capable of a universal mathematisation of exist-

---

30 'Critical philosophy consists . . . in establishing its own claims, in the revelation of pure thought in the foundations and basic methods of the mathematical natural sciences. In this rediscovery of itself consists the irreplaceable first deed of philosophy, by which it develops itself as logic in the widest sense, or as criticism of knowledge. The second deed of philosophy is ethics. . .' Hermann Cohen, 1896, p. 73.

ence (a fear perhaps echoed in Heidegger's charge of 'levelling') is arguably dispelled by a consideration of, for example, Gödel's theorem. 'Logic' is in central respects *arbitrary* (in the proper sense); and the question of what, if anything, makes that arbitrariness still in its own terms 'logical' is one eminently appropriate for consideration by philosophers. This is, perhaps, the logic of reflection, as opposed to the straightforward calculus of 'logic' in the narrow sense.

In certain respects, that is what Heidegger is doing. But his 'arbitrariness' takes off only from the riddles of orientation and datability. The other arbitrariness – incompleteness – lies, so to speak, at the far end of the operations of the understanding. Heidegger seems to assume that formal systems are, as Hilbert had initially speculated, complete.[31] And, I suspect, his whole model of the 'wholenesses' (Ganzheiten) of existence rests on this. But if the understanding is *not* complete – if it creates for itself questions it cannot *analytically* decide, but which are nonetheless *practically* decidable in some determinable 'meta-language' – then Heidegger's insistence on terminality and finitude as the 'horizons' of all 'existence' becomes less convincing.

On the other side, the *dialectic* of the understanding (i.e. its incompleteness), and its shepherding by *reason* (as the general reflexive metalevel, so to speak), is a central ingredient of the thought of Kant and Hegel. We shall now proceed to the second topic of transcendental reflection.

11. Totality and extension

Time and space are the first 'subjective conditions' of conceptuality. They present questions – those of orientation – that cannot be dealt with 'internally' by concepts.

Despite the importance of these topics in Kant's critique of Leibniz (and, similarly, in the breakdown of Husserl's first project, which is effectively what is being echoed in Heidegger's arguments – see below, ch. 3), this is only a preliminary issue in reflection. Kant himself, admittedly, attempted to demonstrate the direct dependence of reasoning on time and space, for example in the transition from the table of judgements to the table of categories. This also lies behind his otherwise rather bold assertion of the synthetic character of arithmetic (the assertion on which, as we shall see, Frege concentrated his critical attention).[32] But the crucial importance of time and space only emerges at a later stage in the transcendental programme,

31 See *SuZ*, 362 for some revealing comments about mathematics as a paradigm of completeness.
32 Cf. *German Philosophy*, 18ff., 25f.

from *within* the operations of conceptuality. Rather than, as with the straight orientational problems, conceptuality being in some way limited by the aesthetic (which is the flavour Heidegger gives to the affair), we shall see that conceptuality *needs* the aesthetic in order to achieve its own ends. It is not that concepts are constrained by orientation (which would be the 'existentialist' way of looking at it); it is more that they need orientation in order to operate at all.

However, this is a rather anthropomorphic way of formulating the situation. The 'subjective conditions' encountered by the understanding can be expressed in terms of straightforward problems in logic and semantics, problems that have been a persistent part of logical debate throughout the centuries. The question is quite simple: what are concepts (names, general terms) *about*?

Part of the problem is that the answer seems so obvious. 'Concepts' are about 'things', one would reply. The general term 'dog' is about anything that is a dog. All the dogs in the world are the 'things' to which the name 'dog' refers. Of course, some 'things' are abstract, in the sense that they are not directly available as objects of sensory inspection. But this is not an insuperable difficulty. 'Anger', for example, is the name of an emotion, and refers to any and all instances of it. The same applies to conceptual acts such as, for example, 'judgement'. A judgement may be a rather rarefied sort of thing compared with a dog; but in principle, at least, and provided we agree on a definition, we can say of anything whether it is or is not a 'judgement'. So the world has 'judgements' in it the same as it has 'dogs', outbursts of 'anger', and so on. This, more or less, seems to be what 'names' are about; and it is difficult to conceive of any kind of reasoning without 'names' used in this manner.

However, the metaphysical interpretation of 'names' is much less straightforward than their grammatical use. The question is this: do names actually identify groups of things, or are they merely labels I affix to things that happen to be to hand, without attributing to those things anything more than a pragmatic and provisional identity? Put more drastically, we could ask: are there *really* 'dogs', or are there merely entities that I determine to be 'dogs' in the context of certain stages of my thinking? And in the latter case: what exactly is the term 'dog' *about*, if its primary 'being' is merely in my conceptual operations?

This, in a nutshell, is what the medieval controversy between realists and nominalists was about (the 'Universalienstreit'). The realist position, that there really *are* dogs, offers an immediate appeal to intuition and 'common sense'. I can imagine, for example, that the things to which a compound term like 'dogs in this village' refers are quite unambiguously identified. I may not know them all; some may be in the process of being born, or of dying; others may be strays that wander between this village and the next. But subject only to such peripheral questions of definition, the 'extension' of the term seems entirely obvious and clear. So: if that is the case, why not also the extension of 'dogs' generally? And furthermore: if we can apply this to materially available individuals, why not also to more abstract entities like outbursts of anger and judgements? The definitional problems may be greater here: but the principle seems to be the same.

The nominalists, by contrast, saw general terms as mere labels, 'flatus vocis' (which might be rendered as 'hot air').[33] For the nominalists, we could say, the world of existent things always and inevitably exceeds the capacity of reason to deal with it. This is not to devalue reason as such, which is clearly a powerful, indeed our only, instrument of pragmatic 'knowledge'. But its metaphysical claims are strictly limited; and the logical structures of our mind are not to be projected onto the 'world' as such. The difficulty here is that the doctrine is counter-intuitive (why *shouldn't* I have an extensionalist doctrine of meaning? – I know a dog when I see one!), and it appears to postulate a realm of 'reality' which is overwhelmingly *there* but at the same time is entirely inaccessible to my thoughts. The result is a kind of metaphysical self-mortification; I know only that my thinking is eternally inadequate to God's universe (hence nominalism's attraction for certain religious directions; this is what Walter Benjamin called 'melancholy').

We cannot go into the *Universalienstreit* here. The formulation that will suffice for our purposes is this: realists think the world is adequately captured by concepts, nominalists think there is always something left over. These positions are not necessarily irreconcilable, as we shall see: the question is not who is right, but how we combine the two. The interest of the question is that the difficulty seems to arise within conceptuality itself, rather than appearing from outside like time and space. How, if at all, does conceptuality account for its own status in the world? What, quite literally, are language and reason talking about?

In modern philosophy this problem has been dealt with in more formal ways. The sensitive point is less, as it has been, the question of whether one is dealing with concrete or abstract individuals (dogs or judgements), although this is still an important way of interpreting the difficulty.[34] The

33 Recent appropriation of this debate has been confused by the fact that 'realist' is often used in a sense diametrically opposed to its historical meaning. The debate is not about whether things 'really exist'; the question is about the relationship between things (which must be 'real', if the word is to have any sense at all) and language's account of them. What Putnam calls *'metaphysical'* (as opposed to 'empirical') realism, for example, should arguably not be termed realism at all, but nominalism (Putnam, 1980, 432).

34 Specifically, the question arises in relation to the reality of 'abstract entities' like classes. Quine defines the 'nominalistic programme' thus: 'One may prefer to regard abstractions as

pressing question is this: what is a totality?

Now, on the face of it a totality is a perfectly obvious thing. For example, it refers to the extension – the whole extension – of one of our terms. The totality of dogs is everything of which 'this is a dog' is true. The same applies to outbursts of anger. Possibly it also applies to judgements.

We can formulate the 'common-sense' position like this. Any discrete totality must have two things: it must have a boundary (I have to know what to exclude), and I must be able to take an inventory of its contents (I must be able to 'see what I've got'). So, 'all dogs' fits these requirements readily enough. I can devise an arrangement for choosing what I deem to be a 'dog'; and were I to get 'all dogs' together in a suitable corral, I would not find it hard to take an inventory (by counting them). This, if you like, is the common-sense conception of a totality (or 'set', in twentieth-century logical terminology).

However, this leaves us with problematic cases. Our 'common-sense' notion of a totality as a container, a 'bag' with 'things' in it, seems to leave out of account, or indeed actively exclude, notions that we might other-wise, and equally intuitively, want to accommodate. The difficulties relate first to the *boundary*, in our metaphor, and secondly to the *inventory*.

12. Conditions and the unconditioned

The problem of the boundary, or the container, is the central topic of Kant's 'Dialectic' in the first *Critique*. Kant's basic metaphor is that of the *conditioned* (cf. B 390). What is conditioned is determined, bounded by what else is conditioned with it. Spatially, a surface is bounded by its neighbours. Temporally, a time-span is bounded by what goes before and what comes after (cf. B 439f). More generally, whatever I am conscious of finds its place in my mind in a reciprocally determined unity. I cannot be conscious in a contradictory manner (I cannot believe both p and not-p); hence everything I am conscious of settles into a pattern of beliefs, things that are consistent with one another and bounded by each other to the extent that I am fully conscious of them.

This can also be represented, in Kant's account, in terms of a chain of causes. Each event causes, or 'conditions', its effect. Displayed in time, the chain of conditions appears as a sequence of delimited events, each one co-existing in a general unity.

The business of ordinary scientific reasoning, in this scheme, is to trace

fictions or manners of speaking; one may hope to find a method whereby all ostensible refer-ence to abstract entities can be explained as mere shorthand for a more basic idiom involving reference only to concrete objects (in some sense or other).' (Quine, 1981, 121). Quine himself is a disappointed nominalist.

the conditions ordering coexistence. In terms of chains of conditions, for example, we move from given present consequences backwards to their proximate and remote causes in an attempt to produce a full account. Kant calls this a 'regressive' procedure (B 438). Although Kant's importation of time and causal sequences here rather confuses the issue, the principle is the same as that of a recursive proof. We are making the contents of our knowledge consistent (and, presumably, discarding what fails the test).

Now, however useful this may be as a refinement of knowledge, what Kant is describing does not exhaust the capacities of consciousness. In particular, consciousness is still able to ask not merely about the condition of any particular determined entity, but about the overall condition of *everything* – the condition, that is, that is not conditioned by any of its sub-conditions and is in that respect *un*-conditioned.[35] We can imagine this in terms of a computer. A computer 'thinks' by progressing in an orderly manner from one state to the next; and its 'state of mind' at any point is co-extensive with the state of its registers. If the 'conditions' are changed – by fresh input, or whatever – then its registers change accordingly. What the computer cannot do is *spontaneously* to review its *entire* state: to put itself, so to speak, outside its own total configuration of hard and software. It may be programmed to do all sorts of sophisticated self-reviews: but then the self-review programme, at least at the moment of its execution, is excluded from what is reviewed. What Kant is suggesting, however, is that human consciousness presupposes that it can 'think itself', as a totality. The 'unconditioned', in our comparison, is the *un-programmed*.

In the 'dialectical inferences of pure reason', Kant has two useful illustrations for this. The first concerns the problem of the knower and the known. Can I 'know myself'? Kant's argument is that I cannot know myself, or at least not determinately, with procedures like 'regression'. What I 'know' in concrete terms is no more 'myself' than the state of the computer's registers is the computer. I may know the contents of my mind, the various containers and boundaries I use to order my consciousness. But I cannot know what it is that contains or bounds those contents as a whole. I know, so to speak, what is 'in' my mind (including intimately personal things like temperament and mood); but that never *exhausts* my mind, because there is always the last, unconditioned step which is at that very moment enabling me to survey the conditioned remainder.

Kant formulates this opposition in terms of the empirical subject and the *transcendental* subject (B 404). The empirical subject is, so to speak, the aggregation of things of which I am aware, of 'perceptions' in a Lockean

35 Kant calls this 'the business of reason' – 'to rise from the conditioned synthesis [i.e. regression] to which understanding always remains tied to the unconditioned which it can never attain' (B 390).

sense – i.e. of internal moods and operations as well as external objects. But it is not a distinct entity over and above those perceptions. Everything distinct must have distinct predicates, predicates such as to make it 'perceivable' either externally or internally.[36] Predicates, though, are limits and determinations; they are Kant's 'conditions'. So if we are talking about something that is by definition *un*-conditioned, it cannot fall within the realm of the knowable. It has *no* predicates; and hence is completely indeterminate even as to 'person' – it could equally well be an 'I', a 'he', an 'it', or even an empty '*x*'.

So this absolute introspection, in Kant's words, ends up with nothing more than

> the simple representation 'I' that is in itself entirely empty of content, and of which one cannot even say that it is a concept. It is merely a consciousness that accompanies all concepts. By means of this 'I' or 'he' or 'it' (the thing) which thinks we imagine no more than a transcendental subject '*x*' of thoughts; and this can only be known by means of the thoughts which are its predicates. (B 404)

Formulaically, my introspective knowledge is only of my consciousness as already determined, never of it as actively determining (B 407). At the same time, though, 'transcendental subject' *is* legitimate, if not as concept or as predicate of anything, then as 'form in general' of knowledge (B 404) – a term that echoes the designation of time and space as 'forms' or 'subjective conditions' of objectivity. The point is not that we should abandon all mention of transcendental conditions, but that we can only approach them negatively, by showing, from within, how they condition and delimit the realm where predicates operate.

In order to follow that, we need to be able to know how thoses limits appear: how, so to speak, reasoning bumps up against limits in the course of its own operations. As Kant deals with it, the problem of the 'transcendental subject' is (like the puzzles of orientation) not generated inside reason, but imposed from outside. There can, as Kant puts it, be no 'rational psychology' (showing that rationality is needed for thinking does not also demonstrate that there is some entity – a soul – which has the attribute of being rational); but this is not a problem for reason so much as for theology, which here finds reason to be of no assistance.

In the four 'cosmological antinomies', however, Kant does adopt a more immanent approach. Their purpose is to show that the understanding (here, in the example of natural-scientific enquiry) *does* run up against limits even when pursuing its own inherent operations. The antinomies revolve around the question of whether discrete cosmological boundaries

36 This, more or less, is the basis for the technique that later emerges more formally in the work of Frege and Russell as the 'theory of descriptions'.

can be established, in the guise of absolute origins, necessary causes and the like. Kant's approach is to deduce contradictions on these questions: statements like 'there is some time-point that is not the successor of any time point', or 'there is some cause that is not the effect of any cause', are shown to be both provable and disprovable in the natural-scientific system. In other words, if natural science is consistent (which we want it to be), then it must be incomplete: it cannot answer questions about its own conditions or limits.

13. Antinomies of totality

Now, Kant's approach to the problem of totality is insufficiently formal for modern aspirations. In particular, the actual derivation of the cosmological antinomies makes too many antiquated assumptions in the field of natural science. Nonetheless, the *goal* of the exercise is still entirely topical. Here we shall try a more formal reconstruction.

Knowledge is determinate: it has boundaries. That is what makes it knowledge. But drawing the boundary ('following the rule', in Wittgenstein's expression) does not itself fall within that bounded determination. To the extent that a boundary is determined by neighbours (i.e. to the extent that a determination has to be *consistent* with my other beliefs), this is not a problem. We need not feel that there is any kind of spontaneity about such a boundary. But what happens when the boundary is no longer determined by consistency? When, for example, we speak of the *totality* of our knowledge, and thus of something that is perforce *not* already positively circumscribed by 'neighbours'? (Ignorance – absence of knowledge or belief – cannot form such a circumscription.) Who or what is drawing that kind of boundary, and according to what rule? Is it a describable boundary at all?

Now, according to Kant's general argument, there are two ways of approaching such a boundary. The first is to adduce what we cannot get to by consistent internal operations alone. This is the argument from 'external' differences. Specifically: what we know 'discursively' (i.e. from the manipulation of predicates) does not exhaust everything we 'know' in some other sense (Kant would say 'intuitively').[37] We could say that discursive knowledge, operating under the rule that any given state of affairs must be consistent, is in principle, and within its own realm, capable of comprehensively extending its determinations. On the other hand, it is not capable of predetermining what is conditional on Kant's 'forms of intuition' – time and space. This (according to Kant) is demonstrated by the

37 For this distinction see B93; further Eisler, 1930, 98.

puzzles of orientation. There is, so to speak, no *reason* why (all other things being equal) a particular snail shell should be right-handed rather than left; and certainly reason does not extend forward in time.

Put in more explicitly metaphysical terms, we could say that orientation is about contingency. We never know determinately what will happen next. Whatever 'logic' is, it is conditioned by time (and, in Kant's view, space). That is why a *logic* of phenomena is impossible, at least 'discursively'. Hence the difficulties of Leibniz's system, and the problems of Husserl's 'phenomenology'. The understanding needs boundaries ('horizons'), and rebels against the notion of the non-finite. Horizons, though, only constitute themselves once we are there; and the getting there was led by something that precedes any determinate horizon: infinite contingency.

That is the 'external' argument. However, reflection proceeds also from the 'inside', from the operations of logic itself. This is where we get to the antinomies.

Kant starts with the hypothesis that rationality (Vernunft) 'demands absolute totality' (B 436).[38] Totality, here, means the full extent of 'possible experience', i.e. what can be covered discursively, by the understanding. Or, more specifically, anything that is given in experience is also 'conditioned' (i.e. subject to the rules of the understanding); and rationality demands that we should follow the whole series of conditions preceding that. That will lead us, eventually, to the unconditioned condition of the whole series. 'If the conditioned is given, then so also is the whole sum of its conditions, and hence also the absolutely unconditioned.'

Kant needs to establish this pull towards the unconditioned preceding the totality of the conditioned because he wants to demonstrate that free (i.e. 'unconditioned') practice, and hence (in the widest sense) ethics, is inseparable even from the understanding. This is unlikely to be an attractive project to many modern thinkers.[39] But the immediate argumentative point is perhaps less contentious. It is the one we have already considered in the context of computers. A computer, presumably, is bounded by the entire configuration of hardware and software that makes up its 'thinking'; a human being, though extensively *determined* by the equivalent mechanisms, is not finally bounded by them. It seems to be axiomatic that a human being must in some sense be capable of disposing of him or herself as an entirety. She must herself be able to generate what are, from the point of view of the 'machine', *truly* random transitions. Practice, in other words, in-

---

38 On the distinction between rationality (Vernunft) and understanding (Verstand) see further *German Philosophy*, 35f.

39 Because ethics, in the usual view, has no jurisdiction over logic, and can at best be subordinated to it or, perhaps most tidily, eradicated altogether by means of some sort of 'determinism'. See Honderich, 1989.

corporates the element of contingency and non-finity already encountered in the puzzles of orientation. To put it in Husserlian terminology, a human being is a machine that creates its own horizons.

For these absolute boundaries to be interesting, we must be able to identify them in some way (rather than simply asserting them, as in Heidegger's appropriation of orientation). This is the function (in Kant's argument) of the antinomies. The antinomies test the limits of understanding from within. They are, so to speak, encouraged to do so by rationality, which can thereby demarcate for itself the extent of its own jurisdiction.

We do not, of course, need to take rationality's demands and encouragements literally. It suffices if the understanding does run up against limits from within, since any such encounter (for the purposes of our argument) serves to demonstrate that the understanding is limited in a way that 'we', or whatever it is that surrounds and 'conditions' the understanding, are not.

Kant's suggestion is that the understanding fails when it tries to encompass absolute totality; and we have considered his delineation of this failure in the 'paralogisms' of psychology, and in the cosmological antinomies. The problem of totality is important in modern set theory. Sets, we may say, are collections (of entities) that can be thought about coherently (in the sense that we can attribute properties to them). When collections are too large (the set of all ordinal numbers, for example, or the set of all sets) they start to behave paradoxically. In 1899 Cantor identified 'the totality of everything thinkable' as one such contradictory collection (he called it an 'absolutely infinite multiplicity'). 'The totality of everything thinkable' seems to be precisely what Kantian 'rationality' wants the understanding to totalise over. The problem of totality (as we shall see in a moment) is at least as topical now as it was for Kant. But its philosophical interpretation, and how it grounds the Kantian ethical universe to which (for example) Habermas and other twentieth-century thinkers appeal is not yet clear. Let us run over the situation again to see how we can get further.

14. Reconstruction of the ethical

I take the basic metaphysical thesis that emerges from Kant's work (whether or not he would have formulated it that way) to run as follows:

> All rationality, including the cognitive operations of the 'understanding', presupposes intersubjectivity – i.e. the interaction of distinct minds.

From such a thesis would follow, *inter alia*, that ethics (the 'logic' of interaction) precedes 'logic' as conventionally understood, and, indeed, that ethics (in the widest sense) is the grounding meta-discourse of logic. In

Kantian terminology, *Vernunft* (reason, or rationality) grounds both ethics ('practical reason') and 'logic' ('pure reason' and the 'understanding' -
Verstand). It is this 'Kantianism' that, for example, underlies the attempts
of Lorenzen to ground logic in 'practice' (see below, chapter 5).

To establish this, 'Kant' needs to show that 'minds' can be substantively
distinct, for otherwise no interaction between them would produce anything not in principle achievable by a single mind. Substantive distinctness
must be distinctness that goes beyond what can be accounted mere ignorance. There must be *legitimate* differences in 'knowledge' between one
'mind' and another, not merely such as can be accounted for by my having
read the newspaper and you not, or you being more practised in mathematical analysis than me. At the same time such differences must not be 'incommensurable': it must still be possible to come to some recognisably
'rational' agreement on the basis of our two knowledges.

Now, Kant himself does not formulate his problems in quite this way;
and the relation between pure and practical reason, and the sense in which
'reason' embraces the two, is never satisfactorily formulated.[40] In particular, intrusions of 'subjectivity' such as space and time, and, later, the puzzles of totality, appear more as simple deficiencies than as 'understanding's'
proper delimitations within a wider, positive realm of 'rationality'.

However, the Kantian project was carried forward in two ways. His successors (in particular, Fichte and Hegel) developed Kant's notion that
knowledge is *tensed*. And the twentieth century has been able to render the
problems of totality more precisely. In the remainder of this chapter we
shall try to identify the main elements of the theory of reflection as it now
stands. This is a skeleton argument, not a sustained exposition. The detail
of the argument will have to be sought elsewhere: either in later chapters of
this book, or in its predecessor *German Philosophy*, or (particularly on
more technical developments in set theory) in the work of other authors.
Much work remains to be done in any event.

15. Totality and unity

The first set of arguments relates to the notion of the mind as a single totality, something where (in Kant's exposition, for example) all elements have
to be able to bear the prefix 'I think'. How do we get from this entirely
abstract notion, which seems to be equivalent to no more than the demand
that 'mind' be *consistent*, to the positive notion of a 'self' capable of interaction?

Now, a predominant twentieth-century notion of mind (as exemplified,

40 See *German Philosophy*, 52ff.

inter alia, by Gilbert Ryle) is that there is nothing that can usefully be called mind. Mind is simply the ordering of pieces of information. *Nihil est in mente quid non prius erat in sensu.* Thinking is the collation of sense data; or, at least, of data that are extra-mental and generally available in some way. Mind contributes nothing substantive. In principle, given the same degree of brain power, the same 'data' produce the same 'knowledge' in all minds. So, for example, the Cartesian claim to derive any kind of personal identity from the fact of cognition is absurd; take away the sense data, and there is nothing in 'mind' left to be aware of.

This would seem to be congruent with the notion that everything that is in the mind (the totality of 'what I am thinking') can be read back to the individual bits of sense data that have been ordered. The view that mental collations – sets – are grounded in the things they apply to, or can apply to, is the basis of the extensionalist approach. The 'mind' is an ordering of things. 'Thoughts' are labels added by the mind, in some conventional procedure or other, to its data. Universal terms, sets, are not aspects of the data; they are only 'real' to the extent that they derive from natural phenomena of the brain or social conditioning; and in that respect they add nothing either to the 'truth' of the things to which they are applied, nor to the identity of 'mind' as some self-contained spiritual entity.

From this point of view, the purpose of philosophical discipline is precisely to *clear away* baggage like 'mind'. The facts must be allowed to stand out in their hard purity; the containers we, perforce, use to order them must be transparent and visibly disposable.

To this end, paradox can be used to show the destructiveness of any interference from mental entities. Russell's programme, and its extreme radicalisation in Wittgenstein's *Tractatus* (see below, chapter 3), is a full exploitation of this. For Russell, accepting classes was a matter of spiritual pain, for classes are mind-entities: the individual things of reality do not form up before us in classes. Wittgenstein was only satisfied by the austere purity of a logic where functions were utterly divorced from arguments. The mind could concern itself only with the things of the outside; to apply itself to its own constructs was a feast of spectres. For both thinkers, the lesson of Russell's paradox was that predicates must never incestuously turn to predicates (or, for Russell, not without at least asserting their credentials through the axiom of reducibility).

16. Individuals and the hierarchy of propositions

In the specific context of naive set theory, the position is as follows. (We shall use the system of *Principia Mathematica (PM)* because of its influence and because it is explicitly philosophical.)[41] There are 'individuals', and there are 'propositions'. Individuals are the simple entities that actually occur in the world. They are not compounded into classes or any other unities that would infringe their simplicity; they are, as Russell says, 'destitute of complexity' (1908, 164). On the other side there are propositions, which are 'essentially complex': they put things together. ('I know that x is F', for example, puts together me, x, and F. *PM*, 43.)

We start with an ontological prejudice in favour of individuals. Individuals are what there is; propositions are merely intellectualised shadows of them. Propositions need individuals in a way that individuals do not need propositions. An individual object 'is' regardless of what else the propositions choose to combine it with. A proposition, on the other hand, cannot achieve 'truth' (which, we assume, is its telos), without individual objects, the entities to which true propositions *correspond* (*PM*, 43). Until it has received its object, the proposition remains 'essentially ambiguous'; it is 'not a definite object . . . it is a mere ambiguity awaiting determination, and in order that it may occur significantly it must receive the necessary determination' (*PM*, 47f).[42]

The deceptiveness of propositions is shown by their disturbing and paradoxical character. For example: the world consists of individuals, and though there are undoubtedly a great many of them, they are nonetheless in some way finite, bounded, and determinable. At any given moment, even allowing for relativity and the mysteries of coming-to-be and passing-away, we would feel that the number of individuals is more or less there, as a single totality, if only in the mind of God.

Propositions, however, are not things but complexes of things, and do not respect this finitude. In fact, the number of propositional complexes vastly, indeed infinitely, exceeds the number of individuals available to be combined into complexes. We can readily see this if we take some combinable entities (without at this stage worrying about whether they are 'individuals'). Red, round and wooden, for example, may be combined so as to produce the notion of red things, round things, wooden things, round red things, red wooden things, round wooden things, things which have all those properties and things that have none of them. In fact, from any collection of n combinables, the profligacy of the proposition will produce 2^n complexes. This means that from the great number of individuals that we

41 The 'Russell' to whom I am attributing the views that follow is something of a cardboard figure. As will emerge in chapter 3, below, I think it is possible to follow Russell's work in a rather different direction. See also Hylton, 1984 and 1990 for more light on a convoluted topic.
42 Actually, in Russell's account, this 'determination' seems to come about not through the fact of correspondence, but through the act of judging (*PM*, 44), which rather dilutes its ontological claims. This, with Frege's 'judgement stroke', was a point to which Wittgenstein objected.

come across in our daily lives, propositional activity can generate complexes which multiply those individuals into ghostly armies. Not merely that: propositional activity can continue to combine the fruits of its activities into yet further complexes. So if we started with n individuals, our first stop was with 2^n complexes of them; but then propositions can be further applied to combine those complexes among each other, whereupon we get 2 to the power of 2^n complexes – and so on, limitlessly (*PM*, 65).

The question is: how do we get this rampaging universe of propositions under control? The valuation implicit in the question gives us the answer. We must ensure that propositions never lose touch with the objects to which they correspond, the 'individuals' which enter at the most primitive level of complex-formation. This, however, is by no means as simple as it sounds.

For Russell, and a tradition that has continued since, the paradigmatic problem of set theory was not size as such, but the paradox of self-reference, or self-membership.[43] Whatever the difficulties of establishing contact with the 'objects', the primary desideratum was clear: propositions must never be obviously confined to their own realm. Propositions must at least purport to 'point to' some real corresponding state of affairs (*PM*, 46). A proposition that produced a complex using itself as an ingredient was obviously offending against the dependent status of propositions – mere ambivalences without the solidity, direct or indirect, of some object.

The almost moralistic repugnance at such self-abuse is visible in Wittgenstein's system: functions and arguments are utterly distinct, and functions can never be arguments.

This approach, however, is excessively austere. In the first place, it leaves out of account the epistemological questions involved in establishing pure and primitive objects as arguments. ('Truly elementary judgements are not very easily found,' as Russell remarked. *PM*, 45) In the second place, it did little to suggest what could take the previous (Fregean) account of numbers as classes of classes (or, as something that seems to require the application of functions to functions).

The more abiding response to the set-theoretical problems was the metaphor of ascent and *hierarchy*. Within this, the central concern is, so to speak, to keep one's feet on the ground – or, at least, on something attached to the ground. The ground is constituted by the objects in the world; and the requirement of the hierarchical principle is that statements should be about the 'ground' or, failing that, about things directly or indirectly resting on it.

43 At *PM*, 60 Russell reviews the paradoxes and concludes, 'In all the above contradictions (which are merely selections from an indefinite number), there is a common characteristic, which we may describe as self-reference or reflexiveness.'

More specifically, we recognise, first, that discourse inevitably and constantly makes statements about statements. For example, we talk about 'sorts of animals'. That is a set of sets of animals. We are not talking about the objects directly (individual animals); we are talking about the classes into which we have ordered them: cows, cats, dogs, and so on. None of these latter entities is an 'object'. But most people do not feel any metaphysical or logical qualms about usage of this sort. Indeed, we would usually be willing to confer honorary objectness on such groupings: 'all cows' may not refer to an individual thing, but it seems a concrete enough notion. In general, 'only the *relative* types of variables are relevant; thus the lowest type occurring in a given context may be called that of individuals, so far as that context is concerned' (1908, 164).

To that extent, we can talk about the reality of 'classes', and indeed, resting on that, combine such classes into further complexes: for example, 'all cows have hooves'. In cases like this, a purist nominalism is usually available to us: we can say that the 'class' of cows here is not really needed; we are simply saying 'for any object, if it is a cow, then it has hooves'. In other words, here we can bring ourselves back to the 'ground', the utter elementarity of statements about individuals. This is not always the case, though: with cardinal numbers, for example, our functions of functions do not permit us such a direct route back to the objects. But this does not matter particularly. The general axiom is that, as Russell puts it, 'all generalised propositions presuppose elementary propositions' (1980, 163f). Within that demand, it does not matter so much that we should in every case be able to get down to ground-level elementary propositions. We can have 'relative' individuals (1908, 164), i.e. entities that form the foundation of any particular logical construction, and which at least enable us to tell which direction the ground is in.

Russell has a terminology to deal with this situation. The various 'levels' in the hierarchy are called *types*. Individual objects occupy the lowest type. Statements about them are called *first-order* statements. First-order statements (of the form, e.g., x is a member of the set 'cats') in turn produce entities of a higher type ('cats'), which can then be put into statements of the second order ('cats are F'), so in turn producing a further logical type. Basically, 'type' refers to the range the variable can take, 'order' refers to the level of proposition required to deal with it. The ontological groundedness of whatever it is we are talking about is established by its type. Superimposed on that (on the type of the 'input', so to speak) are further logical conditions to be observed by the orders of propositions in relation to one another. The general rule is that the 'input' has to be lower in the logical hierarchy than what it is being put into (the propositional complex, function or whatever). You may say, for example, that Simpkin (individual, lowest type) is a member of the set 'cats' (first-order statement); but you may not say that the set 'cats' (second logical type) is Simpkin.

Within this luxuriant ontological thicket further devices restrained unwelcome upward growth. The most celebrated was the axiom of reducibility (see also below, chapter 3). The axiom of reducibility was intended to reduce the order of propositions involved in some statement to the lowest level consistent with the type of the 'input'. This was necessary because of Russell's principle that 'a statement in which a proposition appears as subject will only be significant if it can be reduced to a statement about the terms which appear in the proposition' (*PM*, 48). The statement only satisfied Russell's ontological demands, in other words, if it was at least in principle convertible into a first-order statement about whatever played the role of 'individual' in that context (i.e. whether or not it was 'really' a type one entity).[44] Some statements, however, quantified over functions in ways that did not allow direct 'winding down'[45] to a first-order statement (e.g. identity, in Russell's account). In that case, said the axiom of reducibility, we were to assume (other things being equal, and given unlimited time) that it would nonetheless be possible to find some first-order function which would specify the same set of objects in another way.

The distinction between orders and types, and more exotic accretions such as the axiom of reducibility that went with it, are probably not technically necessary (Quine, 1936). The metaphor of *ascent*, however, continued to characterise this branch of set theory. Quine's image, for example, is that of 'stratification', where the ascending strata take over the role of Russell's types.[46]

Another common way of affirming ontological ground in set-theoretic axioms is some appropriation of von Neumann's axiom IV,2 (von Neumann, 1925, 400; see also Quine, 1981, 165; Quine, 1973, 209). This is usually called the 'Axiom of Foundation'. It requires that the membership relation '∈' should be well founded. Informally, we could say that this is a ban on invoking the membership relation in a situation where everything would purport to be a member of everything else. There must always be something left, at the end of the line, to which nothing else stands in that relation. Generally, for a relation R to be founded, not all elements in the set over which it ranges must be in the image of its converse (for the formula, see Quine, 1973, 101). To illustrate, we could say that the relationship 'less

44 This kind of statement was termed 'predicative' by Russell, following Poincaré. 'We will define a function of one variable as *predicative* when it is of the next order above that of its argument, i.e. of the lowest order compatible with its having that argument.' (*PM*, 53) See also 'The Theory of Logical Types' (1910) in Russell, 1973, at 235.

45 The expression is used by Quine in another application of the hierarchical image (1980, ix).

46 For the set-theoretic system 'NF', see 1980, 90ff. For the system 'ML', see 1981, §28.

than' is founded for any set whose elements are natural numbers (the positive integers). That is because the relationship '$x < y$' holds for most of the natural numbers in a particular group, whether in the position of the x or of the y, but it does not hold for one element – the lowest number – in the 'y' position. In the set of numbers $\{5, 6, 7, 8\}$, for example, nothing is left to stand in the '$<$' relation to 5. 5 is the end of the line, the minimal object, the anchor point of the affair.

The '$<$' relation would not, however, be founded for, say, real numbers greater than 4. It is impossible to settle on a real number for which one could not find another one still smaller: they all can occupy the y position.

The same principle governs whether or not 'ϵ' is to be founded. Obviously entities that are ordered in types, or stratified, will allow 'ϵ' to be founded if we require the variable after the ϵ to be of order $n + 1$, for any variable of order n before the variable. The axiom of foundation achieves this with the requirement:

$$\forall x[x \neq 0 \rightarrow \exists y(y \epsilon x \, . \, \& \, x n y = 0)]$$

In words: for any x, if x is non-empty, then there must be some y such that, if it is a member of x, it is disjoint from x. Starting at the end, the disjointness requirement ($x n y = 0$) means that although y is a member of x, x and y must not have any members in common. We could get this from, say, the relationship between x (sets of animals) and y (cats): y is a set of animals, and hence a member of x, but none of y's members (individual cats) is a set of animals, and consequently x and y are disjoint. We could not get it, on the other hand, from the set of sets that are members of themselves ('$\{x|x\epsilon x\}$'), because every element of that set will also have an element or elements in common with it, and thus offend against the disjointness requirement.[47]

17. Relativity and tense

Naively, we could say that 'foundation' requires us to be able to wind down any collection to the point where we can say: 'I am attributing a to some (or perhaps all) b's, and we already know what b's are.'[48] Or, to put it

47 For the formulation in terms of disjointness, see Quine, 1973, 209 and Barwise & Etchemendy, 1987, 34.
48 This would also cover the *Aussonderungsaxiom* (the 'axiom of separation', glossed by Zermelo as 'sets may never be *independently defined* . . . but must always be *separated* as subsets from sets already given'). Zermelo 1908, 200. Von Neumann says of his axiom IV,2 (the 'foundation' axiom), 'it guarantees that we can treat as "argument" any "function" a that is $\neq A$ [i.e. ϵA] less often than a "function" b that has already been recognised to be an "argument"', and thus 'contains the axiom of separation' (von Neumann, 398).

another way: all legitimate sets are direct or indirect selections from elementary individuals. From 'moving objects in my field of vision' we can select 'animals', from 'animals' we can select 'cats' and 'dogs', from the latter two, and other similar ones, we can select 'mammals', and so on. More abstract sets, such as 'good actions', can in principle always be wound down along chains of that sort: they select from founded selections. Sets like the Russell set, however, do not allow this, because they do not select from a determinate collection, but from the infinity of all sets.

Now, the implicit reproach of 'foundation' is that this infinity is bad because the Russell set selects from a domain in which it is itself included, and thus offends against the ban against thought thinking itself. Moreover, this is held to support the claim that the ontological foundation of sets is essentially non-intellectual – that general terms depend for their legitimacy on how successfully they adhere to entities that are entirely outside cognition. 'Foundation', in other words, is nominalistic in its ontology.

Two points arise against this. In the first place, it is not apparent that self-reference is vicious *per se*.[49] Whatever is 'wrong' with the Russell set, it is not a simple matter of thought referring to itself, and thus failing to be founded in the real world. Even though the set $\{x|\neg x\epsilon x\}$ leads to contradictions, self-inclusive sets can be formed that do not tip themselves out of rationality. Russell's paradox does not support, for example, the ontological assumptions made by Wittgenstein and those, like Carnap or Quine, who followed him (see chapter 3).

The second point is that this kind of nominalism depends heavily on being able to identify what, other than cognitive entities, thought is 'about'. Without such an identification, nominalism is apt to become self-consuming. If the doctrine cannot give an account, other than as a general metaphorical belief, of where cognition is 'founded' (or of what it is for a statement to be 'true'), its own status becomes questionable. This is already implicit in Quine's doctrine of the 'indeterminacy of translation' (see below, chapter 3). It becomes explicit and radical in the work of Paul Feyerabend, or in Davidson's abandonment of the idea that knowledge organises a 'neutral content' common to all 'true' knowledges.[50] Disappointed nominalists become sceptics. Relativism, one could say in a negative assessment, has been rediscovered by some Anglo-American philosophers since 1945.

On the other hand, scepticism can dispel dogmatic slumber. Both these

49 See Barwise & Etchemendy, 1987.
50 'On the very idea of a conceptual scheme', in Davidson, 1984. For Davidson, the 'dualism of scheme and content, of organising system and something waiting to be organised' is the 'third dogma' of empiricism (p. 189f).

developments – the abandonment (by allowing self-reference) of any absolute distinction between thought and its objects, and the move beyond a straightforward correspondence theory of truth – converge on a new and more promising notion. This is the idea that totalities may be *tensed*; that 'what is the case' is not a homogeneous universal space, but something that is in some sense created in time, and changed in time, by rational activity. We can look at this in two cases.

The first case concerns the Löwenheim-Skolem Theorem, and recent comments on it by Hilary Putnam. The Löwenheim-Skolem Theorem says that if you have an enumerable set of sentences that is satisfiable at all, it is satisfiable in an enumerable domain. More freely, we could say that any theory which is going to turn out true at all is going to turn out true of something enumerable. This is a somewhat perplexing result. The problem is that one of the most important parts of mathematics is analysis, which deals with the infinitesimally small, i.e. with *continuous magnitudes* that cannot be exactly measured. For example, you may have a diminishing interval between two numbers (say, as you approach 2 from 1, such that you have 1.5, 1.75, 1.875, etc.). The notion of the continuum presupposes that, however small that interval gets, there will still always be room for a third number between them, ad infinitum (cf. Cantor in Becker, 1975, 278).[51] There is, in other words, no determinate end to how small you can make the interval, and no finite quantity of numbers inside any interval you start from. Furthermore, although you can start work on your interval by proportionate division (e.g. halving the interval you started with, dividing it into three, and so on), the continuum need no longer be accessible to these so-called 'rational' numbers. The 'irrationals' which are at home in the continuum can arrange themselves at will, without regard for any predetermined dispositions (such as 'halve the interval!').

Now, the difficulty with the Löwenheim-Skolem Theorem is that it seems to rule out any way of conceptually getting to grips with the continuum. It seems, in fact, that although we can *define* irrational numbers, as soon as we use set theory to produce statements about them we describe a universe far more ordered than the one we thought we were describing. This is because the irrational numbers are intended, by definition, to be non-denumerable – we cannot, for example, say what the 'first' irrational number is in the interval between 1.5 and 2. On the other hand, as soon as we start running the logical machine so as to derive from our general theory statements about particular numbers, we do so in a denumerable way. Any particular statement can be counted – the first one, the second one, and so on (see Boolos & Jeffrey, 132f). The result will be infinite, but countable.

51 The 'space' clearly *would* get too small at 1.9999... (infinitely). But there are infinitely many numbers before you get that far.

The 'logical machine', in this instance, is axiomatised set theory of the kind we have looked at. Axioms of some kind are necessary to avoid antinomies. But by introducing them, we are also, so to speak, sanitising the real world – and thereby in certain cases leaving out, it seems, just what we thought we were talking about. More specifically, we can define things, but we may not always be able to talk about what we have defined. As Skolem puts it, 'to be an object in B [Zermelo's set-theoretic domain] means something different and far more restricted than merely to be in some way definable'. In general terms, 'every thoroughgoing axiomatisation' involves a *relativity* – i.e. the objects you can talk about are relative to the axiomatic system within which you do so, and any definition that you intended at the outset is relativised by the logical process (Skolem, 1922, 296).

What is sometimes called 'Skolem's paradox' is primarily concerned with infinity and the continuum. Putnam (1980) has widened it to apply to ontological foundations in general: 'One can "Skolemise" absolutely everything. It seems to be absolutely impossible to fix a determinate reference (without appeal to non-natural mental powers) for *any* term at all' (436). In other words, 'theories' can only talk about domains that are preselected by those theories, and which do not contain the 'realities' that we intuitively imagine. For Putnam, this is an argument for what (following Dummett) he calls a 'non-realist semantics' (439), i.e. one which associates truth and 'aboutness' with verification procedures, rather than with correspondence to something absolutely outside. The notion of 'reference', on which correspondence rests, 'begins to seem "occult"' (442).

Conceivably, Putnam's use of Skolem is a little stretched. But the important point is the characterisation of semantics that emerges, though indistinctly. Basically, it is this. Truth-functional semantics presupposes 'models' that are somehow outside the whole cognitive process. A theory is successfully about a bit of reality. It is, in the foundational metaphor, grounded in elementary states of affairs. Putnam's account, however, suggests that theoretical statements are not about truth-functional grounds, but 'about' the procedures in which its users now find themselves. 'Either the use *already* fixes the "interpretation" or *nothing* can' (443). In other words, the vertical metaphor of 'foundation' is replaced by a *horizontal* one, in which truth applies between 'states of the self at more than one time' (436), and not between a state and 'reality'. From that point of view, Tarski's account of truth (any sufficiently interesting language T requires a meta-language to express truth-in-T) sites the meta-language where we are now, such that the formal language expresses things about a restricted part of the universe we now meta-linguistically, but intuitively and informally, occupy (this seems to be the sense of Putnam at 440). In other words, discursive reasoning is 'about', though restrictedly, the richer universe in

which we now are (which is why we can say, ' "snow is white" if and only if
snow is white' without getting lost in regress). It is because we are already
anchored in the richer universe (the one of Skolem's definability) that the
restrictedness, and apparent indeterminacy, of the axiomatically governed
one does not worry us.

We could put this another way. We can imagine or intuit, or, with Skolem, 'define' infinitely many entities. There is, in prospect, a limitless possibility to the numbers we devise to occupy particular intervals. Whenever
we actually identify such a number, however, the limitlessness is displaced
by a specific discursive 'fact'; we have produced something, and the possibility *from* which we produced it no longer obtains. Nonetheless, the possibility, which is what we 'intended' and is in a sense more real than the
account that clusters round the particular actuality plucked from it, remains as the authority behind the whole procedure. The things produced
by the understanding, discursively, are always eluded by the 'totality'; but
the 'real world', if it is anywhere, is more in the totality than in the sanitised
particular.

A horizontal scheme of this nature emerges with greater clarity in Barwise and Etchemendy's discussion of the liar paradox. In Putnam, 1980, the
'vertical' gap between theory and objects (440) is replaced by a horizontal
one between the axiomatised system and the rich meta-language of use and
intention (cf. 423). With Barwise and Etchemendy, the gap is between
classes and *sets*, or, more intuitively, between the *world* as a totality and
situations as the bits of it we can talk about (155). The distinction between
classes and sets, as we saw, is a means of dealing with totalities that are 'too
big'; Barwise and Etchemendy use it to define the boundary between different spaces of rationality, rather as the Skolem paradox distinguishes between what can only be defined and what can also be put into sets.[52] Their
argument is that the liar paradox cannot satisfactorily be dealt with by what
they call a 'Russellian' account – i.e. roughly, one involving a single universe of states of affairs. The problem with the Russellian account is that
the falsity of 'liar' sentences ('I am lying', etc.) seems to 'lie outside the universe of facts, outside the "world" ' (173). In other words, the Russellian
disqualification of sentences of this sort seems excessively drastic. Intuitively, we feel that such a sentence is false, and that its falsehood is in
some sense 'real' and part of a 'world'; but the Russellian account gives us
no model in which to place this falsehood.

The Barwise and Etchemendy account resorts to J.L. Austin's con-
textual notion of truth. In their argument, propositions are about *parts* of
the world ('actual situations'), but never the *whole* world (154f). What can

52 Barwise and Etchemendy call their Reflection Theorem 'a kind of Löwenheim-Skolem
Theorem' (160).

be put into propositions is, so to speak, set-eligible; the rest, i.e. the total-ity, is a class. This gives us an excess space into which unruly propositions like the liar paradox can escape. The liar paradox 'diagonalises out' of the situation it relates to.[53] 'Thus for any actual situation s, the falsehood of its Liar f_s simply cannot be a fact of s.' This, in Barwise and Etchemendy's account, is analogous to the effect of the axiom of comprehension on un-wieldy totalities like the Russell set; they are not barred from the 'world' as a whole – they simply get treated as classes rather than sets.[54] But being barred from any particular actual situation is not as disastrous in the toler-ant 'Austinian' account as it is in Russellian ones; it simply invokes a new situation beyond the boundaries of the old one. Certain sorts of statement, in other words, automatically throw up a boundary around what they re-late to, and *place themselves outside it*. (Gödel's sentence is rather similar; its speaker suddenly finds herself on a meta-level.) As Barwise and Etche-mendy put it, Austinian worlds 'outstrip their constituent situations'.

The interesting question is this: what is the medium in which such bounded situations coexist? It cannot be a homogeneous logical space, because if it was we would simply be in a Russellian universe, and para-doxes would leave the world entirely. The medium of coexistence, Barwise and Etchemendy seem to indicate, is time. Paradoxes consume themselves. But we can keep apart the warring sides of the contradiction by the simple expedient of temporal contextualisation: what is 'true' with respect to one point in time need not be so in another. It is this principle, as Barwise and Etchemendy comment, that makes us able to deal with such otherwise trivial matters as the fact that it is seven o'clock in New York when it is midday in London (171f). These are the problems of *non-persistence* (122) – i.e. 'truths' that relate only to narrow transitory contexts.[55] The overall force of the 'Austinian' argument is not merely that 'things change', but that rationality is *essentially* temporal in that we need time in order to re-concile and manage what would otherwise be mutually destructive states. In particular, we need to be able to recognise and deal with the fact that they are bounded: 'Boundaries of some sort do matter . . . if one is express-ing what we earlier called a non-persistent proposition' (176).

---

53 See chapter 3, below, for 'diagonalising out'.
54 The axiom of comprehension says,

$$\forall x(A(x) \rightarrow \mathrm{Mg}\ x \rightarrow \exists y \forall x(x \epsilon y \leftrightarrow A(x)))$$

In words: for any x, if $A(x)$ is to be a set, then all A's must (already) be members of some y. Put-ting Russell's set ' $\neg x \epsilon x$' for $A(x)$, and substituting y for x throughout the consequent (elim-ination of the universal quantifier) gives us the contradiction. The consequent is false, so the antecedent is also: Russell's formula does not give us a set. But we can still keep it as a class!
55 It is noteworthy, for the 'Kantian' perspective, that 'non-persistence' here also includes our friend spatial orientation! (Barwise & Etchemendy, 1987, 172).

18. Transcendentalism

Let us resume. It would appear that static systems, or at least those formalised by set theory, have difficulties fixing any 'determinate reference' (Putnam). Put more bluntly, we could say that set-theoretic discourse pur-
chases exactness at the cost of realism. Formal systems can never
themselves 'know' what they are talking about.

At the same time, however, there clearly 'is' something we embrace as
truth (or falsity). This seems to have two elements to it. First, 'truth' (like
'reference') does not seem to be containable within one state (certain statements about falsity 'diagonalise out' of the situation, as Barwise and Etchemendy put it). In doing this, however, such statements implicitly throw a
boundary around the situations they relate to: they constitute them as
situations the speaker is no longer in. And 'truth' is something about the relationship between the 'situation' and the 'world'; or, in Putnam's appropriation of Tarski, truth-in-T is about something *in* the 'situation' but
established *from* the 'world'. T is the set-theoretic calculus appropriate to
the 'situation'; and the meta-language is somehow part of the outside in
which we now find ourselves, the 'richer' language of Skolem's *definable*
(though not set-theoretically computable) entities.

It looks, in fact, as though 'truth' is something inescapably sequential;
and 'reference' is not so much to something absolutely outside, as to the
outside of boundaries produced within thought itself. An example of this is
the problem of 'non-persistent' truths. Following Barwise and Etchemendy's appropriation of Austin, this may in fact be the *paradigm* of truth,
rather than an irritating anomaly in Wittgenstein's 'crystalline universe' of
what is the case (see below).

More specifically, we could say this. Set theory fails to show how it can
be ontologically rooted in a 'reality' conceived as the metaphysical outside.
In the course of human reasoning, however, it is apparent that 'outsides'
are created, and that there is an 'excess' of reason over what is exhausted in
the discursive exploration of static systems. That excess is the rational space
from which we, for example, talk about the truth or falsity of utterances related to closed states. Perhaps we could also say that the excess space is the
limitless possibility of choice, whereas discursive understanding concerns
itself with the bounded space (the 'actual situation') of what has already
been decided.

And as we have indicated, it is at this point, with the dialectical antinomies of the understanding, that *time* (Kant's 'aesthetic') returns as the indispensable medium of orientation. Before thinking produces states, it
is done in time; non-persistent certainties are the foundation from which
persistent truths are derived. Transition and process are prior; states are

derivative.

This has certain important correlatives. First, it explains what the nature of the 'transcendental' project is. 'Transcendental' is happily abused in the Anglo-American realm as a synonym for 'systematic' – i.e. as a term for heavy Germanic attempts to foreclose on reality.[56] The 'conditions' discovered by transcendental critique, however, are precisely those which shatter the claim of 'metaphysics' to provide a determinate universal description of the natural and moral universe. The first 'condition' produced by the *Critique of Pure Reason* is time (and space) – i.e. something *indeterminate* and *non-systemic*. The crucial point, though, is not that time undermines logic, but that it is the medium within which logic can happen. And specifically, 'facts' are not external, timeless things, but they are the tensed doings (*pragmata*) of reason itself. Indeed, *all* the constructions of reason are themselves facts in this sense – completed events in time.

This is why neither 'reference' nor set-theoretic 'demonstrations' can hope to explain what 'truth' is about. Truth, as we saw, is some relation across a boundary. The boundary is, in a certain sense at least, thrown up by reason; but it exists in time. What is bounded is a fact. And what governs its 'truth' is not some 'correspondence' or other, but (for example) my view now of what I thought then. Kant's insistence on the role of time in all cognition (including arithmetic, to Frege's unease) is simply an affirmation of that facticity; thought is 'about' facts, but it is *itself* also a fact.[57]

The second correlative is that traditional logic's prioritisation of states over transitions is, metaphysically at least, tendentious.[58] Problems like 'free will and determinism' become less intractable when 'rationality' is no longer defined in terms of a single deterministic state, but as a continuing process that can accommodate even purely random transitions. States, here, are retrospective summaries of certain segments of process. They are abstractions from the course of events, not matrices of it. This is the pur-

---

56 E.g. Rorty, 1980, at 383: 'The primal error of systematic philosophy has always been the notion that such questions are to be answered by some new ("metaphysical" or "transcendental") descriptive or explanatory discourse (dealing with, e.g. "man", "spirit," or "language"). This attempt to answer questions of justification by discovering new objective truths, to answer the moral agent's request for justifications with descriptions of a privileged domain, is the philosopher's special form of bad faith – his special way of substituting pseudo-cognition for moral choice.' Although Rorty excludes Kant from the direct force of this reproach, it remains the underlying motif in his criticism, and the characteristic Anglo-American misunderstanding, of transcendentalism.

57 Dieter Henrich has written important commentaries emphasising that Kant's transcendental 'deduction' is not to be understood as a mathematical 'demonstration', but as something that proceeds from, as he puts it, the 'additional factual element'. See Henrich, 1989, which also contains interesting comments on the concept of reflection (p. 42).

58 It also seems to be an obstacle not only to more rarefied projects in artificial intelligence (see van Benthem, 1990), but also to direct practical concerns such as the production of fast and flexible databases ('Try eating soup with chop-sticks', *The Guardian*, 9.8.90).

port of Lorenzen's 'dialogical' grounding of logic (see chapter 5). The logical constants, in his account, operate like the scores resulting from certain 'game' exchanges. They are a way of describing what you have won (and, other things being equal, could win again). But they no more describe some timeless 'ontology' than '40-15' fixes the 'truth' about some tennis match.

19. Subject and recognition

The basic character of this radicalised version of 'non-realist semantics' would seem to be an order of *transitions*. These transitions are indeterminate; we do not require, for example, consistency between conditions before and after a transition. Purely random transitions are acceptable. (A purely random transition might be an 'arbitrary' decision; or, equally, it might be some unexpected discovery, or even accidental death.) But how, if at all, does this fit into a homogeneous logical space? Is there anything that makes one assertion, one state of mind, commensurate with another? Is there any basis for reasoned agreement?

Traditional metaphysics says that the space is basically that of the 'real world out there', and assumes that the real world is logically homogeneous in a fairly strong way (consistent, obeying the law of excluded middle, etc.). Even if agreement fails in any actual case, it is an article of faith that there must *be* a correct answer, 'out there', on a disputed point.

It is here that non-realist metaphysics returns to the notion of the 'subject'. The subject is the space where contradictions, non-persistent truths, bounded situations coexist. The fundamental condition of 'rationality' in this scheme would seem not to be timeless consistency, but *memory*. Rationality can remember what it has learned; that is the nature of 'identity'. The rational 'subject' is constituted by the condition that, although free in its choices, it holds to its decisions once made. (Like Wotan, it observes its contracts!) This is the further sense in which time is the primary medium of rationality.[59]

We could put the argument like this. There 'is' no completed world, waiting for us to 'know' it. The only foundation of knowledge is something that is capable of moving from state to state, and remembering that it has done so. A non-rational being is directly identical with whatever state it is in; a rational one knows it has moved, and is able to apply predicates like 'truth' by virtue of that and that only. Subjectivity in the stronger sense (knowledge of self) arises only through the *remembered crossing of boundaries*.

59 This position would seem to be axiomatic, or at least quasi-axiomatic, in both intuitionist mathematics and Hegel's *Phenomenology of Spirit*.

'Boundaries' of this sort, however, arise from something stronger than mere effluxion of time. This is the function of a 'dialectic' rather more substantial than the monological puzzles of the antinomies. The basic character of the dialectic – the revelation that there are two sides where once I thought there was one – comes about less through paradox than through the simple phenomenon of *dialogue*, the speaking contest, or *agon* (cf. Lorenzen, 1960). Before it is anything else, logic sets out the rules of dialogue. Dialogue is the most fundamental form of rational activity, because only through it can the empty 'subject' learn that there are boundaries, and that it is itself constituted by its ability to cross them.

Lorenzen's dialogical logic is a recent and more immanently 'logical' version of Hegel's 'master-slave dialectic'. Both are centred on the issue of *recognition*. The claim is, roughly, this. The 'subject' (whatever that is) needs dialogue because only in a contest of this sort can it wrest knowledge from opinion. Unless I try out my assertion on someone else, and win, I have no certainty. (Hegel's version says that I only feel fully autonomous and human to the extent that someone *I* recognise as autonomous and human recognises me.) Rational subjects need each other not as objects of desire or exploitation, but as conditions of truth. Without differences of opinion, there can be no knowledge. In a dialogue *A* must recognise *B*, because otherwise *A* can never be sure that her assertion has been tested as knowledge and has prevailed.

It would seem, then, that intersubjective trial is a precondition of forming a state of knowledge at all. Forming a state of knowledge, equally, is a precondition for moving beyond it. Rational subjects know 'themselves' by crossing the boundary of what they know; and they only *know* anything at all as a result of the intersubjective *agon*.

To the extent that this is sustainable, we establish what we called Kant's basic metaphysical thesis (see above, section 14). 'Logic' is rooted in practice not only for the standard 'intuitionist' reason that it is derived from technical practices (especially mathematics), but for the more fundamental reason that all knowledge is dialogical and hence intersubjective. I *need* other free, healthy interlocutors in order myself to be a human being at all, let alone a 'rational' one. In that sense, ethics (the doctrine of action for the benefit of others) is prior to logic (the technique of forming a consistent body of knowledge).

20. Historicity and reconstruction

Our final point is methodological.

One of the results of recent Anglo-American scepticism has been a reversion to historicism – i.e. to the doctrine that knowledges are completely subordinated to contingent differences like ethnology, language and so on. Bodies of belief from different epochs, up to and including our own immensely 'rational' one, are basically ideologies, and for that reason incommensurable. We cannot translate from one into another; there is no neutral third language; and none of their 'differences' can be rationally resolved.[60] As a further extension of this, the study of history (and particularly of the history of ideas) becomes at best mere antiquarianism, and at worst entirely futile.

This view arises from disappointed nominalism: while we had the aspiration to report on 'out there', all was well, but without that we have no claim whatever for the rightness of our languages. Translation presupposes that we can say 'the same thing' in different languages; but how can we ever establish what 'the same thing' is?

The answer to this is that appeal to an outside 'thing' is an irrelevant metaphysical diversion in the first place. There must, of course, be some 'bridgehead in reality' (to adopt an image from one recent commentator – Hollis 1978). But such a bridgehead is supplied by dialogical rationality – i.e. by my ability to persuade respected opponents of my point of view.

What is more, this is the entire character of knowledge – the laborious accumulation of tested assertions. Knowledge is not 'discovery'; it is *construction*. And the way to appropriate knowledge, to internalise the memory of our collective subjects, is to follow that process of construction. Hence the popularity of the term 'reconstruction' in the tradition of thought we are about to consider. Philosophy does not aspire to be the study of what *is*; that would be metaphysical nonsense. It is, much more modestly, the study of where we have got to; and, possibly, of where we might go next. In that study, one of the most important instruments is the commentary. Commentary, as Habermas says, is (or can be) an intrinsic part of serious systematic thought.

This book is an attempt to implement some of those insights.

60 Rorty is the obvious example of this; but there are many others.

2

Truth in the Present Tense: Frege

1. Introduction

It is, oddly, not self-explanatory that Gottlob Frege (1848–1925) should be considered in a book on German philosophy. That is because 'German philosophy', in the disparaging use of the term, is precisely what Frege (and Wittgenstein) are believed to have laid to rest. Before Frege, in this view, Western philosophy was incapacitated by primitive philosophical logic, and trapped in senseless metaphysical speculation. By the time of Wittgenstein (the Wittgenstein of the *Tractatus*), modern logic was available to all serious thinkers, and philosophers needed never again be tempted by the mystifications of the past. From that perspective, a chapter on Frege or Wittgenstein could only serve to invalidate the work of all preceding philosophers, especially those, like Kant and Hegel, who concerned themselves with logic or metaphysics.

This view has its origins with Bertrand Russell, who was the conduit for Frege's acceptance by a wider philosophical audience, and was Wittgenstein's protector during the early stages of his career. Russell certainly saw himself as someone who had 'overcome' a youthful inclination towards Hegelianism; and he gladly embraced Frege's criticisms of Kant as part of his own general dismissal of idealist metaphysics. Nowadays, it is probably less safe for an anglophone philosopher to be quite as cavalier as Russell in dismissing Kant.[1] But the 'overthrow of Hegel' by Frege is still part of the self-understanding of British philosophy.[2]   In fact, although Frege was

1 See, for example, the brisk and mistaken expositions (and 'refutations') in Chapter LII of *The Principles of Mathematics*, and the more hesitant (he had a Continental audience!) but equally wrong comments in 'The Philosophical Implications of Mathematical Logic' (1911 – now in *Essays in Analysis*, pp. 284-294).
2 'It is undoubtedly true that the overthrow of Hegelianism was a precondition of advance in philosophy, and, in so far as Frege's realistic philosophy played a part in that, that is also an

certainly not a *Hegelian*, much of his life's work was devoted to defending what he took to be a central aspect of *Kant's* thought. Frege's 'Kant', moreover, has a strongly Leibnizian flavour. These exegetical tensions will help us go behind the razamatazz of 'overthrow' and 'new beginning'.

2. Biographical

Frege was, for most of his life, a Jena mathematics professor of no more than modest professional prominence. His interest in philosophy alienated him from his mathematical colleagues while not endearing him to the philosophers. 'The prospects for my book, admittedly, are slender,' he exclaimed in the foreword to his major work, the *Grundgesetze der Arithmetik*:

> At all events, I shall have to give up on all those mathematicians who, whenever logical expressions like 'concept', 'relation', or 'judgement' appear, think 'this is metaphysics, I cannot read it!', and similarly those philosophers who, at the sight of a formula, cry out 'this is mathematics, I cannot read it!'; and, indeed, there will be not a few who react like this. (*GGA* xii)

Frege never moved from Jena. At the age of 31 he became an 'Extraordinarius', and, at 48, 'Honorarprofessor'. He never reached the pinnacle of the German academic system, the position of 'Ordinarius', though this hardly represents the dismal failure that some of his English commentators have suggested. It is probably true, however, that Frege's success among contemporary German readers was very limited. He speaks, for example, of the 'cool reception, or, more accurately, the absent reception' of his work (*GGA* xi), and his posthumous papers contain an article that was rejected by three journals. He had to pay for the publication of his *Grundgesetze* himself. To the dismay of his modern commentators, Frege eventually took refuge in bitter anti-Semitism, and attributed his professional disappointments to a Jewish cabal (see Dummett and Sluga for views on this).

However, Frege found a more attentive audience across the channel. His first and most influential reader was Bertrand Russell, who drew on Frege's work in his *Principles of Mathematics* (1903), and continued to make extensive use of it both in the philosophy of mathematics (*Principia Mathematica*, 1910ff.), and in logic and ontology ('On Denoting', 1905; *The Philosophy of Logical Atomism*, 1918). Frege's discoveries were 'epochmaking', according to Russell (*History of Western Philosophy*, p. 784). The analytical tradition has largely held to this assessment ever since.

ingredient in its historical importance.' Dummett, 1973, 683. For a more sceptical view of analytical philosophy's official history, and of this issue, see Baldwin, 1984.

There is not a great deal of Frege's work, and what there is is often for-biddingly technical. He published three major texts. The first was the *Begriffsschrift*, which appeared when he was 31 and was written while he was still a freelance ('Privatdozent') at the university. In full, the title may be translated as *Conceptual Notation, a Formulaic Language of Pure Thought Modelled on Arithmetic*. The book, as the title suggests, proposes a new system of logical notation. The notation itself, although helpfully in-tuitive, is difficult to print, and no doubt for that reason failed to win general acceptance. The logical principles embodied in the notation, how-ever, and especially the principle of quantification, were immensely signifi-cant, and remained to form the basis of modern logic.

Frege's second book was the *Grundlagen der Arithmetik* ('Foundations of Arithmetic') (*GA*), which appeared in 1884. In it, Frege extended the work he had done in the *Begriffsschrift* in an attempt to explore the idea that arithmetic can be derived from logic. The book does not use symbolic notation; but that, if anything, is a disadvantage for the reader.

Frege's magnum opus was the two-volume *Grundgesetze der Arith-metik* ('Basic laws of arithmetic', 1893 and 1903). In that work, conceptual notation was deployed in a massive attempt to formalise the positions first taken up in the *Grundlagen*. In a sense, the work is a failure, and, though planned to run to three volumes, the third was never completed. This is probably because Russell's paradox, which he communicated to Frege in 1902, persuaded Frege that the project of reducing all mathematics to logic was futile. Contemporaries felt that the project, as it had appeared in the first two volumes, was irredeemably flawed, and that a third volume would be pointless both because the first two would need rewriting, and because Frege's project was by then already being completed by others.[3]

Frege's project is difficult to follow without resorting to these major texts, and, in particular, it is not really possible to understand his argu-ments without identifying at least roughly the purview of his 'conceptual notation'. Nonetheless, the more general aspects of his position are set out in a number of shorter articles in which Frege tried to popularise his ideas, and defend them against critics without such extensive use of symbolism. The articles most commonly read now are 'Function and Concept' (1891), 'Sense and Reference' (1892), 'Concept and Object' (1892), and 'The Thought' (1918).

3 See Philip Jourdain's letter to Frege of 29.3.1913 (*Philosophical and Mathematical Cor-respondence*, p. 76).

3. Psychologism

The notion that philosophy has ended, at least in its traditional forms, is not peculiar to the late twentieth century. It was argued strongly by materialists from the mid-nineteenth century onwards. 'Metaphysics', Marx and Engels wrote in 1846, had 'lost the illusion of independence'. Their celebrated formulation continued: 'It is not consciousness that determines life, but life that determines consciousness ... Autonomous philosophy loses its medium of existence once we start to represent reality.'[4]

Materialism's assault on traditional philosophy reached a crescendo around the revolutionary years of the mid-century. Mostly it rested on a contention that philosophy, and especially 'metaphysics', had been superseded by the discoveries of the 'positive' sciences.[5] The 'vulgar' materialists (as Marx and Engels called them) thought that the world would now be exhaustively describable in terms of mechanics, or at least of chemistry. Karl Vogt, for example, wrote that 'thinking stands in the same relation to the brain as gall does to the liver or urine to the kidneys'.[6] Others contented themselves with popular slogans like 'you are what you eat' and 'no thought without phosphorus' (which was believed to be the chemical involved in ratiocination).

Not until they reached the gates of formal logic did the extirpators of philosophy make an uneasy halt. According to Engels, this, with its companion discipline dialectic, was all that would remain of 'the entirety of philosophy until now'; 'everything else' – and especially, no doubt, the ethical and historical philosophies that had been so prominent in Hegelian metaphysics – 'is absorbed into the positive science of nature and history' (Engels, 1894, 24; 1946, 59).

Even thinking, though not (for sophisticated materialists) comparable with urinating, was in their terms still part of the real world. As such, it was presumably describable by some 'positive science' or other; and furthermore, as Engels intimates in the 'Anti-Dühring', logic would seem to be as historical and changeable as the object to which it relates – the human brain.

This boisterous and politically motivated materialism was not without consequences in the universities. The most prominent academic materialist of the later nineteenth century, F.A. Lange, took over the notion that

---

4 *The German Ideology*, 26f. For more recent speculations, see McCarthy, Bohman, Baynes, 1987.
5 'One leaves alone "absolute truth" . . .; instead, one pursues attainable relative truths along the path of the positive sciences . . .' Engels, 1946, 17. Formulations of this kind derive ultimately from Auguste Comte, for whom 'metaphysics' characterised the second 'epoch' of humanity, while the 'positive' epoch was the third and last.
6 Quoted in Schmidt, 1974, xiii.

thought was in some way an empirical property of the brain. For Lange, the world of our perceptions was the product of our 'sensory mechanism' (Lange 485). The forms of thought were associated with the 'physiology of the sense organs' (482). Kant's categories were to be understood as an inventory of the functions related to our organs of perception (498). This meant, among other things, that statements about the forms of thought had the same merely *probable* status as any other statements of empirical science (481). (Lange proposed, in fact, to do away with the distinction between necessary and contingent truths altogether; absolute necessity could have no role in his system – cf. p. 578.) The aprioristic claims of, say, logic, would remain (Lange identified this as a 'transcendental' as opposed to a 'psychological' matter); but it would be aprioristic because it was the 'essence of *our* intellect' to think that way (473 – my emphasis). Human beings, in other words, were organically programmed to think that way; but other life-forms might do it differently.

This argument encounters a challenge in certain sorts of thought. Principally, there is the question of mathematics. Is mathematics *really* only dealing with a pattern of human thought? Here, Lange had a useful argument from Kant. Possibly (Lange implies) a mathematics based solely on the principle of non-contradiction would make a strong claim to absolute necessity. But formal logic was not, for all its pretensions, capable of this 'magic' (474). Geometry and even arithmetic always had to have recourse to something more – namely, as Kant had argued, intuitions of time and space.[7] And such intuitions could far more readily be assimilated to Lange's doctrine of the *organic* determination of perception (485).

Lange's form of materialism may thus be rendered as follows:

(a) Necessity, if it applies to any truths, applies only to those that are analytic.
(b) Analytic truth is restricted to whatever can be generated by the principle of non-contradiction alone.
(c) Interesting or substantive truths cannot be thus generated. In particular, this is the case with mathematics.
(d) If, despite not being analytical, mathematics is a priori, then this must be because it formalises a universal feature of human thinking. The ultimate ground of mathematical truths is therefore not purely formal, but empirical: indeed, it can be *discovered* by scientific investigation.

Now, although Lange is commonly regarded as the originator of the Marburg tradition of neo-Kantianism, this doctrine does not really accord with the more sophisticated transcendentalism of his successor Hermann Cohen. It is more appropriate to see in Lange a representative of what

7 See section v) of the introduction to the *Critique of Pure Reason*; and *German Philosophy*, 25.

Frege and Husserl later characterised, and combated, as *psychologism*.[8]

All historical and 'psychological' explanations, for Frege, had to be distinguished from the formalism of 'perfect demonstration'.

> We can divide all truths requiring justification into two sorts, where the demonstration of the first is able to proceed on a purely logical basis, while the second must be supported by facts from experience. . . . So the distinction is founded not on the psychological manner of origination, but on the most perfect form of demonstration. (*BegrS*, Introduction, iii)

A logical truth, in Frege's view, was distinguished from a merely empirical one by its independence from perception events, beliefs, and the like. In that sense, logically demonstrable certainties were 'objective', i.e. outside the individual mind, in a way that the 'subjective' truths of experience never could be. This principle is enshrined in his maxim, 'The psychological is to be distinguished sharply from the logical, as the subjective is from the objective' (*Grundlagen*, x).

This critical view of the merely psychological is echoed in Frege's attitude towards natural language. Natural language is an empirical fact, like the processes of perception, and, to that extent, close to the realm of subjectivity. Frege was convinced that if there was, indeed, a pre-subjective realm of 'objective' truths, the logical infrastructure of the world, then there must also be some way of reducing that structure to signs. In this he was encouraged by, most obviously, the example of mathematics, which seemed to offer, for all its defects, a way of formalising truly general statements that exhibited none of the singularity and contingency of natural language. Spinoza, with the axiomatic deduction, *more geometrico*, of his ethics, had appealed to the same enterprise. So had Leibniz, with the project of a *calculus philosophicus* (*BegrS*, Introduction, v).

Frege regarded this tight formalisation as paradigmatic for philosophical enquiry generally. Natural language was an intoxicating illusion, a veil of obscurity over the logical structure of what Frege called the 'thought'. The task of philosophy was to tear aside this unnecessary distraction; and, to do so, it needed a 'conceptual notation' of the sort devised by Frege.

If it is a task of Philosophy to break the dominion of words over the human in-

---

8 This naturalistic reading of Kant is based, like so many since, on Kant's fatal formulation in A – that the laws of nature are 'what we put there'. A naturalistic reading of this comment is incompatible with, for example, the Paralogisms; and a significant part of Kant's re-working of the *Critique of Pure Reason* for the second edition was devoted to blocking this source of misunderstanding (see my *Introduction*, pp. 37ff.). His failure to do so is evident, however, not only from F.A. Lange's comments, but from many others. The interesting ones, from our point of view, are those that testify to the entry of this misunderstanding into the Anglo-Saxon interpretation of Kant. We have already noted Bertrand Russell's reproach of psychologism (*Essays in Analysis*, 292); but the same error is to be found again, more recently, at the foundation of P.F. Strawson's critique of Kant (1966).

tellect ... by freeing thoughts from that which the nature of linguistic expression inflicts upon them, then my conceptual notation, developed further
for this purpose, will be able to offer philosophers a serviceable instrument.
(*BegrS*, Introduction, vii)

Wittgenstein took a similar view:

Language disguises [verkleidet] the thought. It does it in such a way that one
cannot, from the external form of the garment [Kleid], draw conclusions
about the form of the disguised thought ... (*Tractatus*, 4.002)

Because of this, in Wittgenstein's account, 'All philosophy is "linguistic
criticism"' (*Tractatus* 4.0031). There are differences between Frege and the
Tractatus on this issue, but the crucial point remains: for these thinkers,
philosophy cannot safely be done apart from the recognition that the structures of truth and certainty are only very inadequately rendered in natural
language.

Frege's attack on psychologism, and his cautions against the misleading
character of natural language, are a transcendentalist impulse of the kind
that guided Kant. Frege's own impetus, again like Kant's, derived from his
impatience at the irresponsible relativisation of science. His particular concern was the status of mathematics. Frege in fact thought that Kant, by
denying arithmetic the status of being 'analytical', had contributed to the
naturalistic destabilisation of logic and science. Kant's tactic, in fact, had
been to argue that arithmetic was no less empirical than causation, and that
the two stood or fell together.[9] Frege confined himself to arithmetic,
where, as we shall see, his logical innovations did indeed achieve advances
Kant had thought impossible.

Frege's disgust at naturalists and evolutionists is plain:

... We shall soon be at the point where it is thought necessary, when demonstrating Pythagoras's theorem, to take into account the phosphorus content of
our brains, and where an astronomer is reluctant to extend his conclusions to
times long past in case someone objects, 'You are calculating $2 \times 2 = 4$; but the
notion of number has a development, a history! ... How do you know that
this proposition was already established in that time? Could the beings that
lived then not have had the proposition $2 \times 2 = 5$, from which the proposition
$2 \times 2 = 4$ only developed by natural selection in the battle for existence, and
which may in turn be fated to develop to $2 \times 2 = 3$ in the same manner?'
(*Grundlagen*, Introduction, vi)

4. Logic and metaphysics

What is the status of 'laws' of logic?

We might say that the rules of the understanding, as formally described

9 See my *Introduction*, 23ff.

by logic, are conditions of our knowledge of the world. 'Truth' is the successful formation of statements about the world; and logical regularity is a
condition of that formation. So, regardless of the relation between 'our'
minds and anything else (i.e. regardless of epistemology), logic describes an
inescapable structure in the phenomenon 'world'. The things that logic
concerns itself with are 'really' present in the world, at least in so far as we
know the world at all.

Now, within this position there is a crucial variation of metaphysical
emphasis. The basic doctrine is that we cannot experience the world without logic, the rules of the understanding: in that sense, 'the world' and logic
are inextricably linked; there is no irrational world that we can experience.
However, this basic position invites two possible extensions. The first
might be described as passive. Understanding, as structured by logic,
becomes a gate through which knowledge is filtered. This does not, however, exclude the possibility of non-logical worlds; it merely says that we
can have no 'experience' of them, in the special Kantian sense of the term
experience. More particularly, the non-logical parts of the universe seem to
be the source of what actually happens. Logic, and its extensions in science,
explain things, retrospectively, and *predict* other things, prospectively. But
these are generalities; by contrast, the particular contingent events of experience seem to come from elsewhere. This is perhaps most obviously a
problem in relation to the free acts of human beings. These are obviously
not logical or predictable in any very general way. But, beyond that, it
seems that even the individual things of experience are somehow uneasy in
a framework of pure general logic. Trees in general may be explained and
discussed in terms of botany, ecology, microbiology, genetics, and so on.
In each case, the tree figures as a convertible unit in a regular frame. But
what about *this* tree, irregularly shaped, suffering from atmospheric pollu-
tion, one of its branches misshapen from the children's swing suspended
from it? There seems, at this point, to be an uncertainty about the transition
from the regular, scientific and typical to the actual object here.

In logic, this kind of problem is reflected in certain specific areas, usually
concerning the questions of identity and existence. Identity is the judgement, 'This is a tree'; or, perhaps more precisely, 'This thing is the same as
other things that I call trees'. Existence, which, as we shall see, may be
derived from identity, is a judgement such as, 'There is a tree in my garden'
(i.e. more formally, it is not true that there is nothing in the subclass formed
by the intersection of the classes 'trees' and 'things in my garden'). Existence (as we shall find Frege arguing) is very close to enumeration. Bare
existential judgements, such as 'trees exist', are artificial and meaningless.
But enumerative judgements, such as 'there are two trees in my garden' are
entirely meaningful: but also, for the reason we have considered, strangely

puzzling from the standpoint of pure general logic.

Nonetheless, transcendental logic tries to come to terms with riddles like existence and identity. As far as Kant was concerned, judgements of identity would have to remain a mystery deep in the soul of human reason.[10] But he was confident that the notion of existence could be encompassed by logic, and indeed the whole of his 'transcendental logic' is concerned precisely with that. Existence, in Kantian terms, is a matter of time and place. The fundamental distinction between pure generality and particular being is time and place. If something is somewhere, at some time, then that is what makes it 'be', in particular actuality, rather than merely occupy some general slot in logical possibility.

In traditional metaphysics, time and place were the characteristics of matter. Matter was the 'principle of individuation', the component which gave individuality, or particularity, to what would otherwise be a timeless, placeless abstraction. The timeless, placeless abstraction is form, logical structure – the class of trees, for example. Matter was what gave particular individuation to the abstract class, what converted 'treeness' to *this particular tree, here, now.*

Kant's transcendental logic was an attempt to add particularity, or an anticipation of particularity, to the abstractions of what he called 'general' logic. He was trying, for example, to augment bare logical rules like 'a statement cannot be simultaneously true and not true' (the law of non-contradiction), with rules that envisaged the existence of particular things. These latter rules were called the 'categories'; and they included notions like causation, and the subsistence of individual identity across time. Mathematics, in Kant's view, was also part of this extended realm of logic-for-existence. Arithmetic, for example, depended on a kind of abstraction from existence. Rather like the categories, arithmetic *anticipated* particular individual existences. It, so to speak, worked on the assumption that countable individuals would at some stage come along to occupy the slots arranged for them by arithmetic. Kant argued, in support of this, that a person doing arithmetic somehow always had an intuition of objects in space or time. They might not actually be counting apples, or the beads on an abacus, or whatever; but nonetheless the anticipation of such units was a constant underlying factor.

Now, the metaphysics of Kant's logic are, in our terms, passive or resigned because there is an underlying metaphor of reception. Kant's logic, the transcendental logic, waits to receive the offerings of the outside world. It is, perhaps, like a vending machine. The mind, in Kant's account, is designed to receive certain sorts of input, like the vending machine that awaits

---

10 See my *Introduction*, 21f.

coins, and choices expressed by buttons being pushed. When it receives input that it can 'understand', the mind responds in carefully regulated ways. The vending machine issues a ticket; the mind registers an experience.

The point about the vending machine comparison is to emphasise that this view propounds (a) a fundamental discontinuity between the mind and the 'world', and (b) it presupposes a basic degree of fixity in the operations of the mind. As to (a), it says 'I neither know nor care what the outside world "is"; all I can say with confidence is that our knowledge of it will never go outside the rules we have established'. On (b), it imagines that the rules of knowledge, and hence of the knowable world (the world that Kant, and, later, Frege call 'objective'), are somehow self-sustaining and unchangeable.

There is an alternative view to this. It argues that the distinction between what is knowable and what merely 'is', or between mind and the outside world, or between subject and object, is an illegimate interpolation. The situation, rather, would be that the world is both material and formal. Logic is in the world; positing any other, non-logical kind of 'outside world' is a pointless distraction. The world is not made logical by us; it is, intrinsically, logical. And the gap between reason and unreason is not congruent with the gap between 'knowing mind' and 'outside world'; it is, rather, a historical gap, or some other kind of differentiation resident within the world. The force of this will become clearer later.

To recapitulate: the challenge facing any logical doctrine is that of showing how it relates to reality. If logic is form, in all its purity, then where can it throw a bridge across to matter, the messy, unpredictable world of real events? The flashpoint, perhaps, is in the notion of existence. How can logic address actual individual things?

5. Propositional logic

Traditional logic, at the end of the nineteenth century, offered two main resources. The first was what is commonly termed propositional logic. Propositional logic is the purest exercise of the understanding. It is the fundamental logic of combination, the set of rules devised for the application of the law of non-contradiction.

In simple terms, propositional logic concerns itself with combinations of statements. A statement, for the purposes of propositional logic, is something that is either true or not true. It is the task of propositional logic to assess the effect of combinations of statements.

For example, we may wish to state, as a 'law', that thunderstorms are always accompanied by a drop in barometric pressure. We can formulate this in logical terms as a combination of two statements. Statement p is 'thunderstorms happen', and statement q is 'there is a drop in barometric pressure'. We can express this relationship in various ways, both logically and in ordinary language. We can, for example, say 'if there is a thunderstorm, then there must also be a drop in barometric pressure'. Using our letters, this makes 'if p then q'. In symbolic notation, '$p{\to}q$'.

Propositional logic now tells us what other combinations of p, q, and their negations are logically permissible as long as we wish to retain our basic rule about thunderstorms and barometric pressure. This is not, of course, a matter of discovering anything about thunderstorms or barometers; it is merely a matter of ensuring that we have formulated our law in a way that says what we want to say about the relationship between thunderstorms and barometers, and excludes things we do not want to say.

For example, is it consistent with our law to say that the barometric pressure may drop without thunderstorms happening – q but not p, in our abbreviated scheme ('$\neg p.q$', in symbolic notation)? The answer is, yes. It is consistent with the meaning attached by propositional logic to '$p{\to}q$', that one should also affirm '$\neg p.q$', or indeed just plain 'q'.

On the other hand, the rules of propositional logic would usually not (assuming the most common interpretation of the if-then relationship, '$\to$') allow a combination stating that thunderstorms may happen without the barometric pressure dropping. (In symbolic notation, this combination would be expressed '$p.\neg q$'.) This is, in fact, the one thing that is *not* permitted to be consistent with '$p \not\to q$', so much so that '$\neg(p.\neg q)$' ('not p without q') is interchangeable with it.

For a propositional logician, then, the law about thunderstorms says the following. Fine weather, with neither thunderstorm nor pressure drop ('$\neg p.\neg q$') is consistent with the law. Terrible weather, with both thunderstorm and pressure drop is also consistent with the law ('$p.q$'). So is weather where there is a drop in pressure, but no actual thunderstorm ('$\neg p.q$'). The one event that is not permitted by the logical structure of our law is a thunderstorm without a pressure drop ('$p.\neg q$'). In other words, when we formulate a law in the form 'if p then q', we are (or should be) aiming to exclude precisely one event – that of p happening without q. Obviously we are not trying to prescribe laws to nature; we are simply making the most precise possible statement of the event that would require us to reformulate our law. Propositional coherence, in this example, would be a way of ensuring control over the way the theory, and the outturns envisaged by the theory, relate to one another.

The combinations dealt with by propositional logic can, clearly, be far more extensive and complex than in our rudimentary illustration. Propositional logic is not, as with our example, merely a matter of putting into

symbols something that is intuitively obvious anyway; it is a matter of supplying accurate and accelerated routes to determining the consistency of
wide-ranging kinds of combination.

The power of propositional logic is most strikingly visible, perhaps, in
binary arithmetic, which was, by Frege's time, already extensively familiar
from the work of George Boole. The binary system reduces arithmetic to
elementary components. All operations, whether addition, multiplication
or whatever, are achieved by combining two-value positions. All numbers
register as a sequence of positions that are either 'on' or 'off'. And the combination of those numbers is perfomed in exactly the same way as in the
propositional logic illustrated above. This makes it relatively simple to
mechanise the operation, as has, indeed, been achieved in the digital computer. There, each value encounters its combinatory partner in a pre-set
logic gate directly analogous to the 'if-then' combination considered above
(in fact, the logic gates in a computer are *and* [both p and q], *or* [p or q or
both], and *nor* [neither p nor q]). And, as we saw above, some combinations will be acceptable to the gate (and will register positive, or 'true',
or '1'), and others will not be (and will register negative, or 'false', or '0').

6. Syllogisms

The power of propositional logic is also its weakness, because it derives
precisely from the fact that it is so abstracted from the concrete. Propositional logic, as we noted, is built up entirely from the one fundamental rule,
that of non-contradiction. In that rule is enshrined the dual basis of this
logic – the notions of combination and of negation.

With it, however, we still remain at some distance from the real world,
and particularly from *individual things*. Propositional logic, obviously,
does not concern itself with things. It concerns itself with combinations of
statements, which is a long way from concrete individuality. It is not even
as though statements are singular things; they are, at even the most minimal
level, concerned with relationships between entities. 'A thunderstorm has
occurred', for example, directs itself towards the general concept 'thunderstorm', and the temporal specification 'events before the time of speaking'.
This is already a complex affair; by the time propositional logic arrives to
deal with possible combinations between our thunderstorm statement and
others about, say, barometers, we have left the simple individuality of the
thing far behind.

There is, however, another form of traditional logic which does concern
itself with things rather than merely with statements. That is syllogistic
logic.

'Syllogism' is the name of a kind of reasoning conventionally associated with Aristotle, who initiated its detailed study. In contrast to propositional logic, there is an intuitive element in the syllogism. Its basis is not a purely formal principle (like the law of non-contradiction), but the more intuitive notion of inclusion. The syllogism is grounded on an underlying metaphor – that of the sorting of objects. The study of the syllogism is concerned to systematise this intuition: how can objects be assigned amongst differing sorts, in such a way that we can reach legitimate conclusions about the interrelationship of the sorts?

The structure of syllogisms has three elements. In the first place, the inference takes place across three judgements. Two judgements are introduced to provide the premises, and a third is then deduced from the combination of the first two. The first two judgements are derived from 'outside' -either from observation or from the operation of previous syllogisms – and the third is generated by the internal rule of syllogistic reason. The second element of the syllogistic structure is that all the judgements, whether as premises or conclusion, must be formed in one of four basic patterns of inclusion (the 'categorical' forms). These are general affirmation ('all x are y'), general denial ('no x are y'), particular affirmation ('some x are y'), and particular denial ('some x are not y'). The order and pattern in which the three judgements (premise, premise, conclusion) line up to form the syllogism consitutes the 'mood' of the syllogism.

The third element concerns the order in which the terms are presented in the judgements constituting the syllogism. The conclusion, obviously, consists of two linked terms ('all x are y', for example). The other two judgements, the 'premises', each contain one or the other of the terms in the conclusion, plus a third term, the 'middle term', which does not appear in the conclusion. The so-called 'figure' of the syllogism is determined by the pattern adopted by the conclusion terms and the 'middle term' in the premises – that is to say, whether the conclusion terms come before or after the middle term. There are, by a simple process of permutation, four possible 'figures'.[11]

From these basic elements, numerous combinations may be assembled. In the Middle Ages, these were set out, named, and identified as valid or invalid. Some were straightforward and obviously valid, such as the form 'Barbara', which consists of three general affirmative judgements in the first figure (for example, 'All Greeks are human beings'; 'All human beings are mortal'; 'Therefore all Greeks are mortal'). Others involved a more complex mix of judgement types (for example, 'All Greeks are human

11 If we label the first term of the conclusion 'x', the second term 'y', and the middle term 'M', and indicate the syntax of the judgement by |, we get (1) M | y, x | M; (2) y | M, x | M; (3) M | y, M | x; (4) y | M, M | x. The conclusion, of course, is always x | y.

beings'; 'Some Greeks are black-haired'; 'Therefore some human beings are black-haired'). And on the margins lurked doubtful forms like the fourth figure, which, though valid in some moods, is an angular and uncongenial form of reasoning.[12]

The study of syllogisms, historically, lacked any conclusive aprioristic basis. The legitimacy or otherwise of particular inferences is observed, and rules are then devised to capture this prescriptively. There are, it would seem, fifteen valid ways of forming a syllogism (in terms of mixing moods and figures). Various rules have been propounded to generalise the requirements of any valid syllogism (a negative premise must be followed by a negative conclusion, a particular premise must be followed by a particular conclusion, etc.), but syllogistic logicians never appeared to be able to demonstrate the basis of these rules from first principles.

7. Quantification

We come now to Frege's contributions to logic. His outstanding contribution, in the general view, is his establishment of the technique of quantification.[13] For our purposes, however, it is important that this technique was only a means to an end; and it is from this end that we shall start our exposition.

As we noted, Frege starts with a similar goal to that of Kant: rescuing scientific enquiry – and particularly, in his case, mathematics – from the depredations of scepticism. Frege's technique, like Kant's, is what we have characterised as transcendentalism. Transcendentalism is the attempt to ensure that as much of knowledge as possible is grounded in indisputable certainties. Historical principles ('the human mind has evolved into thinking like this') are not certainties of that order. A transcendental certainty is one which can be demonstrated to be, at least, inseparable from anything we would recognise as 'thinking' at all.

One generally accepted certainty, at least in Frege's time, was the law of non-contradiction. But this, as we noticed in its application to propositional logic, is so far removed from 'reality' that it hardly seems to give sufficient defence against encroaching scepticism. The techniques of syllogistic logic, though more concerned with things, also offered no substantial support to the dominion of scientific rationality. In particular, all the really substantial elements of scientific enquiry, from the doctrine of causation to the structures of arithmetic itself, seemed to be based on conventions of one sort or another. They might be conventions at a high level

12 Compare P.T. Geach's comments on the fourth figure, *Logic Matters*, 50-1.
13 See Dummett, *Frege*.

(they were, as Kant pointed out, *a priori* to any particular investigation); but they still relied on resources that were not clearly independent of the historical and the conventional.

In Kant's account of arithmetic, for example, the notions of unit and quantity were made dependent upon an 'intuition' – a convention, in other words, to deal with them as a kind of conventional abstraction from particular things. A unit, in that account, was an abstract representation of something, rather as abacus beads stood for coins, pounds of apples, or whatever. Addition, accordingly, was an empirical generalisation from the spatial accumulation of things like beads. The behaviour of beads was observed, and rules were devised to predict the kind of thing they could be relied upon to do again in the future.

But this approach clearly made no attempt to deduce mathematics from first principles. The problem, as Frege saw it, was that this approach too readily conceded the notion of singularity to sense (*GA*, §12). Sense is, by definition, incapable of generalisation (in the Kantian project, that is the role of the understanding). And obviously, in practice, it is only sense that gives us objects, which are necessarily singular things. But the idea that singularity (and hence also plurality) are *as principles* dependent on sense seemed, at least to Frege, to be a premature surrender.

Frege's answer, again in Kantian terms, was to insist that arithmetic must be not only *a priori* (which would, probably, not be denied even by a sceptic); but that it is also analytic – derivable, in other words, from the absolutely general principles of the understanding, and in no way dependent on conventions of any level. 'Thus, by objectivity [i.e. scientific truthfulness], I mean an independence from our sensibility, intuition, and imagination, from the projection of inner pictures from our memory of earlier sense impressions, but not an independence from reason . . .' (*GA*, §26).

Let us briefly consider what this means. Philosophy is a matter of describing what happens. It may do this for two reasons. Either it wants to distinguish between what has to happen (so there is no point in arguing about it), or, more ambitiously, it wants to establish patterns of legitimation - arguments to support practical options of one sort or another.

Although Frege does talk of the legitimation of judgements (*GA*, §3), his main purpose is the first – description of what happens in order to strip out what is unnecessary and speed up the whole process. In technical terms, his aim is to replace a merely synthetic understanding of arithmetic with an analytical one. Analysis, in his definition, grounds any procedure strictly only in 'general logical laws and definitions' (*GA*, §3). This brings us to a remoter level of abstraction, but it also reduces to a minimum the operations necessary to achieve anything.

The procedure is directly comparable to the replacement of 'analogue' with 'digital' technology. Analogue technology is, itself, a simplification and systematisation of human tasks. The abacus, for example, rids the trader of the need to perform arithmetical operations by piling up coins, vegetables, or whatever. The abacus mimics this operation, in a sense, but also simplifies and accelerates it by transferring it to a smaller number of essential operations.

A similar mimicry can be seen in the gramophone record. Sound is like waves on the surface of a fluid. It can be captured and stored by rendering it as waves on the surface of a disc. This is a great deal simpler than, say, the direct reproduction of a mechanical roll piano; but it is still reproduction by mimicry and hence, perhaps, less precise and economical than it might be.

Digital technology is an attempt to reduce the operations retained in analogue technology still further, to the absolute minimum, and then to build up the same result by combinations of that simplicity. So, whereas the abacus uses beads arranged in 'heaps' of five, the digital technology confines itself to 'heaps' of one. And whereas the conventional sound recording uses a kind of 'representation' of sound waves in the air, digital recording reduces waves to a bare numerical account. The result, in either case, is enormously enhanced speed and storage capacity.

Frege, in a sense, is doing the same thing. For him, the notion that arithmetic was 'synthetic' introduced an extraneous element of analogy into the proceeding. On one level, obviously, this exposed arithmetic to silly arguments that it was in some way a mere historical convention, and subject to change. But, more frustratingly, synthesis dragged down the cool purity of logic, and hampered arithmetic in its quest for analytical speed. From that viewpoint, then, Frege's quest is simply for technical perfection.

He develops his approach in three ways: separation of the empirical from the logical structure of the judgement, separation of the predicate from its 'subject', and separation of statements about things from statements about concepts. In a sense, Frege's approach aims to incorporate the best of propositional and syllogistic logic, with the weaknesses of neither.

8. 'Facts' and the logical structure of the statement

In the first place, Frege insists that the basic logical unit, as with propositional logic, is the statement. Logic has nothing to say about anything that is not a statement. A statement, for these purposes, is something that can be either true or false. The utterance 'house', for example, is not a statement, and cannot be of concern to logic. The utterance, 'this house is mine', however, is a statement that may be either true or false, and consequently is of concern to logic. In Frege's terms, logic deals only with things that have 'judgeable content' (*BegrS*, §2).

Having said that, however, the assertion that something is true is, in turn, to be distinguished from the actual structure of the judgement. Frege emphasises this distinction by means of his notation. The basic judge-mental unit, bare of any assertion, is established by a horizontal line —. This 'content line', as Frege called it in the *Begriffsschrift*,[14] makes no assertion about the truth or otherwise of its contents; it merely offers them up as something that may eventually be asserted or denied. Assertion – the prefix, 'it is true that. . .' – is expressed by a small vertical line at the beginning of the horizontal one: ⊢. This 'judgement line' ('Urteilsstrich') makes no contribution to the logical structure of the statement. It operates on a completely different level, taking the statement out of the speculative, formal arena and into the level of material realities. But this transformation makes no *logical* difference to the statement. 'The judgement line cannot be used for forming a functional expression [i.e. a 'judgeable statement'], because it does not serve with other signs for the designation of an object' (*FuB*, 22n). 'Designation of an object', by which Frege means specification of a state of affairs, is different from asserting that such a state of affairs is really the case.

Frege developed this idea at some length outside pure logic, in his theory of meaning. There, in a famous essay, he distinguished between the sense ('Sinn') and the reference ('Bedeutung') of a statement, or other utterance. The sense, in this account, corresponded to the 'judgeable content' which appeared in his logical notation after the horizontal line. It was a designatory matrix, which might or might not refer to anything. If it did successfully refer to something, then that something would be its 'reference'. Sense, in Frege's usage, was also directly congruent with 'thought'; thought was the 'objective content that is capable of being the shared property of many [people]' ('Über Sinn and Bedeutung' (*SuB*), 32n). Sense was a logical structure, capable of bearing a reference; if it had a reference, that changed nothing in the sense, save in that it confirmed its truth.

Now all referring, in Frege's view, was a kind of naming. That is, a successful reference named an object. The name '10 Downing Street' refers to an object. So, in Frege's view, does any successful designation. '9+7', for example, is a name for the object 16. Part of the point of this doctrine was to explain an aspect of identity. Objects can be referred to in different ways, they can have many 'names' with different 'senses', and yet there is an identity of reference between all those names. So '8+8' would be another name for 16. It may have a different 'sense', i.e. logical structure, from '9+7', but

14 He later rejected this term, and said simply, 'the horizontal line' – *Funktion und Begriff* (*FuB*), 21.

they both designate the same object, and hence the judgement of identity '8+8=9+7' is both valid and, arguably, interesting. This is specially the case in the scientific arena: the discovery that 'the evening star' and 'the morning star' were the same thing, and the judgement of identity expressing it, was logically and scientifically significant.

Frege had a further interpretation of the notion of a 'name' which is puzzling at first sight, but will turn out to be crucial for his logic. The point is this. It is obvious that '10 Downing Street' is a name, and refers to a specific object, just like any other proper name. The notion that '9+7', or indeed '16', could be names, is less obvious, but we can let it go for the time being. But what do we do about complex sentences, like, for example, 'thunderstorms are accompanied by a drop in barometric pressure'? It is obvious that they have a 'sense', and that they contain a 'thought'. But in what way, if any, are they names?

Frege's answer is that any successful sense has a reference, and a 'name' is merely another way of expressing the notion of 'successful sense'. So 'name' is another way of saying 'statement that refers'. This seems to be stretching the term. However, the more insistent question is: to what does a complex sentence, which may contain various names (like 'thunderstorm' or 'barometer'), refer to? Frege's answer is that the referent of a statement is what he calls its 'truth value', i.e. whether it is true or false. A true statement refers to, names, 'the true'. 'Every assertive statement [Behauptungssatz] . . . is to be understood as a proper name, and its reference, if it is present, is either the true or the false. These two objects are recognised, if only tacitly, by everyone who forms judgements . . .' (SuB, 34).

Both of these principles – identity of reference underlying difference of sense, and truth value as the referent of assertions – will turn out to be crucial components of Frege's logical structure. Before we get to this, however, we must consider a more fundamental metaphysical function of the doctrine. This is Frege's insistence on the uniqueness of judgement in its full-blown form, namely assertion. The point is this. For Frege, the little vertical line at the beginning of his horizontal 'content line' may, in one respect, seem rather superfluous, since it contributes nothing towards the actual structure of reference, the 'sense'. Wittgenstein, as we shall see, took the view that the assertion line was, indeed, entirely redundant. For Frege, however, it was the anchor-point of the whole logical procedure. Judgement was the act, the mysterious decision, that confirmed as real what had hitherto only been speculative and, in a sense, mechanical. Judgement, as assertion, was the great step up to the realm of truth and objectivity. 'Judgement is something quite unique and incomparable,' Frege wrote. It represented a 'progression' (SuB, 35), or a 'step from the stage of thoughts to the stage of reference (the stage of objectivity)' (SuB, 34). Indeed, said

Frege in stirring language, judgement was the 'acknowledgement of truth' (*SuB*, 34n). It is this principle – what might be called the supra-logical principle of judgement – that, as we shall see, supplies the real foundation for Frege's doctrines.[15]

Frege's theory of judgement and the primacy of 'Bedeutung' has a further offshoot that coloured his interpretation of his own work, and has had, perhaps, a disproportionate influence on his successors. This is the devaluation of what Frege called 'improper' propositions.[16] On one level, an improper proposition is simply a half-formed thought, a syntactical matrix which might grow into a thought with sense, but which, as it stands, has no 'judgeable content'. By itself, for example, the expression 'a→b' would be an improper proposition in this usage, because it gives us insufficient content about which we could judge, 'this is [un]true'. On the other hand, a proposition that included that same expression – say, 'If a→b, then (a+1)→(b+1)' – could well be a proper proposition because, in this case, it forms a statement with judgeable content.

As far as Frege was concerned, this principle supplied a way of assessing the use of language outside the purely scientific arena. From his point of view, no statement that lacked judgeable content could aspire, so to speak, to the dignity of truth. A statement should at least anticipate, or 'presuppose', that it would achieve meaning ('Bedeutung', *SuB*, 31). In that respect, the use of statements which wilfully abrogated judgeable content was almost an abuse of human rationality. Some of this was harmless, for example the utterances of actors on stage, which everyone recognised as being outside the sphere of truth. Even here, though, Frege seems almost offended by the fact that this kind of speech cannot be bracketed off into its own realm of inconsequence and play. 'It would be desirable to have a particular expression for signs which are only intended to have a sense,' he wrote. 'We could call them, for example, pictures, and then the words of the actor on the stage would be pictures, and indeed the actor himself would be a picture' (*SuB*, 33n).[17]

More significantly, Frege's censorious attitude towards the improper (or 'inauthentic' – *uneigentlich*) use of language extended also to much of the realm of practical relationships and, in particular, to politics. Imperatives, for example, had no 'meaning' in themselves, from this viewpoint (*SuB*, 38). And neither did the extravagant entities invoked by politicians, like 'the will of the people'. This was an 'illusory proper name', a treacherous

15 Frege may have picked up the notion of judgement as 'acknowledgement of truth' from the neo-Kantians (compare Roberts, 1982, 83).

16 See, for example, Frege's letter to Dingler of 6.2.1917 (*Correspondence*, 19-23).

17 There is, arguably, a difference between statements which have no judgeable content, like 'a→b', and the narrations of an actor, which have a judgeable content, but are not offered in order to be judged. This is not, it seems, material.

interloper incapable of designation or 'judgeable content' (*SuB*, 41).

9. Predication

Frege's theory of judgement, then, may be seen as a deferring of the material element. In terms of classical metaphysics, it represents a decision to attend to the formal elements of a statement as fully as possible before turning to the practical elements. Judgement, particularly in the neo-Kantian terms in which Frege presents it, is a practical matter, an act, a decision, an 'acknowledgement'. But we should only proceed to this act once we have established our formal preparations, in constructing the 'sense' of our thinking.

The same scrupulous deferral may be seen in the next, more technical aspect of Frege's approach, his theory of predication. The notion of predication, in essence, is quite simple. It involves, initially, no more than a sharpening up of the old analysis of statements into subject and predicate. The subject is that part of the sentence of which the rest of the statement predicates something. In 'All Greeks are men', for example, 'All Greeks' is the subject, while 'are men' is the predicate. Even quite complex sentences can be analysed in this manner. In 'Samantha is running the water before having a bath and washing her hair', Samantha is, again, the subject, and the rest is the predicate. All the component parts of a syllogism are subject-predicate links.

The problem with the conventional analysis is that the division between subject and predicate is not, when examined closely, as clear as it might seem. (This is, perhaps, an obvious example of the misleading quality of ordinary language.) The point is this. What, precisely, is being predicated of what? Let us take a rather more involved sentence: 'People who live in Greece are mortal'. Grammatically, the predicate is just 'are mortal', while 'people' together with its relative clause are the subject. In Fregean terms, we might say that whole of the first part of the sentence is a 'name' of something that we could also name 'Greeks'. But attribution would seem to be something for the predicate: why does the subject part of the sentence seem to contain far more attributions than the predicate part? In a sentence like this, in other words, there seems to be an ambiguity of role on the part of the 'subject'. It stands and allows itself to be described by the predicate; but it *also* contains a whole package of self-descriptions of its own, outside the ostensible subject-predicate structure of the sentence. The subject seems, as it were, to have jumped the gun. It arrives at the predication site loaded with a pre-emptive set of predications of its own. The same is true even of short single-term subjects, like 'Greeks' (i.e. without the 'all'). Although

'Greeks' is, so to speak, only a punctiform name, it seems in effect to contain an undeclared predication, 'these people are Greeks'.

So in a fully expanded form, with no unacknowledged predications, a statement like 'All Greeks are mortal' might be rendered as '[what we are talking about] is people, and they are Greek, and they are mortal'. The part in the square brackets is, in my formulation, a sort of predication as well. But if we regard it merely as an activation of the subject role, but as otherwise contentless, then we will be approaching the kind of modification envisaged by Frege.

There are clear omissions in our reformulation – the 'all', for example, and the bland 'and' between each predication obviously fails to render the logical hierarchy of predicates. But the essential point is this: for the purposes of logic, it is best for the subject to be utterly subjectual, and accordingly divested of any of the elements to be imported by the predicate.

Now, Frege develops this idea in various ways. In the first place, it has important implications for the predicate part of the sentence. The predicate, now that the subject has been stripped of any pre-emptive concealed predications, contains *all* the predicate structures of any statement. So, as above, there is nothing left in the subject position except a kind of featureless square bracket – the utterly abstract 'what we are talking about'. Frege's analogy for this is the mathematical function. A function would be, for example, $2(x+1)$. This consists of two elements – a kind of logical matrix (the addition of one, and the multiplication of the sum by two), together with an indeterminate something (the 'x') which is to be fitted into this matrix. The matrix part explains in detail what is going to be done. But nothing *is* done until something is put into the slot marked by the 'x'. This 'x', in Frege's account, is analogous to the subject in the subject-predicate link. The predicate contains, so to speak, all the interesting content of the statement; but until we have a subject to predicate this content of, the sentence does not come to life. The appearance of the subject pulls the trigger, it activates the logical mechanism.

The predicate, then, behaves like a mathematical function. It supplies all the significant content that accrues to the subject in its passage through. But it is, in a modification of Kant's famous dictum, empty without the element of sense, the 'matter' which alone gives meaning to the form.[18] Frege's image for this is that the function is 'incomplete' or 'unsatisfied' ('die Funktion für sich allein ist unvollständig, ergänzungsbedürftig oder ungesättigt zu nennen' – *FuB*, 6; see also *GGA*, §1).

What, then, is the 'subject' in this scheme of things? Extending his mathematical analogy, Frege calls the subject the 'argument' of the function.

18 'Thoughts without content are empty, intuitions without concepts are blind' (B75). See also *Introduction*, 17.

The 'x' in '$2(x+1)$' identifies the place where the argument is inserted. The subject in Frege's analysis of the subject-predicate link plays exactly the same role, it is an argument.

Beyond this, the argument is everything that the function is not. In traditional syllogistic logic, as we noticed, the subject term is already encumbered with bits of predication. Here, however, the subject is defined precisely as what does not have any predicative role. This means, in addition, that whereas the predicate is 'unfulfilled', awaiting its subject, the subject itself *is* what Frege calls 'sated' (or 'satisfied', 'gesättigt'). The subject is characterised by Frege as an 'object' ('Gegenstand'). The term 'object' is carefully chosen, for technical reasons, and should not be too hastily associated with any intuitive idea of 'thing'. The basis of the 'object' is its capacity to be inserted as an 'argument' in a 'function'. This means, first and foremost, that the 'object' has, so to speak, no voice in its incorporation into the statement. The function determines, in advance, what sort of 'object' is going to be acceptable as an argument.

In syllogistic logic, we could wander idly through the realm of things, or groups of things (classes), looking for a suitable candidate to fill the 'subject' slot for our predicate, 'are mortal'. In Frege's scheme, we have no such freedom. His function determines precisely, in advance, all the essential requirements of the argument. We are now looking only for something that is (in the above example), human and living in Greece. Indeed, the argument is so exhaustively defined by the function that, in effect, the argument no longer has any independent features of its own. To the extent that it does have them, they are of no concern to the operation of the function. For example, our 'Greeks' may have other attributes, such as (in part) having black hair, or voting for the socialist party, or whatever. But this is of no concern to the function. *Everything* that the function could possibly make use of is established in advance. There is no residue of independent 'subjectness'. In Frege's logic, the subject is truly an empty centre. And the 'object' which fills that subject position, accordingly, is not a collection of attributes. It is a 'thing' only to the extent that the function makes it into one.

Now, the notion of the 'object' does not finish with the definition of the 'argument'. That is, so to speak, the question of what can be put into the function, what triggers it off. But there still remains the question of what comes out of the function at the other end. For Frege, that too is an 'object'. We need to consider this for a moment, for it is, in some ways, even more puzzling than the notion of an object as argument.

The object, then, is 'sated'. What Frege seems to mean by this is that there has been a successful designation of something. Objects are nameable, and named, entities. Functions, that is to say, subjectless predicates, are 'unjudgeable', so unjudged, so without meaning ('Bedeutung'). But something *with* a meaning, i.e. something which designates, is (in Frege's terminology) a name. And what is designated by it is an object. A name, then, subsists in contented, 'sated' relation with the object designated by it. It does not, as does a function, hungrily seek for 'completion'. It merely designates, fulfilled by its objecthood.

So: the object that is placed in the argument slot in a function is something named. Objects, things named or designated, are what can function as arguments.

However, as we saw, these named things are not to be understood as pre-existing bundles of attributes. They are, basically, anchor points for whatever the function chooses to hang upon them. Nonetheless, there is a sense in which they do transfer, or bring with them, the results of previous predications. This comes about because of the operation of Frege's theory of reference.

A meaningful sentence refers to something. In that respect, a correctly formed sentence is a name. What is it a name of? Not, as we saw, of its elements. It is the name of its *truth value*.

The point, then, is this. A function, or predicate, is a procedure for producing significance. On the analogy of mathematics, you put something in (you insert something into the argument slot designated by variables like 'x'), and you get something out. What you get out, the result of the computational procedure, is called in mathematics the 'value' of the function for the particular argument that you have put in. So, on the basis that everything that is not a function is an object, both the input and the output of the function are objects. And furthermore, the object-output of one function may become the object-input of another.

That, obviously, gives us various kinds of 'object'. Since we are starting with mathematics, the first kind of object is a number. (For reasons that will become apparent, it is very important in other ways that numbers should be objects; but, provisionally, we shall just take this as a hypothesis.) The next kind of object is a thing – though, as we saw, an attributionless thing. This kind of object may be imagined as, so to speak, whatever we come up with in our search for something to put in the argument slot. We search; we find something; if it fits what the function is looking for, then we take it, but without concerning ourselves about any other features it may have.

The third kind of object, meanwhile, is the result of any successful search for something to put in the argument slot. That result, as we saw, is the judgement 'this is true'. Such a judgement may arise in two basic ways. In the first way, it may result from our successfully finding something that answers to the function. For example, the function may be, 'There is something that is a person, is Greek, and votes for the Greek socialist party'. If we find one or more 'objects' of whom this can successfully be predicated, then the result of the operation will be a 'value', namely the value *true*. That truth-value, as Frege calls it, is the meaning of the sentence – the 'object' that it 'names'.

The second way of achieving a truth-value is not by finding a thing to fit a functional description, but by expressing a purely logical state of affairs. Obviously, some statements can be true regardless of whether I can go out and find any entities the statement might be alluding to. I can say, for example, 'If all a's are b's, and all b's are c's, then all a's are c's', and this will be true regardless of whether I can somehow demonstrate it empirically. So the statement has a positive truth-value, i.e. an object that it can pass on to become the input of another function.

There is a terminological point to be made here. 'Function' is a mathematical term, and in a sense Frege is only using it as an analogy. What we are fundamentally concerned with is _not_ any operation upon a subject term, but *predicative* operations. Those predicative operations, in Frege's terminology, are always carried out by *concepts* ('Begriffe'). And a concept is a special case of a function, namely one whose 'values' for any given argument are always truth-values (mathematical functions, of course, can yield numerical values) (*FuB*, 20).

10. Second-order predication

So far, Frege's project has been a tidying-up operation. The ragged structure of the syllogism, previously the only available logic of terms, has been systematised by clarifying the allowable input and output of syllogistic statements. A fuller reading of our earlier example would be, now,

> For anything we may talk about, if it is Greek, it is a human being.
> For anything we may talk about, if it is a human being, it is mortal.
> Therefore anything Greek is mortal.

This still has to be wrapped up, of course, in the form of a judgement. Frege would emphasise that this syllogism should, initially, only be understood as a thought, as a judgeable content. It should, therefore, be prefixed with the words, 'The thought that . . .' If we wish to assert that this is true, then we add the further element, 'is true'.

Two things follow from this streamlining process. The first is, as we have noted, that the material nature of the input arguments becomes irrelevant. As long as it fits the function, then that is all we are interested in. We shall see that we may well be interested in, for example, *how many* objects fit the function (i.e. give positive truth-values for it); but we are not further concerned with any other qualities the object may have. The result, second consequence of Frege's tidying, is a radical purification of our logical entities. Instead of ending up, as with the syllogism, with a kind of corral of items, grouped into pens labelled things like 'Greek' or 'Greek and mortal', we finish with a simple truth-value. 'It is true that so-and-so'. That, then, becomes the easily transferred 'object' which each function passes, as argument, to the next stage in the logical process. Things, then, become reduced to bundles of predicable concepts; and these bundles, in turn, can be shifted about as simple positive or negative truth-values. The term logic of the syllogism has thereby become integrated into the combinatory logic of propositions.[19]

In general terms, the effect of all this is as follows. Let us (in a Kantian manner) assume that all experience, and hence everything to which 'truth' ultimately relates, is a kind of internal monologue.[20] 'Here before me is a branch, and the branch has grapes hanging from it, consequently it must be a vine', and so on. Now philosophy, from the point of view of transcendentalists such as Kant or Frege, is the establishment of the necessary and inescapable conditions of experience. Once we have done that, we can be sure that we know what form 'truth' must take. We can formulate scientific, or mathematical laws about the world, secure in the knowledge that their *form* will be incontrovertible, however much may depend also on empirical investigation. Propositional and term logic do, it seems, set out structures that cannot rationally be denied by anyone.

But how far do those structures go? In particular, they do not seem to address the really crucial scientific issues like existence, non-existence and number. The point is not that logic fails to 'predict' the real: we cannot hope to 'prove' that such-and-such a particular thing exists, or exists in a certain number; but, at least in traditional logic, there does not seem even to be any foundation for talking about existence or number. To revert to our previous example: if we can find some Greek who has black hair and votes for the Socialist party, then we shall achieve a positive truth value for our thought, 'there is a Greek who, etc'. That would be a logically successful event. But can we not go further? Can we not say what it would *look like logically* for there, say, to be one of something, or ten, or for one something to be added to another ten? Kant, as Frege points out, left us with the idea of number as being no more than an intuitive generalisation, a sort of woolly conceptual metaphor rather like the syllogism. Frege thinks he can do better. But, first, he needs to make a significant addition to his logical

19 Arguably, this was already possible with syllogisms; but Frege's ruthless revision of the predicative statement was needed to make possible the steps that go beyond the syllogism. See Quine, *Methods*, 94.
20 See *Introduction*, 11.

arsenal. This is what he calls the notion of 'concepts of second order' (or 'second stage' – *GA*, §53; *FuB*, 26f).

The point is this. The subject is an extensionless point, a centre with nothing identifiable in it. Identity comes from outside, from the process of predication. But predication, itself, involves only general terms, concepts. Concepts do not include any element of number, or even of existence. When I say, 'All Greeks are human beings', I am dealing with utterly general terms which do not descend to specifics like number. So, says Frege, existence and number are not things that can be predicated of objects (in the accepted sense). I can say, 'this is a tree', or 'this is a good book', and apply the predicate directly to the object. But existence, or numbers, cannot be predicated at this level. Frege calls a function whose argument can only be an object a 'first-order function' (*FuB*, 27). First-order functions may predicate of their arguments that they fall under this or that concept; but they cannot go further than that, because concepts on their own are general and invoke neither existence nor number. The objects that fall under the concept are disparate. They partake of what Frege calls the 'features' ('Merkmale') of the concept (*GA*, §53), and to that extent they are made homogeneous with one another. Being disparate, the objects are heterogeneous and uncountable. Being united under the concept, they are to that extent one, and therefore equally uncountable. Counting cannot happen at this level. It can only happen, says Frege, as something that happens not to the objects, but to the *concept*.

What is happening here is comparable with Frege's argument about the judgement. Just as the judgement 'it is true' is somehow translogical – it is essential to meaning, and yet plays no part in the structure of the predicate – so also the attribution of existence or number is something different from the basic attachment of a concept to an object-argument. It is, in fact, at a level of secondary reflection; we are, by now, saying something not about the object but about the concept.

When we count, in fact (according to Frege), we are not counting material objects, we are counting something rather more remote: we are counting cases where the argument comes out with a truth-value 'true' for that function. Accordingly, there are two different sorts of things one may say in relation to a concept. At the basic level, one may define it, by enumerating its 'features'. These are what is, explicitly or implicitly, predicated of the object-argument. At the secondary level, we can say something about the concept (or the function) itself. This is not predication; it is the attribution of *properties* ('Eigenschaften').[21] You define a concept by

---

21 See Frege's caution to Russell: 'A predicate is as a rule a first-level function which requires an object as argument and which cannot therefore have itself as argument (subject).' Letter of 22.6.1902, *Correspondence*, 132.

enumerating its features: they are what the concept attributes to the object. But when you say things about a concept in general, you are not defining it, you are bringing something fresh to it from outside. For example, the concept 'trees in this garden' would be defined in terms of features such as tree-ness, being situated in this garden, etc. If there is a 'something' such that it is a tree, and it is situated in this garden, then there will be one or more arguments, 'somethings', that fall under the concept 'trees in this garden'. This latter fact, however – that there are one or more somethings that fall under the concept – is nothing to do with the definition of the concept. It is a kind of secondary reflection which strikes us as we watch the concept ringing up successes. At this point we can say, about the concept, but *not* about the 'somethings', 'the concept covers a range of successes'.

We can look at it another way. The trees in my garden do not wear numbers around their trunks. They do not have labels saying 'I am a tree', or even saying 'I exist'. The actual trees are *logical non-entities*, mere 'somethings'. They only acquire logical identity once they have been converted from being something into being *part of a concept*. The judgement, 'this is a tree, and it is in my garden', however it happens, produces something that was not there before – a named object, an item in my logical inventory. Once it has been produced, by the action of the basic concept, I can start generating further statements about it. But the irreducible basis of my further statements is always the predicate, not the 'something' I originally attached the predicate to. So number, and indeed existence, is a matter of saying 'application of my predicate (or concept) has given me such-and-such a response (in terms of number of successful applications)'.[22]

Existence, in other words, is dependent on logical identification, not the other way round. Once you have named something, you can say whether it exists or not. For nominalists, who teach that we name things once we have found they exist, this would be an odd notion. For our purposes, however, it is the way Frege chooses to formulate his transcendentalism.

11. Existence and number

Let us consider the situation afresh. We are dealing with a logic of how predicates may be linked with things. Although, in a metaphysical way, we are interested in the thing, for all purposes of logic and enquiry it is the predicate that concerns us. This is equally true of older types of logic. The

22 Frege's theory of second-order concepts (i.e. existence, number and the like) can be found most fully explained in *GA*, §§51-3, though see also *FuB*, 26f. Frege thought his theory supplied a refutation of the ontological proof for the existence of God: 'God is [by definition] the most perfect being. Existence is a perfection. Therefore God exists.' But existence, by Frege's theory, is not something that can be predicated of objects (e.g., in this case, God).

statement 'All Greeks are human beings' really just means 'Anything of which we can predicate "Greek" can also have "human being" predicated of it' – and that, for practical purposes, is a statement about the relation between predicates, not between things. That is even more obvious if we render the statement as, simply, 'All Gs are Hs', or even 'All G is H'.

Now the purpose of logic, if we can put it that way, is to anticipate the world. The fuller the anticipation, the more comprehensive our stock of a priori, or indeed analytical, rules about how the world is rationally put together. The best way of considering that rational structure, in Frege's approach, is as a network of predicates. In that way, we shall be able to construct an apparatus which, so to speak, awaits the arrival of experience, and is instantly ready when it comes to process and classify it. '*If* something [the experience] falls in with such-and-such a set of predicates, *then* something else follows.' (Just as, in a vending machine, coins inserted into the machine will be led through various screening devices and will, if 'true' for the purposes of the machine, trigger off a sale.)

The more sophisticated the logic, the more complex the anticipations it will be able to make. Existence as such, perhaps, is not a particularly useful kind of anticipation. Considered as non-nullity, there is a sense in which traditional logics already anticipate it. 'Some Greeks vote Socialist', for example, seems to say that the class of socialist-voting Greeks is not empty. Or, one could express the same thing by simple negation: 'Not (No Greeks vote Socialist)'. But it is unclear how useful this is. Can we get from 'Some Greeks' to 'one Greek'? In terms of our vending machine metaphor, can we make the machine capable, by purely logical instructions, of recognising a condition of 'one' (as opposed to 'some', or 'a handful', or whatever)? Even better, can we make it recognise 'three'? (Obviously a real vending machine would make use of analogue devices, such as cog-wheels and the like. Our challenge is to make it anticipate 'three' without using any analogue devices, not even Kantian intuitions of space.) When Frege declares that existence, from a logical point of view, is the same sort of thing as number, he means two things. First, a mere negation of a general negation (i.e. 'some') does not go far enough; and, second, numerosity is, so to speak, the furthest penetration yet into what had hitherto been the unassailable heartland of matter.

The task, then, is this: how do we produce a logical formula which will register 'true' for a concept which has, say, three things falling under it?

12. Numbers as objects

Producing a logical description of numbers may have several stages to it.

Once the basic project is defined, the precise way of achieving this is perhaps of subsidiary importance. The way that Frege sets about it is not the same as, for example, Bertrand Russell's way. Frege chooses to take three steps. The first involves the determination of what a number might be. The second considers what makes numbers identifiable – i.e. how one can say things like, 'there is the same number of trees as chairs in this garden'. The third considers the definition of any particular number. This step, in turn, has two components – the definition of zero, and the definition of a series, starting with zero, from within which other numbers may be derived.[23]

Numbers, as Frege insists, are objects. What does this mean? In a practical sense, it is important for the functioning of his logic. That is because numbers need to be usable as *arguments* (for functions), and need to be derivable as *values* (from functions). They are, together with truth values and other 'objects', the means for transferring logical results from one functional operation to another.

The second point is that numbers, as objects, are systematically opposed to functions (and concepts, the subset of functions). Objects are 'sated' and 'complete in themselves'; a function, by contrast, is a mere form of a connection, and 'unsatisfied' until it finds things it can connect. This means that there is, ultimately, something rather raffish about a function; it wanders the world, hoping to connect, but may well never succeed. There is nothing *in* the function that establishes it as part of reality; only once it finds an argument can it claim existence, or even number. The concept of 'horned horse', for example, is a kind of bohemian fantasy, charming but remote from the more serious levels of 'truth'. So, says Frege, it would be quite inappropriate to classify numbers with these unsteady characters. Concepts may come and go at the whim of the imagination; but numbers are a substantial part of the realm of truth.

So, like schoolmasters, the 'second-order concepts' only confer the dignity of existence, or number, on their first-order subordinates as a kind of reward for success. And these second-order concepts are not predicates (i.e. first-order characteristics); they are 'properties' achieved by those concepts which are raised to the level of truth. Existence and number, as we have already noted, supervene *after* the elementary logical struggle, not

23 From this point on, we shall use logical notation to help in the exposition. Familiarity with this is not essential. Frege's own notation is not in general use, and raises considerable printing difficulties. The main difference, in terms of content, is that Frege's schemata are expressed as a series of conditionals. This makes a great deal of sense, in that Frege is emphasising that *if* an argument gives the function a positive truth-value, *then* the logical conditions envisaged by the function apply. But it is perhaps easier to read schemata where '→' is not the main connective, and, in any event, the whole 'thought' can be understood as conditional without also needing to be expressed as conditional in all its elements. So we shall adjust Frege's schemata as necessary.

before it. That is both why they cannot be directly predicated of things, and also why they are secure from the wayward contingency of first-order predicates.

So, numbers must be objects in order to preserve them from the instability of being mere functions. The world, in Frege's transcendentalist vision, does not consist of brute 'things'; they are just the indeterminate 'x's' which, as arguments, trigger successful functions. Nor does it somehow consist of all the random concepts dreamt up in first-order predication (this is the basis of his hostility towards the ontological proof). It consists only of the two together – the indeterminate x's and the first-order predicates that give them form and visibility. Number is the recognition and confirmation of that coming together – something remote both from the 'things' and the predicates, but achieving, as a kind of elemental judgement, the basic foundations of the world. Number, the affirmation of truth and existence, is the basic logical ingredient of the material world.

It is all very well to say that numbers are objects – but what sort of objects? Frege explains this in terms of his theory of 'extension' ('Umfang').

13. Extension and class

Let us take a function, 'Something is a tree and is in this garden'. The 'something' is the indeterminate variable x. We can substitute whatever we like for x, as the function's argument. A few objects will give a positive value for the function; in other words, there is a group of somethings of which treeness and situation in this garden can successfully be predicated. That group is called by Frege the 'Umfang' of the concept 'tree in this garden'. It is, in another terminology, the *class* associated with that concept: the class of trees in this garden.

Now a class, in Frege's view, is obviously an 'object'. The four trees in my garden are conclusively and successfully 'named' by virtue of the function taking them as its arguments.

There is in fact a question here, as soon becomes clear.[24] A class can be regarded extensionally, in which case it is the collection of objects described by its concept. That seems to imply that the collection can, at least on some level, be comprehensively identified. That makes sense with, say, the trees in this garden; but it is less easy to envisage the objectivity of the collection 'good books'. The alternative understanding of a class is intensional – that is to say, 'class' is a shorthand for describing the result(s) of applying a

24 See, for example, Russell's discussions in *The Principles of Mathematics* (1903), pp. 69, 101-7, etc.

concept – but, in that respect, class is less obviously an 'object'.

Frege (and Russell, in 1903) thought this came to the same thing in the end, a view that he expressed by law V of his *Basic Laws* (*GGA*, 36)

$$(\forall a(Fa=Ga)) \leftrightarrow (\{x|Fx\} = \{y|Gy\})$$

In words, this states that to say that all F's are G's (an intensional relation, expressed by '$\forall a(Fa = Ga)$') is the same as saying that the class of F's is identical with the class of G's (an extensional matter, here expressed by '$\{x|Fx\} = \{y|Gy\}$'). As Russell's paradox later demonstrated, concepts do not always behave in the way envisaged by this equation, and extensions can end up with an indeterminate membership. An indeterminate extension would not seem to be an 'object' in quite the same comforting way as, for example, the four trees in the garden in front of me. Whether this indicates a difference between intension and extension or not, it does seem to undermine the reliability of any passage from concept to object.

Frege was aware of this uncertainty from the beginning. In *Function and Concept* he admitted that the relationship between functions and their extensions had to be regarded as a 'basic logical law' (p. 10), i.e. an indemonstrable though seemingly self-evident axiom.

Now, in any event, numbers do not attach to the extensions of first-order predicates as such. In Frege's view, a number is a name for a quality shared not by any particular extension, but by a class of such extensions – the class of extensions 'equal in number to' whatever it might be. In other words, a number is a name for a class of classes. All concepts with a four-fold extension, for example, fall under a second-level concept 'four'. (Equally, all concepts with an extension of at least one would fall under a second-level concept 'existence'.)

14. Numerical equality

So far, we have only considered what sort of thing a number might be. Now, we have to try to define it, logically.

The first requirement, according to Frege, is to identify number in terms of what it is things with the same number share. This cannot be done directly. There is no intuitive notion of numbers which could be used as a touchstone for determining whether something else was of that number. In this respect, Frege says, number is like direction. There is no absolute direction. All there is is the direction of other lines. So any particular direction is best considered not in some abstracted way, but as a collection of lines sharing the same quality, or, more particularly, *parallel* with one another. In other words, rather than starting with 'direction' and looking for objects to match it, you start with a collection of objects in a relation of identity to one another (in being parallel), and then attach a name to that collection – say, 'North-West'.

So what are things sharing the same number equal in? How do we define such a relationship without resorting to number (given that an undefined number must at this stage still be some illegitimate intuitive entity like Kant's points in space, or whatever)?

Frege's answer is to produce what he calls a relationship of 'non-ambiguity' ('Eindeutigkeit'), which he says can be defined logically. Groups of things that are in a 'non-ambiguous' relation reciprocally with the members of another group are, in Frege's account, 'equinumerate'. And if you have a class of equinumerate things, you have things that share a common nameable entity, namely number.

Frege's formula for this relationship is (*GGA*, §23; also *GA*, §72):

$$((d)(a)(e)(Fda.Fde{\rightarrow}a{=}e)).((a)(d)(b)(Fda.Fba{\rightarrow}d{=}b))$$

This is the definition of a relation F such that any object '*d*' will only stand in that relation to one other object, and any object '*a*' will only have one other object stand in that relation to it. If two classes are such that this relation applies to any member of one class, for any argument taken from the other class, then the two classes are in a reciprocal non-ambiguous relation.

The point is this. With the aid of such a 'non-ambiguous' relationship we can, so to speak, 'pair off' any particular member of one class with a particular member of another one. If they are equinumerate, then we shall run out of members of both classes at the same time, and the 'non-ambiguous' relationship will still hold. If, on the other hand, the classes are not equinumerate, then the reciprocity will cease to hold at some point, i.e. when one group has run out of members and the other has not. Frege's example is the relationship of the knives to the forks laid on a table. Each knife is in a 'reciprocal non-ambiguous relation' to each fork. We know the two groups are 'equinumerate' not because we count either of them, but simply by virtue of this relation of identity. Once that is established, we can take the two concepts ('knife on this table' and 'fork on this table'), assert that their extensions are equinumerate, and then proceed to affix a number to this fresh class (the class of 'extensions equinumerate with the class, "knives on the table"') as its name.

In principle, we could adopt any name for this class. We could call it 'yurtl', to designate the class of classes equinumerate with the knives on the table. But, of course, there are already numbers available as names for our knives and forks. What we need to do now is to define how any particular number might, logically, be defined, and then offer it as a calibration point.

15. Definition of particular numbers

The first number to define, in Frege's view, is nought (*GA*, §74). To do this, we could take any extensionless concept, such as, perhaps 'unicorns'. 'Nought' would then be the name we attach to the class of classes equinumerate with the class 'unicorns'. But this would be a rather contingent sort of notion; after all, perhaps there are unicorns. The safest kind of extensionless concept is a contradictory one. There are no square circles. Or, more formally, nothing is non-identical with itself. The concept, 'things not identical with themselves' has a null extension. So any other class with an extension equinumerate with the extension of that concept can, from now on, safely be credited with membership of the class we call 'nought'.

The next thing is to define the rest of the whole numbers. Frege does it in a way that is rather difficult to follow, and before considering his method, it is worth pointing out easier ways. Russell's approach, for example, is more immediately illuminating. In 'On Denoting', he produces what is in effect a concept that can only have an extension of one. It goes as follows:[25]

$$(\exists x)(Fx.(y)(Fy \rightarrow y=x))$$

In words (a little loosely): there is some x such that x is an F, and if any other object is an F then it must be the same as x. Put another way: anything that purports to be an F can only be the first object we thought of as an F; however many instances of F are alleged, they are all identical, i.e. the one same object. The extension of this concept must, then, be one and one only. So any class equinumerate with the extension of the above expression can safely be labelled 'one'.

A concept ϕ with a unit extension could also be devised as follows:[26]

$$(\exists a)(\phi a.(F)(x)(Fa. \neg Fx: \rightarrow: \neg \phi x)$$

In words: there is some a such that a is a ϕ, and for any other property F, and for any other object x, if a has that property and x does not, then x is not a ϕ.[27]

Frege, meanwhile, uses the notion of series to define numbers after 0. This, of course, has the advantage of avoiding the need to define every

25 This is more or less a rendering of Russell's examples about Charles II's father (*Essays in Analysis*, 106f). The actual formulation is in Quine, 1974, p. 223. In fact, the whole thing is already present in *GA*, §79(4).
26 Russell in 'Is Mathematics Purely Linguistic?' (*Essays in Analysis*, 295-306), p. 301.
27 Russell glosses ϕ as being the 'unit property'. In Fregean terms, objects could not have the property of being 'one'. But, at the time Russell was writing this article, he was anxious to avoid use of the relation of identity, '=' (p. 298); and this of course rules out the first schema.

number separately. Once you have one number, and the principle of generating a series, then any number in that series should be attainable.

16. Series and number

To follow Frege's deduction, we shall have to go back again to an earlier
point. In the *Grundlagen*, Frege's reasoning goes as follows.

Frege starts with various principles from Leibniz. The first is the definition 'Eadem sunt, quorum unum potest substitui altera salva vertitate' –
things that can be substituted one for another while preserving truth are the
same (*GA*, §65, applied in §6). The second is the series of representative
definitions of (small) cardinal numbers by means of successive additions of
one. For example, $2=$[i.e. is defined as] $1+1$, $3=2+1$, $4=3+1$. On this basis,
according to Frege, any number and any arithmetical operation can be
defined by breaking down any higher number into its component aggregations of '1'. As an example, we can take the addition of $2+2$. Here we can
substitute (by our definition of identity and by our definition of 2) '$1+1$' for
one of the 2's. That gives us $2+1+1$. In that formulation there is something
we recognise from our initial definitions – '$2+1$' has already been offered as
a definition of '3'. So, for $2+1$ we can substitute 3, and we get $3+1$. '$3+1$' is
also something we should recognise – it is the definition of 4. So by using
our initial definitions, and carrying out pure substitution (according to the
identity principle) we can derive 4.

Now this still leaves open the question of what a number is, and, furthermore, how the series of numbers is to be regarded.

We have already discussed Frege's definition of numbers as objects, and
also his definition of nought. We can now proceed to the way he reaches
'one', following the principle that any one number can be derived by performing a '$+1$' operation on the preceding number.

Working on this basis, how does Frege reach 1 from 0? His definition of
two numbers adjacent to one another in the series of natural numbers is
this:

> There is a concept F and an object x that falls under it, such that the number
> that accrues to the concept F [i.e. the number of Fs] is n, and the number that
> accrues to the concept 'falling under F, but not equal to x' [i.e. the number of
> Fs without x] is m. (*GA*, §76)

Filling this in a little, 'the number that accrues to the concept F' is the extension of F, i.e. the number attributable to the class of objects giving a positive truth-value for the expression, 'is an F'. Similarly, 'falling under F, but
not equal to x' is a concept, and Frege is interested in all those things of
which it can be truly predicated that they are Fs, but without being x

(which we have, so to speak, already counted). Frege calls this relationship the f-series (*GGA*, §43).

In the case of nought and one, we get the following. If the number of things falling under a concept is one, then the number preceding that will be the number of things under the concept not counting the one already counted, i.e. in this case, nought. The usefulness of the concept 'equal to nought' in this context is that we know, analytically, that it has an extension of one – there can only ever be one class with nothing in it. (Or, to put it another way, empty classes are indistinguishable from one another; so, for all practical purposes, there is only one of them.)[28] In other respects, though, Frege's use of the concept is rather confusing; any other concept with an extension of one would do.

To sum up, then: if we can define the notion of being adjacent in the series of natural numbers, and if we have a definition of a natural number, then we can get to its neighbour. Since we have a definition of a natural number, namely nought, we can reach 'one' by considering it in its capacity as successor to nought.

17. Natural numbers

It remains to define natural numbers as a class. So far, we have the relationship of proximity, such that we can define any given natural number in terms of its neighbour. But what about numbers as a whole? It is important to have an analytical definition of this, in Frege's project, in order to preserve the notion of numbers as independent 'objects', defined only in terms of series starting with nought. In particular, it is important that numbers should be defined exclusively with reference to what he calls the 'f-series (f indicating *Folge* – succession), and should not be subject to any contingent limit. Accordingly, the final part of Frege's laying of foundations, in the *Grundlagen* and at the beginning of the *Grundgesetze*, is his definition of the notion of 'ancestry'[29] – in practical terms, the notion of a class structured by the repetition of one operation. The operation is '+1', and the task is to define a class with reference exclusively to the operation

28 See Quine, *Mathematical Logic*, 237.
29 Why 'ancestry'? In *BegrS*, §24 (p. 58), Frege illustrates what he means by reference to (1) the relation of being a child and (2) the property of being human. In such an example, if *x* is human, then everything which stands in the relation of 'being a child' to *x* is also human: the property of humanity is *inherited* through the relation of being a child. In that sense, any given human being is the 'ancestor' of all those who stand towards him, directly or indirectly, in the relation of 'being a child of'. (This is explained by Quine in 39 of *Mathematical Logic*. It is worth noting, however, that his example of Napoleon's ancestry is confusing. Although, empirically, Napoleon's ancestors are, of course, his ancestors, in the logical sense intended by Frege *Napoleon* is the ancestor in the series.

and to one member. If that is possible, then the class will not be subject to any contingent external limit.

The definition of such a class is as follows (from *GGA*, §45):

> If the statement: 'If any object which stands in the f-relation to *x* is an F; and if anything which stands in the f-relation to any F is itself an F; then *y* must be an F' is true generally of the concept F, then we say that *y* follows *x* in the f-series.

This definition can be looked at as follows. First, we know that anything to which *x* stands in the relation f will be an F. Say (to take a rather feudal example) the f-relation is 'oldest surviving male child of', and F is 'presumptive heirs'. Once we put *x* in this context (this is a name of something, rather than a variable in the strict sense), then the class of Fs will be anchored, so to speak, to *x*. F becomes 'presumptive heirs of *x*', rather than just presumptive heirs. So the first part of the definition states that anything which bears to *x* the relation 'oldest surviving male child of' will itself be an F, i.e. a presumptive heir of *x*.

That, however, takes us only one f-relation (one 'generation') beyond *x*. What about *x*'s oldest surviving great-great-grandsons? Are they still presumptive heirs to *x*'s fortunes? This is dealt with by the second part of the definition. It states that *anything*, if it stands in the f-relation to an F, will itself be an F. In other words, at any stage in the proceedings, if an F (a presumptive heir) stands in f-relation to something (has someone who is his oldest surviving male child), then that further something (the oldest son) will also be an F (a presumptive heir).

If we put the two together, then the character 'presumptive heir of *x*' will be passed along whenever such an *x*-heir stands in f-relation to something, i.e. has an oldest son surviving him. This means that we can, of any accredited *x*-heir and any oldest son surviving him, establish a succession: the last generation can claim, by virtue of his immediate neighbourhood to an *x*-heir, that he stands (indirectly, unless the *x*-heir is *x* himself) in the f-series in relation to *x* himself. This is a logical version of the apostolic succession. Christ laid his hands on the apostles, and sent them out into the world as His representatives. The spiritual heirs to Christ's apostles (the bishops) have all acceded to this title by having hands laid on them by their predecessors. Any bishop today knows two things: his predecessor was a spiritual heir to the apostles, and that predecessor confirmed him in office by the laying on of hands. And the final legitimacy that can be inferred from this is that he, the modern bishop, is heir in the series of laying-on-of-hands that started with Christ. So the legitimation of *y* (the bishop) is that he is able, from (a) knowledge of the origination of the f-series (laying on of hands) and (b) knowledge of his predecessor's title (spiritual heir to Christ), to infer the existence of an f-series chain leading from Christ (*x*) to him. He is, therefore, a successor to Christ in the f-series.

Now, the final stage in the actual definition is the inference, 'y is an F'. This merely slots in the second element so that, for any series, we have both a beginning and an end. Again, y is not a variable as such: it is a name for some value, and our task (as with Christ and some particular bishop or other) is to determine the relationship between x and y within the series. The point is this. *If* we can establish from our two data in the antecedent part of the definition (i.e. we are talking about x-heirs, and x-heirship passes in the f-series) that y must be an x-heir, then we are talking about a series in which x precedes y.

There is, in other words, an implication within an implication – which is, in part, what makes it so difficult to put into words. The other difficulty is that the inference does not express, in the premises, why we should infer that y is an F. That is because the particular reasons why we should do that in the case of y are secondary to the purpose of the definition, which is just saying, *if* we are compelled to make this inference (for whatever reason), then x and y are in such-and-such a relation. The structure of the definition is this:

1) Outer implication: whenever we can truthfully say the following of the two values x and y, then we are dealing with a series in which x is at the beginning and y is at the end.
2) Inner implication: we must infer from x's being the progenitor, via the f-series, of Fs, and from the fact that F-hood is passed down the f-series, that y is an F.
3) Unspoken justification for the inner implication (for example): an F stands in the f-relation to y.

The application of this is that it makes possible (given a properly rigorous exposition of what we have just been considering) the further extension of logic to mathematics. The advantage, in the realm of numbers, is that it rids us of the need to review every intermediate member of a series in order to conclude that a later member (a higher number) is part of the same series as the low ones. 'If, for example, it is given that, in the f-series, b follows a and c follows b, then we can conclude from our explanation that c follows a without having to know the intermediate members' (*GA*, §80).

To start once more. We are trying, in this case, to determine the properties of a class solely in terms of the analytical ingredients that make it up. Those are, first, the notion of unit increase. That is given by the procedure we have already seen, of defining each cardinal number in terms of an increase of one over its predecessor. Second, the elementary cardinal number is nought. If we can relate any given higher number, say 587,000, back to those elements in purely logical terms, then we shall save ourselves the tedious job of crawling towards 587,000 by one-at-a-time incremental definitions. And, more importantly, we can at a stroke vindicate the independence of cardinal numbers from some external ceiling or other, an absolute (but probably non-logical) limit.

Specifically, we can look at the application of our definition of ancestry to numbers in the following terms. We are, here, concerned with establishing that numbers can be defined, analytically, as a homogeneous group. The elements of this are the f-series (i.e. the series of unit aggregation) and one of the members, namely nought. Nought is the first of the cardinal numbers; in this context, we are not interested in any number 'before' nought. The purpose of our enquiry will be to establish that, given nought and the f-series, any subsequent member is part of the same class (of natural numbers).

So, using our definition, and substituting 'nought' for x, the series of unit aggregation for f-series, 'natural numbers' for F, and 587,000 for y, we get the following (compare GA, §81). First, anything generated from nought by means of unit aggregation will be a natural number. Second, anything that is generated from a natural number by means of unit aggregation will, in its turn, also be a natural number. Third, if, from the first two principles, we can conclude that 587,000 must be a natural number, then we can say that 587,000 follows nought in the series of unit aggregations. (And we will conclude that 587,000 is a natural number, because we know that we can get it by unit aggregation from 586,999, which, in turn, we know is a natural number ultimately derivable by unit aggregation from nought.)

18. No last natural number. Recapitulation

We must finally establish the infinity, or, better, the non-finity (no contingent limits) of the series of natural numbers; specifically, Frege wants to prove that there is no final member of the series of natural numbers (GA, §82; the explanation, as usual, proceeds more smoothly in GGA, §46, but is couched in Frege's rather forbidding notation).

Frege's technique for demonstrating non-finity may seem cheap at first glance. All it consists in, at bottom, is this:

> Take any sequence of integers, say the sequence ending with five. If we take the extension of the concept 'is a natural number less than or equal to five', we will find that the extension has the number six. That is because, *if we count nought*, there are six arguments giving a positive truth value for the concept – nought, one, two, three, four, and five. If this is true for all members of the series of natural numbers, then any natural number n must be followed by a further one, namely the number accruing to the concept 'natural numbers in

the series ending with n'. This proves that no natural number can be followed by itself – or, in other words, that the series of natural numbers cannot end with any determinate number.

Let us briefly recapitulate. Frege's intention is to reconstruct arithmetic analytically, on the basis of 'pure thought' alone. This means that he must eschew recourse to *intuitions*, i.e., to that use of sensory, picturable 'external things' which seemed to play a role in Kant's 'synthetic' account of arithmetic (*GA* §58). He achieves this, fundamentally, by the doctrine that the *truth values* attached to statements have an objectual status commensurate with that of the *things* indicated by names: and, moreover, any instance of a statement coming out true constitutes an 'object' of which we can predicate properties just as much as does the sensory thing of which we predicate 'features' (*Merkmale* – above, p.74). (This doctrine is the core of basic law V; see below.)

On this basis arithmetic concerns itself with the properties of concepts; or, more particularly, with the properties that arise by virtue of the instances in which a statement containing a function is true. The general property, in terms of which all concepts may be compared, is *numerousness*. We get to this via the relation of 'equinumerousness', which may be predicated of any two concepts' *extensions*.

The other arithmetical properties follow. Our point of calibration is the number *nought*, which we define as the number attributable to any concept with an empty extension. We further determine the relation of being *adjacent natural numbers*, which gets us to one, and thence to any other particular number. And finally we determine the property of being a *member of the series of natural numbers* (which, additionally, we see to have *no last member*). With that, we have 'analytically' established the 'objective' status of the natural numbers, and provided the groundwork for the laws of arithmetic.

The critical issue, however, is this. Frege's account may not be intuitive in the direct Kantian sense (invoking existences in space and time), but it *is* intuitionistic in the sense that it tries to reconstruct arithmetic from basic elementary certainties. This would be the essence of his opposition to purely formalist projects such as Hilbert's (see the *Correspondence*); and, by the same token, it is what brings Frege into our transcendentalist purview. The problem, however, is that Frege's hostility to psychologism (and his correlative dislike of any *temporal* dimension to 'logic') leads him to take as his elementary 'intuition' something far less self-evident than he initially thought – namely, truth-values as ideal objects. This we shall now consider.

19. Russell's paradox

Two questions arise at this point. The first, more general one is at the basic metaphysical level. It is this: if we assume, for the purposes of argument, that arithmetic is set firm in the indissoluble truths of logic, then what does this tell us about the world? Is the world also set in reason, or is reason itself merely a 'convention' of some kind, adopted by human beings? Does the assimilation of arithmetic to reason really tell us any more about reason?

Frege himself was clearly conscious of this question, and he was aware that mathematical logic, in itself, does nothing to answer it. The other side of his philosophy, couched in a polemic which accompanied his work on logic, was his doctrine of Truth. In general terms, this was articulated in his attacks on 'psychologism', and his insistence that 'the laws of truth are not psychological laws, but boundary stones fastened in an eternal ground' (*GGA*, XVI). In the later work, this became elevated to a kind of Platonism. In the essay 'The Thought', for example, he insisted that thoughts, in the technical sense we have encountered, were components of a timeless 'third realm'.

> Thoughts are neither things of the outside world nor representations. . . . A third realm must be acknowledged. Whatever belongs to it accords with the representations in that it cannot be perceived by the senses, and with things in that it needs no bearer, to the contents of whose consciousness it would belong. So, for example, the thought that we express in the pythagorean theorem is timelessly true, true independently of whether anyone believes it to be true. It needs no bearer. It is true not only since it was discovered; just as a planet has been in reciprocal interaction with other planets since before anyone saw it. ('Der Gedanke', 69)

Any failure to accept this doctrine, in Frege's view, would result in what he called idealism (*GGA*, xix) – i.e. a general scepticism, and inability to decide what was true and what was not.

In certain respects, Frege is obviously right, though whether this metaphysical position actually follows from his logical insights is perhaps debatable. The metaphysical consequences of the attack on psychologism were more fully investigated by two other thinkers we are concerned with: Wittgenstein and Husserl. And in a more fundamental sense, of course, the problem of relativism is the metaphysical problem *tout court*, so we shall be seeing more of it.

The more specific of the two questions raised by Frege's work is also one he had anticipated. It is more technical. It is generally identified with the tag 'Russell's paradox', in honour of the philosopher who illuminated the difficulty most clearly.

The problem is this. We noted, at the very beginning of Frege's progress, through the laws of logic, to the elements of arithmetic, that one of his basic moves was to pass from the notion of predication to the notion of that group of things of which the predication is made. Frege will pass, for example, from the function 'x is a tree in this garden' to the class of actual objects that can truly be inserted for the variable x. That class, then, is the extension of the concept 'tree in this garden'. Having once got the notion of extension, as we saw, Frege is then able to derive all the other elements of number and arithmetic.

Frege was never, however, happy that this kind of passage was the same kind of solidly 'logical' move as were, say, the moves that could be generated by application of the law of non-contradiction in propositional logic. Can we really claim that the statement 'all Fs are Bs' is saying the same, no more and no less, as the statement that we can identify the things we call F with the things we call B (which is what 'basic law V' amounts to, *GGA*, §20). If nothing else, it does appear that 'things', units, subsistent entities have crept in in a rather unlogical way.[30] Frege was quite open about his own doubts here, though without being able to suggest any remedy (*GGA*, vii).

In due course, the half-expected refutation of basic law V arrived in a letter from Bertrand Russell, containing the celebrated paradox. It goes as follows.

Classes may be divided into two: those that do not include themselves and those that do. (Or we could also say, extensions that are not members of themselves and those that are.) For example, the class 'horses' is not itself a horse: it does not include itself. On the other side, the class 'not horses' is, indeed, not a horse; so it may be said to include itself. In this example, at least, the two classes seem to adhere to the law of non-contradiction: whatever an entity may be, it will not simultaneously be both 'horse' and 'not horse'.

Consider next, however, the class 'classes not including themselves' (i.e. more precisely, the extension of the concept 'class not including itself'). Does this include itself or not? It would seem, at first, that we can truly predicate of such a class that it is a 'class not including itself', just as we can truly predicate of the horse that it is a 'horse'. If we do so, however, we have a contradiction, because we would be saying that this class included itself, whereas this class is distinguished precisely by the fact that it does *not* include itself. What, then, if we say that the class does not include itself? In

---

30 This is precisely the point that Kant makes in his transition from judgement, pure and simple, to the categories. See my *Introduction*, 18f. And, indeed, the reason why Kant concluded that arithmetic was 'synthetic' was precisely this, and not any sentimental attachment to the abacus.

that case, it is a member of the class 'classes not including themselves', in which case we are back again with the same contradiction as above.[31]

It is uncertain, in other words, whether the class is or is not a member of itself. It could be; but it could equally well not be. Russell argued that the same line of paradoxical reasoning could generate further striking illustrations: it could be shown, for example, that 'the concept *bicycle* is a teaspoon, and *teaspoon* is a bicycle' (*Principles of Mathematics*, 102). So the law of non-contradiction, indispensable foundation of logic, is violated (*GGA*, II, 254).

Both Frege and Russell thought they had answers to the paradox, and subsequent thinkers have offered other solutions.[32] What is important for our purposes, however, is that Frege's belief in the objectness of numbers was severely shaken, and, with it, his confidence in the ability of science to distil the rational structure of reality. For some, this disappointment has been a ticket for a Nietzschean dismissal of the concept world.[33] For those more familiar with the Kantian tradition, however, paradoxes and riddles remain what they always were: a reminder that philosophy, if it is to do its job, cannot confine itself to what appear to be elementary certainties.

20. Critical assessment

The principle of form and content

Frege's approach rests on the premise that *formal elements and elements of content are disjoint*. It is this axiom that enables Frege to derive his argument for the analyticity of arithmetic; and, arguably, faults in it make possible the derivation of the Russell paradox and, hence, Frege's 'failure'. The position is as follows.

It is an old notion that grammar, logic, and (perhaps) ontology seem to fall into a fundamental distinction – that between form and content. The ontological distinctions are those between matter and form, or between substance and attribute. The grammatical distinction is that between subject and predicate. Statements (formulae capable of being true or false) seem to consist of 'subject' and 'predicate' (as the entities can be named). Furthermore, subjects cannot, it seems, be used as predicates. 'Socrates is

---

31 *GGA*, II, 254. See also Russell to Frege, 16.6.1902 (Frege, *Philosophical and Mathematical Correspondence*, 130f). The paradox is an ancient form of philosophical conundrum. The classical version is the paradox of Epimenides the Cretan, who said that all Cretans were liars (so was he, a Cretan, lying or not?).
32 See also Geach's comments in 'Class and Concept' (*Logic Matters*, 226-235).
33 See Hilary Lawson, *Reflexivity*.

mortal' works; 'something mortal socratises' does not.[34]

Frege's distinction, as we have seen, is between *function* and *argument* (above, §9). This helps avoid the ontological ballast of terms like 'subject'. It also sharpens up the distinction. For example, although the subject-predicate distinction, and its irreversibility, is quite evident in 'Socrates is mortal', sentences like 'all swans are birds' and 'some birds are swans' seem to blur the issue. In Frege's formalism ('for any x, if x is S then x is B'; and 'for some x, if x is B then x is S') the clear demarcation between arguments and predicates is restored.

This position, which we shall call the weak principle of form and content, may be rendered as:

> In any predicate calculus, the set of values over which the object variables range is disjoint from the set of values over which the predicate (or higher order) variables range.

Now, if that was all that Frege was saying, then his position would be unexceptionable. It seems evident that for any sentence of any calculus, the relation of 'function' to 'argument' is non-symmetrical. However, Frege wants to go further than this rule of calculation. In particular, he wants to strike down psychologism. Psychologism rests on the assumption that we can coherently say things about thinking itself. To rule this out, something stronger than asymmetry of the function-argument relation is needed. Frege achieves this strengthening by *interpreting 'functions' as 'thinking'*. This semantic interpretation involves an ontological commitment. The distinction between functions and arguments becomes an ontological one. So the asymmetry of the relation is 'explained' by saying that the entities denoted at either side of the relation are themselves, ontologically, distinct. There are function-entities, and there are argument-entities. As a result of this ontological move, the rule ceases to be a formal rule of calculation, and becomes a declaration about the *necessary properties of certain entities*. Thoughts, in a word, are ontologically distinct from their objects; and that is why *thoughts may never be arguments*.

Frege's stronger, 'ontological' principle may be rendered as follows:

> Nothing that has been or may be a member of a predicate or higher-order set of values may ever, in any calculus, appear as the value of an object variable.

(This deals with psychologism because we can now say: anything we can put in the 'argument' position is not a function-entity, not a thought. So if we purport to describe thinking, or to explain it in terms of empirical cate-

---

34 See Tennant, 1990, 22, which states the topic in terms derived from F.P. Ramsey. The issue is of course much older; in Aristotle, it is expressed as the difference between 'first substance' and 'second substance' (see *Categories*, book v). Strawson, 1974 is a representative modern treatment. See also *German Philosophy*, 17, 19.

gories, then whatever we purport to describe is by that very token not the formalism of pure thought. Ultimately, as Wittgenstein emphasised, thought in this sense can only be *shown*, or demonstrated in practice; it can never have things *said* about it.)

Bedeutung

The centrality of Frege's 'ontological' strengthening of the asymmetry of argument and function appears from his doctrine of *Bedeutung*. The imagery underlying this doctrine exhibits and clarifies Frege's rule that thoughts may never be arguments.

The basic point is this: although the distinction between thinking and its content is mainly argued by Frege on the syntactical level (in 1892b, for example), an ontological distinction is clearly insinuated (by Frege's use of terms like *Gegenstand* for the content). Thought is absolutely inward, whereas its contents have the correspondingly absolute *externality* (as 'Gegenstände' – literally, 'what stands opposite you').

Thoughts can 'make sense' even when not significant. They can have, as Frege puts it, 'sense' (*Sinn*) even without 'reference' (*Bedeutung*). The calculus of logic and the grammar of natural language have generality even in the absence of significant application. 'Sense,' as Frege puts it, 'can be the common property of many and is thus not a part or modality of the single soul' (1892a, 29).

But cognition is characterised by what might be called its gravitation towards the object. The crucial element, which removes cognition from the grasp of psychologism, is *judgement*. Cognition is completed neither in representations (*Vorstellungen*, i.e. the physiological aspects of consciousness), nor in the noncommittal formality of 'sense', but only in judgement. A representation is 'an inner picture formed from the memory of sense impressions I have had, and from inner and outer activities I have carried out' (1892a, 29). As such it is entirely contingent and subjective, and therefore not cognition. However, sense, or (in Frege's earlier use) 'thought' is also not enough. 'The thought alone yields no cognition (*Erkenntnis*)' (1892a, 35). What is needed is the assignment of truth-values; and that is something that goes beyond both representation and formal calculus. It can happen only in judgement, which Frege defines as 'the progression from a thought to its truth-value' (ibid.). As such, this act is 'something quite unique and incomparable'. In the end, it results in what Frege calls the 'recognition' (or even 'acclamation', *Anerkennung* – 1892a, 34n.; 1918, 63) of truth.[35] In this respect, then, 'truth' is not primarily to do with things in sensuality; it is an

35 Frege's notion of judgement draws heavily on neo-Kantianism. See Sluga, 1984, e.g. 342f; and Roberts, 1982, 83.

intellectual or even spiritual event. Nonetheless, it is essentially passive, after the model of 'discovery'; truth is 'entering into a relation with' something that 'already existed before' (1918, 69n.).

Now, Frege's doctrine of *Bedeutung* legitimates thought (or, more narrowly, 'scientific' statements) in terms of objects. Statements become legal tender in the realm of cognition (so to speak) to the extent that they are backed by things. If they signify something, they can properly enter the calculus of thought. This requirement is absolute. It is easy to follow in the case of concepts that describe or identify. 'Tree in my garden', for example, signifies the 'extension' of the concepts combined in that phrase. This is, as Frege argues, analogous to a process of naming. True concepts name in that, like proper names, they 'belong' to an individual or group of individuals. The individuals are already there; and they acquire a name as part of a process of labelling. The legitimacy of the labels rests on the autonomous objectivity of the individuals they label. And the conceptual dispositions of logic, rather like the notional intermediate transactions of double-entry bookkeeping or commodity brokerage, depend on the principle that they are merely ways of moving from one labelled objective state (a 'value') to another. At the conclusion of each conceptual manoeuvre, however abstract the movements detailed in the course of it, the account always shows a balance that can be withdrawn in hard cash, or coffee, or, logically, in actual entities truly labelled ('signified') by the concepts.

The concomitant of this is that even subordinate operations, such as the intermediate stages in a proof, have to be in the directly convertible currency of *Bedeutung*. No concept may be introduced without ensuring that it has a *Bedeutung*; and no operations may be carried out that obscure the *Bedeutung* of the concepts that are being dealt with.

> Of a logically perfect language (a conceptual notation) is to be required that every expression that grammatically forms a proper name from signs already introduced should actually denote an object, and that no sign can be introduced as a proper name without ensuring that it has *Bedeutung*. (1892a, 41)

Loss of *Bedeutung* entails loss of 'value'. 'The thought loses some of its value for us as soon as we recognise that one of its parts lacks *Bedeutung*' (1892a, 33).

Equally, function entities can only become argument entities through the mediation of the things they denote. If a function is capable of having an extension, then it is capable, by being represented by that extension, of appearing as a name or argument. This is obviously only an indirect appearance: thoughts themselves never become the subjects of predication. But at the same time it establishes the basis on which mathematical concepts can become 'objects'. Whatever is capable of having an extension is, by that token, capable of being 'objectified' in that extension.

Describability

The theory of *Bedeutung* gives the grounding for conceptuality's operations. The currency of *Sinn* is underpinned by *Gegenstände*. That, then, deals with one side of the argument-function disjunction. The other side is accounted for by what could be described as the principle of absolute describability. At its simplest, this simply means that thought, understood as the general concepts deployed by predication, exhausts the realm of what may appear in consciousness at all. This, perhaps, is the force of Quine's 'to be is to be the value of a variable', where one would need to add 'in a function'. Whatever can be dealt with, can be dealt with, and only be dealt with, in functions. The thinkable is coextensive with the conceptual. So just as objects (the anchors of *Bedeutung*) are absolutely external to ratiocination, conceptuality (or *Sinn*) is absolutely internal to it. And because it is absolutely internal, all that is must be encompassed by the *Sinn* of concepts. Internally, grammatically, the *Gegenstand* named by the argument is *completely* featureless. There is nothing that can be said about it that cannot be said in the subject-predicate form of concept deployment.

This notion is developed later in Russell's 'Theory of Descriptions' (Russell, 1905) and in Quine's elimination of singular terms (Quine, 1974).

For Frege, the positive force of this lies in the principle, as one might call it, of *discovery*. Truth follows the paradigm of discovery. Everything that is true rests in a timeless realm of 'it is the case that. . .'. The event itself may be dated; but once 'discovered', its status changes from becoming to being. The battle of Hastings happened a long time ago, and will not happen again; but 'William defeated Harold in 1066' is true now, and forever, out of time. This, as Frege explains, is the 'tempus praesens' of truth: 'So the present in "is true" does not indicate the present of the speaker, but is, if the expression is permitted, a tense of timelessness . . . The truth whose recognition lies in the form of the assertoric sentence is timeless' (1918, 76).

Describability may be rendered thus:

D0   Whatever is, is describable in subject-predicate form.

We have already explained this. It has two derivatives. First,

D1   Time 'is', and is hence describable.

Things 'fall under' concepts of time and space in the same way that they do under any other concept, it would seem. 'In the same way, expressions for concepts that embrace places, etc., may be formed' (1892a, 42). Frege appears to be suggesting that places and times may have general time-concepts predicated of them in the same way that anything may have colour, warmth and so on predicated of it. Perhaps, 'happening at 9 p.m. on 26th November 1990' would be an example of such a predicate.

By virtue of D1, we can also state the second derivative:

D2   For the purposes of logic, truth is assertoric.

In other words, the only statements that fall under the purview of logic are statements that make assertions about what is the case (now, in actuality). This covers not only statements about present situations ('it is raining'), but historical statements like the one we saw as well as forecasts like, '[it is the case that] it will rain tomorrow'. It rules out (obviously) fictional statements and others that make no claims to truth. More importantly, though, it rules out problematic ('it is possibly the case that. . .') and apodeictic ('necessarily. . .') statements. Such *modal* statements are not statements about what is actually the case.

In Frege, this is enlisted as part of the same *ontological* project as the strengthened form-content principle. We could call D2 the 'mind of God' principle. Its force is: some mind, if sufficiently large, could know all truths assertorically. The entire extent of truths is available to be known now, as an *actuality* in the 'tempus praesens' of truth. This is not a claim about whether a mind of such power does or could exist; it is a way of ruling out the 'Darwinism' Frege attributed to the psychologists.[36] If anything is a truth, it is true now (together with a time determination, if needed). 'Discovery' relates to the time when a truth is formulated; but it was always a truth even before it was formulated. 'Truth, whose recognition lies in the form of the assertoric sentence, is timeless' (1918, 76). The notion that truth *itself* could be subject to qualifications ('it is possibly true that. . .') is ruled out by this notion. We may, in any given situation, be unable to state something with certainty; but this is a purely contingent qualification: the truth itself persists timeless and independent. 'The truth of a sentence is, indeed, not the fact of its being thought' (1884, §77).

Analyticity

The full force of Frege's position on form and content, and on describability, is as follows. Clearly, the world is full of things that change and flow and can, at most, be comprehensively cognised by God. Nonetheless, all 'things' can be inserted into predicative formulae – or, in Frege's terms, appear as 'arguments' to 'functions'. Furthermore, this appearance is exhaustive; there is no residue that eludes functional description. Because of

36 For Frege's attack on the 'historical method' in philosophy, see 1884, vii. 'This conception pulls everything into the subjective and, if taken to its conclusion, cancels truth.'

this exhaustiveness, such patterns or 'laws' as appear in thought are absolutely general; we cannot 'think' anything that does not accord with them.
And, furthermore, since time and space are among the predicates disposed
by conceptuality, they are instruments *belonging to* the mind rather than,
as seemed to be the case with psychologism, conditions *imposed upon* it (by
the historical development of the brain, or whatever).

'Logic', then, is justified as being that part of the pattern of cognition
which is completely general. 'Things' become absorbed into predicates
(through atomic judgments of some kind); and 'logic' then is the pattern by
means of which the predicatively absorbed things are further manipulated
by the mind. Once you get past the atomic judgements, you are dealing
with a realm of completely general laws. 'Thought is in its essence everywhere the same: we do not have to consider conceptual laws as differing
according to their objects' (1884, iii).

This becomes the basis of Frege's claim to ground arithmetic 'analytically'. Analytical truths are those that rest on 'general logical laws' (1884,
§3) – those, in other words, that deal with objects already absorbed into
predicates. Arithmetic is analytical (according to Frege) because it makes
statements about concepts with particular properties (*Eigenschaften*; 1884,
53). For the purposes of arithmetic, as we saw, the properties of concepts
concern their extension – crudely, whether and how many objects are in
the concept's extension. The law of form and content is obeyed because the
properties, strictly, are not predicated of the *concepts*, but of their *extensions*.[37]

Space, time and predication

As we saw, analyticity in the pure form envisaged by Frege does not work.
Russell's paradox demonstrated that concepts and extensions are not related in the simple way Frege had hoped. What does this tell us about his
'logicist' project in general?

One thing it does *not* reveal is that Frege has an inadequate or naive attitude to epistemic questions. Probably Frege does not have an account of
how a particular atomic statement ('this is a table') can be established as
'true' without circularity or regress. But Frege's system does not stand or
fall on a satisfactory answer here. 'To justify speaking of a sign's *Bedeutung*
it suffices in the first instance to indicate our intention in speaking or thinking, even with the reservation: if it has one' (1892a, 31f). The difficulty is

37 'The distinction between concept and object remains implacable' (1892b, 201). But concepts have truth-values proper to themselves, and *they* are objects (1892a, 34). As a result, 'The
extensions of concepts are also objects, although the concepts themselves are not' (1891, 19).
On that basis numbers (the extensions of properties of concepts) are also 'independent, recognisable objects' (1884, §56).

best approached through Frege's attitude to time and space, and, in particular, to principle D1. Is time an object *of* description, or is it a condition *on*
description? Frege's explicit statements on this (especially 1892a, 42) are
not entirely clear; but D1 seems to be a premise of D2, Frege's 'Platonism'.

The claim would appear to be that time predicates act in the same way as
any other general concepts within 'functions'. So, just as I could say, '*x* is
red', I could also say, '*x* is at two o'clock'. There seem to be two problems
here, however: first, the *eliminability* of time (and space) in terms of other
conceptual determinations; and second, the indispensability of *orientational* distinctions as an ultimate means of differentiation.

First, it would seem that, within a discourse using only general terms as
predicates, spatial and temporal distinctions can always be eliminated. For
example, specification by calendars and clocks does not appeal to *time* as a
general concept (like *colour*, say), but to something other than time,
namely to devices for recording and measuring. This seems to reflect a kind
of dependence. Time is nothing without the events that fill it; and time only
constitutes a homogeneous 'entity' to the extent that we devise ways of
slicing it up (e.g. by counting years or the rotations of a clock hand). Bare
temporality seems blind, in Kant's term. It is unclear to what extent time,
or even time-points, can be 'objects' (as Frege suggests).[38]

In that respect, it is also unclear how they can have general concepts predicated of them. Concepts, as Frege says, have 'sense' through their capacity to 'refer'. So 'red' is capable of referring to any red thing. As Strawson
has said, a general concept can be 'exemplified in any number of different
particular cases' (Strawson, 1974, 15); in this case, anything red exemplifies
the concept 'red'. But what is the analogous procedure in time? It is not apparent how time can be 'exemplified' in anything, unless one is going to
claim that anything that exists 'exemplifies' time. Time does not appear to
have the 'sense' that Frege demands of concepts. 'Redness' seems to be an
immediately applicable notion in the way that 'temporal' (if that is the
appropriate 'predicate') does not. Indeed, the time determination on its
own seems to have precisely the blind quality about it that Kant attributed
to 'intuitions', *as distinct from concepts* (cf. B 75).

The same problem seems to apply to space. Things can 'exemplify' space
only to the extent that they exemplify properly general concepts. Space
alone cannot determine anything. What we loosely objectify as 'space', the
coordinate grid stretching out to the farthest reaches of the universe,
appears 'conceptually' as a relation between the objects we perceive in the
universe, and is beyond that and 'in itself' neither an object, nor a relation,

---

38 'Places, time points, time intervals are, seen logically, objects; furthermore the linguistic
denotation of a particular place or a particular moment or interval is to be conceived as a
proper name' (1892a, 42).

nor any kind of generality.

This might tempt us to regard determinations of time and space as, in logical terms, redundant. This is allegedly what Leibniz thought;[39] and it is implied by the reduction of spatio-temporal determinations to conceptual descriptions that seems to be envisaged by Frege. The objection here, however, is that we cannot assume general concepts alone to be sufficient to distinguish particulars: the ultimate ground of differentiation is always spatio-temporal (Strawson, 1974, 17). We need not discuss this further here: it is the argument on *orientation*, illustrated in chapter one, above, by Kant's 'incongruent counterparts' and by Heidegger's theories on time and datability.

Modality

How does this help us interpret Russell's paradox?

The point would seem to be this. Frege's 'platonist' metaphor of discovery insists on timelessness because the stock of truths 'out there' is, ultimately, fixed. We may, for empirical reasons, not yet have discovered all of them; but this reflects merely the constraints of being mortal and living in time, not the fixed status of the truths awaiting discovery.

The problem seems to be, however, that the 'out-thereness' of truths (their 'content-hood' according to the principle of form and content and their timelessness according to D) is not as self-evident as Frege thinks. Certain sorts of truth, at the very least, seem to depend in some way on our acts in knowing them. Or, to put it another way, there is no syntactical reason why 'analytical' objects should not be generated spontaneously by our intellects. Self-referential concepts seem to be an example of this. But if that happens, of course, the element of timeless discovery disappears. Furthermore, any rule or axiom introduced purely to forbid such spontaneous generations must be a dubious creature. Can it claim to be a timeless truth, freshly discovered? Or is it merely reactive, i.e. spontaneously ad hoc and so no different 'ontologically' from what it is designed to suppress? We shall return to this problem, that of reflexivity, in the next chapter.

39 See Leibniz's fable of the leaves: Strawson, 1974, 15; *German Philosophy*, 15. The notion that temporality, or the 'flow of time', is 'unreal' is central to the position taken up in Mellor, 1984. Mellor's view is diametrically opposed to the phenomenological account of, say, Heidegger. Mellor thinks that 'dates' (Heidegger: 'calendar time') are real, whereas 'tense' (Heidegger: 'datability') is not. A phenomenological reply to Mellor would, I suspect, concentrate on his premise that 'tense' already includes an element of absolute quantity ('*how far* events are, past or future, from the present' – Mellor, 1984, 14; my emphasis). Without quantity, Mellor's conversion of tensed expressions into 'tenseless facts' would be impossible (p. 44f). With it, however, Mellor seems to have imported an element that, in Heideggerian terms at least, belongs to *calendar* time, not to 'datability'. So his elimination of tense rests on a *petitio principii*.

It is mainly a problem for platonistic logicism, however. A less intense concentration on the single modality of *assertion* makes us more flexible in our ontological commitments.[40]

The point is this. 'Truth' does not have to be seen as something bare and unqualifiable, something that, once discovered, is ruthlessly compelling of all adversaries. In particular, 'the true' (as Frege calls it – 'das Wahre') does not have to be seen as a state whose vast extension is mapped by some idealised consciousness moving gradually across it. 'Truth' is something that arises in *movements* rather than states; and in that respect the metaphor of discovery should, perhaps, be replaced by one of ordered transition. The dancer is not interested in states and discoveries, but in how to combine movements smoothly. Less intuitively, we can localise the problem in Frege's implicit assumption that 'truth' is assertoric and actual, and that other modalities fall outside logic. The position is as follows.

Traditionally, true statements may take three forms. They may be assertoric ('p is the case'), problematic ('possibly p is the case'), and apodeictic ('necessarily p is the case').[41] These are three 'modalities'. They can be reduced to two because possibility and necessity can be defined in terms of each other ('possibly p' is equivalent to 'not necessarily not p'). From that perspective, one can also say that the two primitive sorts of modality have the ontological dimensions of *actuality* (assertions) and *possibility* (problematic and apodeictic statements).

Frege confines himself to assertoric statements.[42] From the point of view of a logic which includes modality, however, Frege's 'Sinn'-bearing statements have a kind of concealed modal operator: 'actually . . .'. If one regards Fregean logic as bearing with it an unacknowledged modality, this provides one location for the residue of time (and perhaps space) that seems to elude simpler notions of the subject-predicate link.

This raises technical semantic questions. Informally, however, the position seems to be as follows. Assertoric statements can be regarded as a subset of the set of all logically relevant statements, with the other subset being 'modal' in the narrow sense (apodeictic or problematic). We could, alterna-

40 To some extent, what I am suggesting echoes Strawson, 1950.
41 Cf., for example, Kneale & Kneale, 1984, 82; Kant, B 265f.
42 By implication if not expressly. This is because non-assertoric modal operators are not truth-functional, as required by the doctrine of *Bedeutung*. In a sentence containing only truth-functional operators, the truth value of the whole is completely determined by the truth value of the components. For example, the truth-value of 'it is raining and the sun is shining' is determined by whether it is raining and whether the sun is shining. (We could say, the assertion either 'discovers' the actual state of affairs, or it does not.) Non-assertoric operators are not truth-functional in this way, however. The truth-value of 'Possibly it is raining and the sun is shining' ('It is possible for it to rain while the sun is shining') is not determined completely by the fact this is precisely what is now happening (though it would normally be valid to infer possibility from actuality: $p \rightarrow Mp$).

tively, regard all logically relevant statements as containing a modal operator (in a broad sense); although assertoric statements, by convention, omit
any express mention of it. We would then have a means of situating those
elements of meaning that do not seem to accommodate themselves to naive
subject-predicate (or 'argument-function') accounts. (The difficulty with
time 'predicates' is an indication of this incomplete accommodation.)

Our outline of modality follows the approach taken in Eley, 1985. Eley
draws on elements from Kant, and particularly the suggestion that modality is directed towards the *empirical application* of the understanding (cf. B
266).

The understanding and its empirical application

The besetting difficulty of modal expressions is to decide *what they are
talking about.*[43] If, for example, I say, 'If it freezes tonight, the plants may
die' ('Possibly: Frost tonight→Plant death'), what does the possibility relate to? Am I attributing some ontological property to frosts (*de re* modality), or am I saying something about the statement itself (*de dicto*)? In the
de re case, I could probably express the idea without resorting to a modal
operator (e.g.: 'Frost is expected tonight; some frosts kill plants'). In the *de
dicto* case, it is unclear what 'modal' utterances about my statement can
add: the statement is either true or not, and whether it freezes and whether
the plants die is a purely external matter, and has nothing to do with the
character of my statement. (I could, of course, interpret 'possibly' as meaning 'on the evidence available'; that, however, is a comment on the present
lack of data on which to complete a truth-functional determination, not a
comment on the statement as such.)

Modality has more plausibility if it is considered as a comment about the
set of assumptions on the basis of which one reaches a conclusion. Even for
a resolute nominalist, this would have an application in the context of irredeemably abstract objects such as numbers (i.e. objects whose mind-
dependence is not merely contingent, as in the case of forecasts underdetermined by data). One could, then, use modal expressions to distinguish between statements made from the background of different sets of
assumptions. If you are comparing rational numbers and real numbers, for
example, you could say that it is *possible* to enumerate the numbers in the
interval between one and two if you confine yourself to the rationals,
though not if you use the reals. Similarly, you could say that for numbers in
either system it is *necessarily* always the case that for any two numbers x
and y, either $x < y$, $x = y$, or $x > y$. Here, the ontological question as to
whether one is talking about 'things' or 'statements' is less pressing: we are,

43 See Haack, 1978, 178ff. for a more detailed discussion.

even from a Fregean point of view, talking about entities that are, as it were, suspended between the status of *res* and *dictum*. So, 'possibly' means we can do something if we adopt the appropriate set of assumptions about numbers; 'necessarily' means we can do it whatever assumptions we adopt.

This, however, can only serve as a preliminary example. Even if we regard numbers as fictive entities, the difference between reals and rationals seems too slight to dignify with the distinct logic of modality. After all, reals include rationals in the sense that rationals are simply a restricted application of reals. So we are talking about the same thing; it is merely that using rationals is more convenient for elementary applications. You do not need a word processor to write a shopping list.

The sense, intuitively, is that modal expressions should indicate really distinct contexts, rather than more or less restricted views of the same one. This expectation of realness (Haack calls it 'epistemological independence' – 1978, 190) finds one expression in the term 'possible worlds'. Possible worlds (in this account) are situations that are conceivable, though not actual. The easiest intuitive notion of such a situation is a counterfactual or 'third conditional' one: something that might have been the case even though in fact it is not. There is a certain solidity – 'epistemological independence' – about this; what might have happened if I had got my shares application in on time is a 'world' of more than mere fairy tales. D.K. Lewis, 1973, indeed, argues that such counterfactual worlds are 'real' in quite a strong sense.

Most standard semantics for possible worlds revolves around this intuition of a tensed narrative: what would have happened if someone had decided differently (cf. Stegmüller, 1975, II 231). Haack (1978) suggests that, 'without paying attention to considerations of tense and mood, one has difficulty in understanding even modal statements with single modal operators' (p. 198). One further trend has been to assimilate modal operators to intuitionistic notions of 'provability' or 'conceivability'; and the dimension of tense then reflects the stage-by-stage accumulation of knowledge.[44] Truth is what I know now, or could know now, on the basis of the objects in my present world and the rules I have for 'knowing' them; possibility is where I would be if I added to or subtracted from those rules or objects; and necessity applies to me now and in any stage I could possibly move to (cf. Hughes and Cresswell, 1972, Ch. 10). More generally, this could be regarded as a series of stages in the growth of science, displayed in 'possible temporal succession' (Tennant, 1990, 108).

It is uncertain how satisfactory this is as an interpretation of modality, or, more importantly, as a resolution of the difficulties we saw over time. A

---

44 See van Dalen, 1986, 246; Tennant, 1990, 106ff.

miss is as good as a mile; the fact that something never came about would seem, on one level at least, to remove it utterly from the actual world, and to annihilate its interest for serious inquiry.

The basic problem would seem to be that most of the interpretations of 'possible worlds' presuppose a Fregean ontology (as we have defined it), and this is not compatible with modal semantics. In particular, the doctrine of describability does not leave anything over to be reflected in differing modalities. Time, for example, is exhaustively describable in the Fregean scheme; and the temporal interpretations of modality cannot be reconciled with that view. Either the world 'is' some way or other, or it is not; there is no room for 'must' and 'might'. This is also true if modality is related to provability. If proving things is, in some sense, 'discovering' things about the conceptual apparatus that fits the world best, then the fact that those discoveries happen over the course of time does not make its various stages intrinsically interesting or 'epistemologically independent'.

These issues will be explored further in chapters four and five. Meanwhile, however, we can summarise the difficulties in the following terms. First, positing 'possible worlds' against the Fregean background has all the weaknesses of the Leibnizian project (see chapter four). The actual world, in that scheme, always 'wins' because it contains all the conceptual and empirical data of the one real world. Possible worlds, by comparison, are in some way deficient, and, ultimately, uninteresting. What makes possible worlds different is a *conceptual limitation* of some kind (there was something we did not know; there still is something we do not know, and so on). The object world, only worthy object of logic, remains unchanged. To the extent that we do not encompass all of it in our current thoughts, it persists as the object of as yet *unthought thoughts* (the thoughts of God – Eley, 1985, 61). Whether thought or unthought, however, the world subsists eternally in 'tempus praesens'.

But this is the kind of ontological commitment criticised by those in the Husserlian tradition as the 'illusion of presence [*Vorhandenheit*]' (e.g. Eley, 1985, 152).[45] Another solution, urged by past passages in philosophy, is to follow the transition from 'Leibniz' to 'Kant', or, as we have traced in this book, from 'early' to 'late' Husserl (these are all conceptual rather than biographical markers). The basic move in that transition is the *abandonment of 'the world' as a repository of truths awaiting discovery*. Nothing is true independently of the point of its formulation in human consciousness. To the extent that 'truth' has a context, this context is not the 'world' of discoverable facts, but the 'subject' that formulates statements. Briefly, we can reconstruct this position in terms of the principle of *reflection* and of the

45 See also Heidegger's comments on the notion of 'Vorhandenheit', and the correlative notion of 'nature', in Heidegger, 1976, esp. §21.

notion of *partiality*.

The principle of reflection can be stated thus:

R   Use of the understanding (predicating concepts) is particular.

This is what might be called the anti-description principle. The principle of describability (above, D0) asserted that everything may be described conceptually ('being that can be understood is conceptual', to modify a dictum of Gadamer), or, metaphorically, that everything may be 'wrapped up' by concepts. R, by contrast, asserts that whatever is conceptual is conditioned by particularity. There is a localisation, or a particularisation, that *precedes* any use of the understanding; and this localisation eludes the generality of concepts. In that respect, the truth of conceptual predication holds only subject to a context of particularity.

The term 'reflection' derives from Kant, and denotes the search for 'subjective conditions under which we can arrive at concepts' (B 316). This issue is discussed in greater detail in chapter one, above. It is worth noting that R involves what can at first seem like a reversion to 'psychologism', which held that conceptual activities were particular to the organism (the brain and so on) in which they took place. However, psychologism's incoherence rests not in its particularism, but in what might be called the category-mistake of relying on empirical resources (neurophysiology) to describe particularity.

A better way to approach the particularism suggested by the principle of reflection is in the notion of *partiality*. Partiality holds that

P   No truths absolutely transcend their context: even 'necessary' truths relate to some particular set of worlds.

All truths are partial; and there is no point in believing in absolute truths even as a limiting case. To do so is to fall into Platonist or Fregean ontology.[46]

The question, then, is how to understand this partiality. The obvious way, again, is to think of it in terms of *time*. There are (in this perspective) things that are always true, things that are sometimes true, and things that are true now. Kant, with many others since, associates these with necessity, possibility and actuality, respectively (B 184). This would be a clear intuitive interpretation of the notion of truth contexts.

However, faced with the case of time alone Platonist, Leibnizian or Fregean ontologies simply interpret partiality as cognitive inadequacy; an integral 'world' embracing the totality of 'facts' remains. To rule out this ontological leap, P must be strengthened with R, and the two must be

46 Van Benthem, 1988, thematises partiality (55ff.), though I have radicalised his position in 'ontological' terms.

understood as barring *any* speculation about non-contextual totalities. This is best achieved by interpreting partiality as the partiality related to a knowing *subject*. A 'subject' here may be anything that can 1) undergo transitions from one state (of 'knowledge') to another and 2) take into account the states or transitions of other subjects in doing so. That is broad enough to encompass not only the biological human individuals often associated with the term 'subject', but also computers (data modified by programs, fresh data, etc.), 'bodies of (scientific) knowledge', and common consensus of a political, religious or aesthetic kind. This 'subject', in other words, is not individualistic or even 'humanistic'. Models for it may be found in 'epistemic' logics,[47] in artificial intelligence,[48] in the philosophy of science,[49] in aesthetics,[50] and in the philosophy of history.[51]

Consequences

The argument may be schematically recapitulated as follows. The problem in Frege's project surfaced in Russell's paradox. Russell's paradox showed that the distinction between 'arguments' and 'functions' was not as clear as Frege had thought: and, within Frege's framework, the paradox could only be avoided by stipulating rules that lacked the initial distinction's self-evidence.

Russell's theory of types is an answer more technical than philosophical, as Wittgenstein's dissatisfied response (see next chapter) makes clear. The first step towards a philosophical answer (if one disregards the rather barren purism of the *Tractatus* itself) seems to emerge in a revitalised calculus of modality. This can be used to loosen the abbreviated (merely assertoric) account of 'truth' inherent in Frege's project.

The 'Husserlian' interpretation, in turn, embeds the modal calculus in a constructive or intuitionist semantics (cf. Eley, 1985, 148f, using Lorenzen, 1975). That suffices to deal with Russell's paradox: in intuitionism, 'only previously defined objects may occur as members of a species' (Heyting, 1931, 57). (This is an aspect of the intuitionists' rejection of 'unthought thoughts', or 'unknown truths' – Brouwer, 1949, 90.)

The final step is to interpret the modal-constructive calculus not as relating to *time*, but as relating to *subjects*. Time is merely one way of formulating the partiality that is ultimately attributable to the locatedness of truth

47 See van Benthem, 1988, 44 for comments on Hintikka's work in this area.
48 See van Benthem, 1988, 19.
49 Michel Foucault's 'epistemes'; T.S. Kuhn on paradigms.
50 For example, Kant. See *German Philosophy*, chapter 1.
51 This is the force of Hegel's notion of 'Geist'. Reason (as opposed to understanding) is the interaction of subjects. Here lies the fundamental importance of the 'Master-Slave' episode in the *Phenomenology of Spirit*. See *German Philosophy*, chapter 2.

in a plurality of subjects. It is, as Kant's project shows, a means of situating the 'subjective conditions' of 'concepts'; but it is not itself some mysterious half-determinate arena. 'Epistemic logic' is a step in this interpretation; a fuller one is perhaps the reconstruction of 'natural deduction' (Gentzen, 1934) in terms of a logic of *dialogue* (Lorenzen: see chapter 5, below). This replaces the semantics of truth tables, and comes closest to the intuition that truth 'happens' in the interaction of 'subjects' bearing 'knowledges' (rather than in the interaction of 'consciousness' with 'world').

A final point, in anticipation of further discussion below, is that the reflective derivation of 'subjectivity' is neither solipsistic nor irrationalist. An uncritical appropriation of this notion of the 'conditions' of rationality tries to subordinate rationality to something primordial yet still somehow describable. This category-mistake is visible in Heidegger's appropriation of the Husserlian 'Lebenswelt' (his term for the pre-scientific context of conceptuality) for irrationalist doctrines of 'Being', 'fate', and so on.[52] (A similar difficulty, at an earlier point, emerges in Schelling's doctrines of the 'unprethinkable' – see *German Philosophy*, chapter 3.) But 'subjectivity', here, is a cautious attempt to substitute a less dogmatic and restrictive ontology for the one exemplified by Frege; and it is intended to be substantially *weaker* in its ontological commitments, and not to introduce all sorts of entities supposedly moving in a 'pre-rational' space. If understood correctly, the project is directly compatible with that of Kant; if incorrectly, we revert to the same incoherence demonstrated by psychologism.

---

52 Heidegger is aware of this danger on a more formal level; but his ethical and political engagements from 1927 to 1933 show that he failed to avoid it where it mattered.

3

The Invisible Subject: Wittgenstein

1. Introduction: class and calculus

The problem for metaphysical philosophy, broadly speaking, is to match intuition with calculus. 'Intuition' covers what can be brought under the umbrella of common sense. To what extent is throroughgoing determinism intuitively acceptable, for example? Solipsism would seem to be another case that goes beyond the boundaries of common sense. Our metaphysical account must describe a world in which there are other people, and where 'freedom' (in some sense) is possible. At the same time, the calculi of logic, mathematics and the natural sciences often make intuitive accounts diffi-cult. Calculi insist that we know things that seem incompatible with our common-sense world; or, more frequently, they exclude certain sorts of knowledge, and reproach us with interpreting more into our calculi than they can sustain.

The calculi of science exercise a relentless pressure on intuition, but are met by the solid resistance of habit and belief. In this conflict, one response leans towards scepticism (we retain our faith in the 'real', common-sense world, but at the cost of our confidence in the ability of calculi to give us in-formation about that world). The other moves to idealism: for the sake of reason, beliefs in the absolute autonomy of a 'world out there' have, if necessary, to be ceded. In scepticism, intuition and common sense emerge as the winners; in idealism, confidence in what reason tells us, even at the expense of intuition, retains a hold.

The destruction of Frege's system by Russell's paradox is a blow from calculus against intuition. The 'intuition' underlying, and weakening, Frege's system can be seen in various ways. We have already considered his assertoric account of truth. Another aspect of his same basic intuition is his approach to *class*. This will give us more direct access to Wittgenstein's interpretation of mathematics, and his extension of that interpretation to the problems of intersubjectivity and ethics.

As we saw, Frege believed that thoughts signified objects, and that there was an elementary disjunction between the two: no thought could be an object, and no object a thought. Further, it was precisely because of this disjunction that objects could successfully be manipulated in thought.

The basic relation that made this manipulation possible was *naming*. Thoughts, as concepts, named. And, like paper documents or electronic data in a banking system, thoughts could be backed up by values, and thus be used to move logical credits and debits around the conceptual framework.

The 'intuition', here, enters as another aspect of what we called the ontological premise of form and content (above, ch.2 §20a). This, essentially, is the assumption that there is an intimate and constant relation between the form (the name, or the concept), and the 'thing' that it denotes. The two are ontologically distinct; but they are bound together by the relation of naming.

The notion that knowledge stands in a naming relation to things is, of course, one of the most fundamental intuitions of all. It reaches an early expression in the creation myths of the first book of the Bible; and a more technical one in 'mirroring' theories of knowledge. The common strand of these doctrines is the claim that names and things are *isomorphic*: a change in either side is reflected in a change in the other.[1] ('Horse', for example, denotes a certain collection of things; if I change it to 'horse with horns', I designate another thing – in this case, an empty collection. Correspondingly, a change in things designated is matched by a change in the designation: everything has its name.)

In more technical terms, the relation between names and the things named is expressed in the terminology of intension and extension. Intension, very loosely, is 'meaning'; extension is the collection of things meant. The 'intuitive' assumption would be that any 'intension' corresponds to an 'extension'. For example: 'anything of which I can predicate "is a bicycle" is a member of *the class of bicycles*'.[2] It may be fictitious ('unicorns'), impossible ('round squares'), or empirically unverifiable ('angry Martians'): but these are all still determinate extensions. The notion is, in other words, that there is always some determinable relation between any 'meaning' I happen to dream up and entities in the world independent of that meaning. And the importance of this is that it gives us a justification for *relying on* our tools of 'meaning'; they do, intuitively, intervene pre-

1 On mirroring and isomorphism see Vossenkuhl, 1986, 134ff.
2 Which might be expressed as '$Bx \rightarrow x\epsilon\{y|By\}$'; though, perhaps, that presupposes a particular interpretation of 'ϵ'. See Quine, 1969, 16; Lemmon, 1965, 202.

dictably in the 'real world', even if in particular cases the outcome of this intervention cannot be specified. The rule that intensions have their extensions is a rule of ontological access: meaning and names, however 'private', have a determinable passage into the real world.

This assumption is, of course, fundamental to Frege's project. Arithmetic, in his account, is a calculus concerned with the *sizes of extensions*; and the assumption allows him to claim that manipulating intensions will have an exactly determinable isomorphism in the outside world. He needs this, because without those isomorphic extensions the principle of 'value' is lost; and arithmetic's claim to be 'analytic' (universal by virtue of purely conceptual laws) fails.[3] It is embodied in 'law V' of the 'Basic Laws of Arithmetic', which states, roughly, that relations between intensional expressions are equivalent to relations between classes formed from the same functions (Frege, 1893, 36; and van Heijenoort, 1967, 126). And this law, as Frege was always aware, was the point at which, if anywhere, his intuitions were showing. 'I believe it is purely logical. But this, at all events, indicates the point where the decision must fall' (Frege, 1893, vii).

The 'decision' fell in the shape of Russell's paradox, with the demonstration that not all predicates (apparently meaningful designations) can be associated with classes. We can say of an entity that it is 'not a member of itself' without offending against the rules of grammar or intension; but the membership of any class associated with such a predicate is indeterminate, because we cannot say of the 'class' of entities satisfying the predicate whether it is or is not a member of itself. So the isomorphism of intension and extension is broken, not because the class is empty, or contingently (empirically) indeterminate, but because it is *necessarily* indeterminate. The concept is intensionally legitimate (we 'know what it means'); but it does not have – cannot have – an extensional 'value' ('Wertverlauf') in the Fregean sense.

2. Russell's 'types'

From the viewpoint of the calculus, this need not be a problem. If some sorts of predicate cannot be associated with classes, then we simply stipulate as much. A standard formula might be an 'axiom of comprehension', which stipulates that classes (or, more usually, 'sets') have in turn to be members of some larger collection.[4] As it stands, however, this is a syn-

---

3 It remains universal; but the assumption that it can import that universality from the conceptual realm fails, because the isomorphism is no longer absolute.

4 '$\forall x(A(x) \to Mgx) \to \exists y \forall x(x \in y \leftrightarrow A(x))$' – 'For set-hood ('Mg') to follow from a function A there must be something y of which that set is itself a member.' This would rule out ' $\neg x \in x$' for A, because the consequent produces a contradiction. Reinhardt & Soeder, 1974, 29.

tactical prescription, and does not display the intuitive interpretability that characterises Frege's original project (though it could be interpreted along the lines of the distinction between 'situations' and 'world', as we saw in chapter one). In particular, on the face of it at least, such a stipulation fails to be self-evident.

Russell tried to rescue the situation by means of what he called the theory of types. His project has four components. First, it is part of a re-treat from the notion that 'classes' could be relied on to contribute to logic in the simple way envisaged by Frege. For a time, before fully embracing the theory of types, Russell toyed with a 'no-classes' theory. The force of this doctrine is sceptical rather than idealistic: it is not that things do not exist, but rather that our conceptual approaches to them (e.g. classes) are inherently inadequate. Within the theory of types itself, this scepticism persists in the notion that 'class' is not some elementary given, but has to be reconstructed from our more fundamental intensional grammar (by means of the axiom of reducibility, which Russell also called the axiom of classes – 1908, 168).

The fundamental feature of predication that Russell identifies as self-evident, and as carrying with it a means of ousting the paradox, is distilled into his distinction between *propositional functions* and *generalised functions*.[5] A propositional function, basically, is just a function that gives the values true or false, though without having any variables bound by quantifiers (i.e. it is what Quine calls an 'open sentence'; cf. Quine, 1974, 121). For example, the propositional function 'is a bicycle' is true (or false) of any object of which it is stated. A generalised function, on the other hand, is one with all its variables bound by quantifiers: for example, 'For all x's, if x is a bicycle x has two wheels.'

For his interpretation, Russell leans heavily on Frege.[6] The point is this. A function (following Frege) is not a thing; it can only play the role of a thing through its 'values'. Values are things of which functions can be true. Until we, so to speak, start collecting those values, the function is entirely bare of thinghood; but once the function displays its values, it itself becomes a value, the possible argument to another function.

This, it appears from Russell's account, is the difference between 'propositional functions' and 'generalised functions'. He suggests (again using Frege – 1893, 35) that an open sentence, say 'Fa', can be read as '*anything* is F', while a closed one, say '$\forall x (Fx)$', would be read as 'for *all* x, x is F'. The 'all' introduced by the quantifier ('some' would have the same effect) assimilates the function to its values, and makes it into a new value itself, analogously to the role of the *Wertverlauf* in Frege. The 'any' of a propositional

5 On this topic, also as it relates to Frege and Wittgenstein, compare Hylton, 1984.
6 Especially 1893, pp. 31ff., where Frege deals with introducing and eliminating quantifiers.

function, on the other hand, indicates the self-effacement of pure thought, thought that *cannot* play the role of a function.

That, at least, appears to be the basis for Russell's distinction between the two kinds of 'function'. It has been strongly criticised by Quine (cf. van Heijenoort, 1967, 150f, and elsewhere). Its purpose, though, is to retain Frege's original insight, and continue to use it in a way that avoids the paradoxes. The importance of propositional functions, according to Russell, is that they cannot form the basis of paradoxes involving self-membership. This is because expressions involving *any*, rather than *all*, invoke no 'course of values' that would enable them to become subjects of predication. 'All' expressions, by contrast, can be reflexive precisely because they themselves constitute 'new values' that can, seemingly, act as arguments to themselves.

> In the former [propositional functions], we merely affirm an undetermined one of the propositions of the form "*p* is true or false", whereas in the latter [generalised propositions] we affirm (if anything) a new proposition, different from all the propositions of the form "*p* is true or false". Thus we may admit "any value" of a variable in cases where "all values" would lead to reflexive fallacies; for the admission of "any value" does not in the same way *create new values*. (1908, 158; my emphasis)

Having established this distinction, Russell's scheme works by presenting 'propositional functions' as fundamental and 'generalised functions' as derivative. This seems to be evidenced, among other things, by the contention that all *deduction* – the basic chains of human reasoning – operates with propositional functions (1908, 158; and see Frege, 1893, 31; 'modus ponens' is a primitive rule of inference). The effect of the priority of propositional functions is this: generalised functions derive from them, and furthermore they derive from them the domain of values they may take as arguments.

> The fundamental *all* is 'all values of a propositional function', and every other *all* is derivative from this. (1908, 161)

So, because a propositional function cannot take itself as a value, generalised functions implicitly derive the same incapacity from the propositional functions embedded within them, despite the fact that from their grammatical form they might otherwise appear to be self-referential.

We can resume the argument as follows. In Russell's view, the set-theoretic paradox that damaged Frege's project was attributable to self-referentiality. Accordingly, some device was needed that would bar self-reference, but without this seeming mere technical interference (and hence intuitively – 'philosophically' – uninterpretable).

The problem with the 'axiom of comprehension', arguably, is that it is merely technical – a procedural rule not derivable from the self-evident nature of thought. Russell emphasised that he wanted to find 'some *natural restriction upon the possible values of . . . the function, . . . and not needing to be imposed from without*' (1908, 161; my emphasis).

Russell thought this '*internal* limitation . . . , given by the nature of the function' could be traced to the propositional function. As we saw, the propositional function cannot be self-referential because it 'is' nothing that could be the value of an argument.

Moreover, the propositional function is primary. *Reasoning* works with propositional functions (or, as Russell expresses it in an equivalent formulation, '*all deduction operates with real variables*' – 158). (The suggestion is that quantifiers have to be eliminated in order to allow deduction – cf. Frege, 1893, 31. Quantified statements review states, perhaps, while deduction itself always breaks the scope of the quantifier. To infer by modus ponens, for example, Russell says, 'we have to pass from the apparent to the real variable [i.e. from quantified to open sentences] and then back again to the apparent variable' (158). We start and finish with quantified statements, but the actual deductive step in the inference is bare of quantifiers. To do Barbara, for example, we have two quantified premises (all humans are mortal; all Greeks are human) and a quantified conclusion (all Greeks are mortal), but the deduction depends on eliminating the quantifier scope ('all') in favour of the universality of the propositional function's 'any'. So the actual reasoning takes place with 'any Greeks are human', etc. Such would appear to be the force of this argument.)

The goal of Russell's argument, at any event, is to emphasise that propositional functions are both primary and ontologically self-effacing. They are instantiated; but they do not 'exist', as *Wertverläufe* or whatever. For example, 'There is no one proposition which *is* the law of contradiction (say); there are only the various instances of the law' (158).

So: a propositional function automatically, 'naturally', excludes itself as a possible value for its arguments. This is the crucial component of what Russell calls its 'range of significance'. Every function, propositional or otherwise, carries with it the range of significance established by the propositional function;[7] and no function, propositional or derived, can include itself because the propositional form never admits such self-reference. Furthermore, the range of significance need not, indeed cannot, be explicit, for every explicit determination of a range of significance merely introduces a further implicit one (161). The fundamental conditions of logic can only, as Wittgenstein later said, be 'shown'; they cannot be made

7 The range of significance is not what the function is true of, but what it can meaningfully be predicated of, whether truly or not. So 'this table' is within the range of 'is red' (and may be true or false); 'five' is not, and is neither true nor false, but meaningless.

objects of 'saying'.

The 'range of significance' of a function, then, is Russell's basic category; and this range, as he argues with the aid of the 'propositional function', can never include the function itself. With that exclusion, the legitimate range of arguments is termed by Russell a 'type': 'A *type* is defined as the range of signifance of a propositional function, that is, as the collection of arguments for which the said function has values' (163).

Now, the notion of a type carries no particular ontological prescriptions. Arguments to a function may be individuals, as in the case of a function like 'is red'; or they may be remoter objects, such as the range of significance of a function like 'has an integer square root'. Thus far, Russell seems satisfactorily to have preserved the self-evidence of Frege's project, while avoiding the paradoxes associated with an uncritical account of set membership. He has, in particular, avoided assumptions about the entity 'class', which reduces his exposure to ontological commitments.

3. Reducibility

Class rears its head again later, however. To see this, we should briefly recapitulate the course of the argument so far.

The 'natural' way of looking at predicates would be to assume that each predicate corresponds to a class of objects that exemplify it. Some of those classes may be empty ('unicorns'), but the main point is that, for any specified entity, it should be possible to determine whether or not it is a member of some class. It turns out, however, that this membership relation is, in certain instances, absolutely impossible to determine. For example, is 'the class of x's such that $\neg x \epsilon x$' a member of itself?

In view of this, there seem to be two possible reactions. First, we stick to classes, but view them as in some way fictional, without abandoning our underlying commitment to a 'real objective world'. This is a development we can see in Quine. Alternatively, we abandon classes, and try to reconstruct notions like membership in terms of a general fundamental logic (i.e. one that still embraces 'reality' *tout court*, rather than withdrawing to the procedural realm of calculation). This is more consistent with Frege's project; and it is the path preferred by Russell in his theory of types.

Russell does this with the distinction between propositional and generalised functions, the force of which is to underline the difference between pure operations of thought and those creations of thought that acquire grammatical objecthood. The distinction is precisely analogous to Frege's distinction between concepts and their *Wertverläufe*, except that Russell makes *no* commitments about the objectual status of 'extensions'. For

Russell, some things can be arguments of bound variables, and other things cannot; but this grammatical rule makes no determination one way or the other about such things' status as 'objects', even fictitious ones, in a 'world'.[8]

In parallel terminology, we could say that Russell puts intension rather than extension at the base of his analysis. The a priori of thinking is not the existence, 'out there', or extensions to our concepts; it is the construction, intensionally, of ranges of significance.

> What is necessary is not that the values should be given individually and exten-
> sionally, but that the totality of the values should be given intensionally, so
> that, concerning any assigned object, it is at least theoretically determinate
> whether or not the said object is a value of the function. (Whitehead and
> Russell, 40)[9]

Now, the difficulty with this is that it makes certain sorts of intuitively unobjectionable concepts hard to manage. If our ontology is reduced to the basically grammatical relation between 'function' and its potential 'arguments', certain manoeuvres become problematic. In particular, what do we do when we want a predicate whose 'range of significance' does not accept the argument we need to use? Where, in other words, we have the argument, and we have the function, but the argument is not the kind of entity that the function is supposed to be significant about?

In Russell's account, this can come about in the following way. Functions, as we saw, eject themselves from their own ranges of significance. This, at bottom, is because of the ontological self-effacement of the propositional function – the kind of function from which all others derive. But other characteristics also enter here which, taken together, Russell calls the 'hierarchy of functions'. This 'hierarchy' can be seen in two contexts.

First, the 'types' indicate a general quasi-ontological scale of entities. The ranges of significance of particular functions coalesce into a general order of Being. This is because any function ejects from its range of significance not only itself, but also any other entity for which it is meaningless. That embraces, essentially, any other entity on the same rung as itself of a grammatical scale of attributions. For example, any function that is significant only for sense data ejects all other functions with the same range. So

8 A significantly different view emerges in Quine's dictum, 'To be is to be a value of a variable' – (i.e. of a variable bound by a quantifier: 1974, 234). Russell's purpose is precisely to avoid 'ontologising' the objects over which variables of quantification range.

9 This is in line with the traditional definition of intension. Arnauld, who called it 'la compréhension' (in opposition to 'l'étendue'), wrote in the so-called Port-Royal logic, 'J'appelle compréhension de l'idée, les attributs qu'elle enferme en soi, et qu'on ne lui peut oster sans la détruire, comme la compréhension de l'idée du triangle enferme extension, figure, trois lignes, trois angles, et l'egalité de ces trois angles deux droits, &c.' *La Logique ou l'art de penser*, Paris, 1662, 62.

not only can 'is red' not be predicated of itself; neither can it be predicated of any other comparable functions ('hardness is red').

However, this aspect of types is, for Russell, of secondary interest. More important is the further hierarchical ramification which can arise. The point is this: for the purposes of assessing things like the paradoxes, the important question is not the initial type of the argument, but the way it is dealt with by functions. The argument might be an object of sense experience, or it might be a number. The latter is, presumably, a higher 'type' in Russell's sense (assuming, with Frege, that numbers are classes of classes); but this is not critical to the problem of paradoxes, which are mostly concerned not with varying types of input argument, but with varying orders of function.

For practical purposes, says Russell, the 'input' of our functions in any particular context is to be classed as an 'individual', where this is more a grammatical category ('destitute of complexity') than an ontological one (164). The ramification of orders arises when we (roughly) make statements about something, then make statements about those statements, and so on. For example, if our initial argument-individuals are human beings, then our first function might be some generalisation involving 'wise' ('for some person x, x is wise'), whereupon a second-order function might be to say of wisdom that it is a cardinal virtue (for this example, see Kneale & Kneale, 658).

Now, as part of the hierarchy of functions Russell makes a central stipulation, namely, that no generalised function may range over variables of more than one type (164f). This is the case even with functions like 'is true', which may appear to be one function ranging over many types but 'is really many analogous functions with different ranges of significance' (162). So each range of significance has, so to speak, functions proper to it; indeed, it would almost seem that each range only comes about because of the 'intension' which evokes it. The important point of interpretation would seem to be this: since we cannot rely on 'classes', as pre-existing objects of whom it can always be determined whether or not they have some attribute, we must scrupulously observe the grammatical ('intensional') circumstances within which our entities arise.

Russell terms functions that are proper in this sense *predicative*. Specifically, a predicative function 'is of the order next above that of its argument' (165). The metaphor of 'next above' is probably not central for Russell; what is being emphasised is that the function is a *different* order from its arguments (163), and also that it is the one whose generalisation applies specifically within the type of its arguments (166).[10]

10 Kneale, for example, questions the legitimacy of the 'next above' (Kneale & Kneale, 658); and we have considered the role of this metaphor in other contexts above, chapter 1; but the

The problem, however, is this. Although 'generalisation can only be applied within some one type' (166), *non*-generalising functions (propositional functions, in particular) are not restricted in this way. They can, as long as they eschew generalisation (they stay with 'any', not venturing into 'all') take any argument, irrespective of its type. That much is legitimate. The difficulties arise when we find functions that purport to generalise across more than one type. Certain functions make attributions to arguments of one type that can only be gained by generalising over arguments of another type.

Examples might be as follows.[11] First, in order to say that two things are identical, we need to say that one has all the properties of the other. Our underlying type, then, is constituted by the things of which we are predicating identity; but we need to generalise over their properties, which are of another ('higher') type. ('For all properties P possessed by x, y possesses P'.) (See Whitehead and Russell, 57)

Another example is the statement 'Napoleon had all the qualities that make a great general' (ibid. 56). To say that Napoleon was brave, persistent, and a great general would be acceptable: those are all first-order functions of a type one object. Equally, to say that bravery and persistence are qualities of great generals is acceptable: that is a second-order function of type two objects. But the statement as it stands purports to generalise over two types – great generals and qualities of great generals. Are we saying that Napoleon possessed certain qualities that we have designated, independently, as 'qualities of great generals' (analogously to the cardinal virtues)? Or are we saying that 'qualities of great generals' are those possessed by Napoleon and certain other individuals, dispensing with any generalisation over 'qualities' in the abstract? It seems we are doing neither. We have, so to speak, half an eye on the individuals and half an eye on the qualities: and the totality of 'qualities of great generals' only arises during the course of the generalisation.

More technically, we could say that ranging over two domains of types has the effect of threatening the principle that functions eject themselves from the type over which they generalise. For example, in the case of identity, 'being identical with y' is one of the properties of x that is being generalised over. So the function generalises over itself. In the case of Napoleon, the property of 'having all the properties of a great general' is one of the properties of great generals being generalised over. So, again, the

critical notion here is the intensional link between a range and its function, not that of ascent from empiry into abstraction.

11 These are the less technical examples from *Principia Mathematica*. Those in 1908 are only mathematical (167). In the literature, the standard example is that of the least upper bound of a set of real numbers (Kneale & Kneale, 662; Quine, 1969, 249).

function is included in its own generalisation.[12]

Now, this is only a problem because of the intimacy, in Russell's 'intensional' account, of the relation between functions and their possible arguments. A function is blind, so to speak, to arguments outside its range. If one imagines functions as containers, then the containers are non-transparent. I can see what I am putting into them as I do it (first-order predication); but by the time I start putting the first containers into other ones (second-order predication) the original arguments are no longer visible to me. This would not be the case, however, if I could still 'see' the original arguments. If that were so, everything I say is still essentially about them: the arguments persist as entities regardless of the 'orders' of any intermediate functions I apply to them.

This is, indeed, the force of what Russell calls the *axiom of reducibility*, or the *axiom of classes*. This states that 'every propositional function is equivalent, for all its values, to some predicative function' (1908, 167). In other words, we do not have to worry about the fact that attributions of identity, or whatever, appear to range impredicatively over more than one type: we simply assume that there *is* always some fixed range of values from some harmless predicative function which provides a well-formed totality precisely equivalent to the one we want. (E.g. 'great generals' already 'are', and an appropriate predicative function might be a disjunctive listing of all their instants of birth.) How this is supposed to accord with Russell's intensional scheme is unclear, because it flies in the face of his aprioristic grammar. The effect is to reinstate much of the metaphysical dogma of class, even though Russell disguises it as a technical axiom rather than as 'assuming that there really are such things as classes' (1908, 167). Classes remain outside the scheme, but only at the price of an assumption that seems almost as disreputable. In practice, it does in the end amount to an 'admission of classes', however 'grudging' (168).

Quine has construed the axiom of reducibility as Russell's abandonment of the 'constructivism' with which his theory of types started (1969, 253). Certainly a major technical defect threatens: once the axiom of reducibility is granted, there is no need anyway to postulate functions other than 'predicative' ones (Quine, 1969, 253f). And that, of course, leaves the 'propositional function', from which Russell derives his 'types' and their ontological grammar, up in the air.

---

12 Quine's example is that of the 'average Yale student' whose own grades contributed to the computation of the average he then matches (1969, 243).

4. The 'cleavages' between logic and set theory

At this stage, as before, we find the sceptics diverging from the non-sceptics. The sceptics, exemplified by Quine, would give up any attempt to ground arithmetic in logic, and would draw attention to 'the major cleavages between logic and set theory' (Quine, 1969, 257) as one more reminder that reality always exceeds the capabilities of reason.

The non-sceptics, meanwhile, continue trying to find common ground between the real and the rational. The most persistent theme here is, indeed, constructivism of some kind. Constructivism concentrates its attention on arithmetic. Arithmetic is obviously *real* (it is inconceivable that it should not always 'work'); but we have yet to prove it *rational* (i.e. derivable from equally unshakeable logical necessity).

Russell's attempt was constructivist in the sense that it tried to derive arithmetic from the foundational logical activity of predication. Wittgenstein, as we shall now see, followed the substantive elements of this. The difference is that he was far more purist than Russell, and this overrode any sustained attempt to reconstruct a workable 'logical' set theory. The result, in the *Tractatus*, was a work more of metaphysics and ethics than of mathematical logic; and this emphasis became more pronounced in the later work.

What joins Wittgenstein to our general theme is, as we shall see, his method, which we are characterising as *irreflexivity*. Frege's distinction between concept and object, and Russell's notion of the self-effacing propositional function, are sharpened by Wittgenstein into an absolute boundary between logic and things. This amounts to a doctrine of the invisible subject; and certainly it is in ethics that it reaches its distinctive development. In general, Wittgenstein's position represents the opposite extreme to that of, say, the later Husserlians (chapter 5) or Hegel; but they are all on the same continuum (of 'constructivism'), and, as every good Hegelian knows, the extremes touch!

5. The 'zero method'

Wittgenstein's own response to these problems was characteristically purist. The important point, moreover, is that the basic structure of his response remained the same throughout his life. In the *Tractatus*, his central project is, with Frege and Russell, still a 'logicistic' rescue of arithmetic. This is something he later abandoned. But the underlying move – the rejection of what, in the *Philosophical Investigations*, he called 'second-order philosophy' (§121) – remains consistent throughout.

In the *Tractatus (TLP)*, Wittgenstein attempted a pure first-order account of mathematical logic, in which entities like classes were entirely ruled out, whether as 'real' in their own right, or even as grudging assumptions of the Axiom of Reducibility variety. That was Wittgenstein's technical ambition; but it stands for a more radical metaphysical project that persists throughout his work.

The point, essentially, was this: Wittgenstein refused to accept that 'logic', or 'mathematics', contributed *anything* of content to knowledge. 'Theories that allow a logical sentence to seem as though it has content [gehaltvoll] are always false' (*TLP*, 6.111). There was, literally, nothing in logic that could be talked about. Logic, he said, was like 'punctuation' (*TLP*, 5.4611); it accompanies what we say about the world, but it is itself entirely insubstantial. Or, as he also put it, logic in itself *says* nothing (*TLP*, 5.43). There is nothing in it that can become an 'object' of some statement in its own turn; negation, for example, is not the 'object' of further negation in the expression '$\neg\neg p$' (*TLP*, 5.44).

This is what might be called the doctrine of the disappearing logical constants (*TLP*, 5.441).[13] 'Logical constants' are the traditional name for the non-empirical bits and pieces that reasoning adds to any cognition – in symbols, things like 'v', '$\neg$', '&' and so on. The term 'constant' is, in a sense, loaded, for it is usually contrasted with 'variable'; constants, in such usage, are specific fixed entities, while a variable is, so to speak, a mere gap waiting to be filled. So the temptation (as Wittgenstein would regard it) is to regard the 'logical' constant as an entity of some kind, if only a formal one.

Against this, Wittgenstein argued that there was 'no such thing as "logical objects", "logical constants" (in the sense of Frege or Russell)' (*TLP*, 5.4). Truth-functions (the things expressible in truth tables) were 'not material functions' (*TLP*, 5.44), and logical relations such as 'v' or '$\rightarrow$' were merely 'apparent relations' (*TLP*, 5.461). In general, logic was a 'zero method' (*TLP*, 6.121), in that it allowed content to articulate itself, but added nothing.

6. Mapping; the 'picture theory of meaning'

This is the substance of Wittgenstein's so-called 'picture theory of meaning'. The picture theory has this name somewhat misleadingly. Although Wittgenstein speaks of what can be translated as 'pictures' of facts ('Bilder

13 Strawson, 1982, comments on one aspect of this, though it is doubtful whether Wittgenstein would have agreed that logic was derived from 'pure reflection on the general nature of statement' (p. 15), since this formulation attributes to logic precisely the content that Wittgenstein hoped to avoid.

der Tatsachen', *TLP*, 2.1), the force of 'Bild' lies not in the notion of painterly representation suggested by 'picture', but in the very different associations of structure or form. More than that: 'Bild' is, in fact, German for what English logic calls 'image'. Wittgenstein has a very specific metaphor in mind here, and the use of expressions like 'picture' obscures the role of this doctrine in the *Tractatus*.

In particular, the relation between 'Bild' and things is not one of depiction, but of *abbilden*.[14] The meaning of *abbilden* in the context of logic is quite clear: it means *mapping*, i.e. what a function does as between the domain of the variables and the range onto which they are mapped. Once we realise this, the purpose of the so-called picture theory (which would be better termed the theory of mapping) becomes clearer. In particular, this is not an epistemological doctrine, but a logical one.

So we have a function ('Abbildung') and the image ('Bild') it produces. What the function does is to assign, to each object in the domain of things ('Gegenstände' – *TLP*, 2.131), a value (its 'image', 'Bild'). Once things are, so to speak, processed by the function, they become 'elements' of the image (*TLP*, 2.13). *Elements* are members of *sets*. This means, among other things, that they fall within the requirements of Zermelo's axiomatisation of set theory, and become acceptable variables for logical operations. Wittgenstein summarises the relationship between things and their logical images thus:

> 2.1514 The functional relation [abbildende Beziehung] consists of assignments between the elements of the image [Bild] and the things [Sachen].

This is all fairly metaphorical. But what Wittgenstein means is this. The basic cognitive manoeuvre is this assignment of things to 'logical space' (*TLP*, 2.11). Logical space is the range within which values for functions of things can fall. A thing enters logical space as soon as a function of it receives a value. For most things, the range of values is simply true or false, e.g. for any x, the functional expression 'x is a table' will assign either 'true' or 'false'. So logical space is filled with elementary statements of the form, '"x is a table" is true for . . .'. These functions ('is a table', etc.) are what establishes the link between logical space, with its 'images', and reality. Wittgenstein specifies:

> 2.17 What the image [Bild] has to have in common with reality, in order to map [abbilden] it according to its manner – truly or falsely – is its functional form [Form der Abbildung].

14 Depiction would be 'vorstellen', or 'darstellen'. Wittgenstein does use 'darstellen' here (*TLP*, 2.173f), and it is clear that he is playing with the ambiguity of 'abbilden'; but the metaphor draws its force from the set-theoretic use of 'abbilden', not its more conversational connotations.

7. Non-reflexivity; functions and operations

The 'function' is the device by means of which objects are first introduced into logical space. (Wittgenstein's term for function is both 'Abbildung' and 'Funktion'.) The resulting sentences (e.g. 'this is a table') are *elementary sentences*. These are intensely empirical; they make immediate statements about things (they 'assert the existence of a state of affairs' *TLP*, 4.21). And it is only in the context of elementary sentences that *names* appear (*TLP*, 4.23); names are, perhaps, points of the most direct connection between language and things.

Elementary sentences consist of functions of names, and names only (*TLP*, 4.24).[15] The strong suggestion is that names can only be applied to individuals. Classes, in other words, do not have names. This is fundamental, because it means that Wittgenstein is excluding anything above first-order functions, in Russell's terms. There are various ways in which we can see this working.

'Abbildung', the first-order function, is what the image has in common with reality (*TLP*, 2.18). It is, so to speak, the bridge between reality and language.[16] But because the role of 'Abbildung' operates only between things and first-order statements, that is the realm to which it is restricted both logically and ontologically. There is only one domain of real individuals; and it is only upon these natural empirical individuals that the function, as 'Abbildung', may operate.

Because of this, the function cannot say anything about itself. Its role is exhausted in importing reality into discourse. Once it has done that, its mapping ceases. The function cannot be applied to concepts. So it is not possible to describe, reflexively, what the function as 'Abbildung' is doing. The function cannot, as it were, operate at a meta-level. Wittgenstein puts it like this:

> 2.173   The image represents its object from outside (its standpoint is its form of representation), and for that reason the image represents its object truly or falsely.
> 2.174   But the image cannot place [stellen] itself outside its form of representation [Darstellung].

In other words, the 'place' of the 'Abbildung' is fixed upon 'darstellen'. It is, perhaps, like the lens of a microscope; it makes sense applying it to speci-

---

15 To revert to the 'mapping' theory, using this new term: the function (Abbildung) now assigns a value in logical space (the image, or Bild) for any individual in the domain (which may, also, have a name). So, for 'Aristotle', the function 'is Greek' assigns the value (image) 'true'.

16 The function is sometimes represented graphically by means of arrows spanning the gap between the domain and the function's range of values (the image). See, for example, Reinhardt and Soeder, 1974, p.32.

mens ('from outside', i.e. from a different set of coordinates), but it would be absurd to use it for reading a book, or looking at one's interlocutors.

This might be called the principle of non-reflexivity: the proper role of functions is the representation of objects, and they cannot be applied to themselves (reflexively), or even, Wittgenstein implies, to second-order entities at all.

Various things follow from this. In the first place, Wittgenstein is in clear agreement with Russell's veto on the reflexive use of functions.

> 3.332   No sentence can say something about itself, because the sentence sign cannot be contained within itself, (that is the whole 'theory of types').

And indeed, that much is consistent with Russell's position. But Wittgenstein goes further. Russell's theory of types rested on the contention that there are individuals, and then there are first-order functions, second-order functions, and so on. So the basic distinction would be between individuals and functions; but (subject to the theory of types) there was no restriction on the ascending hierarchy of orders, with each level supplying acceptable variables for the next one up.

Wittgenstein's position, though it is not stated entirely clearly, is more radical than this. As we have seen, the base units of language are things (which may be named) and functions (Abbildungen); they come together in elementary sentences. Now, because functions are, most properly, only for mapping real things, the elementary sentences do, in effect, include the entire extent of 'logical space'. Whatever there is to be said, is already contained within the elementary sentences, the functionalised 'images' of reality.

This, then, is the logical-ontological basis for Wittgenstein's theory of the disappearing logical constants. There is no *room* for more 'content' once the functions have done their job on the individuals. There is no such 'object' as 'logic' that could appear in the elementary sentences.

The only way it appears is as a purely formal 'punctuation'. And, furthermore, this punctuation is already fully contained within the elementary sentences. Wittgenstein explains:

> 5.47   [...] After all, the elementary sentences already contain all logical operations. For 'fa' says the same as '($\exists$x).fx.x=a'.
> Where there is composition, there are argument and function, and where these are, all logical constants are as well.

The point is this. Once you have arguments (the things) and functions (the 'Abbildung'), you have all the components of logic as well. At that point, moreover, the hierarchy of types comes to an abrupt halt. The substance is already exhaustively present in the first 'image'. The only thing that can be changed is the punctuation, the particular logical form. But that is not the same as, for example, quantifying over functions and moving into higher orders. 'Operations' are ontologically innocuous.

It is from this vantage point that Wittgenstein can mount his campaign for logic as a 'zero method'. Logic is about operations, not about functions. Operations and functions are quite distinct, he insists:

> 5.25   The occurrence of the operation does not characterise the sense of the sentence.
> The operation, after all, *does not say anything* ['sagt nichts aus' – my emphasis], but only its result does, and that depends on the bases of the operation. (Operation and Function must not be confused with one another.)

And the problem that logic does seem to need to create rational entities, to do arithmetic, for example, is only an apparent problem. That is because functions as such are not (or should not) be involved; it is merely the spectral hand of the operations giving an illusion of reflexivity:

> 5.251   A function cannot be its own argument; though the result of an operation can be its own base.

8. Showing and representing

The distinction between functions and operations is congruent with another distinction that is less technical, and that becomes particularly important in Wittgenstein's later work. It is the distinction between showing and representing.

In the immediate logical context, this follows directly from Wittgenstein's hierarchy of names, functions and operations. As we noticed, functions ('Abbildungen') make it possible for the images to 'represent' ('vertreten', *TLP*, 2.131, or 'darstellen', *TLP*, 2.173) objects in logical space. Operations, on the other hand, do *not* have a representative function. This restriction on the ontological relevance of operations is fundamental to Wittgenstein's thought. This emphasis is quite clear. In relation to the logical constants (the 'visible' aspect of logical operations), he writes:

> 4.0312 [. . .]   My basic idea [Grundgedanke] is that the 'logical constants' do not represent [vertreten]. That the *Logic* of facts cannot be represented.

Now, obviously Wittgenstein does not mean that it is impossible to say anything about logic; logic is, after all, the theme of the *Tractatus*. The point is this: statements 'about' logic are different – ontologically different – from 'normal' statements. 'Normal' statements (the term 'normal' is one Wittgenstein uses unselfconsciously in the later work) are functional applications to the real world. But statements about logic are not about the real world; in fact, they have *no object*. The things any 'meta-logic' would presume to talk about are characteristics of the logical space in which the world exists for experience. But they are not separable from it. As soon as the world appears in logical space, the 'logical' bits appear with it ('Where there is composition, there are argument and function, and where these are, all the logical constants are already', *TLP*, 5.74).

It is in this sense that logic is, in a quite Kantian sense, 'transcendental' (*TLP*, 6.13); it is a condition of the possibility of any experience. But the transcendentality of Wittgenstein's logic differs from Kant's in that there is nothing you can say about it in abstraction from experience. In this respect, Wittgenstein's logic is transcendental in the sense of the transcendental aesthetic, rather than in the sense of the transcendental analytic. The transcendental analytic leaves scope for, e.g., the table of categories. The transcendental aesthetic, however, simply establishes that there is a certain irreducible something about the form of our experience – time and space. And the force of that non-discursive, non-reflexive something is that we cannot talk about it. We only know time and space through the objects of experience; and we only know the objects of experience through time and space. We cannot speak of either in isolation from the other. Equally, for Wittgenstein, we cannot talk of 'logic' in isolation from the things it is given with – the elementary sentences.

Wittgenstein puts this as follows:

4.12   [. . .] In order to represent [darstellen] logical form we would have to position [aufstellen] ourselves with our sentence outside logic, and that means outside the world.

In other words, if you are in the world, you are using elementary sentences about natural empirical objects. If you try to talk about anything else, with the manner of objectifying representation, you place yourself outside this world, and, thus, outside sense.

There is, however, a sense in which logic becomes apparent, and that is by means of what Wittgenstein calls 'showing'. Even though we cannot talk about logic as though it were a determinate object, we can, so to speak, become aware of it as something that 'shows' itself.

4.121   Sentences cannot represent [darstellen] logical form; it is mirrored in them.
Whatever is mirrored in language cannot be represented by it.
Whatever expresses *itself* in language is something that *we* cannot express through it.
The sentence *shows* the logical form of reality.

The distinction between showing and saying is congruent with that between operations and functions; and it is equally fundamental.

4.1212   What can be shown *cannot* be said.

Talking about things, i.e. applying functions, is utterly different from the demonstrative gestures of logical form.[17] And, in a strange reversal that we shall encounter again, it is through these soft and harmonious gestures that logic appeals outside itself, to a level of *feeling*:

> 4.1213   Now, too, we understand our feeling: that we are in possession of a correct logical apprehension just as long as everything in our symbolic language harmonises [stimmt].[18]

9. Formal concepts, truth tables, boundaries

Before we start to investigate the further implications of Wittgenstein's technical position, we need to look at three ways in which it sets him against competing views.

In the first place, the notion of 'disappearing logical constants' carries over into what Wittgenstein calls 'formal concepts'.

A concept is, usually, something that is 'represented' by a *function* (*TLP*, 4.126). The concept 'table', for example, is represented by the function 'is a table'. Certain things, however, are only apparently 'concepts' in this sense. These apparent concepts (Scheinbegriffe) include terms like 'object', 'fact', 'function' and 'number' (*TLP*, 4.1272). If (says Wittgenstein) you follow Frege or Russell and use these terms as though they were real concepts, you get senseless sentences. For example, according to him you cannot say 'there are objects' (presumably, '$(\exists x)Fx$', with F for 'is an object'). Equally, he refuses to allow 'one is a number'.

We shall consider later whether this is sustainable (in the way Wittgenstein puts it). Clearly, though, it follows from the position we have been tracing. These 'formal concepts' are pale casts of logic and 'operation', not the red-blooded concepts engendered by function and experience. Wittgenstein suggests that they are the attendants of the 'variable', the coordinates, so to speak, of the spot in logical space where real objects enter our 'world'. But to imagine that these coordinates are themselves capable of existence (*TLP*, 4.1274) is to be frightened by a spectre; notions like 'number', in Wittgenstein's view, are Gogolesque dead souls.

Wittgenstein's hostility to any notion of 'logic' as the bearer of sub-

---

17 As we are seeing, and shall see further, the saying/showing opposition runs throughout Wittgenstein's work. Earlier readers did not always appreciate its centrality, however. Russell, indeed, did not. To him, Wittgenstein wrote, 'Now I'm afraid you haven't really got hold of my main contention, to which the whole business of logical propositions is only corollary. The main point is the theory of what can be expressed [gesagt] by propositions – i.e. by language (and, what comes to the same, what can be *thought*) and what cannot be expressed by propositions, but only shown (gezeigt); which, I believe, is the cardinal problem of philosophy...' (Quoted in Anscombe, 161). See also Schulte, 1989, 79ff.
18 See *TLP*, 4.411, 6.1223, 6.1232 for similar appeals to 'feeling'.

stantive content is also evident in his probabilistic interpretation of the syntax of truth-functions. One of the technical contributions of the *Tractatus* was to demonstrate the use of truth tables in propositional logic. '$p{\rightarrow}q$', for example, can be rendered in tabular form as in *TLP*, 4.442; and this technique is valuable for analysing complex expressions. For Wittgenstein, however, this was a further specification of the ontological status of logic. He defined 'sentence' in the following terms:

> 4.4   The sentence is the expression of correspondence and non-correspondence with the truth possibilities of the elementary sentences.

This notion of 'truth possibilities' was entirely statistical. A sentence such as '$p{\rightarrow}q$', for example, when expressed in a truth table, was a visible demonstration of the probability of a certain combination of events occurring.[19] This particular sentence, as we immediately see from the table in *TLP*, 4.442, indicates that there is a 75% probability of a valid combination occurring (of the four possible combinations, p & $\neg q$ is excluded, but the other three are all acceptable).

Obviously this is not a magical predetermination of what is the case; it is simply a way of fixing the relationship between language and its objects. Language, through truth-functions, delimits the logical space in which events may happen (*TLP*, 4.463); or, to put it the other way round, the success or failure of language is gauged by this kind of probabilistic correspondence. This 'doctrine of probabilities' (*TLP*, 4.464, 5.1) is axiomatic for Wittgenstein's account of the ontological status of logic.

10. A space bounded from within

The third aspect of Wittgenstein's ontology of logic is fundamental to our understanding of his work. It is his treatment of reflexivity, and, specifically, of the problem of self-delimitation.

The point is this. Any particular logical construction, as we saw, delimits the logical space within which 'facts' can happen; the sentence is 'like the space which is bounded [begrenzt] by hard substance, and within which a body has its place' (*TLP*, 4.463).

This is true of any particular sentence because, as we saw, sentences are compounds of elementary sentences, and elementary sentences themselves *include all the logical operations* (*TLP*, 5.47). They are, in that respect, passively self-delimiting; the operative structure that they contain, as a result of the *functions*, already implies the spatial delimitation expressed by com-

19 See also 6.122: 'We can get by without the logical sentences, since, with the appropriate notation, we can recognise the formal properties of the sentences by merely looking at them.

pound sentences. Put more simply, we could say that the empirical world, the ground of the elementary sentences, is already a bounded, delimited thing. The sentences merely reproduce ('represent') those bounds more or less successfully; they do not actively create them.

The universe is implicitly bounded by the totality of things in it (more on this later). And any individual statement, in turn, witnesses to a delimitation. But we cannot generalise this. Thought cannot get outside itself and talk about 'everything that is thinkable', because it would then be putting itself outside its own boundaries.[20] So although the task of philosophy (as Wittgenstein says, echoing Kant's dictum about making room for belief),[21] is to define the realm of reasoning (or, more narrowly, of sentences, or *language* – *TLP*, 5.61), it can only do this *from the inside*.

> 4.114 It [philosophy] must bound [abgrenzen] the thinkable and thereby also the unthinkable.
> It must delimit [begrenzen] the unthinkable by the thinkable from within.

A boundary seen from within, though, is not really a boundary, because anything we can determine *as* a boundary is also something we can 'get outside' (I don't *know* I've got out of the maze until I am out of it). Since the rules about second-order philosophy will not allow us to say things about merely conceptual totalities like 'the thinkable', we are restricted, in our understanding of the boundary, to an intuition arising from repeated collision with the senselessness of second-order statements.

> So the book wants to draw a boundary round thought, or rather – not around thought, but the expression of thoughts: for in order to draw a boundary round thought, we would have to be able to think both sides of this boundary (so we would have to think the unthinkable).
> So the boundary will only be able to be drawn in language, and whatever lies beyond that boundary will simply be nonsense. (*TLP*, Foreword)

11. Reflexivity

The 'boundary from inside' argument is immensely important, partly because of the 'metaphysical' conclusions Wittgenstein draws from it in the *Tractatus* itself, but mainly because it forms the heart of a whole cluster of logical and technical assumptions that dominate Wittgenstein's later work and, arguably, that of an entire subsequent tradition.

Wittgenstein contends, as we saw, that the business of logic is exhausted

---

20 See also *TLP*, 5.61.
21 'Ich musste also das Wissen aufheben, um zum Glauben Platz zu bekommen.' B XXX.

in its dealings with the things of experience, and that it has no application beyond immediate, natural experience. Now, this is not an unfamiliar position. Basically, it is identical with Kant's account of the understanding; the understanding, in Kant's argument, was properly applicable only to what was given to it by sense, and any attempt to extend the understanding beyond sense led to the metaphysical entanglements of the 'antinomies'. The doctrine is encapsulated in Kant's famous dictum, 'Thoughts without content are empty, intuitions without concepts are blind.'[22]

Wittgenstein's position differs from Kant's, though, in its radicalism. Kant, as is well known, did not confine himself to the understanding; like the *Tractatus*, the *Critique of Pure Reason* attempts to delimit the realm of the understanding, but it does so from a 'higher' vantage point, namely that of *reason*.[23] In Kant, reasoning is able to *reflect* upon itself; 'reason', in the narrow sense, reflects upon the role of 'understanding'. This, however, presupposes that the instruments of reasoning, in the sense of 'meaningful utterance', extend into more than one realm. For Wittgenstein, such a presupposition is unacceptable. In his world-view, language is *univocal as to type*: the veto on 'second-order philosophy' includes in its purview any reflection by language on itself.

The basic position is that logic has its ground and justification in elementary sentences, and elementary sentences are about immediate natural experience. (This is the force of Wittgenstein's famous declaration, 'The general form of the sentence is: the situation is such and such' *TLP*, 4.5.) So logic must not be used to try to talk about logic. The *Tractatus* itself escapes this anathematisation by confining itself to criticism; the conclusion of the work, famously, is that once we have gone through all our discussions we shall realise that there was never really anything there to talk about in the first place. Logic is there to produce 'sentences of natural science'; if you use it to try to say anything else you just produce 'metaphysics', because you will, inevitably, be using terms without 'meaning' (*TLP*, 6.53; by 'meaning', Wittgenstein is thinking of his first-order functional mapping from a domain of natural objects). There *is* 'philosophy', in some sense; its most important task, perhaps, is to clear our vision for what is there before us, *showing* itself with naive immediacy, in the logic of our speech. Beyond that, in 'metaphysics', the only true philosophy is what pushes itself out into the realm of the inexpressible, and there falls silent.

Now, this ban on reflective use of language includes a wide variety of statements other philosophers might allow. They may be listed as follows:

---

22 B 75. See *German Philosophy*, 17ff.
23 See *German Philosophy*, 32ff. for a more detailed discussion.

Second-order statements

As we have seen, Wittgenstein was extremely hesitant about the role of second-order statements. The attempt to clear them out of mathematics is a major part of the *Tractatus*'s technical agenda. In 6.031 he declares, with bravado, that 'the theory of classes is entirely superfluous in mathematics'. It is perhaps questionable whether his 'operative' deduction of numbers, in the previous paragraphs, works, or, indeed, whether it gets by without covertly resorting to functions of functions anyway (e.g. in the notion of 'numerical equality'). Elsewhere, another arithmetically useful function which cannot usually be dealt with without second-order statements, namely identity, is supposedly defined in terms of first-order functions.[24] 'Thus the equality symbol is no essential component of our symbolic language,' he concludes with gusto (*TLP*, 5.533). The whole theory of 'formal concepts', as we saw, is also an attempt to clear away abstract classes.

Self-referring statements

Such statements, which are already disallowed in Russell's theory of types, are excluded by Wittgenstein on purportedly technical grounds. For Russell, of course, statements which were *apparently* self-referring from a formal standpoint were acceptable provided we distinguished between the types of the variables involved. According to Wittgenstein, however, self-referring statements were always an abuse of formal syntax (*TLP*, 3.33f, which is, however, less enlightening than its brusque manner would suggest).

There is one particular kind of self-referring statement excluded by Wittgenstein that is interesting for our purposes, namely statements which say of themselves that they are true ('It is impossible for a sentence to say of itself that it is true,' *TLP*, 4.442). This introduces wider perspectives in the theory of truth predicates, of which we shall have more to say later. Let us just say here that Wittgenstein is clearly right, in an immediate sense. He would exclude the sentence for syntactical reasons. Others, such as Russell from the theory of types, or Tarski or Kripke in the theory of truth predicates, would prescribe ways in which the sentence was to be interpreted. But Wittgenstein himself is obviously not really allowing for these solutions; and, in particular, his doctrine does not seem to allow even for the more modest sort of (Henkin, or Gödel) sentence that says of itself that it is *provable* (or not provable).

Generally reflexive statements

pAnother kind of statement that Wittgenstein objects to is the one that says something about the logical status of itself or of other statements. This takes various forms. One obvious source of irritation to Wittgenstein was the 'judgement stroke' ('⊢') introduced by Frege, and retained by Russell. 'Frege's "judgement stroke" is logically meaningless; with Frege (and Russell) it just shows that the authors think that sentences marked that way are true' (*TLP*, 4.442). The problem, in Wittgenstein's view, was that the judgement stroke constructed a 'meta-statement', distinct from the statement itself, and having the form 'the truth-value of the statement p is W'. But, says Wittgenstein, a sentence does not denote a thing (a truth-value) whose property would be either 'true' or 'false'; the verb of a sentence is not 'is true' or 'is false', as Frege believed, but whatever 'is true' must already be contained by the verb. (*TLP*, 4.063)[25]

In other words, sentences are not 'about' truth-values; they are 'about', if that is the right preposition, first-order functions. A sentence, 'This is a chair', is only about being a chair, and not about a mental entity such as truth. Knowing, indeed, *adds* nothing to what is known. ' "A knows that p is the case" is meaningless, if p is a tautology,' says Wittgenstein (*TLP*, 5.1362). If p is true under all possible interpretations, then the fact that A 'knows' it changes nothing (although some other verb, such as 'believes' or 'has realised' might – in a first-order way – tell us something about A's intellect).

This modal problem is linked to questions of intensionality. An intensional use of language claims to identify purely intellectual entitities. For example, the notion that you could attribute to a sentence the property, 'is true', suggests that such things as 'true sentences' 'exist'. ('Chairs' exist because there are things to which I can attribute the property of being a chair; so, presumably, 'true sentences' exist because there are sentences to which I can attribute the property of being true.) If you allow that, then you may also be tempted to allow that 'believing' a sentence is a further legitimate truth-functional combination – which Wittgenstein would fiercely deny.

Wittgenstein's comments on this issue – in 5.54ff. – are not easy to follow. The basic problem about modal sentences like 'A believes p' is that the two parts ('A believes', and 'p') appear to be, but are not, part of the same truth-functional structure. Broadly, we could say that whether or not the first part is true raises issues that are distinct from whether or not the second part is true. This means that the two parts cannot be integrated into a truth-functional compound of elementary sentences in the way that Wittgenstein generally requires.[26]

25 On this, see also Geach, 1972, chapter 8.
26 '$p{\to}q$', for example, is a quite clear truth-functional, probabilistic combination of two elementary sentences. The net effect of various truth-values for the two parts is expressed in the table in 4.442. But you cannot simply add in the 'believes' part as though it was another ele-

Axioms

Axioms, traditionally, are statements that are self-evident in the sense that there is no point in trying to 'prove' them any further.[27] In a modern context, and particularly in post-Fregean attempts to ground arithmetic without falling into paradox, axioms are simply stipulations, whether 'self-evident' or not, that serve to keep a theoretical structure in some kind of shape.

Russell used his axiom of reducibility, which was not at all self-evident, to define identity; and he needed an 'axiom of infinity' to cope with another complication of the theory of types.[28] But generally, Russell tried to avoid being overly axiomatic, and (like Frege) saw arithmetic as the representation of some real ontology, rather than as merely the expression of a game with human rule makers. This rapidly changed, however, with the development of modern set theory, where axioms became almost entirely pragmatic ('If it works, let's assume it!'), and thus, from an ontological point of view, essentially arbitrary. The arbitrary nature of this view of numbers and their existence was well put by Hilbert, one of the protagonists of the 'axiomatic' method, in a letter to Frege:

> As long as the arbitrarily posited axioms do not contradict each other with all their consequences, they are true, and the things defined by the axioms exist. For me that is the criterion of truth and existence.[29]

Wittgenstein is hostile towards axioms.[30] In the *Tractatus*, this results partly from a lingering Fregean belief in the ontological necessity of logical structures. But the more important reason for this hostility, and the one that carries over into the later work, is the doctrine of irreflexivity. Axioms are objectionable simply because the understanding cannot know how it knows. To do so would be to get outside itself. We can see logic (as it 'shows' itself); and we can 'feel' that it is right; but we cannot make general statements about it from outside.

In part, this is because of the rule that logic is syntactically non-reflexive: 'The logical laws may not themselves be subject to further logical laws.' (*TLP*, 6.123) Beyond that, however, the rules of logic can never be arbitrary (in the sense of *arbitrium*, free will: 'In logic it is not *we* who express . . .

---

mentary sentence on the same level (on the lines, e.g., of '$p \to q$. A believes $p \to q$'). Because of this, the two parts of the sentence fail to satisfy Wittgenstein's demand (in 5.54) that sentences within other sentences should 'only occur as a basis for truth-functional operations'. 'Reference and Modality', in Quine, 1980, is a celebrated skirmish in this area, from a Wittgensteinian standpoint.

27 In Pascal's formulation, they are 'perfectly self-evident' (Meschkowski, *Einführung*, 10).
28 See Kneale & Kneale, 668f. This is different from Zermelo's axiom of infinity.
29 Hilbert to Frege, in Frege, 1980, 39ff. See Hilbert's self-characterisation also in Hilbert, 1904. Meschkowski has a clear and well-illustrated discussion of these developments.
30 See 5.535 (Russell's axiom of infinity), 6.1232 (the axiom of reducibility).

what we want. . .' *TLP*, 6.124). Logic has no substantive independent content, and hence cannot itself form part of a deed or decision. It is simply
given, irresistibly, with the elementary sentences; it cannot be manipulated
as an instrument. Our logical world is not created by deliberate acts of will.

In other words, Wittgenstein is not arguing that logic is underwritten by
some kind of Platonic ideal. In this respect he has abandoned the positions
of Frege or Russell. He seems to be prepared to concede that aspects of
logic may be 'arbitrary' (*TLP*, 6.124), in the looser sense that they are (perhaps) not absolutely necessary.[31] But that does not make them subject to
our *arbitrium*; they are given to us with the elementary sentences, and over
that we have no control. This, rather than the purely logicistic impulse, is
what determines Wittgenstein's attitude towards axioms and 'language
game' rules, here and later.

Distinctions of type

Russell's theory of types involved the doctrine of 'ambiguity of type'.
Basically, this meant that foundational logical terms like 'class', 'function',
'truth' and so on were all to be regarded as ambiguous, in the sense that
they mean one thing in one order of judgement and something different in
another. Or, more precisely, statements of differing orders are not 'true'
(for example) in the same way. 'The words "true" and "false" have many
different meanings, according to the kind of proposition to which they are
applied,' he wrote.[32] This doctrine has the obvious disadvantage that it
seems to set up a multifarious universe of disparate entities, most of which
are probably as much intellectual as empirical ('Truly elementary [i.e. first-
order] judgements are not very easily found,' Russell commented – Whitehead and Russell, 1962, p.45).

Wittgenstein's doctrine of irreflexivity, as we have already seen, would
be enough to make him reject the doctrine of types. Higher-order predication, for Wittgenstein, was not the reflection of some hierarchy of
being; it was simply a misuse of logical syntax. This is what lies behind his
somewhat perfunctory comment in *TLP*, 6.123:

> Contrary to what Russell thought, there is not a law of contradiction that is
> peculiar to each 'type'; one is enough, for it will not be applied to itself.

Also, though, Wittgenstein's rejection has to be attributed to his instinctive
metaphysical monism. There is only one world; and the functions are a

31 Though in 6.1232 Wittgenstein seems to adopt the logicistic view that logical generality,
stricto sensu, is 'essential', whereas other sorts, including (by implication) axiomatic generality, are ultimately 'contingent'. This, of course, is not compatible with his later views. But
neither does it follow from the throughout more fundamental doctrine of irreflexivity.
32 Whitehead & Russell, 42, 64.

first-order mapping of it. Consequently there is no room for distinctions of type. It is difficult for Wittgenstein to attack the doctrine of types from this standpoint, though, without making 'metaphysical' statements of the kind he rejects. To understand this position we shall have to look more closely at what has been called Wittgenstein's 'axiom of finity'.[33]

12. Finitism

Wittgenstein's attitude to infinity was intuitionistic.

Are there infinitely many things in the universe? Or is there a finite number of things, even though we can never get round to counting them all? This question is, of course, an old one. It is the subject of Kant's first antinomy (B454ff.). Kant regarded it as insoluble, and, moreover, as an indication of the point at which understanding reaches its limits, and has to defer to *reason*.[34]

More recently, physics seemed to be reaching the conclusion that the world was finite, at least in the sense that it did not extend throughout infinite space. The theory of relativity suggested that astronomical space might be curved and hence, in a non-Euclidian way, return to itself rather than carrying on to infinity. Wittgenstein was in this latter sense an ontological finitist.

In the *Tractatus*, Wittgenstein's finitism serves as a way of preserving the fine purity of first-order logic. The point is this. The heart of the *Tractatus*, as we have seen, was the technique of truth tables. By means of them Wittgenstein hoped to reduce logic to something entirely manifest; that is to say, it would justify itself by its own evident purity, rather than by having to appeal to any kind of outside grounding. In the truth tables, logical form 'showed' itself.

There were two problems here, however. The first, which we have already discussed in detail, was the problem of second-order statements. Could logic talk about itself? Wittgenstein's answer was firmly that it could not, on the basis that language consisted of two utterly disparate elements – 'about' elements, the representational functions, which were directed exclusively outwards, and 'operations', which were directed inwards. This makes for difficulties in arithmetic, which we shall consider again in a moment.

Before that, however, quantification posed a difficulty for Wittgenstein. It is essential for predicate logic that there be some way of binding variables. This was the major advance of Frege's logic. But what is the status of

33 More generally, on finitism, see Nagel and Newman, 1958, 33.
34 See *German Philosophy*, 41-44.

such quantifiers – formulations such as 'for any x, . . .', or 'for some y, . . .'? Although inextricable from any worthwhile logic, they did not seem to fit into the austere purity of the truth tables; and, indeed, Wittgenstein insisted, 'I distinguish the concept *all* from the truth-function' (*TLP*, 5.521). In the *Tractatus*, Wittgenstein attempted to derive quantification from the finity of the universe. This worked as follows.

If we assume that physics is right in saying the world is finite, and if we furthermore say that the 'functions' which underlie the elementary sentences are exclusively concerned with the outside world, then it follows that there is a finite number of elementary sentences. There is only a limited number of things (given that functions are not allowed to be 'about' logical or intellectual things) that elementary sentences can be about. Notionally, at least, they form a denumerable totality.[35]

Now, if we have a denumerable, or closed, totality, then all sorts of logical manoeuvres become much simpler. In particular, the notion of quantity is ontologically pre-defined; we have no need of a 'logical' quantifier, because there is already a generalisation implicit in any function. Suppose, for example, that the objects of my universe were restricted to coloured cubes on the table in front of me. My 'elementary sentences', in Wittgensteinian terms, would consist of statements like 'this is red', 'this is blue', 'this is on top of that', and so on. That is a finite number of statements, and each one generalises over a distinct group of objects – those that are red, those that are blue, those that are on top of others, and so on. The 'quantity' is given immediately, ontologically, with the function. Furthermore, the number of combinations of these functions in non-elementary sentences would also be given; it would be a large, but finite number (G^F where G is the number of objects, F the number of functions, assuming both are finite).

(The point is, of course, that this does *not* happen with an infinite universe. In such a case, problems of the transfinite ensure that functions do not automatically bring any determinable, quantifiable set with them. Wittgenstein is, so to speak, reading the universal quantifier as 'for *all x*, . . .', rather than as 'for *any x*, . . .'.)[36]

So, for Wittgenstein, quantification follows automatically from the ontological link of the 'general sentence form' of elementary sentences:

4.5   [. . .] The general form of the sentence is: such and such is the case.
4.51   On the assumption I had *all* the elementary sentences, then one could simply ask what sentences could be formed from them. And that would be *all* the sentences and *that* is how they would be bounded [begrenzt].

35 It is questionable, of course, whether we are allowed to say that, in Wittgenstein's terms. But he does.
36 Russell made this distinction; see Russell, 1908, 156.

4.52 The sentences are everything that follows from the totality [Gesamtheit] of all the elementary sentences (and, of course, from the fact that it is the *totality of all* of them). (So one could say in a certain sense that *all* sentences are generalisations of [i.e. quantifications over] the elementary sentences.)[37]

Given this ontology, the relationship between quantification and propositional junctors is not hard to determine. It is possible, claims Wittgenstein, to get into quantification by negating the range of values of a function; if you do so, according to him, you obtain the existential quantifier in the form of its negation – 'nothing exists such that . . .' (*TLP*, 5.52).[38]

Another way of looking at it is that if you have a finite domain of objects, the existential quantifier is equivalent to a disjunction ('this is red, or this is red, or this is red, etc.'), and the universal quantifier is equivalent to a conjunction ('this is red, and this is red, etc.').[39]

13. Cardinality

The next problem concerns cardinal numbers. From the point of view of the early Wittgenstein, counting things is a natural-ontological link with the actual world. If we are bounded in a finite world of objects, 'represented' in the functions and elementary sentences, then enumerating them would seem a basic activity.

Explaining numbers was, inevitably, one of the principal challenges facing the *Tractatus*. How could the set-theoretic paradoxes be avoided? If numbers are classes of equinumerous classes, then second-order logic, with all its pitfalls, lay across the philosopher's path. Russell, as we saw, resorted to the hierarchy of types. The basic disadvantage of this, though, is that the world seems to be forcing logic to do things – in particular, to be 'ambiguous' in the face of those types. If logic rests on pure unreflexive self-evidence (as Frege, Russell and Wittgenstein all believed), then why should its forms be dictated by a heteronomous ontology of 'types'?

The theory of numbers comes at the climax of the *Tractatus*, in section 6,

37 See also *TLP*, 5.5561: 'Empirical reality is limited by the totality of objects. The limit shows itself again in the totality of the elementary sentences.'
38 In a finite universe, a function such as 'is red' brings with it all its actual values – the elementary sentences 'this is red', 'that is red', and so on. In Wittgenstein's account, the negation of this (which he expresses by N(§)) indicates 'nothing satisfies the function, "is red"'. There are, in other words, no red things. This gives us, expressed in quantifier notation, '$(x) \neg Fx$', which is in turn equivalent to '$\neg(\exists x)Fx$'. So we have a basic explanation of the two quantifiers and the position of the negative.
39 Wittgenstein appears to resist this interpretation (which, despite his comment, is not obviously attributable to Frege or Russell) in *TLP*, 5.521, presumably because of his declared wish to distinguish between quantification and truth-functions. But he later seems to say of himself that he did endorse it (*Wittgenstein und der Wiener Kreis* – *WWK*, 39). See also Quine, 1974, 116.

where it is followed by the book's 'metaphysical' culmination in death, ethics, and so on. 'And *thus* we come to the numbers,' declares Wittgenstein with finality (*TLP*, 6.02).

Wittgenstein's theory of numbers is 'operative'. He does not explain in detail how this works, either in the *Tractatus* or elsewhere.[40] Essentially, though, it rests on the notion of performing a repeated operation. Operations, as we saw, are distinct from functions. Functions are exclusively first-order, and cannot be applied to other functions. Operations, on the other hand, *can* be applied to the results of other operations (*TLP*, 5.25ff.). So, although we cannot say things like 'the class of chairs in this room is equinumerous with any class in the class of classes named "five"', we are allowed to make successions of statements where nothing changes except the repetition of a logical 'operation'. We could, for example, say 'this is a chair, and this is a chair,' and so on, where we do not intrude any additional functions (such as, 'that makes a class equinumerous with "five"'), but simply build a purely formal conjunction ('. . . and . . . and . . . etc.', five times).

The 'five' in such an 'operative' context is, then, strictly tied to the world it reflects. We are not pulling down the notion of 'five' from some Platonic realm of numbers; we are simply registering, in a series of primitive responses, the occurrence of elementary sentences. This, then, is an 'abbilden' (imaging, function) in the more literal and less technical sense. Numbers in the real world are reflected, transposed, into quantities of signs at the conceptual level. 'In accordance with these sign rules we can thus write the series x, Ω'x, Ω'Ω'x, Ω'Ω'Ω'x, . . .' (*TLP*, 6.02; 'Ω' is the sign for 'operation', here performed on the variable 'x'). In this account, then, numbering is saved for the first-order 'functional', imagistic level.

Wittgenstein continued to emphasise this in his later thinking on mathematics. 'The indication of a number is the indication of how many and not of equinumerousness,' he declared (*WWK*, 222). The most appropriate indication of number was not through the abstract conceptuality of 'the class 5', but, for example, through lines on the page – '|||||'. And these lines on the page were not to be taken as 'representing' the 'class' of '5' – that would constitute an infiltration of second-order functions – but simply as a *picture* (*WWK*, 223). The lines, like the repeated 'Ωs', perform as a *self-showing*, in the way required by Wittgenstein of logical form. They do not comment, by reflexive predication, on other levels of logical activity; they simply *make manifest* ('zeigen' rather than 'sagen').[41]

40 But compare Meschkowski, 50ff.
41 Lines and sequences of 'Ωs' are the most obvious ways in which numbers 'present' themselves. But, according to Wittgenstein, the formulaic representation of particular numbers can have the same intuitive pictoriality. In the expression

So, says Wittgenstein, the number five

> presents itself [stellt sich dar] in the five of the lines ['|||||']. Here we grasp the
> numerical sign immediately as a picture [Bild] . . . The road back to a pictorial
> [bildhaft] presentation of numbers must remain open through all the arith-
> metical symbols, abbreviations, operation signs, etc. The symbolism of num-
> ber-presentation is a system of rules for translating into the pictorial. (*WWK*,
> 225f)

14. Induction; infinity

The central concept in Wittgenstein's work on mathematics is that of *induction*. Induction, essentially, is a means of defining a series. The most
basic series is the series of natural numbers – '0, 1, 2, 3 . . .'. The basis of the
definition of the series of natural numbers, as of any definition of a series, is
twofold: the first member of the series (here 0) must be defined, and, for
any member (including the first), the successor must be defined. Thus, for
example, '0' names the class of classes equinumerous with the null class
(which can be defined as the extension of a contradiction such as '$p \& \neg p$',
which is true of nothing); and '1', the successor of '0', names the next
natural number, which is (for example, in Frege's definition – *Grundlagen*,
§77), the extension of the class '0' – i.e. that single class of classes equinumerous with the null class.

This notion is at the foundation of Frege's instauration of mathematical
logic (see §§23ff. of the *Begriffsschrift*; §§76, 79-81 of the *Grundlagen*,
etc.). For Frege it represented the great achievement of his logic. With it, he
thought he could generate the truths of mathematics in pure thought, without recourse to intuition:

> . . . we see how pure thought, irrespective of any content given by the senses
> or even by an intuition a priori, can, solely from the content that results from
> its own constitution, bring forth judgements that at first sight appear to be
> possible only on the basis of some intuition. (*Begriffsschrift*, 55)

Wittgenstein's notation of 'operation' is a rendering of this principle of
series. For any member of a series, Wittgenstein writes the expression
'[a,x,O'x]', where 'a' is the first member of the series, 'x' any member of the
series, and 'O'x' the successor of 'x'. In terms of Frege's derivation of the

---

$(\exists x,y).fx.fy. \neg (\exists x,y,z).fx.fy.fz$

(there are two f's), says Wittgenstein, 'the number 2 appears as a depictive trait of the symbolism' (*WWK*, 223; strictly, we should also add ' $\neg(x=y)$). The notion of logical forms as 'traits'
('Züge' – i.e. non-reflexive, pre-intentional manifestations) is familiar from the *Tractatus*
(4.1221).

successor function for natural numbers, Wittgenstein's symbolism can be read as follows:

> Where 'a' is the first member of the series, 'a' is to be defined as '0', which names the extension of a contradiction.
>
> The operation 'O'x' (the successor function) means: the class of classes 'equinumerous with the extension of the function "natural numbers in the series ending with x"'

Already in the *Tractatus*, Wittgenstein felt that the notion of series was sufficiently important to be regarded as 'the general form of a sentence' (*TLP*, 6). The 'sentence', then, was to be regarded as a general formula for specifying a member of some series. The formula was to define the first member of the series, and the operation by which one progressed from any member to its successor. The operation was to be a truth-functional operation on elementary sentences. Wittgenstein abbreviated this as 'N', but its full expression would be in truth-tabular form (*TLP*, 5.502, and see 5.101). By this means the series operation would adhere to the principle of logical 'showing' (i.e. making evident).

In principle, induction goes far beyond the derivation of the series of natural numbers. In effect, induction refers to any procedure for doing something in a series of steps. It may be understood, basically, as a procedure that says where you start, and how you continue. Those two things must be certain; but that is all that is needed. Given that, the steps will be countable, which is the index of our 'control' over the whole procedure. If we always know where we are to go next, we can express how many steps we needed to get from the start to where we are now, and how many we would need to get to any given conclusion. 'Infinitely many' is a good enough answer, e.g. in the case of the series of natural numbers, provided we know that we are moving up the series. What is not allowed is confusion over whether we have taken a step at all, as would be the case with the real numbers; there is no 'next' real number, and the series of real numbers is not only infinite, but transfinite. We shall have more to say about this later.[42]

Now induction, being so very general, is also very powerful. The natural numbers are defined, inductively, by a function specifying the starting point (zero) and what value you get for each successive step thereafter (number of natural numbers mentioned so far). Step one, therefore, is zero, step two is the number of numbers mentioned so far, i.e. one (we've mentioned zero), and so on. The 'steps' are described as the 'domain' of the function; what you get out are its 'values'. The 'domain' must, for an inductively defined function, always be expressible in natural numbers; you

---

42 See Boolos & Jeffrey, chs. 1, 2.

cannot have a first step followed by a 'one-and-a-halfth' step.

The values, however, can be anything, and do not necessarily need to be numbers at all. They could, for example, be pages of this book starting on this page and going backwards. As long as you know the starting point and what to do next, the inductively defined function holds proceedings firmly, even mechanically, in its grip. In the case of a function taking the pages of this book as its range of values, the function will cease when it runs out of pages to proceed to. But the function does not have to stop in this manner; it can quite happily go on ad infinitum, as indeed it will in the case of the natural numbers when they form the range of values. All that matters is that it should continue to proceed countably, step by step.

The other point about induction is that you do not, as in the examples of the book, or the natural numbers, need to remain within one function. There are many functions that can be defined inductively, including the functions of arithmetic (such as sum and product), and it is perfectly possible to combine them. Or, to put it another way, it is possible to define immensely complicated functions which incorporate manipulations such as sum and product, but which still always yield precise values for any given argument (i.e. in our image, at any given step). Gödel's notion of PROOF (for some argument), which we shall be looking at later, is one such complex function. In his exposition, it requires 45 lines of definition (Gödel, 606).

So, with sufficient care in the definition, an inductive function will (it seems – this is the essence of Church's thesis) deal with anything that can be regarded as 'logical' at all.[43] This is the justice in Wittgenstein's faith in the notion of series. The delight of the thing, for Wittgenstein and for others since then, is its apparently mechanical character. He regularly describes the operation of such systems – of proof, mathematical calculation, and the like – as a 'technology', a 'process', or an 'automaton' (*BGM*, 178, 68, 187). The inductively constructed machine, once set in motion, performs smoothly and without human intervention.

The further point about induction, and related notions like proof (which is the demonstration that some statement is a theorem of some system), is that, like a machine, it gets on with doing things without talking about it. Induction and proof show, but do not reflect upon that showing (see *WWK*, 135). A proof, says Wittgenstein, is like a 'cinematographic picture' (*BGM*, 159); it pictures, or demonstrates, but silently and without trying to justify itself. The compelling nature of a proof rests not in any attempt to justify something from some outside, 'theoretical', point of view, but simply in the automatic reproduction of the same process (*BGM*, 186f).

43 It will not, as we shall see, deal with everything that is *expressible* in logical notation. But the notion of induction seems to be coextensive with that of, for example, provability.

The only problem with induction is its capacity to generate misleading ontologies. This is the same problem that we saw with the 'logical constants'; these are but the pale cast of thought, logical things do not *exist*.

The focus of these difficulties is the notion of infinity, in Wittgenstein's view. The power of inductive laws is their capacity to produces rules of procedure – infinite rules. Wittgenstein compares the result with a spiral; I know the rules by which I can generate this spiral, and, with them, I can go on indefinitely. But does this mean that the infinite spiral *exists*? Clearly not, says Wittgenstein. If we look at one turn in the spiral generated by my rule, and a set, say, of ten such turns, we can say that there is an 'analogy' between that set and the set contained in 'the whole spiral'. 'But that is only an analogy, and this has led people to introduce the notion of infinite classes or sets' (*WWK*, 72).

This is reflected also in the ambiguity of the term 'all', as found, for example, in the universal quantifier. Such an 'all', says Wittgenstein, is an indication of 'infinite possibility' (*WWK*, 135); but this should not lead us to infer any kind of infinite actuality. The distinction, says Wittgenstein, is between a *system* on the one (logical) hand, and the *empirical totality* of objects on the other. The system is an infinite possibility, because we only need one rule of procedure to set in motion an unending process. 'If we know the principle that is at the root of a system, then we know the *whole* system' (*WWK*, 216). Empirical totality, on the other hand, is the object of a necessarily finite experience.

The distinction between functions and operations is useful here as well (*WWK*, 217). Operations, which may be applied to their own results, are infinitely repeatable. Functions, though, are the generators of elementary sentences *about experience* (Wittgenstein also calls these sentences 'statement functions' – i.e., in Quinean terms, sentences with bound variables). They yield a (finite) totality; operators, though, and mathematics in general, express 'nothing factual'. Consequently the 'all' of mathematics (which Wittgenstein glosses as that of 'perfect induction' – *WWK*, 53) has nothing ontological about it.

This is the reason for Wittgenstein's endorsement of 'finitism' (*BGM*, 142). He links this doctrine with behaviourism – here, the principle that human action is best understood in terms of what we can see, rather than in terms of imaginary attributions of 'intention'. Both finitism and behaviourism, says Wittgenstein, 'deny the existence of something, both for the purpose of getting free from a confusion'. The infinite set, for philosophy, is the same speculative abstraction as 'intention' is in psychology.

15. Systems and language games

Wittgenstein's conception of logic is based on his understanding of the series and of inductive functions. That has its most obvious application to mathematics; and Wittgenstein's mathematical illustrations are the least mysterious of his teachings. Nonetheless this mathematical understanding of logic carries over into a far more general philosophical position with applications, as is well known, in quite remote areas like ethics and aesthetics. In order to understand how this works we need to look briefly at the generalisation of 'system'.

A system, probably, is what later writers have called a 'theory' (see Boolos & Jeffrey, 106), that is an axiomatic system closed under rules of inference of some kind. This is an implementation of the notion of induction (now more commonly referred to as recursivity). Basically, a system is a collection of provable statements ('theorems'), generated in some essentially mechanical way from, probably, a set of 'axiomatic' sentences.[44]

Now, this mathematically grounded notion of a system has a number of consequences for Wittgenstein's general views, and we shall be unravelling these in the remainder of the chapter. The most important one is that such a system is extremely precise about what falls within it and what does not. The system, in other words, has a clear conception, from within, of its own boundaries. We shall look at this in greater detail after considering the other important aspect of the system, namely its capacity to determine 'knowledge'.

Mathematical knowledge, as far as Wittgenstein was concerned, is governed by mathematical techniques. We only 'know', in maths, what we have a technique for knowing. This is already clear in the *Tractatus*, where he compares knowledge to a 'measure' along which the known world displays itself (*TLP*, 2.1512). Whatever the world may be beyond that measure is not for us to know.

Wittgenstein was less concerned with this in the *Tractatus* than he was later, as it became apparent that mathematics was axiomatic, and that the logistic project – to use logic as the root discipline for all human calculation – could not be carried out. Both logic and mathematics were systems, but they were distinct, and mathematics was not included in logic.[45] Whatever the nature of the world, there was more than one way of 'knowing' about it. So Wittgenstein's rather optimistic early view that he had solved the

44 Wittgenstein explains the notion of 'system' in this way in *WWK*, 145f.
45 *WWK*, 218. In the *Tractatus*, Wittgenstein did try to reduce number theory to logic; by the time of his conversations with Schlick and Waismann, he thought mathematics was doing something analogous, but different.

problems of philosophy by purifying one overriding logic gave way to a recognition that 'systems' had to be seen in the plural.

Thus, by 1930 Wittgenstein regarded physics as one or more 'representational systems by means of which we describe reality' (*WWK*, 231). In the *Remarks on the Foundations of Mathematics*, Wittgenstein questioned whether there was any such thing as a 'fact' independent of the system we used to described it. Arithmetic, for example, taught us to see particular sorts of 'fact' (*BGM*, 381); and counting, far from resting on empirical fact, could be regarded as determining what those empirical facts *were* (*BGM*, 383).

It is this notion of a mathematical system, as something that is in some way self-contained and self-grounding, however much it may 'accompany' empiry (*WWK*, 231), that underlies Wittgenstein's more famous conception of the 'language game'. A game, like a system, is something that has rules. It arises in the doing, not by conscious devising or initiation. And, furthermore, it makes possible the consciousness that fills it; language games are forms, not instruments, and they determine, to a greater or lesser extent, what we know through them.

16. Rules

So, what are these 'systems', or 'games', with their 'rules'? Clearly, they are conditions of our knowledge, in some preliminary Kantian sense. But the real philosophical question – are the rules general or local, and, if local, who makes them? – has yet to be answered.[46]

In the *Remarks on the Foundations of Mathematics*, Wittgenstein repeatedly plays with the idea that systems and games are a natural phenomenon – part, as he says, of the 'natural history' of human beings (*BGM*, 92). We are, perhaps, born with such systems, or we develop them through custom and education, but they do not have any claim to absolute, Platonic truth. Elsewhere, Wittgenstein wonders whether the principles of mathematics might not be 'anthropological' – empirical descriptions of how human beings reason and calculate (*BGM*, 192).

However, Wittgenstein rejects this suggestion, at least in its fully naturalistic form. Attributing logic to natural history, he says, is 'incompatible with the hard logical "must"' (*BGM*, 352). More specifically, and more 'transcendentally', he comments that basic structures cannot be an object of experience. 'How can we describe the foundation of our language

46 Kant dealt with these questions in the Transcendental Dialectic. Wittgenstein's discussions come closest to the topics of the 'Paralogisms' and the 'Antinomies'. See *German Philosophy*, 38ff.

through statements of experience?' he asks (*BGM*, 236). We do not, in other words, have any choice about the rules of our 'games'. For whatever reason, we have to follow them. They are not simply things we find *in* experience; they are conditions of our having experience at all.

Another way of expressing this is to say that our cognitive 'techniques', the inductive rules that govern our systems, are a 'fact *of* natural history', though they do not have the role of statements *in* natural history (*BGM*, 379). In other words, wherever the rules come from, they are not things we can report on at arm's length, as we might report, empirically, on natural-historical phenomena. This seems to echo Wittgenstein's conception in the *Tractatus*, of logical signs being 'naturnotwendig' – i.e. natural, but at the same time necessary conditions of knowledge (*TLP*, 6.124).

The most basic rules are those we cannot imagine otherwise. Wittgenstein's objection to the axiom of reducibility, in the *Tractatus*, was that a world in which this axiom did not apply was perfectly thinkable (6.1233). Regardless of the origins of the axiom, the objection to it was that it was not compelling, and as such it sank to the level of a comment on experience and the contingent. Wittgenstein refused, for the same reason, to allow that Newton's laws were axioms: 'One can easily imagine that the situation might be different' (*BGM*, 225). 'We give a different kind of recognition to axioms than to statements of experience' (*BGM*, 226).

At the same time, Wittgenstein *did* accept Euclid's parallel axiom, even though it was, in a sense, 'disproved' by modern physics in exactly the same way as Newton's laws (*BGM*, 223). But 'disproof', as we shall see, was precisely not the sort of thing that could affect the rules of a 'game'.

Wittgenstein also played with other characterisations of rules, couched in more psychological terms. Rules, then, are not devised instrumentally, nor even discovered; they are, so to speak, the most familiar things – things we have always possessed. 'When we formulate a rule, we always have the feeling: you have known that for ages' (*WWK*, 77). That is one reason why, as Wittgenstein says, 'There can *never* be surprises in logic' (*TLP*, 6.1251). At the same time, though, the rules are not things we are consciously or deliberately familiar with. In Wittgenstein's image, we stand 'with our backs to them', rather than facing them critically (*BGM*, 243). Rules are not in the first instance concerned with truth and falsehood, and thus cannot be assessed in terms of whether they themselves work in that regard. The fundamental feature of rule-understanding, indicates Wittgenstein, is 'immediate insight, whether of a truth or a falsehood' (*BGM*, 241). That, at least psychologically, is the character of rule-recognition – the assimilation of some basic technique, or system-generating inductive process.

17. Irreflexivity of systems

So what is 'truth'? Or, more specifically, is truth local to a system, or are there general criteria? This raises the question of to what extent it is possible to reflect on the performance of systems, either from within or from outside, perhaps by means of other, 'higher' systems. If truth is general, it must be possible to express it in different systems, and the difference will be one of idiom rather than of substance. For that to be possible, though, systems must be either reflexive (able to report on themselves), or translatable (able to be reported by others).

As we already know, Wittgenstein is strongly resistant to reflexivity. In the *Tractatus*, where, admittedly, he still felt that one system (that of 'logic') sufficed, he argued that the system could not say anything about itself (*TLP*, 4.12; see above). He took the same view even when he no longer propounded the monolithic claims of 'logic'. 'We cannot step outside our logical world in order to observe it from the outside,' he continued to insist (*WWK*, 226). In relation to any axiomatic system, he declared, 'These . . . axioms, and whatever is generated from them, are, so to speak, my whole world. I cannot get out of this world' (*WWK*, 146).

The reason why this is not possible is the basic thematic distinction between functions and operators; in application to itself ('reflexively'), logic can only use operators. But operators cannot 'report' (or represent, 'darstellen'); for that you would have to use functions, which Wittgenstein disallows. Logical systems consist of smoothly running operative *forms* which produce *calculations*, not *statements*. What a system does is manifest, it 'shows' itself, we feel that it is right – but we do not comment on it, and neither do the systems comment on themselves. The purity of logical form is beyond reflection; it simply *is*. 'The essence of complete induction in mathematics does not find expression in the shape of a sentence or of a system of axioms, but is *inexpressible*' (*WWK*, 34, my emphasis).

The rules of a system or game are not the same as axioms. Some axioms may express rules, but rules cannot always, or even generally, be reduced to axioms. This is the sense of Wittgenstein's emphasis on unreflecting 'technique'. Games are things people *do*. Their rules are deeply internalised, they need not be expressed, and possibly they cannot even be expressed.

> What we find in mathematics books is not the *description of something*, but the thing itself. We *do* mathematics. Just as one speaks of 'writing history' and 'doing history', there is a certain sense in which one can only do mathematics. (*WWK*, 34n)

Because the rules of a system are probably inexpressible, there is no obvious way in which disparate systems can be compared. According to

Wittgenstein, then, even apparently very close systems, at least within mathematics, have to be regarded as quite distinct. In relation to the natural numbers, for example, the integers represent something 'entirely new' (*WWK*, 36). The same may be said of the rational numbers in relation to the integers (*WWK*, 129), or of calculations by stroke and calculations in decimal notation (*BGM*, 184). This is so even when we have, say, two systems with explicit and apparently comparable sets of axioms.

> It is not the case that I have the two systems . . . in front of me and can compare them with one another from outside.

Wittgenstein allows that there may be a way of bringing two such systems (e.g., here, integers and rationals) into one system; but, even now, the result is not a reflective insight into the 'content' of the old systems, but simply a new form of *calculation*.

> And the sentence, 'The one class [*scilicet* of numbers] is more extensive than the other,' does not occur in that calculation. That is the prose that accompanies the calculation. (*WWK*, 129)

The prose commentary, in other words, has little to do with the poetry of calculation itself. Calculation is a movement, a dance, which neither comments on itself nor pedantically 'includes' other systems. That is why Euclidian geometry and counting with natural numbers remain perfectly worthwhile systems despite the complexities of modern mathematics. We can never claim to possess a universal system that supersedes all its predecessors, nor, ultimately, imagine what such a universal system could be.

> The new system does not complete the old one. The old system has no open places. What one does not yet have, one does not have at all. (*WWK*, 36)

That means, furthermore, as far as any system is concerned, that it is, so to speak, not self-conscious. It does not know what its own rules are (systems with explicit axioms are, in this respect, a special case), and neither can it make general statements about its own capacity to reach the 'truth'.

> I cannot say of a sentence that it belongs to a system. I cannot say in the language of the first system what is solvable and what is not. The question does not even exist. (*WWK*, 36)

And in that sense, then, truth is local to each system:

> A sentence that cannot be proved in Russell's system is 'true' or 'false' in a different sense from a sentence of the *Principia Mathematica*. (*BGM*, 118)

18. Translatability, theory, grounding

In a radical sense, then, systems are not comparable with one another. Systems are things that are 'seen' (*WWK*, 135), rather than consciously constructed or proved; they are rules of action rather than sets of explanations. A transition from one system to another, says Wittgenstein, is 'in a certain sense fortuitous' (*WWK*, 146).

Translation, then, is generally impossible from one system to another. (This is the Wittgensteinian thought which lies at the base of Quine's project in *Word and Object*, to demonstrate what he calls 'radical indeterminacy' in the translation of natural languages.) But just as translation 'sideways', from one system into another, is generally impossible, so too is translation 'upwards', into more general systems.

Every reasoned account has to take place within a system. But because of the irreflexivity of systems, it is never possible to attribute absolute 'truthfulness' to any particular one, even to such a very general one as the 'logic' of the *Tractatus*. No particular system can claim for itself, or, indeed, for others, that it is exhaustive. Systems are irreflexive techniques of calculation, not disposable and deliberate instruments. 'By means of rules I can only ever determine *a* game, never *the* game,' Wittgenstein said (*WWK*, 133).

This meant that the notion of a 'theory' of a game, as something that somehow stood outside the game and 'explained' it, was incoherent. Either you were in one game, or you were in another; there was no 'meta-game' (*WWK*, 121, 134). In chess, for example,

> what is called the 'theory of chess' is not a theory that describes something, but a kind of geometry. It is, of course, another calculus and not a theory. (*WWK*, 133)

The same could be said of algebra; it was a totally new system of calculation, not a 'theory' that somehow 'explained' arithmetic:

> The system of calculation by letters is a new calculus; but it does not relate to normal numerical calculation as meta-calculus to a calculus. *Letter calculation is not a theory*. That is the essential thing. (*WWK*, 136)

Indeed, argued Wittgenstein, the whole project of 'founding' a system such as mathematics, by means of explanatory generalisations, was absurd. That covered Frege's logistic attempts, in particular. 'Why does mathematics need a foundation?' he exclaimed (*BGM*, 378).

Much of this was directed against then fashionable attempts to see mathematical axiom systems as in some way hierarchically ordered. The theory of numbers, for example, was structured in levels of ascending generality, from natural numbers at the bottom to complex numbers at the top (*BGM*, 134 'there is no super-system [Über-System]' Wittgenstein protested). The same applied to Cantor's theory of ascending alephs (transfinite cardinalities – *BGM*, 135). 'In the same way, Hilbert's "Metamathematics" reveals itself to be disguised mathematics' (*WWK*, 136).

19. Contradiction

Wittgenstein's position, as we have seen, rested heavily on the notion that a properly working system justified itself. It was a technique, a practice, and any rules, explanations or other reflective comments were ultimately redundant. The difficulties arise, however, when the calculation starts to go wrong. Here, once more, we return to the realm of the paradoxes. Our first concern is with Cantor's set theory which, although not 'paradoxical', nonetheless is disruptive of the notion of induction.

Cantor's theory of the transfinite, developed in 1874, is central to modern number theory. It is a method for giving precision to notions of infinity. Its basic technique is *diagonalisation*, which can be used to show that certain numbers (the so-called 'real' numbers) are not only unending (infinite in the sense that you need never stop counting, which applies to natural numbers as well), but uncountable. There are always more 'real' numbers than you can think of, let alone count. That is what the 'transfinite' is.

More specifically, diagonalisation works by showing that it is impossible to make a list of real numbers. A proper real number is one that cannot be understood as the quotient of two natural numbers (i.e. the result of dividing one natural number by another; quotients can be listed – see Meschkowski, 42). In practice, that means it is an infinite, non-repeating decimal – like π, for example, or $\sqrt{2}$, though not a recurring decimal like 1/3 (0.3 recurring), which is an ordinary quotient.

You cannot make a list of real numbers because, as each one is infinitely long, there are infinitely many points at which you could specify a digit different from the one you already have (in a number in the existing list). For example, if you are making a list of real numbers between 1 and 2, and you have reached the stage of listing, say,

$$1.00000$$
$$1.00001$$
$$1.00002$$
etc.

you can always, infinitely, insist on putting another number between each of the numbers you have already listed. In childish language, 'whatever you say, I can tell you one you've missed!'

The diagonal method is a way of describing, in precise formulaic terms, a number that is not included in any list so far drawn up. Basically, it says: take the nth number in the list you have made; go to the nth digit after the decimal point; and my new number, even if the same everywhere else, will be different at that digit (in some way we can specify).

The method is called diagonal because, if one imagines the numbers written down in an ordered list, the digits will form columns if one looks vertically, and the numbers will form rows if one looks horizontally. Since the diagonal formula always specifies the same number of column (n digits across) as of row (n numbers down), each digit located will be one across, one down, i.e. diagonal, to the one before. The method is so delightful because, however many numbers we write down in our first list, we can always specify one that differs, at the nth digit in the nth row, from each of them.[47]

The interesting point about diagonalisation is that it makes it possible to specify infinity, or non-finity, in an entirely finite and precise way. The 'anti-diagonal' numbers are clearly defined; or, at least, the method for generating them is; but the results are not so definite. There is, indeed, more than a whiff of paradox about it: it is an orderly way of producing disorder.

It is this contrast between the precision of the method and the oddity of the results that also, perhaps, makes diagonalisation seem slightly disreputable, rather like the magnetism exploited by eighteenth-century mountebanks. Wittgenstein, in the *Remarks on the Foundations of Mathematics*, commented that it was useful to imagine diagonalisation as something that schoolchildren might have been familiar with (*BGM*, 131).

Now clearly the use of a mathematical system to produce uncertainty was not something that fitted well with Wittgenstein's views; in particular, it tempted us to say something about the system from the outside. If we say that a technique 'doesn't work', then we raise the question of where we are standing in order to be able to say that. As we have seen, Wittgenstein's conception of rules and systems does not allow for this.

Consequently, he tried initially to argue that 'contradictions', by which he meant various currently discussed paradoxes or mathematical oddities, were always in some sense internal to the game which engendered them (cp. *WWK*, 124). He seems to have felt that as long as the 'game' was able to continue, nothing of any moment had occurred. And, if the game continued, one must assume that the rules somehow included provision for what people worried about as 'contradictions'. Alternatively, if the game stopped at that point, one could still say that the rules, in some way, provided precisely for that – stopping when something called a 'contradiction' arose.

> The game reaches a kind of conclusion when a certain figure called 'contradiction' arises. In that case, it just means I determined the game that way in the first place. There is certainly no question of a contradiction in the sense of

47 See Boolos and Jeffrey, ch. 2; Meschkowski, 41ff.

making the game impossible. (*WWK*, 202)

Wittgenstein also seems to have felt, at least initially, that the 'contradictions' that most worried people were not systemic and mathematical-technical, but simply the results of loose language. This, in particular, is how he regarded the antinomies of Russell and Burali-Forti: 'For the antinomies did not arise in calculation, but in normal everyday speech, precisely because one was using words ambiguously' (*WWK*, 121f). Russell's paradox, indeed, was simply a consequence of the hypostatisation of logic:

> Russell's contradiction is not worrying because it is a contradiction, but because the whole growth at the end of which it appears is a cancerous growth without purpose and sense that seems to grow out of the normal body. (*BGM*, 370)

20. Wittgenstein and Gödel

The straightforward view that contradictions were verbal and of no practical impact on 'calculation' was not really tenable in the long run, however. The year after Wittgenstein's comments on Russell and Burali-Forti, Gödel's celebrated paper 'On formally undecidable propositions of *Principia Mathematica* and related systems' was published.

Gödel managed to show that an entirely strict calculus, using the inductive procedures commended by Wittgenstein, could be made to generate a sentence that was true, but at the same time manifestly never demonstrable in terms of the calculus that generated it. In other words, the sentence did precisely what Wittgenstein had always said systems, or sentences from them, could not – it went beyond the boundary of its own system. In Gödel's comment on his own result, 'The proposition that is undecidable *in the system PM* still was decided by metamathematical considerations' (Gödel 599).

We cannot attempt here to render Gödel's proof, but it is important to see how compelling it is. Gödel's sentence, roughly, is 'something is not provable in the system'. The question is: can we replace 'something', in that sentence, with the sentence itself? The answer, obviously, is undecidable. If we suppose that the result is true, then the sentence must be provable, and the sentence is false. If we say that it is false, then we are agreeing with what the predicate says, the sentence is true, and we are thrown back to the first supposition. So neither possibility works; the sentence is undecidable. But if it is undecidable, it is unprovable (in the system); and consequently, what the sentence says is *true*!

On one level, as Gödel acknowledged, the sentence is very similar to antinomies Wittgenstein had dismissed as merely verbal (Gödel, 598). The point is, however, first that Gödel reaches his result by a process of close calculation which cannot be discredited as ambiguous use of terms, and second that the sentence makes manifest a distinction between systemic provability, and extra-systemic 'truth', which the conventional paradoxes never reach. And it is this capacity to say something *about* the system though not *within* it that lets Gödel's sentence exemplify reflexivity.

Gödel's close calculation, in fact, makes use of the same diagonalisation Wittgenstein disliked in the context of Cantor's work. This is possible because Gödel devises a way of correlating all the elements of a logical language with natural numbers. This 'Gödelisation' is in a sense arbitrary; it serves to convert any formula into a number that (although immensely large) is unambiguously associated with just that one formula. If we keep to finite formulae (i.e. we may not have infinite applications of f, the successor function), we shall have, as Gödel says, 'a one-to-one correspondence by which a finite sequence of natural numbers is associated with every finite sequence of primitive signs (hence also with every formula)' (Gödel, 601).

That means that formulae are countable, and can be correlated with each other. In particular, we can construct an array of all the single-variable formulae, in which (for example) the columns downwards are the formulae as variables, and the rows across are the formulae as (in effect) predicates. At the intersection of any row and column we can indicate whether the row formula is true of the column formula (and that, in turn, becomes a new formula, with its own number).

The formula expressing 'is not provable in the system' is complicated. Gödel only gets there by means of forty-five preliminary definitions, any one of which would generate some quite staggeringly large Gödel number (see, for an example, Kneale & Kneale, 715). But despite this, the location of the number is quite unambiguous, and there is no difficulty about saying, 'for any number n, the formula at position n down may be predicated of the formula at position n across'. The n thus unambiguously defines all such predications, which of course lie on a diagonal down the array.

However, Gödel is not using this like Cantor, to construct an 'anti-diagonal' set. It is more the result of a manoeuvre to ensure that the notion of provability becomes a one-variable predicate.

The more interesting aspect of Gödel's result is its application of induction, or recursive definition. Induction, as we noticed, is the process whereby a direct line is demonstrated from the basic presuppositions of the system, via the rules of procedure, to the theorems (a theorem is a provable formula). When such a line is demonstrable, the formula may be regarded as proved. In the propositional (basic truth-functional) calculus, theorems are the 'tautologies' Wittgenstein claimed all logic to be, and it is easy, by means of truth tables, to decide whether any given formula is such a tauto-logy or not. The tautologies of the propositional calculus are the proved theorems.

In the case of the predicate calculus, which includes the kind of logic necessary for Gödel's discussions, and indeed for any of Wittgenstein's mathematical systems, this is not the case. There is, in fact, no finite proce-dure for deciding whether any given formula of the predicate calculus, though otherwise well formed, is a theorem.

Nonetheless, induction makes it possible to climb up through the for-mulae of any given system, drawing a clear line of proof. Induction, or re-cursivity, is roughly a matter of proceeding by combinations of what you already have, and not introducing anything new. (A more technical defini-tion is given by Gödel at 602.)

The practical result of Gödel's series of forty-five recursive definitions is that the formula he arrives at, 'x is a proof of y', is an absolutely un-objectionable theorem of the system. It is as possible to calculate whether the two variables x and y are related in this way as it would be, for example, to calculate whether '$x = \sqrt{y}$' was true for any two given arguments. There is, in other words, no vagueness in the procedure to be followed, or the time it will take to complete.

The forty-sixth definition, which is the one that matters, is not, however, recursive. That says, quite simply, 'there is something that proves y'. That is analogous to saying 'y has an integer square root' – which is not a state-ment whose correctness can always be calculated in a determinate finite number of steps. More technically, the forty-sixth formula is not recursive because there is no bound on the existential quantifier.[48]

In other words, although we know exactly what we mean when we say, of two formulae, that one is a proof of the other (or, at least, we do once we have read Gödel's forty-five line definition), the statement that something *has* a proof is of a different nature. Nonetheless, this does not lead to the formula's ejection from the system; it simply shows that clearly meaning-ful formulae can be devised whose correctness is not automatically certain. In fact, as Gödel shows, it is not only uncertain – in certain situations it is certainly *undecidable*.

Now, this argument was much more of a challenge for Wittgenstein's theory than the conjuring tricks of ordinary diagonalisation. In particular, Gödel's paper showed that it *was* possible for a system to say something about itself. It could make statements encompassing everything that it

48 As it would be if, for example, the 'something' was stated to be some formula with a Gödel number less than such-and-such – see Gödel, 602, Theorem IV, and 603n. The bound makes for recursivity because it enables the function to be calculated in a finite number of steps. On recursivity, see Boolos & Jeffrey, and Metschl.

might be able to prove – and, by implication, drawing a line between that and the things it could not prove. This is not easy to reconcile with Wittgenstein's views. In the *Tractatus*, he said that 'A sentence cannot possibly say of itself that it is true' (*TLP*, 4.442), which, strictly, is true even in Gödelian terms, but does not allow for it saying of itself that it is provable. The underlying doctrine, that 'No sentence can say anything about itself' (*TLP*, 3.332), seems to be refuted in any event.

Wittgenstein's express reactions to Gödel were disappointing, though he clearly found him disturbing. The only directly technical attempt to dislodge Gödel seems to be the comment that, 'Gödel's sentence, which says something about itself, does not *mention* itself' (*BGM*, 386), but this is not entirely enlightening.

At the same time, Wittgenstein was clearly aware of the import of Gödel's paper for his own work – specifically, for the idea that systems are closed and internally delimiting. Gödel's sentence, as we saw, can only be understood as something true that is not calculable within the system itself. The sentence itself is not very interesting. But it does seem to demolish the doctrine that systems of thought are local and univocal to the one system.

Wittgenstein was aware of this, as we see in his comment,

> To say 'This sequence of words has no meaning' excludes it from the realm of language and thereby delimits the area of language. (*PU*, §499)

In other words, tentatively – words *can* place themselves 'outside' the limit. But Wittgenstein is unwilling to allow this very profound objection to his system any further. Failing help from elsewhere, he resorts to the earlier argument that the drawing of a limit will, if useful at all, have a purpose that retains it within the limits of some game after all: 'It could belong to a game, and the boundary is there to be jumped by the players . . . If I draw a limit, I have not thereby yet specified why I drew it.'

And that, ultimately, is Wittgenstein's answer to Gödel: all games are practical techniques, and they are to be judged by how well they achieve their goals. Merely intellectual considerations are beside the point. 'As long as I could carry on playing, there was no problem,' as he said in an earlier comment on contradictions (*WWK*, 125); a problem you do not know about is a problem that does not exist. What was the *point*, he asked, of the notion that something could be true but not provable, and added:

> It is as though someone concluded, from certain principles of natural form and architectural style, that there should be a little baroque chateau on Mount Everest, where, of course, nobody can live. (*BGM*, 122)

As far as the practice of philosophy was concerned, he concluded, the philosopher must make sure he 'got past' the mathematical problems, rather than running up against one that would have to be sorted out before he could continue (*BGM*, 301). Gödel's sentence, in other words, was a purely speculative conundrum, another intellectual growth that should be avoided. Otherwise people would again be tempted to believe that thought could achieve something real.

21. Logic and ethics

In terms of the problem we set at the beginning – what is logical necessity? – this represents, provisionally, Wittgenstein's answer. The abandonment of second-order philosophy has reduced 'logic' to something that is untouchable precisely because it is completely formal. In Wittgenstein's account, logic is pure, and hence necessary, because it adds nothing to the world. Logic is necessary because there is nothing in it to be contingent. The various entities (classes, types, etc.) that Frege and Russell had left lying around in logic were hostages to contingency; and their weakness was revealed precisely by problems like the paradoxes, and by Russell's resort to un-self-evident intrusions like the axiom of reducibility. Logic can cheerfully admit the brutish uncertainties of the outside world, but remain unsullied by them precisely by refusing to contribute to them.

For the philosopher, to understand logic and its role is to understand the thrall in which the things of our 'world' ('the world is everything that is the case') are held. It is the melancholic insight that the world is chained to a spectral dance. The steps in the dance are the rules of logic, remorselessly present in even the most elementary sentence. Or, to use an image that the Schopenhauerian Wittgenstein might more readily adopt, logic is the warp and woof of the veil of Maya.

Logic is, at most, 'punctuation', a 'feature' ('Zug' – *TLP*, 4.126). There is nothing there to talk *about*. The price for this abstemiousness is that you cannot talk about logic, or the logical universe. The reward, on the other hand, is the stern certainty of the *via negativa*, the insight that you can throw away this particular ladder once you have climbed it. 'God does not reveal himself *in* the world' (*TLP*, 6.432). The vainglory of reason is the most dangerous pride of all.[49]

At the end of the *Tractatus*, Wittgenstein turns to ethics and aesthetics, and says that ethics is 'transcendental', and that, like logic, ethics 'cannot be enunciated [sich nicht aussprechen lässt]' (*TLP*, 6.421). Reflection about the world has revealed that we cannot use logic to say anything about itself, or about the world in general. This reflection is an insight, but it is an insight that places itself outside logic, and outside any possibility of artic-

---

49 Wittgenstein's refusal to countenance intellectual entities is comparable with Adorno's reading of the dialectic. See *German Philosophy*, ch. X.

ulation. The insights of philosophical reflection fall in the domain of silence.

The same argument serves to locate the philosophical 'subject' (the free human agent, in this instance). Wittgenstein declares that the boundaries of my language are also the boundaries of my world (*TLP*, 5.62); and that the subject is what constitutes those containing boundaries (and thus itself falls outside them – *TLP*, 5.632). The reasoning here is not entirely clear. What is more cogent is the 'solipsism' argument. As has been pointed out, this is not really a refutation of solipsism. But it does serve to specify the location of the transcendental ego, in Kantian terms. Solipsism (according to Wittgenstein) is meaningless because there is no 'I' in the experienced world for it to belong to; I cannot experience myself as the 'owner' of my universe. 'The I of solipsism shrinks to an extensionless point, and there remains the reality coordinated with it' (*TLP*, 5.64). All we know about the I is that it is never an object of experience.

That, of course, is something it has in common with logic; and that is the sense in which ethics, the branch of philosophy concerned with freely acting subjects, is 'transcendental' along with logic (*TLP*, 6.13, 6.421).

22. 'Im Anfang war die Tat'

What, then, is the 'purpose' of Wittgenstein's own 'calculus' – the ban on reflexivity? When confronted with Gödel's work, this ban emerges more as an article of faith, an 'axiom', rather than as something compellingly self-evident. So why does Wittgenstein hold to it so firmly?

The basic principle would seem to be this: there is an absolute and unbridgeable distinction between practice and logic. The reason why 'systems' are *techniques*, rather than reflexive *objects*, is that they should not be allowed to become part of the world of practice. If, which Wittgenstein denies, one were able to judge the value of systems (e.g. by saying, 'the theorems proved by this system are *true*'), then one would be acknowledging a logical event as a real one. And that, in turn, implies the possibility of logical practice.

This is what Wittgenstein consistently rejects. Logic, in his terms, operates unthinkingly, 'automatically', 'without surprises', in a world which is given to it *from the outside*. In the later work, this world becomes plural, and 'logic' is fragmented into a diversity of systems, games and so on. But still the same principle applies: rules are pre-reflexive, they are the edicts of a radically alien praxis which, so to speak, can be neither judged nor resisted. This intense passivity affects even mathematics, which he sees as the subordination to ultimately quite arbitrary *commands*:

> I think of the matter in this way: mathematics is carried on entirely in the form of *commands*. 'You must do *that and that*' ... (How human beings came to this method of prediction is quite indifferent.) (*BGM*, 232)

This intense passivity characterises Wittgenstein's position from the *Tractatus* onwards. There is, he insists, 'no *logical* connection between the will and the world' (*TLP*, 6.374). 'If good or bad desires change the world, then they can only change the limits of the world, not the facts; not those things that can be expressed in language' (*TLP*, 6.43). No rational *intervention* in 'the world' is possible, because the world is utterly dependent on the 'limits' set by an inscrutable and inaccessible practice. 'Ethics has nothing to do with punishment and reward in the usual sense,' as Wittgenstein says Calvinistically (*TLP*, 6.442). 'God does not reveal Himself *in* the world,' and there is consequently no point in our believing that our own 'practice' is any more than the twitching of truth-tabular probability. 'For all events and being thus are contingent' (*TLP*, 6.41).

The later theory of language games does not alter this melancholic vision.[50] The non-comparable, untranslatable games, whose only connection is through a hermeneutic 'Verstehen' (rather than univocal 'substitution' – see *PU*, 531f), re-enact the *Tractatus*'s ban on causation by reason. There is, in this view, no 'rational' behaviour, only a fragmentation of hermetic local practices.

The only 'philosophical' reaction to this state of affairs is to recognise the limit for what it is, and not to try to overcome it. The understanding, though intoxicating, is ultimately just a further scourge in our earthly passion. Salvation lies only in those things that lie beyond the limits of the knowable.

> Anything sayable can a priori only be nonsense. Nevertheless we run at the limits of language. Kierkegaard too saw this running and described it in similar fashion (as running against the paradox). Ethics is this running against the limits of language. (*WWK*, 68)

In the light of this, Wittgenstein's adoption of the Faustian motto – 'In the beginning was the deed' (*ÜG*, §402) – is a cruel misrendering of Goethe's sense. For Faust, practice was the logical self-transcendence of reason. For Wittgenstein, it is merely the remote instauration of a calculus we are condemned to perform without reflection or responsibility. For Wittgenstein, as for the other Schopenhauerians of his time, the only appropriate response is speechless apathy. 'What one cannot speak about, of that one must be silent.'

50 Wittgenstein's Schopenhauerism is, indeed, 'melancholic' in precisely the sense identified, and criticised, by Benjamin in *Ursprung des deutschen Trauerspiels*. See Roberts, 1982, IIl1.

4

Subjectivity and 'Life-world': Husserl

1. Introduction

Frege stated the project of logicism – that the conceptual instruments with which we talk about the world (e.g. mathematics) should be derived from those of pure thought (logic, in the narrowest sense). The purpose of this, implicitly, would be to show that certain kinds of knowledge are free of contingency and hence, potentially, free of error. It rested on the assumption that there is an 'interior', of the understanding, and an 'exterior', of the world of events. A theory of truth would show what continuity, if any, ran between them.

The project ran into trouble initially with Russell's paradox. Russell's paradox seemed to show that the scope of 'pure thought' would have to be restricted if, for example, mathematics was to be derived from it. In particular, it could not be applied to certain kinds of objects. Russell tried to deal with this apparently arbitrary restriction with the theory of types. Wittgenstein, more radically, insisted that language could *only* talk about 'outside' things, and never things of the 'inside'; only an immediacy of this kind could guarantee the integrity of language.

Husserl's project is in many respects congruent with that of Wittgenstein – both in its early aspirations and in the rather different conclusions that emerged in the 'late' work.[1] The search, after the initial failure of logicism, was to find unblemished 'objects' for logic. The structures of logic themselves seemed satisfactory enough; but the problems arose with the objects to which they were applied. Wittgenstein's 'picture theory' provided a typification of the sort of object that logical operations could

1 Historically, of course, Husserl came first, and may well in some indirect way have 'influenced' Wittgenstein. But Wittgenstein is more familiar and, in certain respects, clearer to understand.

digest; Husserl, in a more vigorously systematic way, engages in the same kind of search. 'Phenomenology', as Husserl develops it, is in its origins a system for generating objects acceptable to logic.

The interest of Husserl's initial project lies in its more or less admitted *failure*. Husserl's attempt to separate the pragmatic from the logical (as typified in his attack on 'psychologism') did not succeed; pure logic could not provide the 'foundations' he sought. This, as we shall see, is highly instructive. We can say at once, however, that the relativistic lesson Husserl himself drew, though it impressed a series of successors and continues to inspire much contemporary French thinking, will not be ours. Husserl's work assumes that rationality operates on the model of an inductive formal system, and that anything uncomputable (so to speak) is also unreasonable. Hence his resort to historicism – the doctrine that human history is *properly* 'beyond reason'.

As we shall see, however, this is not a view we need be convinced by.

2. Biographical and preliminary

Husserl, who lived from 1859 to 1938, was a major philosopher. As with Wittgenstein, however, his influence has been greater outside the German-speaking countries. His importance for French thought, in particular, would be hard to overestimate. Derrida's work is centrally informed by the phenomenological project; Merleau-Ponty and Levinas are two other names inextricably linked with Husserl's.

Nonetheless, his influence has been indirect, and the precise import of his thinking is not widely familiar. The study of his actual work seems to have fallen mainly to specialised schools. Husserl's immediate followers still take at face value his assessment of phenomenology as the programme for the new philosophy, and continue to labour towards its fulfilment. Elsewhere, Husserl's project, which looks a little like a rehabilitation of the Aristotelian categories, has proved attractive to Roman Catholic philosophers. In Anglo-American circles, Husserl plays a role, with Meinong and Russell, in the debate about the nature of propositions, and, beyond that, he meets a bemused tolerance because of his lifelong interest in the philosophy of mathematics, and his early inspiration from Frege.[2]

Husserl was not well served by historical circumstances. An assimilated Jew, his career coincided with the growth of German nationalism. The scope for the acceptance and indeed prominence enjoyed by, for example, a

2 Husserl's habilitation dissertation was 'The Philosophy of Arithmetic' (Halle, 1887). He subsequently corresponded with Frege, and seems to have moved away from his initial 'psychologism' as a result of Frege's criticisms.

liberal Jew like Hermann Cohen was already strongly declining in the first decade of the century. Husserl only escaped the fate of the ejected Ernst Cassirer because, by 1933, he had already retired.

He did, however, suffer from never being fully topical in his own country. He lacked the sustained embattlement that would have thrown his work into sharper public focus. His early work, in particular the *Logical Investigations (LU)*, did meet resistance; but the revisionary ardour of his successors, such as it was, has been slow reaching full public articulation. In any event, Husserl's career, and his work in general, were marked by professional modesty. He seems to have seen himself, at least until late in life, as a technical philosopher intent on correcting and perfecting rather than overthrowing. What is more, during his academic tenure Husserl's phenomenology eschewed concern with practice, whether in ethics, politics or aesthetics.[3]

Phenomenology as a doctrine was not publicly complete until 1913, with the publication of *Ideas* and of the first two volumes of the revised *Logical Investigations*. Its fate thereafter is, to some extent, visible in the third revised volume, which did not appear until 1921, and then with a preface explaining that the author was 'only able to bear the war and the ensuing "peace" with the most general of philosophical pursuits. . .' and that one of his principal students and assistants had been killed in the fighting. Husserl did not mention that one of his sons was also killed, and another injured, in the war. A further point, perhaps, was that the philosopher of the German trenches was Nietzsche; at this stage, phenomenology did not provide comfort under fire or inspiration for self-sacrifice.

Subsequently, Husserl's most prominent revisionary successor was Heidegger, who was his protégé and took over the chair of philosophy at Freiburg when Husserl retired in 1928. Here, Husserl was again unlucky. Although Heidegger's *Being and Time* first appeared in the *Yearbook for Philosophy and Phenomenological Research*, and certainly *did* represent a significant engagement with the master, any debate that might have developed at the time was quickly swallowed by 1933, when Heidegger became immersed in the Nazi system, while Husserl, the Jew, was anathematised by it. Embarrassment at this whole affair (notoriously, for example, Heidegger deleted Husserl's dedication from *Being and Time*) has inhibited full-blooded debate of Husserl's work, at least in Germany. It looks almost as if he has passed into the classical pantheon without refinement in the flames of topicality.

Nonetheless, Husserl's work was and is topical. In the first place, as we

---

3 'These are, admittedly, discoveries that lack any dazzling brilliance; they lack immediate application to practical life or to the development of higher aspirations of the feelings. . .' (*Logische Untersuchungen – LU*, IIi 12).

see from Heidegger and associated thinkers like Klages, Husserl was an important factor in the turn against positivism and (in their case) towards a paganistic symbolism. The attempt to reach metaphysical bedrock in the early twentieth century took many forms. The displacement of *causation* as the dominant category of 'science' (*Wissenschaft*) was, however, the most important; and the phenomenological project gave it conceptual substance.[4]

Second, Husserlian phenomenology re-established, in the human sciences, disciplines that were lost during the epoch of positivism. In this regard it is the inspiration behind movements as diverse as structuralism and New Criticism, and indeed behind successful contemporary work in the history of philosophy.

Before we look at Husserl's work, it is perhaps worth saying that he is not an easy philosopher to read. He writes without beauty or, indeed, real precision. For the sake of simplicity I have referred to the *Logical Investigations* and the *Ideas* as the 'early work', and to the *Cartesian Meditations*, *Experience and Judgement*, and *The Crisis in the European Sciences* as 'later work'. Tracing discontinuities between the two is a treacherous business; but I hope that enough emerges to substantiate my view about the 'failure' of the early work.

3. Psychologism

What is logic about? *Judgements*, would be one answer. Judgements seem to be the most general form of human rational activity. Whether I say, 'Taxation without representation is wrong', or 'If we cannot have A without B, and we have A, then we must also have B', I am making judgements. So, presumably, there must be general rules about this activity. Traditionally, those rules have been called logic.

But what are judgements? At the time of Husserl's project, there was a tendency to regard judgements as in some sense personal acts, and then to look for ways in which these acts could be legitimated. The neo-Kantians, for example, regarded judgements as the acts by means of which human beings invoked a realm of transcendent values, thereby escaping mere subjectivity. A judgement was 'valid' precisely because it was accommodated to these values. Humanity's capacity to form judgements made possible the world, and informed it with the 'values' that supposedly structured objec-

4 Simmel's *Philosophy of Money* has a similar orientation. Lukács (1973) later said that Schopenhauer was the dominant philosopher of this epoch. Whether that is historically true or not, certainly Schopenhauer's critique of Kant and causality was sympathetic to the tenor of the age.

tivity.[5] The problem, though, was that this seemed a rather remote and arbitrary event. The values thus invoked might, as claimed, be absolute and universal; but nothing in the logical procedure itself seemed to guarantee it. It might just as well represent the personal decision of the judger. Indeed, that seemed to be the emphasis placed by the neo-Kantian account of judgement. Judgement, for them, may not have been arbitrary in the sense of being purely individual; but it was arbitrary in the sense of arising from its historical and cultural context.

Husserl's project directed itself against this kind of relativism. His explicit target, however, was not neo-Kantianism, but 'psychologism'. Psychologism is a form of positivism; for Husserl's purposes, it is the doctrine that all 'science' is ultimately empirical. Concealed in this doctrine is the notion that empirical science is primarily concerned with causal explanations. So, just as the falling of the apple is explained as the effect of gravity, so too phenomena in the mind are explained as the effects of neurochemistry, habituation, or whatever. This is a popular view of the world. It is still widespread among natural scientists, and not uncommon among philosophers.

Psychologism seems particularly plausible if we regard mental phenomena as acts. An act, understood as an event in time, seems to fit well with the model of science as concerned with all things that arise within a time-bound causal nexus. Human thoughts arise as the effect of some cause or other, and proceed in their turn to have further effects. Logic, from such a standpoint, is merely the study and, perhaps, manipulation of such causal sequences (*LU*, I 52).

Nineteenth-century positivism is most readily linked with Auguste Comte. In the German context, however, it had certain quite distinct associations, namely political radicalism. Feuerbach was one obvious early proponent of a positivistic naturalism (the species-related characteristics of humanity govern the way it thinks).[6] Engels, in the *Anti-Dühring*, was perhaps the most notorious. The same association of positivism with left-leaning politics also emerged in Friedrich Lange, an early neo-Kantian and author of the polemical *History of Materialism*. Lange was one neo-Kantian expressly identified by Husserl as an opponent (*LU*, I 93).

Husserl's most often identified opponent, however, is John Stuart Mill, who stands for the doctrine that logic is part of psychology. Specifically, as Husserl sees it, Mill contends that logic is the technical part of psychology, it is the 'craft' of which psychology is the science (see *LU*, I 51). If psycho-

---

5 See, for example, Rickert, 1928. Rickert and Husserl collaborated on the new journal *Logos* (1910ff.), and Rickert recommended Husserl as his successor to the chair in Freiburg. He was a leader of South-Western neo-Kantianism, and influenced Max Weber, Lukács, and others.
6 See *Introduction*, p.192f.

logy is the science of the mind in general, logic is the craft of good thinking. 'How the mind works' would then be the foundation of logic, rather as physiology might be regarded as the science of which sport is the technique.

Husserl's initial arguments are devoted to a relocation of the metaphysical foundations. This consists, first, in demonstrating that the empirical foundations presupposed by psychologism (and positivism generally) are incoherent; and, secondly, in establishing an intensionalist doctrine of ideal objects.

4. Infinite regress

Logic cannot be founded on the empirical observation of psychic acts, says Husserl. Logic is not the formulation of 'laws of thought' (*LU*, I 105). Attempts at this kind of account lead either to vicious circularity or to infinite regress (*LU*, I 84).

Infinite regress arises when the answer given to a question turns out to raise the same question once again. For example, 'How do you know this is an oak tree?' Answer: 'Because it resembles something I already know to be an oak tree.' Question: 'How did you know that was an oak tree?' And so on.

In his attack on psychologism, Husserl combines this argument with an argument against the use of causal explanations. Psychologism, he alleges, states that the 'laws of thought' are 'motor causes' of thinking. 'They are causal laws of thought, they express how we have to think in accordance with the nature of *our* minds' (*LU*, I 67). So logical correctness, in such an account, would mean thinking in accordance with the causal demands of the human mental organism. And yet – what guarantees the correctness of the demands programmed into the organism? The mind's efficient performance of its tasks, without disturbance from extraneous causes (fatigue, boredom), is no more than a local physical fact, and tells us nothing about the legitimacy of the tasks in terms of *logic*. Husserl uses the example of a calculating machine. The fact that a calculator calculates as programmed tells us nothing about whether the program is right or not (*LU*, I 68). So we have to 'regress' to the program; and what do we use to evaluate that? The programs in some previous machine? And how do we justify them?[7]

7 Leibniz uses a similar argument to explain what he means by a 'perception'. If the mind was like a machine, and one could expand the machine sufficiently to go in and inspect it, one would still only ever see wheels and cogs, never a perception as such. A perception, at least as something which might be 'true' (as opposed, for example, to an action which could be held up as evidence for appropriate response), is in this view never reducible to what is mechanically observable.

Husserl uses the reproach of regress more directly in his attack on empiricist attempts to explain identity in terms of resemblance (*LU*, IIi 113ff.). How do we predicate general terms of individuals? The 'empiricist', according to Husserl, says this happens through resemblance: the individual object resembles other objects contained in the extension of some predicative term. The predicative term, it would seem, arises as a kind of reflexive response to the existence of a group that then becomes its extension. But how do we ever get as far as that identity, on the basis of simple resemblance? Any individual object 'resembles', in terms of what may be predicated of it, infinitely many other groups. So how does any particular predicative extension – a well-defined set, perhaps, rather than a loose aggregate of individuals – ever get started?

Or, to put it another way, how can any individual become part of experience (and amenable to predication) unless it already has some predicative 'handle' enabling it to be picked up. It would seem that 'things' never come naked to experience; they are always already 'selected' in terms of some prior predicate or other.

In any event, these predicates constitute *identities* behind which we cannot further enquire. Reading identity as resemblance merely defers the question of what identity the individual resembles; and refusal to state the identity leads to infinite regress (*LU*, IIi 116). So, just as reference back, by means of causation, to factually prior 'programming' leads to infinite regress in the context of logical rules, so too reference back, by means of similarity, to factually prior groups leads to infinite regress where general terms are to be explained.

5. Circularity

Vicious circles arise when a definition or explanation presupposes the thing that is to be defined or explained. For example: 'Sleep results from soporific forces', where 'soporific' is merely another name for 'sleep'.

As Husserl was aware, the reproach of circularity is not immediately conclusive in the context of logic. One may offer the general reproach that logic cannot be explained by psychology, since psychology, like any science, itself presupposes logic. So the thing that is offered as an explanation presupposes the thing that is to be explained. But, expressed in these terms, the same reproach can be made to logic itself. If logic is the foundational discipline, then how can it be explained without presupposing itself? (*LU*, I 57)

This is part of the general problem of reflexivity, and, in this context, is reducible to the question as to the nature of 'axioms', or foundational rules.

It is clear, to 'psychologists' as much as to anyone else, that you have to have rules. For example, you probably need the 'law of non-contradiction' to reason at all. That is one of the axioms of propositional logic – '$\neg(p \& \neg p)$'. It seems, intuitively, to be entirely formal. A system of reasoning which did not contain this axiom would, literally, end up saying anything; and that does not seem to be very useful. So if the negation of the law of non-contradiction is unacceptable, then, by another 'rule' – that a negation is cancelled by a subsequent negation – we 'prove' the law of non-contradiction.

So the law of non-contradiction, at least, seems unassailable. It is reflecting on the most general character of thought. In a sense, this would appear to be a circular justification. From another perspective, though, it has the advantage of being confined to the field of pure thought, and in that respect thought may be said to have a clear view over itself. It is not, so to speak, making any claims about things that lie outside its own purely discernible confines. So although, in this instance, thought is saying something about thought, and in that sense lifting itself up by its own bootstraps, the principle seems vindicated by absolute self-evidence.[8]

But this is not the case once 'logic' strays much beyond the bare calculus of relations between true and false statements. To produce a calculus for dealing with the relations between subjects and predicates, for example, we need to start introducing axioms which are rather less directly self-evident. To do set theory, without which even apparently basic notions like identity cannot be formulated, we seem suddenly to be confronted with disconcertingly 'metaphysical' rules about what entities exist in the world. 'Metaphysical', here, means straying beyond the ideal of a pure calculus, beyond formal self-evidence, and into 'about' statements.

Husserl deals with the problem of circularity in terms of non-contradiction. His argument is not entirely explicit, but amounts to this (*LU*, I 58). Logic has to be self-justifying, since it is the fundamental discipline and there is nothing more fundamental in terms of which it can be justified. This need not, however, be viciously circular. There are two ways in which something may be grounded argumentatively. The first way infers from antecedent to consequent ('if *a*, then *b*'). Husserl expresses this as inferring 'from' (*schließen aus*). The psychologists, for example, would infer from the necessity of non-contradiction for successful reasoning that it was a 'law of (human) thought'. If the necessity of one thing is guaranteed, then the necessary existence of the other (the 'law') is also guaranteed. This is probably not circular; though it does, among other things, raise a problem of regress (what makes non-contradiction necessary?). But it would be cir-

8 According to Pascal, only 'perfectly self-evident' things should be accepted as axioms. See Meschkowski, *Einführung*, 10.

cular if one tried it on a purely logical level; because logic is entire, and to justify any one part by necessary inference from another would indeed be circular (like providing a leg-up for oneself).

Inference 'from' is one form of reasoning. The other, however, is inference 'by' (*nach*). In inference 'by', you make no judgements about the necessity of something. Your system simply has a rule. It need not be explicitly adopted as an axiom. It simply exists, tacitly, in the system; and it emerges, if at all, through reflection rather than through inference or proof. Husserl uses the example of an artist painting beautiful pictures with no conscious knowledge of aesthetics.

Husserl is, in effect, offering a transcendental argument at this point. A principle is transcendental not because it has been grounded as a law of nature, nor demonstrated to be universally necessary, but because not accepting it would offend against some fundamental intuition. The law of non-contradiction expresses our fundamental intuition that reason cannot encompass the simultaneous truth and untruth of a sentence. That is, in the transcendental account, all that there is to be said. We do not infer the law of non-contradiction *from* anything; we merely intuit, by reflection, that it is part of any system of reasoning. (We do not infer from one thing that another thing 'must' be; we intuit by reflection that it 'is'.)

The law of non-contradiction, then, is a transcendental condition of scientificity. It is a rule 'according to which science must proceed in order to be science at all' (*LU*, I 58). In its guise as a 'possibility condition' (*LU*, I 110ff.), the law of contradiction appears for Husserl as the requirement of *consistency*. Consistency is what we have explained: the principle according to which no system may be allowed to produce contradictory statements.[9] Husserl uses consistency rather more widely. For him, it covers all 'laws that are founded purely in the concept of theory'. This involves truth, sentence, object, predication, relation, 'and so on'; all these are concepts that 'essentially constitute the concept of theoretical unity'. Denying these laws – presumably he means any or all of them – is, according to Husserl, 'equivalent' to saying that terms like truth or theory were 'devoid of consistent sense'.

6. Insight and eidos

Husserl's argument is guided by the metaphor of *sight*. The suggestion, essentially, is this. We cannot ground certainty empirically, because

---

9 Specifically, this is because, under the standard axioms of propositional logic, any conclusion follows from a false condition. If the system is able to generate a statement of the form '$p \& \neg p$', it will be able to generate any statement. *Ex absurdo quodlibet.*

empiricism either refutes itself (by getting involved in infinite regress or circularity), or else it leads us to what needs justifying, but is then at a loss how to go further (e.g. by claiming that non-contradiction is universal). Against this, Husserl argues that we have to accept that some things are primordially certain; there is no way of inferring them *from* anything else.

This primordial certainty is characterised, in Husserl's terminology, as a kind of absolute visibility. His most usual term for it is *evident*. To some extent, this is presumably an echo of the standard account of axioms as 'self-evident'. In Husserl, however, this essentially metaphorical argument is widely extended. 'Evidence' (*Evidenz* – the character of being self-evident) is, he claims, 'the final authority in all questions of cognition' (*LU*, IIi 100). And the legitimacy of consistency is precisely that it falls within evidence; Husserl speaks of 'the evident possibility conditions of any theory whatever' (*LU*, I 110).

From this point, the metaphor is taken up across more and more layers of the argument. We shall pursue this as we go. Meanwhile, however, it is worth anticipating the main lineaments. The term most closely associated with 'evidence' is 'intuition', which in German is *Anschauung* – 'looking at'. 'An intuition', for Husserl's purposes, is 'a looking at something self-evident', an apprehension of absolute visibility. This is the sense in which he can say, for example, that logical concepts are 'intuitive' – a formulation which sounds contradictory in, say, Kantian terms.[10]

Phenomenology, as we shall see, is concerned with what shows itself – what makes itself visible, in other words. 'Phenomena' are the objects of sense (specifically: of sight, in Husserl's metaphor), rather than the invisible 'causes' that supposedly lie behind them. The particular sort of investigation is termed by Husserl 'eidetic', or related to the 'eidos', or (Platonistically) *visible essence* of things.[11]

Meanwhile, the form of reasoning appropriate to such investigations is not, as we saw, inferential, but *reflexive*. It does not thrust abruptly into the dark secrets of causation, but, simply, looks at itself. Reflection is the self-showing of reason.

On the other side, inference and causal explanation are lost in darkness and inexactness. This is the central reproach against them. 'How,' asks Husserl, 'are we to have *insight* into causal laws?' (*LU*, I 65; my emphasis). Causes are occult things, liable to lose themselves in the infinities of regress, and unwilling to present themselves in the light of consciousness.

10 'Logical concepts as valid units of thought have to have their origin in intuition' (*LU*, IIi 5). The association of 'Anschauung' with understanding is a Schopenhauerian motif (*Introduction*, 166). Schopenhauer's influence on Husserl is important and little appreciated.
11 Again, see Schopenhauer on this. *Introduction*, 167.

This elusiveness is most evident in the 'problem of induction', central difficulty of empiricism. Induction systematises what has happened in the past, but can never hope to make absolute predictions for the future. Its 'laws' yield probability, not necessity or universality (*LU*, I 62). This is inevitable for the natural sciences, which cannot expect to 'see' more than imperfectly; but it seems a poor basis for logic, which aspires to absolute certainty.

7. Communication and 'meaning'

Logically secure statements, in Husserl's view, carried a 'meaning' (*Bedeutung*) that was entirely independent of time and place. 'Whatever this statement says is *the same* whoever may speak it in assertion [i.e. judge], and under whatever circumstances and times he may do it . . . In this identical meaning, whose identity we can always bring to evident consciousness whenever we repeat the statement, we can simply find no trace of judging or of a person judging' (*LU*, IIi 43).[12]

Meaning, then, is independent of times, places, and, pre-eminently, persons. In pragmatic terms, obviously, speech is primarily concerned with communication; and communication presupposes mutual recognition between persons (*LU*, IIi 32f). This raises important questions in itself; but, at the foundational level, we cannot build up our notion of truth on a pragmatic or communicative basis. Truth is, so to speak, no respecter of persons or their relationships. 'We call an expression objective if . . . it is comprehensible without taking into account the person uttering it or the circumstances of its utterance' (*LU*, IIi 80). Indeed, expressions have just as much meaning in the 'lonely life of the soul' (*LU*, IIi 24), outside all human communication; the introspections of the philosopher need not lack the plenitude of meaning.

An expression retains its purity of meaning, so to speak, as long as it remains uncompromised by mere sensuality. 'The word only ceases to be a word when our exclusive interest is directed towards its sensory side, towards the word as a mere figure of sound. But as long as we live in the understanding of it, it expresses its same identical meaning whether directed to someone else or not' (*LU*, IIi 35).

The point to bear in mind is this: for Husserl, 'truth' is not only not empirically legitimated, it is also unrelated to practice. Just as the task of the logician, in founding his or her discipline, differs from that of the psychol-

12 Despite Husserl's rejection of the terminology of 'judging', the programme corresponds directly to Frege's: 'The truth of a sentence is not the fact of its being thought.' (*Grundlagen*, §77)

ogist (because he or she disregards experience), so too the content of logic is essentially *non-practical* (*LU*, IIi 81).

8. The 'proper kingdom' of logic

According to the principle of 'evidence', then, the task of philosophy is to reach the intuitive (absolutely visible) constituents of knowledge, and not to seek to go behind them by means of metaphysically occult 'explanations' such as causality. This is probably best understood as a rule of semantics. 'Meanings' are complete. They are not caused, nor in any other way contingent on something else. To the extent that we can talk of an external world at all, that world must be understood to be *absolutely* external to cognition. There is no alternative way to it. It is not possible meaningfully to compare our intuitions with the world, whether by looking for the brute facts that 'cause' cognitive responses, or by delineating practical processes which engender them. For the purposes of cognition, meanings are final.

We could call this Husserl's doctrine of the *univocity* of meaning. This is the notion that 'meanings' are inherently rigid. They are not, so to speak, labels to be applied at the whim of a language user. They have a final meaning, anchored in 'evidence' and intuition. Equivocity, or any use of terms to designate objects not envisaged in the original rigidity, would in this respect be arbitrary and derivative. Among other things, it would seem from this doctrine that language cannot describe its own actions: for no language of rigid designators can have a term for an act that it has not yet performed (that obviously does not exclude terms like 'noun'; but it does exclude notions like 'this sentence').

Husserl's second set of assumptions follows from this. They are, basically, that the scientifically accessible world is single and homogeneous. Together, this amounts to an axiom of completeness: 'science' can answer all questions that arise within its realm. Husserl expresses this in the image of a 'kingdom of truth' that is 'proper' (*eigen*) to pure logic; a kingdom, in other words, where reason can survey its territory with the clarity of absolute evidence (*LU*, I 60). What is more, this territory has a territorial integrity. The power of reason may be limitless; but there is nothing it cannot encompass, and in that sense its realm is 'closed' (in the sense of complete – filled with its unique authority). It should be the logician's aim, suggests Husserl, to show that 'The logical laws and forms belong to a theoretically closed (*abgeschlossen*) sphere of abstract truth. . .' (*LU*, I 38).

More specifically, Husserl states that reason has 'no limit'; 'everything that is, is knowable "in itself"'; being is suffused with 'predicates and relations that are firmly determined in themselves' (*LU*, IIi 90). The logical truths, obviously, are infinite; but they, like the 'series of numbers', form a 'concept' (*Inbegriff*) that is 'clearly delimited' and 'ideally closed' (*LU*, IIi 105). The logical truths, it would seem from Husserl's account, are infinite but denumerable (he mentions counting in connection with the series of numbers). As far as this reasoning is concerned, all the truths of science are essentially unitary. Pure logic deals with objective 'meanings'; and these are the 'homogeneous matter' from which all the particular sciences derive (*LU*, IIi 95).

Univocity is a feature of logic and the realm of 'meaning' generally. This follows, for Husserl, from the insistence that the truth of a statement is independent of the time and place of its utterance. Under appropriate circumstances, the 'ideal unity' of a meaning reaches a 'univocal and objectively firm' expression. In common usage, of course, we cannot hope for this univocity, because statements about experience are always 'subjectively opaque [*getrübt*]' (*LU*, IIi 91). But the underlying character of 'meaning' is, says Husserl, its *identity* – 'it is the *self-same* in the strictest sense of the word' (*LU*, IIi 99). If nowhere else, this kind of absolutely secure identity is to be found in mathematics, where

> something objective and ideal is expressed, . . . something that can appear in manifold possible thought experiences as the same intentional unity, and which stands before us, in the objective-ideal contemplation that characterises all thinking, as, self-evidently, the One and the Same. (*LU*, IIi 45)

Husserl's assumptions about completeness and univocity would probably not stand up to scrutiny in strictly logical terms. In particular, Gödel's 1931 paper would seem to put paid to them. Arithmetic is not complete, in that, regardless of how far the axiom system is extended, it can always generate questions which cannot be answered within any given system. It is hard to know how the homogeneous kingdom of logical verities could be accommodated to this.

The underlying point, which we have already noted and which is probably more important, is that such systems are also not straightforwardly univocal, at least if univocity means some constant mapping of the set of logical symbols onto the set of what Husserl calls the logical 'objects'. The difficulty with this view is that a formal system strong enough to do arithmetic is also strong enough to talk about *itself*. So there is a fundamental equivocity in the symbolism of such a system as to whether it is talking about 'objects' (of whatever kind), or itself; and this would seem to undermine the substance of Husserl's notion of 'identity'.

9. Experience and essence

We are now at the beginning of the phenomenological project itself. We bring with us two basic principles.

The first is the distinction between meaning and experience. Empiricism, and variants such as positivism and psychologism, build an implicit hierarchy into the universe, a hierarchy derived from empirical reality. The metaphysical elements are derived from physical objects that are present and to hand. This, however, is not good enough (in Husserl's view). The merely present world is inchoate; it has yet to acquire 'meaning'. And this is something that can only be supplied in a pre-empirical world of pure identities. So although, as Husserl repeatedly emphasises, his goal is a return from metaphysical occultism to 'the things themselves' (*die Sachen selbst*), these 'things' should not be understood simply in terms of present physical realities. In particular, the sphere of 'objects' (*Gegenstände* – this term echoes Rickert's neo-Kantianism) includes what Husserl calls 'general' objects as well as individual ones. This is not, he insists, a Platonistic 'metaphysical hypostatisation'. General objects are not to be sought in heaven (a *topos ouranios*), or the mind of God; rather, the term is simply 'an indication of the validity of certain judgements, namely those which judge about numbers, propositions, geometrical structures, etc.' (*LU*, IIi 101). More strongly, though, Husserl insists that the predicate 'existence' is quite properly attached to 'ideal objects' (*LU*, IIi 124), and, as we shall see, these ideal objects are not in any way restricted to pure mathematics.

The second principle is the rejection of causality in logic. The rules of our understanding are not 'caused'; meaning is not, so to speak, implemented, whether by us or by some outside force. It is simply there, or, as Husserl says, *given*, in evident cognition (*LU*, IIi 92). In other words, meaning is something towards which we have an essentially passive, contemplative relation. It is there, and we should not try to obscure it with positivistic 'explanations'.

Important elements of Husserl's position here are not as explicit as they might be. They are, however, constitutive of the 'flavour' of his project, and need to be borne in mind. The point is this. Empiricist philosophies seek to derive everything from experience. Experience is understood as the field of objects that exist, as individuals, in a realm of causes and effects. The rules extracted from this foundation – whether of the natural sciences, logic, or whatever – are inductive generalisations. In a certain fundamental sense, moreover, they are rules of conduct – practical norms of experience. 'I have learned from experience that it is best to behave in such-and-such a manner.' This empiricism, according to Husserl, characteristically interprets logic as a 'technique' (*Kunstlehre*), and science in general as 'normative'. In all respects, science is harnessed to the demands of *interest*.[13]

Empiricism's underlying metaphor, it would seem, is an infinite field of causally interacting billiard balls. The natural sciences are the general model for a description of this field: they try to identify causes and regularities, and predict future interactions. The human sciences deal with the same basic matter, but directed towards the specific concerns of a more complex billiard ball, the human being. The interests of this particular billiard ball are, so to speak, concerned with maximising its interactive efficiency, or 'getting what it wants'. Scientific description of the interactive circumstances makes that easier. So logic, or familiarity with the 'laws of thought', facilitates the movement of each billiard ball among its fellows and through the general field of the natural world.

Now Husserl, as we have already seen, does not think this makes sense as an account of the nature of logic. Logic cannot be grounded causally or empirically without landing in infinite regress, and so on. Beyond that, however, the whole image of the world projected by empiricism is something secondary and derivative. The philosophy envisaged by Husserl is in the first instance concerned not with experience, nor with causes, nor even with individuals. *All* these components of the 'billiard ball' view are swept aside in the 'metaphysics' of phenomenology (though Husserl is loath to use this word – *LU*, IIi 21). 'To the extent that purely theoretical interests have the constitutive role, individual singularity and its empirical linkage count for nothing . . .' (*LU*, I 235).

If we anticipate Husserl's development of his position a little, we can say this. Purely 'logical', 'a priori', 'abstract' sciences (such as, in Husserl's view, arithmetic and geometry – *Ideas (Id)*, 135) are obviously not concerned with experience, causes, or individuals. In that respect, they stand as models for the kind of 'essential' (certain and non-empirical) knowledge to which philosophy aspires. The only trouble, though, is that the world is full of many more things than can be encompassed by the axioms of geometry. Are they all to be consigned to unaccountable experience? If so, we have scarcely progressed beyond the scepticism of a Hume, who after all would have agreed about the analytical verities of mathematics.

No, indeed, says Husserl. The critical distinction is not between 'exact' disciplines like mathematics and 'vague' ones like phenomenology, but between eidetic and empirical ones; and the eidetic disciplines can encompass anything *short of judgement*. Or, more specifically, where the empirical

---

13 'Normative interests govern us . . . particularly in the case of real objects considered as objects of practical valuations; hence the unmistakeable tendency to identify the concept of the normative discipline with that of the practical discipline, or technique . . . The technique represents that particular case of a normative discipline in which the basic norm consists in the attainment of a general practical goal.' *LU*, I 47.

disciplines 'posit' the existence of individual objects (and, indeed, of the scientist observing those objects) as sites of infinite causative interaction, the eidetic disciplines neither make nor endorse any judgement, whether of existence or anything else. In other words, while the empirical disciplines see themselves as in some sense participants in the great causal interactivity of the billiard table, the eidetic ones observe but do not get involved.

This, itself, mirrors what is in effect Husserl's own basic 'metaphysical' commitment. The things of 'consciousness' (understood as the logical forms, meanings, and so on) *exist* in the full sense of the word. On the other side there is 'reality', understood as the place where individuals battle on through the causal nexus. But the two things are not commensurate; they do not form a whole; between the one and the other there yawns 'a verit- able gulf of meaning'. In particular, consciousness has nothing to do with causality. It is something 'into which nothing can enter and from which nothing can escape; that has no spatio-temporal outside and cannot be in- cluded in any spatio-temporal connection, which can experience causality from nothing and which cannot exercise causality on anything. . .' Ulti- mately, moreover, the 'real' world only exists as a kind of secondary image, as the object of intentions – 'beyond that it is Nothing'.[14]

10. Epoché

To resume: philosophy sets itself to explore a realm of absolute certainties. Its model is 'logic', in some sense. It derives its content from intuitions, which are final. Its form, also, is final. None of its concerns are contingent upon the decisions or actions of individual human beings.

Within this general scheme of things, we must now follow the way Husserl assembles his system. It has, basically, two components. The first is *epoché*, by means of which Husserl hopes to guarantee the finality of the contents of his logic (of the intuitional 'meanings', that is to say). The second is the notion of the *horizon*, which is the formal order in accordance with which individual intuitions coexist.

'Epoché' is the term used by Husserl to describe his basic method. The method consists in 'bracketing out' the natural attitude's assumptions about existence. Human beings in their day-to-day dealings assume, and indeed affirm (according to Husserl) the existence of the things they ex- perience. But this affirmation is something that has no place in transcen- dental philosophy. An object's existence or non-existence is extraneous to the concerns of philosophy as strict logic. For the concerns of philosophy, we can say all we need to say about something without interpolating state-

14 *Id*, 92f. Husserl does not talk in these terms in *LU*.

ments about its existence or non-existence. The whole field of intuitions, and the laws of their interrelations, are not affected by questions of existence.

In detail, the procedure works as follows. As we have already noted, a pure empiricism (at least in Husserl's view) is difficult to sustain. A pure empiricism would say that the mind is entirely passive, and that cognition arises, in a more or less mechanical way, in response to stimuli from the external world (Husserl calls this 'nominalism' – *LU*, IIi 156). 'Ideas', in this view, would be a matter of habit and convention. Husserl's criticism, essentially, is that it is difficult to account for generalisation on the basis of contingently arising sense impressions. How does 'objectivity', as a realm of shared and assured concepts, ever arise, and what basis could it have for its legitimacy? The puzzles of circularity and regress are, in Husserl's refutation, the contradictions that a purely empiricist, or nominalist, view falls into.[15]

Now, the answer to nominalism, in Husserl's account, is that the mind is *active* in dealing with the world. There is, of course, an 'outside world', and that is where we all, as individuals, live and die. But the outside world only comes to our consciousness through the activities of the intellect. Thus, in any thought, we are always dealing with two components – the thing of which we are conscious, and the *mental act which brings it to consciousness*. And, furthermore, the mental act has an absolute priority over its contents by virtue of the fact that nothing could even *become* 'content' without mental acts.

Husserl's predecessors had adopted this distinction, but had fallen into confusion (according to Husserl) by regarding the mental act as something accessible to empirical psychology. If the mental act was itself an actual or potential object of acts, the argument went, then it could not have the same status of absolute knowledge-constitutive agent, and we were again exposed to circularity. The empirical cannot legitimate the empirical.[16]

15 This is, of course, an area of fundamental debate. I do not wish here to assimilate Husserl's terminology of 'nominalism' to its current use by philosophers like Quine (e.g. *FLPV*, 14ff.), Putnam or Rorty. But Husserl's discussion is quite closely congruent with that of contemporaries like Russell over whether 'truth' is a matter of extensions or intensions. The extensionalist (Husserl's 'nominalist'; in later writings, 'empiricist') would say that 'truth' is what happens when we find arguments that give us positive values for some function. In that respect the origin of the function is purely subjective, and its metaphysical status is provisional and pragmatic. The intensionalist, by contrast, would say that the process by which the function arises is more important than its particular encounters with pieces of the outside world; and that 'truth' is something to be sought, initially at least, in the conceptual activities of the mind.

16 F.A. Lange, otherwise a thinker whom Husserl repudiated, argued for this same absolute division between the *acts* of the mind and its contents. The axiom of identity, for example, was 'the basis of all cognition, though not itself a cognition, but rather a deed of the mind, an act of originary synthesis'. See Ollig, 1982, 53.

So, any truly philosophical investigation must start with the mental act qua act, not as some neurological phenomenon. How, though, can we know about things that are absolutely non-empirical? Husserl's answer is that we acquire this knowledge through *reflection*. Reflection, in a use which goes back at least to Locke (see *Essay*, IIi §4), is the knowledge that the mind has of itself and its own operations. The critical thing in Husserl's account, though, is that the mind does not come to know its operations as content, in the ordinary sense, since they are not empirical. This gives a distinct coloration to Husserl's use of the term.

'Experience' (i.e. the realm of the empirical) is defined by Husserl as *co-positing of real existence* ('Mitsetzung von realem Dasein' *LU*, IIi 399). This, obviously, is a rather specific use of the term experience. Husserl is arguing that when we, in the natural course of day-to-day life, experience things, we 'believe' in them, and attribute real existence to them. More broadly, we could say that the 'natural attitude', as Husserl calls it, believes that it is, so to speak, a real thing in a network of real interacting things. When I, in my natural attitude, do something, I believe that I do it to really existing things, and that I am one amongst those really existing things. This can apply even to purely cognitive deeds such as judgements (for example, I believe of myself that I have, really, formed an opinion).

Now, reflection, which is concerned only with the operations of the mind, can escape the empirical simply by not believing in (or 'positing') real existence – for anything.

How can this work?

The formulaic answer would be to say that existence is not a 'real predicate' (as Kant said, and see *LU*, IIiii §43), and hence that removing it makes no difference to logic. For example, the judgement 'this is a table' is not affected one way or another by adding 'and it really exists', or even, arguably, by prefacing it with 'it is true that'.

Practically, of course, suspending our belief in existence *does* make a difference. This kind of 'reflection', Husserl concedes, is 'unnatural' (*LU*, IIi 9). But it is precisely this kind of unnaturalness that he wishes to achieve. For it is our practical engagement in a world of real things, a world in which we passionately believe, that hinders us from seeing genuine truth and rationality. Clearing out the baggage of the natural attitude ('bracketing' our belief in existence – *Id*, 57), clears the way for a better insight, namely the insight into the 'acts' of the mind and their status as 'objects' of a higher order (*LU*, IIi 9).

So Husserl characterises the phenomenological discipline – this process of suspension and reflection – in basically practical terms. It is an 'opting out' (Nicht-Mitmachen), which converts the reflecting I into a 'disinterested observer' (i.e. one with no practical commitment to what is going on – *Cartesianische Meditationen (CM)*,37).[17]

11. 'Acts' and the given

There are important correlatives we must note here. In the first place, although Husserl uses the terminology of 'acts' for the operations of the mind, he does not mean particular actions like judgements, utterances or whatever.

> As far as the terminology of acts is concerned, one should, obviously, no longer think here of the orginal sense of *actus*; any thought of activity [Betätigung] must be absolutely excluded . . . We reject the 'mythology of actions [Tätigkeiten]'; we define 'acts' not as psychic actions [Betätigungen], but as intentional experiences. (*LU*, IIi 379n)

In other words, the actions of the mind are not to be understood as pragmatic interventions by individuals. As far as any one 'mind' is concerned, in fact, these acts are experienced in passivity. This becomes more apparent in the notion of intuition developed by Husserl in the *Ideas*. Husserl contrasts his 'legitimatory source' ('Rechtsquelle', p. 36) with that of the empiricists. For them, it was experience, and the direct grounding of knowledge in an external world. Whatever 'true' knowledge was, its claims to that title were grounded in experience. That world was the given; our cognition was the derived.

Husserl, as we have seen, disputes the pure givenness of experience. Experience, in his definition, is cognition with the added element of existential positing. But that positing, in terms of meaning, is redundant. Experience is not pure and given; it is regular cognition framed, and probably distorted, by commitments about existence. Empiricism's attempt to ground knowledge in things themselves, rather than in fallible subjective accounts of them, was laudable. But its belief that 'things' were the objects to which we apply ourselves in day-to-day self-interest was an illusion. Things, 'die Sachen selbst',

> are not to be identified simply with *natural things* [Natursachen], nor is reality in the habitual sense to be identified with reality in general. . . (*Id*, 35)

'Die Sachen selbst' were better sought where the commitments of practice had not interfered, and where there genuinely was a given, undistorted world. That givenness, perhaps paradoxically, was to be found in in-

---

17 This may well owe a good deal to Schopenhauer, whom Husserl read at an early age, twice gave courses on (Bernet, Kern, Marbach, 1989, 217f), and whom he cites in *LU*. This indebtedness is not merely a matter of Schopenhauer's quietism; his 'Pythagorean' attitude to the constructions of reason also seems close to Husserl's project.

tentional acts. They provided the 'originary giving intuitions' which the existential commitments of empiricism obscured (*Id, 36*; the English translation talks of 'primordial dator intuitions'). Phenomenology, in other words, looked 'inwards', to the intentions of the mind, rather than outwards, to a world that could no longer be regarded as neutral ground. But this inward looking was not individual introspection; it was, in some sense, reflection on the absolute, trans-individual structures of objectivity.

12. Real time[18]

Despite Husserl's definition of experience as the co-positing of real existence, it is not directly obvious what difference it makes to suspend this co-positing. If existence is not a 'real predicate' anyway, and if the natural attitude is mainly a practical, rather than a cognitive, matter, then the attribution of existence would seem to make no particular difference one way or the other.

In fact, Husserl is making rather stronger claims than this about the natural attitude and the effect of phenomenological reflection. The problem of what is involved in the attribution of 'existence' is not something new in the history of philosophy, and the question of whether it is a 'real predicate' or not has been thoroughly discussed, in various terminologies, for a very long time. One account which would have been familiar to Husserl from the work of Brentano, whom he admired, is that of scholasticism.[19] The scholastics, by which we mean Thomist Aristotelians, took the view that there were general terms, manipulated by logic, and there was individuation, which so to speak attached concreteness to things. Each thing was intelligible because it partook of logical generality, the 'ideal'. And it was singular, an individual manifestation of the ideal, because of *matter*. Ideas were general; therein lay their power. To become part of the world of things, they had to lose this absolute generality; and they did so by joining something quite different, namely matter. In that sense they needed matter, the 'principle of individuation'.[20]

Now matter, in this context, has its usual connotation of physical stuff. More precisely, though, it is defined as what is extended, or as what 'has

---

18 Most of my reading here is taken from *LU*. In the *Ideas*, Husserl starts to distinguish between 'objective' or 'cosmic' time, which is what we are concerned with here, and 'phenomenological' time, which is the 'unitary form of all experiences' (161). Phenomenological time is part of the structure of the 'horizon': see below. Husserl's treatment of time became obscurer as his project progressed. In the *Ideas* he expressed relief that the 'mysteries of time consciousness' did not have to be dealt with in his 'preliminary analyses' (163).

19 Husserl attributed 'genius' to Brentano (*LU*, IIi 367). The theory of intentions has its origins in scholasticism. See Bell, 1990 on Brentano's influence.

20 'Principium individuationis'. Thomas Aquinas, *De ente et essentia*, ii, 254.

dimensions'.[21] Extension does not embrace only things in space, but also matter in time, the 'fourth dimension'. So matter is the condition of being in time and space.

In scholastic terms, then, to attribute existence is to say that something is an individual thing, i.e. that it is in time and space.

This, furthermore, is what Husserl also understands by 'positing existence'. The being of species, or, generally, of the 'ideal', is *timeless* (*LU*, IIi 124). The ideal is counterposed to what Husserl terms the 'real', i.e. the existent. Within the realm of the real, the 'individuating determinants' include, pre-eminently, temporality and spatiality (*LU*, IIi 158). Reality is characterised by being *individual*; by having a presence in space and time, or, in the conventional formula, being *'here and now'*; and by *temporality*.

Of these, the last is in fact a sufficient characterisation; 'Real being and temporal being may not be identical concepts, but they are equivalent' (*LU*, IIi 123). Husserl evidently took the view that space, despite problems like orientation, was basically recoverable by logic (the 'ideal'), whereas time was irredeemably un-logical. So time becomes the locus of 'matter', to use the old term. In Husserl's terminology, we may call it the site of the real.

> . . . let us simply define reality as temporality. For here we are only concerned with the timeless 'being' of the ideal. (*LU*, IIi 124)

This, then, gives us a more substantial account of what phenomenological 'reflection' might be: it is the recovery of cognitive acts into the realm of the ideal – i.e. without regard to their appearance through individual things in time. The *epoché*, then, precisely does not interfere with the thoughts I have as I pass through life; it merely removes any judgements about their 'reality'. And it does so by suspending any views I might be tempted to form about real hereness and nowness.

In the *Ideas*, Husserl contrasts his epoché with sophistic or sceptical responses to the world:

> I do not negate this 'world', as though I were a sceptic, and I do not doubt its existence, as though I were a sceptic; but I practise the 'phenomenological' *epoché*, which entirely blocks any judgement by me about spatio-temporal existence. (*Id*, 56)

In other words, I do not make negative or doubting judgements about existence, I eschew any judgement whatever. Thus no additional intentional activity (negating or doubting) flows into my 'intentions', and they remain pure and unalloyed.

Anyway, the extraction of time and space from my thoughts does not, in

---

21 'designatio individui respectu speciei est per materiam determinatam dimensionibus . . .', Thomas, op. cit., ii, 92. For more on all this, see chapter 1 of *German Philosophy*.

Husserl's contention, make any serious difference to them. As parts of thought, and perhaps even as parts of practical life, they remain unimpaired. Even such intimate and personal thoughts as the proper name of a friend do not depend on 'existential co-positing'. 'Does the individual [individuell] proper name also imply the individuating [individualisierend] determinants, i.e. for example, temporality and spatiality?' Surely not, Husserl argues, for otherwise the proper name would have to change its meaning with every step taken by its bearer (*LU*, IIi 158). 'In any event, the here and now, when we are looking attentively at a piece or at an object's characteristic features, is often enough a matter of indifference.'

13. Truth and foundedness

Given these starting points, what exactly are Husserl's criteria for, in the widest sense, truth? The most obvious way of looking at truth is pragmatic; truthful statements are those that express some sort of useful information about the world. 'Usefulness' is inseparable from that view; 'information' is something that can be tested and used.

This view is not open to Husserl. In the first place, this kind of pragmatism instals an *interested agent* as the subject of knowledge. The test of truth is whether such an agent can realise his or her interests with its aid. But this clearly conflicts with Husserl's aspirations. The realm of the 'ideal' is not reducible to the interests of individuals. The aim of philosophy is precisely to transcend the particularity of 'judgements *hic et nunc*, linked together by motivation' (*LU*, IIi 26).

In the second place, pragmatism preselects the 'players' in its truth scenario. The 'world' and the knowing subject are both taken as given; in Husserl's terms, their existence is co-posited. But this, of course, preempts the whole discussion. For Husserl, the 'objects' of truth must 'be' truthfully. The natural attitude's co-posited entities have a pragmatic being, but such pragmatic existence is by no means the same as truthful being. This sounds elliptical, if not metaphysical. But Husserl's point is that one cannot hang a whole theory of truth on one model – that of a relationship between world and knowing subject – without first clarifying what these supposedly irreducible entities are. If truth accounts for what 'is', then the nature of 'being' has to be determined before we can attribute it to the entities that are supposed to explain it. There is a degree of circularity here. And its debilitating effects, says Husserl, are visible in the misunderstanding that there is 'a real process, or a real relation, that played out between consciousness, or the I, and the matter that it is "conscious of"' (*LU*, IIi 371). Whatever the correspondence theory of truth has to offer, it cannot lie in describing the passage of one existent thing into the cognitive processes of another.

So Husserl's aim is to discover an 'ideal' level of truth which is not obscured by an unthinking pragmatism of the ad hoc. His method, essentially, involves the discovery of the fundamental objects of knowledge, and the relative subordination of the activities of the understanding, which Husserl regards as combinatorial rather than substantive. This project is not all that far removed from that of the British empiricists (to whom much of *Logical Investigations* IIi is devoted). His attitude to the understanding is closely comparable with Wittgenstein's account, a few years later, of logic as a 'zero method' (see above). And, indeed, both of these thinkers share the kind of idealism which sees 'things' as essentially non-practical – as 'pictures', in fact, rather than as *pragmata*.[22]

14. Logical objects

The foundations of Husserl's ideal universe are set in what he calls 'objects' (Gegenstände). This is what he has in mind, for example, with his slogan of a return 'to things themselves' ('auf die Sachen selbst', *LU*, IIi 6). It is also what is meant by his otherwise rather puzzling use of the tag *adaequatio rei ac intellectus* (*LU*, IIi 8); the 'adequation' envisaged is not that of primitive empiricism, i.e. of a correspondence between 'real' things and their depiction in the brain, but of an adequate intellection of 'things' understood as *ideal objects*.[23]

The ideality of these objects is underlined by Husserl's insistence that they are constituents of the *logical* universe. When, for example, I am talking about 'four', I have it in mind as a species, which means that I have '*it*, objectively [gegenständlich], before my logical gaze, i.e. I am judging about it as an object (*subjectum*), and not about anything individual' (*LU*, IIi 140). Husserl defines further:

> To make something objective [gegenständlich], to make it the subject of predication or attribution, is only another expression for *representation* [vorstellen], and indeed of representation in the sense which, though not the only one, is determining [maßgebend] for logic altogether. (*LU*, IIi 140)

The suggestion is that meanings, ideal objects, emerge in a context which can be described as 'logical'. A logical 'representation' is something that

22 Or, as Husserl says, independent of the *fact* (*CM*, 72) – which, etymologically, means the same. In *Id*, 12, Husserl opposes fact (Tatsache) to Eidos – which means image.
23 *Adaequatio*, for Husserl, is when we perceive what we intend. This turns correspondence, which is interested in whether we intend what we perceive, on its head! (*LU*, IIii 118); but see below.

can be situated in a predicative sentence. Representation is 'determining' for logic because its variables have to be given values. Equally, though, 'things' only emerge as such because there are logical structures which anticipate them as possible values for variables. Either way, these objects are the 'most primitive building blocks of the logical process, out of which our world is built up' (*EuU*, §12, p. 59).

We have, if we pursue Husserl's metaphor, two components to the 'world'. First we have the bricks (the 'objects'), and secondly we have the structure. How do we interpret this?

Starting with the objects, then, if representation is the 'determining' element, clearly what cannot be represented has a weaker claim on logical objectness than what can. Unrepresentability is a fate suffered by, for example, 'forms of connection' ('Verknüpfungsformen', *LU*, IIi 238). More generally, Husserl argues that the 'categorial forms' have no 'objective correlatives'. ('Categorial forms' seem to include the logical connectives, as well as the predicate 'is' – *LU*, IIii 138f.) In Husserl's view, we would never be able to perceive anything corresponding to them. We obviously can never hope to perceive an 'or'; and in Husserl's view, this applies equally to 'being' (I perceive that something is coloured; I do not perceive 'being-coloured' – *LU*, IIii 137).

The temptation at this point would be to dismiss operations of the understanding entirely from the realm of 'objectivity'. Indeed, Husserl allows some force to the objection that certain purely synthesising functions do not change the 'object itself', and that consequently they should be regarded as merely part of our 'subjective dealings' ('subjektives Betätigen' – *LU*, IIii 158). But, in the first place, he asserts that there *are* categorial or ideal 'objects of a higher order' (*LU*, IIii 145, 156); indeed, it would be difficult to conceive of how a number might be an object otherwise.

Secondly, the categorial forms are indispensable for the structure of Husserl's building – what he terms its 'grounding' (*Fundierung*; in the English *Ideas*, this is also translated as 'consolidation'). Husserl asserts a 'fundamental distinction' between categorial form and what he calls 'sensually grounded matter of cognition' (*LU*, IIii 145). The grounded matter consists of the objects, the building bricks. They are the 'objects of the lowest stage of possible intuition'. They are objects with possible correlatives in perception, i.e. things we might see. They provide the content, while 'categories' supply the form. In other words, they are the atomic elements of a structure held together by the glue of logical connectives. This atomic elementarity is reflected also in Husserl's notion of 'simple' ('schlicht' – *LU*, IIii 147) intentional acts. These direct and simple intuitions supply the building blocks, and guarantee the foundedness of the building, while the complex 'founded acts' grow out of the combinations and relations of categorial form.

In accordance with this view, Husserl insists on the need for such simple intuitions in any true statement. Whatever is complex must, ultimately, be composed from what is simple. These simple elements are what Husserl calls the 'finally founding acts of *any* complex act' (*LU*, IIi 497).[24]

15. Apophansis[25]

How do we recognise these 'simple' acts? For an empiricist, the answer would be easy: simple acts are direct observations of reality. Because of Husserl's insistence on freeing logic from practice, however, this is not a route open to him. The 'reality' so blithely observed by the empiricist is merely something posited by the natural attitude. 'Perfectly simple objectifications,' says Husserl, 'are free from all "categorial forms"' (*LU*, IIi 483). But this cannot mean a direct passive apperception, because the mind is active, and in that sense always applies a form of some kind. What is needed is a form that is as rudimentary (Husserl says 'einfältig') as the content it conveys.

That is to be found, it seems, in the elementary predicative judgement '*S* is *P*' (or '*Fx*'). That part of logic which deals with such predications is called by Husserl, following Aristotle, *apophantic* logic (*LU*, IIi 331n.; *De Interpretatione* IV, V). Apophantic logic, in Husserl's view, is 'fundamental' precisely in the sense we have been considering. Historically, he claims, it has been 'in the centre of formal logic' (*Erfahrung und Urteil (EuU)*, 1), and any philosopher must ponder the extent to which 'the predicative judgement is the preferred and central theme of logic, such that logic is necessarily, in its core, apophantic logic, the doctrine of judgements' (*EuU*, 5).[26]

What Husserl means by this is less clear than it might be. Roughly, though, the distinction is again one between form and content. Pure formal logic, in the conventional sense, is termed by Husserl 'ontology', that is to say, the logic of 'somethingness [Etwas] in general and its transformations' (*EuU*, 2). It covers notions such as object, property, relation, plurality; and, beyond that, it is associated with the formal-mathematical disciplines (*Id* 249).

As a general formulation, ontology is concerned with the 'categorial forms', which we have already met (*EuU*, 2). Possibly we could say that

24 Husserl's insistence on the priority of content over logical form is also exemplified by the *Ideas*'s emphasis on 'noema' (things known) over 'noesis' (cognitive processes). 'Relating the problem to the *acts*, the noeses, is inadequate,' he says, for example (263). It is the noema that has its 'peculiar objectivity' (265), and a 'content', through which it relates to the object (267).
25 The theory of 'apophansis' is only explicitly developed in the later work.
26 See also *LU*, IIi 481: predicative synthesis is 'a particularly pre-eminent form of synthesis'.

'ontology' is concerned with the logical connectives (quantifiers plus '→' and '⊥', minimally), while 'apophantics' are concerned with the predicative atoms that make a propositional calculus possible in the first place. All judgements, says Husserl, are ultimately reducible to 'copulative' judgements, in the basic form '*S* is *P*' (*EuU*, 6).

In another account, Husserl suggests that ontology looks at the rules for preventing 'senselessness' ('Unsinn') while apophantics concerns those for preventing 'nonsense' ('Widersinn'; – *LU*, IIi 334f). Ontology directs the possible *forms* of meaning, and prevents syntactically senseless formulae such as 'King but or similar and'. Apophantics, by contrast, concerns the 'possibility or impossibility of the being of signified objects . . . in so far as it is determined by the proper *essence* [Wesen] of these meanings, and is thus open to insight through apodeictic evidence'. In other words, it prevents semantically unacceptable formulae such as 'a square is round'.

The force of this lies in Husserl's insistence that the semantic, or apophantic level is dealing with absolute foundational intuitions. These are the 'final substantive [sachhaltig] cores of meaning'. Elementary predication rests on 'ultimately originating objective evidence' (*EuU*, 15). It is the stage at which 'objects' first come to light; and it is only by virtue of this objectification through predication that derivative and complex forms of judgement acquire meaning. Elementary predication is the point where both logical form and material content become manifest. Hence the fundamental character of its claims:[27]

> Here lies the deepest of the sources from which the *universality of the logical*, and ultimately the universality of the predicative judgement, is to be illumined, [. . .] and from here we can also understand the ultimate reason for the very universality of logic's dominion. (*Id*, 244f)

In the later work, Husserl increased his emphasis on the primordial apophantic judgement, as distinct from derivative or manipulative ones. He called the elementary judgements 'cognitive' (erkennend), as distinct from 'mere' (bloßes) judgement, which mechanically reproduces a judgement once, but no longer, cognitive and entire (*EuU*, 15f). Cognitive judgement is utterly distinct from judgement as mere subjective activity. 'Mere' judgement, the subjective action, simply repeats the same, mechanically. Cognitive judgement, on the other hand, 'is something "immanent" in the sense that it is given, itself, in the repetition as an identical object' (*EuU*, 16).[28]

27 The co-origination of both the object and its logical form, and their inextricability from one another, is also part of Wittgenstein's 'picture theory' (see above).
28 'Immanent' is Husserl's way of identifying the thought that takes place on its own ground, the ground of logic and the ideal. 'Transcendent', by contrast, relates to concerns with the 'real'. The natural attitude persists in looking to the transcendent. Psychologism, too, describes conceptual matters as though they were physiological, 'real', events. The Husserlian epoché is the discipline of maintaining oneself within the immanent.

Cognitive judgement marks the appearance of something identical, irreducibly itself and pristine, not a mechanically reproduced gesture of ratiocination. Such an object is 'immanent [i.e. immanent in the logical process, rather than injected by transcendent practical considerations], but in an unreal and timeless way, not as something *reell* or individuated'[29] (*EuU*, 16f).

So: elementary predicative judgements give us the ideal 'identities' that underlie knowledge. This gives us a basis for determining conditions for truth.

16. Picture, name

Elementary apophantic judgements, then, are the entry points for foundational intuitions. They are not, however, foundational by virtue of the conceptual act itself, but by virtue of the objects they, so to speak, allow in.[30] We are, as Husserl puts it, not concerned with 'these acts as objects, but with the objects of these acts' (*LU*, IIii 141).

At this point, Husserl allows himself recourse to the metaphor of the *image*, part of the ancient stock in trade of what is generally called Platonism.[31] If there are ideal objects, then what sort of thing are they? The suggestion at hand is that they are in some sense visually representable; they have a 'form' (as Plato's term *idea* is often rendered), and we can, among other things, 'imagine' or *picture* them. This notion is urged by Husserl's use of ocular metaphors of 'intuition' ('Anschauung') and 'insight'; and it surfaces explictly in his use of words like 'looking at a picture' ('Bildbeschauung' – *LU*, IIi 460) or 'imagination' ('Einbildung'). It is probably something he took over from Schopenhauer, who propounded exactly this kind of idealism.[32] Substantively, Husserl invokes the theory of disinterested contemplation used in Kant's aesthetics, i.e., here, the (for him) useful conception that one can have a visual intuition of something without positing its existence (*LU*, IIi 491).

The suggestion, then, is that that the imaginary ('das Einbildende') is inseparable from the judgement itself, 'das Fürwahrhaltende' (*LU*, IIi 489). All true judgements have 'counterparts' in an imaginative act; and, indeed,

29 I.e. that is part of the cluster of empirical phenomena within the conceptual process, but is not part of any ideal 'object'. On terms like 'real' and 'reell', see *LU*, IIi 398f.
30 Heidegger's commentary on *apophansis* in *Being and Time* 32ff. is a helpful interpretation of what Husserl is getting at.
31 Husserl was willing to be associated with Platonism. See *Ideas*, 117, where he also mentions logicism.
32 See my *German Philosophy*, 162ff. But note Husserl's (weak) caution about taking 'picture' too literally – *LU*, IIi 490ff. See also *LU*, IIi 424 on 'imagination' and 'Einbildung'. Heidegger's discussion of Kant on Einbildung (in his Kant book) seems to be a development of this.

it is this that makes it possible to speak of truth or falsehood.[33] In the *Logical Investigations*, Husserl's general term for this imaginative act is 'representation' (which, again, emphasises how close some of his thinking is to certain traditions in British empiricism). Representation, he defines, is 'that act in which something becomes objective [gegenständlich] to us in a certain *narrower sense*' (*LU*, IIi 459). As such it is also systematically opposed to the judgement, which, most generally, is 'an act of concluded predication where it appears to us that something *is* or *is not*' (where, of course, the 'being' apparently expressed by the copula is merely combinatory and never 'objective').

It would seem, however, that direct intuition is not possible. A judgement, at least in the form of a 'cognitive judgement' (as *EuU*, puts it), has to come first. The apophantic event is a precondition for the emergence of the image. In that sense, at least, the 'logicality' of the procedure is preserved (though perhaps in a rather arbitrary way). It is further preserved in the process by means of which ideal objects, once released by the primitive judgement, become available for further manipulation. Husserl's term for this process is 'modification'.

Modification, generally, is an operation where something changes its syntactical form, with or without also changing its semantic content. For example, a predicative judgement ('The table is white') could be converted into a noun ('The white table') before, perhaps, being incorporated into some further sentence.

In this case, Husserl is only interested in the kind of modification where no semantic alteration takes place. Here, it converts any assertoric judgement ('*p* is the case') into a 'mere representation' (*LU*, IIi 480). The judgement becomes modally indifferent; it is, as Husserl describes it, a 'neutral putting forward [Dahingestellthaben] of the same state of affairs' (*LU*, IIi 490). In the passage from predication to noun, we are dealing with a particularly important case that Husserl calls 'nominalisation'. In nominalisation, the synthetic aggregate (subject and predicate) is reduced to a new 'single-element' act and thereby to one that is 'simply represented' and 'objective in the fullest sense' (*LU*, IIi 482). In the case of elementary predication, nominalisation gives us our root intuitions, and they are associated with *names*.

We now have the basic elements of our grammar. Ontologically, we have elementary apophantic judgements and their counterpart 'representations'. The same distinction repeats itself at a syntactical level in the pair: propositions (Aussagen) and names. This gives us our rules for sentence

---

33 In the *Ideas*, 'purely imaginary [einbildende] intuitions' are closely associated with the Eidos, the 'pure essence', which in that book is Husserl's general term for ideal objects. See *Id*, 12.

formation, and for truth conditions.

17. Semantic rules

The first rule is that there is a basic and essential difference between formal elements and elements of content. We have noted this in the context of elementary predicative judgements and the representations associated with them. The same applies in the difference between propositions and names (*LU*, IIi 467). Names are, as he puts it, a 'crystallisation' ('Niederschlag') of judgements (i.e. they always have their origins in elementary apophansis); but, analytically, they are to be 'strictly distinguished' from these origins (*LU*, IIi 468).[34] Names, let us assume, are the sentence elements associated with representations. They are, in other words, the closest point to 'objectivity'.

The second rule is that sentences involve form. They must involve form, since they incorporate logical acts, either directly and explicitly (as synthesising judgements of some kind), or indirectly (as 'nominal acts', i.e. as crystallisations of previous judgements). There are no brute non-predicative intuitions; or, if there are, they are not philosophically interesting. As Husserl puts it, 'representing' *is* 'to make something objective, to make it the subject of predications or attributions' (*LU*, IIi 140).

The third rule is that all sentences must involve content. Contents, as we have seen, are the objects given in elementary apophansis. So what the rule amounts to is: all sentences must contain one or more objects of this kind. This can be expressed either semantically, in terms of representations, or syntactically, in terms of names. So: 'Every act is either itself a representation, or it is founded in one or more representations' (*LU*, IIi 461). For example: 'A judgement has at least one representation as its basis [Grundlage], just as every fully articulated proposition has at least one "Name"'. In more metaphysical language,

> the individual is required, purely logically, as the primordial object [Urgegenstand]; it is the logical absolute towards which all logical combinations [Abwandlungen] refer back. (*Id*, 29)

Individuals arise in the simple 'objectifying acts' which found the possibility of truth. They are the bearers of names; and it is as names that these

---

34 Husserl appears to regard 'judgements' partly as a subset of 'propositions' (Aussagen), and partly as what propositions express. Propositions express acts, and thereby make claims about the world. These acts are representation and judgement, 'the acts which give names and propositions meaning and fulfilling sense' (*LU*, IIi 477). The claims made are distinct, of course, from 'real' existence claims; but they are claims about 'ideal', act-founded existences of some kind.

simple acts enter the universe of logical combinations. 'All simple acts are nominal' (*LU*, IIi 497; & cf. 498f).

18. Objects

Now, in Husserl's exposition all sorts of 'objects' are possible. The move from empiricism means, in principle at least, that we are not restricted to objects in sensory experience. An object is anything that arises in originally giving intuition.

This gives us the following situation. There is a sensory manifold. Husserl situates it with the aid of terms like 'primary content' and 'primary intuition' (*LU*, IIii 162, 180; *Id*, 172). Whether this has any epistemological significance is not clear. Do we 'know' individual bits of the sensory manifold, or not? Husserl expressly leaves the question unresolved. The point to bear in mind is that the 'objects' which alone allow us to speak of truth are intentions, acts of the mind rather than impositions of the body. So whether we have sensory 'knowledge' is irrelevant to the question of whether something is true or not; at most, the sensory aspect is a completion of what is already established in intentionality.

Objectivity arises in the actual intuition of generality, which sweeps away the mere manifold of the sensory. The confusion and uncertainty of sense is replaced by actual identity. This happens by an act of what Husserl calls 'ideational abstraction',

> in which, instead of the dependent moment, its 'idea', its generality, comes to consciousness and to *actual givenness*. We need this act so that rather than the manifold of single moments of one and the same kind, the kind itself, as *one and the same*, may stand before our eyes. (*LU*, IIii 162)

The paradigmatic core object, so to speak, is grounded in 'external sensory contents' (*LU*, IIii 179). But these may be quite remote. And, in any event, we have to consider a whole class of 'syntactical objectivities' or 'empty substrates'. These are, as Husserl puts it, 'derivatives of the empty Something' (*Id*, 28); and they include things like numbers and all the states of affairs (Sachverhalte) that belong to 'logic as *mathesis universalis*'.

Husserl's view of what legitimates 'syntactical objectivities' is not entirely clear. In *Experience and Judgement* he argues that they are founded in relations such as containment, 'greater than', and so on; and that relations 'are in that respect founded objects; ultimately they refer back to objects that are not relations' (*EuU*, 285). But Husserl does not make it clear whether relations are 'founded' because they can be applied to foundational objects, or whether they are themselves intrinsically capable of being foundational. This would seem to raise particular questions in the context of things like numbers. Frege's project, after all, was to show that numbers existed in a full sense, despite, or precisely because of, their 'grounding' in no more than the pure laws of thought. The further problem is that after the emergence of the set-theoretic paradoxes, and the difficulties that Frege's project encountered in Russell's paradox, arithmetic seemed anyway doomed to reliance on axioms. And axioms, or at least those of set theory, are not altogether easy to incorporate into a scheme based on absolute intuitions.

However, this difficulty only matters to the extent that Husserl is committed to a Platonistic logicism; and his later work, as we shall see, effectively abandoned claims in that direction.

19. Modification and reflection

The axiomatic and indispensable part of Husserl's doctrine of objects is his notion of grounding. What an object is, and, in particular, whether they are Platonistic or conventional, matters less than the assertion that there *are* such things, and that 'truth' is a fabric woven from them. This entails certain crucial interdicts, which we can best see in Husserl's discussion of 'modification'.

Modification, as we noted, is the procedure by which the phenomenologist disengages him or herself from the fact of judging, which is a contingent and ad hoc matter, and enters the realm of pure objective intuition.

> To every judgement belongs its modification, an act which merely *represents* what the judgement *asserts* [für wahr hält], i.e. which makes objective [gegenständlich hat] without any decision as to truth or falsehood. (*LU*, IIi 480 – my emphasis)

The most interesting kind of modification is called by Husserl 'qualitative' or 'conforming'. This modification suspends the existential positing present in a judgement of experience (its 'quality'), but without affecting the 'material' of the judgement, i.e. its objective core (*LU*, IIi 484f). The result is that qualitative modification brings us back to the things that make truth true.

This is only possible, of course, because there are such cores of objectivity to return to. This shows itself, among other things, in the fact that you only return once, so to speak. Once you have reached bedrock, any further reflection on your intellectual position ceases. Qualitative modification is complete with the founding intuition, and the suspension of any 'positing' of or 'belief' in the external object. Qualitative modification is 'not iterable', says Husserl:

> Once 'belief' has turned into 'mere representation', the most we can do is re-

turn to belief; but a modification which repeats and continues itself in the
same sense does not exist. (*LU*, IIi 487)

Now, 'qualitative modification' is important because of its proximity to
the centre of all phenomenological methodology. It is the ladder down
which we climb to reach the 'things themselves', the foundations of our
world. But it imposes significant restrictions on what is permissible to logic
and to *reflection*.

In the *Cartesian Meditations*, Husserl uses 'reflection' in connection
with the phenomenological epoché. In certain respects, though, reflection
in the traditional sense is precisely what Husserl is ruling out. This applies
in particular to the notion, familiar since Leibniz, that reflection is the
observation of the intellect by the intellect. In the *'Monadology'*, for
example, Leibniz defines human beings precisely in terms of their capacity
to perform 'reflexive acts', and to consider 'what are called Me, substance,
soul, spirit, in a word, immaterial things and truths' (§ 5).

In Husserl's scheme, however, observation of the intellect, as such, is
impossible. 'Truth' attaches to objects of one kind or another; the 'acts' of
the mind are primarily the 'intuitions' within which these objects arise.
Those intuitions, then, constitute the proper and indeed only content of
complex statements. The mind *does* do more than receive intuitions, of
course: it forms judgements, commits itself to existential positings, and the
like. But these activities cling strictly to the intuitions, and have no 'existence' in their own right. In that respect, there is nothing in the cognitive
activities of the mind to observe. Obviously I can 'observe' intuitions related to the mind; indeed, I can observe my own state of mind in terms of
intuitions; but those are always already objects, not subjects.

Husserl makes two principal points about this. In the first place, the 'I' is
phenomenologically invisible. Whenever I observe something, he argues, I
am 'consumed by' ('aufgehen in') the observation. All I am conscious of is
the content of the observation, not of 'myself' as involved in it (unless, of
course, I am observing myself, but then I am still not visible to myself *as
observer*).

> If we, so to speak, live in the act in question, if we are consumed for example in
> the perceptive observation of an appearing process, or in a play of fantasy, in
> the reading of a fairy story, in the carrying out of a mathematical proof etc.,
> then there is no sign of the I as a point of relation for the completed act. (*LU*,
> IIi 376)

This invisibility is equally apparent in the phenomenon of 'representations of representations' (*LU*, IIi 486-8). One of the things that qualitative
modification is not, says Husserl, is a representation of a representation.
Qualitative modification suspends an element of the judgement; the other

adds something to it. Husserl's example is introspective awareness: I represent to myself that I am representing something. Is this either a recovery of some foundational level, or an observation of the subject? In Husserl's terms, it is neither. It is simply an additional intuition; another 'object', namely a representation of something, appears in view. It is, so to speak, as though I painted a painting of a painting. The object on the first painting is not recovered more truthfully; and neither is the activity of painting; we simply have another, rather more complex, object.

We shall consider shortly what the wider implications of this are. For the moment, let us bear two things in mind. First, Husserl is making a quite concrete point: namely, that modality is not part of his logical universe. The argument is primarily concerned with questions not about introspection, but about the nature of logical truth. The 'I as a point of relation' is, so to speak, the system, or the possible world, within which the statements attached to it are true. Husserl, by excluding any explicit dealings with this reference point, is insisting that for the purposes of logic statements are either true or not true, forever. Relativising them to a particular moment is not an option interesting to logic. As we have seen, expressions such as 'it is true that' (which, in this context, is probably equivalent to modal operators such as 'possibly') are precisely the ones that Husserl wishes to 'modify out' of his universe.

The interesting point, which we shall be developing, is Husserl's very close identification of this procedure with a 'metaphysics of the I' (*LU*, IIi 361), which includes the psychologists' assimilation of truth to individual cognitive acts. Husserl's project, as we have seen, is the extirpation of the practical from the logical. Modification, characteristically, is a 'neutralising' (*LU*, IIi 490), a procedure by means of which the judgement, as individual event, is eliminated (*LU*, IIi 468). The notion of reflection as individualistic introspection is, perhaps, one which can be traced in predecessors like the psychologists or, more remotely, Romantic philosophy. But Husserl's association of modality with empirical individuality represents a distinct tactical move.

20. Leibniz

Husserl's basic position, then, is that there are founding verities of some sort. They consist in simple intuitions which emerge in elementary apophansis. Those intuitions, though (or precisely because of being) ideal, are what constitutes 'objectivity'; and merely contingent or pragmatic events, *including* the procedures of ratiocination itself, are confined to the 'subjective'. 'Truth' attaches to propositions insofar as they can be derived from 'objective' foundations.[35]

This has quite distinct effects on Husserl's cosmology. They may be identified through his use of Leibniz. Leibniz, said Husserl, was the philosopher to whom he stood closest (*LU*, I 219); and in his later work he adopted the terminology of the *monad* (e.g. *CM*, 69ff.).

Leibniz, as is well known, was the philosopher of 'possible worlds'. The point of this is roughly as follows. The actually existing world seems to be a place of irredeemable contingency. Of anything that happens, we can ask why that should have happened and not some other thing. Parallel to this, however, we can conceive of contexts where any event stands in precise relation to other events. The natural sciences have the ambition to sketch such contexts. Before any science applies itself to the actual world, it attempts to construct its own internal world of regularity and predictability where things happen in uniform order. In certain respects, whether any particular science succeeds in predicting the *actual* course of events is secondary. The first fundamental is that its predictions should be uniform and internally consistent with each other. Such a science (it is conjectured) would take the form of a closed system, composed of a finite number of elementary, 'simple' atoms, and an infinite number of entitities 'composed' from them according to rules of combination.

Without this regularity, a science is no use even if it *does* fit with the facts. Astrology, perhaps, is precisely such a non-science. What matters is not its pragmatic successes, which may be considerable, but its internal lack of rigour. Without that rigour, astrology is not even a *possible* account of the world.

A 'possible world', by contrast, is precisely a uniform account of the world, or a part of it, closed under some consistent set of principles. 'Possible', here, means as much as 'conceivable'; and conceivability embraces far more than the finity of what is actually the case now. Leibniz speculates that

> there is an infinity of possible ways of creating the world according to the different designs that God could form, and that each possible world depends on certain archaic or teleological designs by God which are proper to it, i.e. on certain free primitive axioms [quelques decrets libres primitifs], conceived *sub ratione possibilitatis*, or laws of the general order of this possible universe to which they are appropriate [auquel elles conviennent] and of which they determine the notion, together with the notions of all the individual sub-

35 This would seem to be similar to Kripke's theory of 'grounding' in 'Outline of a Theory of Truth' (1975). It also excludes things excluded by Kripke, e.g. circular or self-referential statements. In Husserl's terms, beliefs or actualities are logically vacuous; so statements involving such elements are not capable of founding others. In Kripkean terms, ungroundable statements have no truth value.

stances which have to appear in this same universe. (To Arnauld, June 1686; Gerhardt 2.51)

The pragmatic success of the possible world is entirely secondary. We may not, as things stand, be able to account very successfully for the actual world. But this does not mean that the actual world is *genuinely* beset by contingency. It merely means that the descriptive schemes we have managed so far have not been very successful. So we can conjecture that we *might* devise a 'possible world' to account for the actual world comprehensively, perhaps if we had limitless conceptual resources, or if other fortuitous restrictions were lifted. In any event, we can say that the actual world is a realisation of some closed systematic account of the kind conjectured. It is, in other words, a realisation of some possible world.

So the contingency of the actual lies not in its disorderliness, which is only apparent. It lies, rather, in the choice of *that particular* possible world rather than any other. Why, in Leibniz's terms, did God not choose some other one of the infinitely many possible worlds at his disposal?

Leibniz's answer, as is well known, is that God chose the best possible world to actualise (e.g. *Principes de la Nature et de la Grace*, §10). That, perhaps, is a matter of opinion. But the crucial point, to which we shall be returning, is that Leibniz (and Husserl) see contingency as residing in the choice *between* worlds, rather than in the events within them. The reason why worlds cannot allow internal contingency is that they all have to obey the rules of consistent formation 'proper' to them. Leibniz has various celebrated formulations to emphasise this. In particular, he says that monads (which mirror the structure of their world) are 'windowless'. Nothing – i.e. no contingent external intervention – enters or leaves them. Like components in a great machine, they simply perform the rationality vested in them. Free spaces, where discontinuity or unpredictable change take place, occur only outside worlds, beyond the frontiers of the regular universe.

The correlative to this is the crucial doctrine of internal differences (e.g. 'Monadology',§9). In this doctrine, things are differentiated, or individuated, not by extrinsic non-rational things like matter, but by laws of specification. Individuals, in this scheme, are derived from elementary atoms combined according to the rules of composition. In that respect, any individual is describable according to generalities and laws; 'each possible individual of any world contains in its notion the laws of its world' ('Remarks on a letter from Arnaud', Gerhardt, 2.40). What Leibniz means to exclude by this doctrine is any notion that individuation results from matter and contingency – specifically, from time and space.[36]

36 See my *German Philosophy*, 15, for more on this.

The ultimate aim of this doctrine is the subjugation, so to speak, of time. God foresees all things because everything is but the realisation of a possible world, closed under a homogeneous system of rationality (*Theodicy*, §360). 'The present is great with the future'; all things are related with a 'perfect connection'. For God, time is of no concern, since he is able to calculate all combinations, and envisage all events, in an instant. We are in a different condition because of the burdens of physical and sensory existence. Owing to those restrictions, our knowledge, though it extends throughout the infinity of our world, is 'confused' (*Principes* §13); and to us the complexities of the universe only unfold in the sensory medium of time.[37]

21. Monadology

Husserl enlists Leibniz's term 'monad' to develop the cosmology of possible worlds (*CM*, 69). The monad should be seen in terms of *monadic systems*. A monadic system is a theory, or a language closed under rules of inference.[38] It is more than a purely abstract concept, in that it is ontologically founded. That is to say, not all of its sentences have equal weight. Some of its sentences are atomic and intuitively certain, and they form the basis from which all the other sentences are derived. A monad is, so to speak, a theory with a finite number of privileged axioms – the atomic intuitions. In accordance with this, the system thus has a semantic and ontological commitment: the monad is not merely consistent, it is *true*.

The interest of monadic 'possible worlds' is that they can express things about existence without needing to be *actually correct* in a pragmatic sense. The monadic system is modally neutral. If (with Husserl) we regard modality as something essentially pragmatic, involving (for example) the *assertion* that such-and-such is the case, then a monadic, non-pragmatic system can dispense with modality.

Within monads, the pragmatic is uniformly un-asserted. Monads are modally homogeneous internally, and sentences within them are modally neutral with respect to each other (i.e. it is not the case that some sentences are necessary, others possible, etc.). This neutrality only disappears if we, so to speak, want to climb out of our monad into another system. This *does* happen every time we venture into pragmatic worlds, for these constitute different systems. Once there, we then evaluate our original one. For example, the assertion that such-and-such is the case is an assertion about a

---

37 'On pourroit connoitre la beauté de l'univers dans chaque ame, si l'on pouvoit deplier tous ses replis, qui ne se developpent sensiblement qu'avec le temps' (ibid.). See Gilles Deleuze, *Le Pli*, for more on this.
38 See above, ch.3; also Boolos & Jeffrey, 106.

sentence in a monad, from the vantage point of another system (cf. *EuU*, 364).

The expression 'possible worlds' indicates the modal neutrality of monads. They are neither 'actually true' nor 'actually false'; they are simply not impossible.

In the first place, this withdrawal into a de-modalised world is (in Husserl's eyes) a matter of philosophical neatness. It is a way of excluding as many irrelevant considerations as possible. The most irrelevant and most disturbing consideration of all is the consideration of actuality. Only if we exclude it as a starting point can we hope to develop a truly 'scientific' approach. Historically, this rigorous de-actualisation starts with Descartes' method of doubt about the universe of natural convictions; and only with this radicalism did rigorous modern science become possible (*Krisis*, 83).

Husserl's own method, the *epoché*, is a continuation of Cartesian doubt. It systematically converts facts (the *pragmata*) into possibilities:

> We transfer, so to speak, our real perception into the realm of unrealities, of the as-if, which the pure possibilities supply us with, purified of anything that binds us to this fact or to any other fact whatever. (*CM*, 72)

Beyond this, however, the possible world, the monad, has a positive ontological status. This is because of Husserl's principle of foundation: there are foundations, and they lie in the primitive atomic intuitions, not in 'experience'. Truth, ultimately, *only* happens with the aid of those foundations; and in that respect the intuitive input into possible worlds guarantees their status. Modal assertions that 'such-and-such *is* the case' are, in Husserl's account, at a twofold remove from the foundational level. The foundational level, what Husserl calls the 'primordial form' (Urform), is characterised by 'the most simple certainty' (*EuU*, 110). These are the apophantic elements, the ideal objects in their primordial emergence. Husserl also describes this level as 'pre-predicative' (*EuU*, 111). Being pre-predicative, of course, this 'simple certainty' cannot be described as modal either (modality is a property of judgements, not of objects).

Predication, if we consider this as a derivative manoeuvre rather than as primordial apophantic predication, destroys this simplicity. In Husserl's phrase, the initial certainty becomes 'split' (zwiespältig). The certainty has become a judgement with two components – subject and predicate. And because of this, it is 'broken by doubt' (*EuU*, 110).

This level, then, is the level of the epoché – the level at which foundational atoms become combined in sythesising operations of the understanding, subject, however, to a general 'doubt'. They have lost primordial certainty, and they anticipate confirmation in a pragmatic necessity. Their own modal status is entirely uncommitted, though doubt, if we understand it as 'possibility', does represent an initial 'modalisation of the primordial form' (*EuU*, 111).

The final, assertoric stage represents a 'decision', and a 'spontaneous engagement by the I' (*EuU*, 110). In other words, the initial emergence of the object, and then its entry, with predication, into logical space (though only in the modally neutral form of doubtful possibility), is overtaken by activities which, logically and ideally, have nothing to do with the primordial foundations. The ego, so to speak, appropriates something to its interests; but the two (ego and object) are ontologically distinct; the result is a fundamental 'modification' of the primordial condition.

This derivative and almost secondary status of the assertoric is emphasised by Husserl's account of predicates such as 'is real' or 'exists'. These predicates are attached to sentences, he says, rather than to objects. A house, for example, is not 'determined' any further by having 'reality' attributed to it (*EuU*, 364). So the correct grammar would be, not 'this red house is real', but 'the sentence, "this is a red house" is real'. The 'object' house, as an intuition, is always real ('every class of objects is a class of realities' – *EuU*, 365); the question here is whether sentences about it are real, empirically based ones or not. But, of course, such empiricality is never more than a local 'co-positing' by an interested I; for the phenomenologist, the interesting aspects of truth lie much deeper.

In this respect, the actual, empirical levels of factual necessity are secondary. Husserl compares phenomenology with geometry, which has no interest in 'methodically establishing' the actual chalk lines on the blackboard:

> Geometry and phenomenology as sciences of pure essence make no ascertainments about real existence. This is related to the fact that clear fictions provide data that are not only just as good, but to a large extent better than the incidents of actual perception and experience. (*Id*, 153)

This all serves to confirm the superiority of the world of possibility over that of actuality:

> The old ontological doctrine that the cognition of 'possibilities' must precede that of realities, when properly understood and properly applied, is in my view a great truth. (*Id*, 159)

22. The elementary disjunction of form and content

Husserl's philosophy says that the world is twofold: there are objects, and there are combinations of objects; or, there is content, and there is form. The crucial point is: these are disjoint. No content can ever be form, and no form can ever be content. Further: philosophy has to account for both form and content at the same level of elementarity. Neither can come first, because neither can be derived from the other (as they are disjoint).

From this all else follows. In the first place, objects may not be allowed to precede forms; forms cannot be derived from objects. 'Nominalism', for example, or psychologism, or any kind of naturalism, are ruled out because they fail to account for form. In naturalism, the processes of the understanding are psychological or conventional. But, in Husserl's view, that makes such processes *objects*, not *forms*; so the essential *formal* element of the world is omitted.

In the second place, no object can be originally derived from form; purely formal variations do not generate new objects. This, perhaps, is the really critical point. The first thing is that all 'objects' are of equal standing, regardless of their 'formal' components. The distinction between 'real' objects and objects 'in the mind' is either a modal one, and as such a result of different combinatory forms. Or it is a matter of different objects; the intention 'centaur', for example, is a different intention, embedded in a nexus of different intentions, from the intention 'horse'. This is not, in other words, an *ontological* distinction. It is a pragmatic one, explicable in terms of differing formal constellations of objects. This is why, first, the distinction between 'external' and 'internal' phenomena is not a fundamental one; and, as part of that, there is no metaphysical mileage to be got out of traditional epistemology's distinctions between 'subject' and 'object'.

Further, forms can never become contents (this principle is close to Frege's ideas; see chapter 2, §20). This is the basis of Husserl's notion of reflection. The cognitive 'I' is not distinct from its contents; there is nothing 'in' the cognitive 'I' that can become an object of reflection. Even if, as an explanatory metaphor, we talk about 'acts' emanating from the 'I', this entity can never be presented as something, let alone some kind of agent, that we can inspect. Everything that is separable from my momentary intentions is either another object, or it is the abstract elementary form *unity* – and that can never become an independent object in its own right. So to talk about reflecting on an 'I' which, as Leibniz puts it, 'adds something to the objects of sense' (Gerhardt, 6.488), is in Husserl's view entirely misleading. In Husserl's terms,

> . . . if we confine the purely psychic I to its phenomenological content, then it reduces to a unity of consciousness, i.e. to the real complex of experiences which we (each of us for his own I) partly find present in us with evidence, and, for the rest, assume with good reasons. So the phenomenologically reduced I is nothing distinct [nichts Eigenartiges], which sways over the manifold of experiences; it is simply identical with its own relational unity. (*LU*, IIi 353)

So the phenomenological method consists in resorting neither to explicit objects (particular privileged entities such as 'laws of thought', or whatever), nor to implicit ones (the synthesising acts of consciousness), but to segments where everything is taken precisely as it 'gives' itself in a unity of consciousness. This is the purpose of phenomenology's modal reduction to possibility. Possibility leaves all objects and all forms untouched; what it ensures is that the modal judgements which arise from importing another world context – the interests of the pragmatic I – are suspended. Furthermore, this suspension in possibility works for moments of intense practical action just as much as it does for abstract scientific contemplation. There is no obstacle to phenomenologically 'reducing', say, the consciousness of a moment of crisis; all the conceived dangers remain; the only essential is that I should bracket out my judgement *now*, in another 'world', on whether the dangers conceived then were real or imagined.

23. Immanence

We can try to summarise the situation as follows. Every segment of consciousness forms a whole in which content and form are distinct but not separable. Form, at its most elementary level, is the 'unity' within which consciousness is alone possible; but this unity is not conceivable apart from the things that it unifies. Content, at its elementary level, consists of objective intuitions; but these intuitions only appear in logical, formal space (the 'unity' of form). This could be described as a rule of inseparability; it says that things may only appear consistently with form, i.e. in a homogeneous logical space. This, roughly, is a version of Kantianism.

Beyond this, however, Husserl also has what we could term a rule of disjunction, which says that form can only be filled with content, not with itself. There is nothing 'in' form that could ever be converted to content. The only aspects of form that *seem* to be 'objectifiable' – judgements, for example, or affirmations – are actually fresh objects in their own right. If, for example, I say something about a judgement I have just formed, I am no longer forming the judgement, I am saying something about the intuition 'judgement I formed'. I am, so to speak, reporting on an event inside my head; but I am no longer involved in the judgement itself. In another terminology, I am mentioning it, but not using it.

The actual logical categories which serve to combine objects can never be objects themselves. The most important is the category 'to be'.[39] To be, as

39 *LU*, IIii 139. The rest of the list is not entirely enlightening, since it seems to contain elements of first-order logic such as quantification ('Allheit'), negation and conditional ('Grund, Folge') alongside 'number' ('Anzahl'), which goes a good deal further.

we have noted, adds nothing to the object of which it is predicated. To the extent that we can talk about a category of this kind at all, we have to abstract not from the 'acts' (*scilicet*, sentences) in which these categories appear, but from the objects which appear in them. 'Not in these acts as objects, but in the objects of these acts do we find the abstractive foundation for realising such concepts.' To put it another way: categories such as 'to be' are merely shorthand for ways in which things can appear in logical space. They are, in another expression he uses, merely 'derivatives of the general notion "something"'. Husserl seems to think they can all be reduced to the general notion of unity.[40] So although they are essential for the appearance of things in consciousness, they are not themselves convertible into things that can appear. Meanwhile the sense of 'to be' in an everyday sense is only derivable from the individual pragmatic nexus in which each such judgement arises: from the objects which 'found' the judgement, in other words, not from the forms they assume in it.

For phenomenological method, the whole thing can be expressed in terms of what Husserl calls *immanence*. Immanent analysis observes the phenomena of consciousness in terms of the objects that are there, not in terms of the objects that might be there. The objects that might be there are 'transcendent', in the sense that they exceed the limits of the consciousness being reflected on. Most obviously, transcendent objects are 'real things'; but logical objects are also transcendent if they are conceived as real parts of an active I.

24. Truly existent objects

Husserl's principle of immanence allows him to make claims about 'existence' which would otherwise sound rather fanciful. 'The real' *transcends* the logical space deployed by consciousness and the intuitions admissible in it. It stands in relation to 'truth' as the chalk marks on the blackboard do to the geometer's proof – i.e. it is purely external, pragmatic, illustrative. To determine 'truth' we have to abandon the 'real' and look in the realm of the immanent and the ideal. As we have noted, 'to be', the logical copula 'is', is for Husserl a logical category, something within intuitional space. So, if we are looking for 'things' that 'are', we are perfectly entitled to proceed from within; and in that sense, 'existence' can be treated as an immaterial, logical thing, rather than as a pragmatic material one.

For Husserl, accordingly, the paradigmatic 'object' becomes the ideal *species* (which is specified by predication) rather than the real *individual*

---

40 Which would give us non-contradiction, and thence, arguably, the combinatorial resources of propositional logic. See *LU*, I 110ff. on theoretical unity, consistency, and so on.

(which is individuated by matter). Husserl calls species 'general objects':

> Anyone who has become accustomed to understand Being only as 'real' Being, and to understand objects only as real objects will find our talk of general objects and their Being perverse; on the other hand, nobody will find this talk objectionable who simply takes it as an index for the validity of certain judgements, namely those which deal with numbers, sentences, geometrical formations, etc., and who now asks himself whether here as elsewhere the title 'object that truly is' ['wahrhaft seiender Gegenstand'] cannot be attributed to them as a correlative of the validity of the judgement. (*LU*, II 101)

In other words, objects that can be specified from intuitions, consistently with the homogeneity of logical space, 'truly are'. Husserl regards this kind of 'true being' as fully equivalent to 'existence'. 'The ideal objects . . . truly exist' (*LU*, IIi 124). Even entities that are barred from logical space by consistency (such as 'round square') can be said to have 'existence', understood as 'Being in the "world" of ideal meanings' (*LU*, IIi 326).

The wider meaning of 'existence', then, for Husserl, is immanent logical possibility. In developed intentional contexts, of course, the abstract possibility of notions like 'round square' is soon ruled out; but the 'existence' of the primitive intuitions ('round' and 'square') remains foundational. Ultimately, it is from *this* level of existence that more complex levels derive their status. What Husserl calls the 'existential law' ('Existenzialgesetz' – *LU*, IIi 330) is the procedure by which inferential operations such as 'complication' and 'modification' generate further 'existences' of 'deductively secure validity' (*LU*, IIi 331). For Husserl, it would seem, existence follows from theorem-hood in a deductive system.

From certain aspects, Husserl is even prepared to claim the *equivalence* of the two:

> . . . not only are 'object in true being' and 'rationally positable' equivalent correlatives, but so are 'truly positable' and 'object positable in some original perfect rational thesis'. (*Id*, 296)

Pragmatically, it would seem that most 'objects', at least in everyday life, are far from being 'rationally positable', or theorems in some deductive system – and in that respect Husserl's claimed equivalence seems hopelessly strong. But Husserl regards this as something to which 'science' can at least *aspire*.

> In principle (in the a priori of absolute essential generality) the *idea of a possible consciousness*, in which the object itself is graspable in an originary and perfectly adequate way, corresponds to *every 'truly being' object*. Conversely, if this possibility is guaranteed, *eo ipso* the object truly is. (*Id*, 296)

In other words, if the object 'is', then it must be perfectly graspable in a possible world of logically ordered intuitions. That includes not merely mathematical species such as numbers and geometrical forms, but 'every particular object that comes to consciousness in the manifold of concrete experiences' (*Id*, 296). So, the things of our world are in principle exhaustively convertible into theorem-hood. And, conversely, everything that is in our world, everything of which it is predicable that it 'is the case', is included in the totality of ideal objects:

> If we think of the totality of such ideal objects, we thereby have the totality of the pure 'essences' [Wesen], of the 'essences' [Essenzen] of all ideally possible individual objectivities (existences). (*LU*, IIi 252)

25. Perception

Now, obviously there has in practice to be some restriction on this. What, in ontological or epistemological terms, is the position of things we do not know as strictly deducible theorems?

This is a question which also arises within Leibniz's system, and as his answer is simpler and more direct than Husserl's, it may be helpful to give it first. As we noted, God's universe is characterised by 'perfect order' (Gerhardt, 6.606). That is to say, it is a 'possible world' in the sense of being a closed deductive theory. (It is also, according to Leibniz, the best of the possible worlds. That is not something that concerns Husserl, though it will concern us.) Now, if it is closed in this sense, it must in principle be possible to know all of it. God (for Leibniz) knows everything in the world, all at once. We, however, do not; or, more precisely, we do not know everything *clearly and distinctly*. Each monad (mind) is a mirror of the whole universe; but the knowledge reflected in that mirror is 'perspectival' (Gerhardt, 6.616), i.e. it sees clearly what is nearby, but the more distant things are indistinct. Also, perspective means that things that are, in themselves, fixed identities, 'look' different from the different standpoints of different monads.

Leibniz's comparison is with our perception of the noise of waves at the seaside. As we walk along the beach, he says, we hear *all* the sounds that the wave makes as it falls. Nonetheless, we hear them 'confusedly'; we cannot *discern* one sound from another, and it all sounds like a great confused roar (Gerhardt, 6.604). This is the inevitable consequence of our intellectual inadequacies. We need time to separate the noises from one another; if, so to speak, the wave fell in infinitely slow motion, we might be able to cope; but as it is, we simply have a confused and indistinct perception.

The plausibility of Leibniz's account rests at least partly on its importation of God. The crucial component of this doctrine is that 'the world' is an ideal, theory-like structure – a 'possible world'. But we do not, cannot ever, know it that way, except in very limited areas. So how do we know that the world, or even any part of it, is like that? For Leibniz, it is an axiom; and this he expresses by saying that *God* knows the world like that. Furthermore, since God is absolutely different from us, the fact of our 'confusion' poses no particular difficulty. God is conceptually infinite, and is thereby able to compute everything computable at a stroke. We are slower, and only manage to compute minimal amounts at any time. And this distinction – effectively, our slowness – is placed there by God as an external fiat; it does not change what happens in the universe, but it slows down our capacity to know it. In Leibniz, the distinction between God and humanity is a kind of axiom of materiality; and it has a roughly equivalent role to that of matter in the Thomistic system.

But without this absolute difference, how do we account for 'confusion'? What is it? Is it, so to speak, internal to the system? Or is it external, an 'accident' or a 'contingency'? In that case, where does it come from, and are the explanatory boundaries of the system quite as comprehensive as, say, Husserl's doctrine of 'objects' and 'existence' suggests? *Are* there events and influences that he has left out, and indeed can never reach? If there are, the system suddenly seems incomplete in a rather damaging way.[41]

Husserl is aware of this problem, though seemingly in a rather indistinct way, and his solution is not clear. One obvious place that it surfaces is in the difference between purely conceptual objects and the objects of real life. The one group seems to be much more 'distinct' than the other. A carefully defined geometrical form, at least in Husserl's view, is more precise, say, than a more pragmatic notion like 'tree'. Husserl calls the one 'exact', and the other 'vague' (*LU*, I 61; IIi 88; etc.). But why *should* there be this difference? After all, the distinction between 'purely conceptual' and 'empirical' in this context would seem to breach the rule of phenomenological immanence. Husserl declares that the problem is 'a task that has not yet been seriously taken up'; and leaves it at that (*LU*, IIi 246).[42]

More persistently, the problem arises in the question of *perception*. If knowledge, pre-eminently, is a matter of species knowledge, then what role does the experience of real individual things play? Husserl is as coquet-

41 It may not be necessary to define the boundaries of one's system. Wittgenstein, for one, thought it was not. But things get difficult when entities that can *obviously* not be explained within it present themselves. With God's instauration of human conceptual inadequacy, the Leibnizian account provides a boundary and a view of what happens outside it. Furthermore the notion of the *best* of possible worlds also identifies an area of 'meta-systemic' discursivity. Husserl has neither of these things; and both cause him serious difficulties.
42 Husserl himself uses the phrase *clara et distincta*. See, e.g., *CM*, 85.

tish with the notion of perception as he is with that of existence. He suggests, for example, that 'an extension of the concept of perception beyond
the bounds of sensuality' is called for (*LU*, IIii 5). The distinction between
imagination and perception, he claims, is 'an *internal* difference between
acts' (*LU*, IIii 116) – not one, that is to say, which turns on whatever happens to be the case, contingently, in an 'external' world.

Husserl's actual analysis of perception occupies the long chapter six of
Logical Investigation VI. It takes two approaches. One is the notion that
perception is a 'fulfilment' ('Erfüllung') of some logical state of affairs.
'Meaning this fulfils itself in perception' (*LU*, IIii 20). In other words, you
'intend' something, and the sensory perception of what you intend then
'fulfils' the intention. To some extent, this may be an echo of Frege's notion
of 'satiation'; but, even so, this does not help us greatly. What is this object
that is doing the fulfilling? Or: what is the *logical* status of an 'external' entity? A real object, Husserl defines, is 'a possible object of a simple perception' (*LU*, IIii 151).

The second element in Husserl's approach is a perspectivalism similar to
the kind Leibniz uses. Husserl calls it 'toning', or 'shading' ('Abschattung')
– the metaphor is that intense colours overlay others, or that the 'front' side
of things gets in the way of the back (*LU*, IIii 117). Toning happens along a
continuous scale towards an 'ideal limit' of complete fulfilment. With complete fulfilment we achieve

> the genuine *adaequatio rei et intellectus*: the objective is *really 'present'*, or
> *'given'* as what is intended; no partial intention which might be lacking its ful-
> filment [e.g. the 'back' of the object] is implied. (*LU*, IIii 118)

As we noted, this is most obviously feasible in the case of intellectual
objects like mathematical entities. But Husserl emphasises that it can apply
to anything. In this 'absolute plenitude of content',

> The object is not merely indicated [gemeint], but is in the strictest sense *given*,
> just as it is indicated and set as one with the indicating; beyond that it is imma-
> terial whether we are dealing with an individual or a general object . . . (*LU*,
> IIii 122)

The difficulty with this is that the 'giving' appears still to be a basically 'internal' matter. Perception is, so to speak, the delightful vision of what you
intended all along; but if there is no material difference between this and
imagination, except perhaps in the intensity of the delight, then what is the
status, if any, of an external world?

We shall return to this problem.

26. Orders of compossibility; the horizon

Let us return, then, to the question facing Husserl's monadological ration-alism. If the weight of 'truth', and indeed of 'existence', falls so heavily on ideal intuitions, then what are we to make of the messy and informal world of real things, spread before us in time and space? Can Husserl account for anything beyond abstract levels of theory formation?

Husserl characterises his work as 'phenomenology'. In the first instance, he does this in order to emphasise his 'bracketing out' of real being. The contents of consciousness, the totality of the experienced world, remain as they are, but without any commitment to their 'reality'. They are reduced, in other words, to appearances – 'mere phenomena' (e.g. *CM*, 22).

This disqualification of experience as merely phenomenal immediately raises the question: what, then, is not appearance? Where is true Being? We have already seen Husserl's answer: true Being lies in essential intuitions and their combination into unitary logical fields.

This answer, however, raises the next question: what about the non-logical, the phenomenal? Why, and in what way, is it distinct from the formal purity of 'essence'?

Leibniz's answer (if we may call him to our aid again) has the virtue of straightforwardness. The only 'substances' (entities with true being) are the souls, or monads. These substances perceive the world; they are the 'mirrors of the universe'. What they perceive is not substantial: it is merely phenomenal. The phenomena are not arbitrary, of course, because the universe being reflected is perfectly ordered by God. So the perceived world is phenomenal, indeed, but each phenomenon is 'well founded': 'all these bodies and everything that we attribute to them are not substances but only well founded phenomena' (Gerhardt, 3.622). In other words, the pheno-mena do adhere to logical order (perception is defined by Leibniz as 'the representation of the manifold in unity'). Indeed, they also adhere to the absolute logical order of the 'possible world'. But that is only known to God. Created souls, by and large, are restricted to appearances, i.e. the order of the *empirical* as opposed to the order of *necessity* (Gerhardt, 3.623).

The order of the empirical, and of appearances, is the order of time and space. Time and space form the display cabinet, so to speak, in which appearances arrange themselves. It is precisely because they are in time and space that they are appearances; absolute logical order need not resort to such devices. But direct insight into that order is only given to 'spirits', who are created in the image of God; and most of the time they too are restricted to the empirical (3.623). Perception through empiry is characterised by perspective: appearances appear differently to different observers; essences remain identical and constant.

Perspective happens against the coordinates of time and space. Time and space display the absolute order of the universe in a way that is perceivable by lower minds. They are themselves *not* essential, or substantial; but they serve to render, crudely, the world's logical articulation. 'Space, far removed from being a substance, is not even a being. It is an order, like time, an order of coexistence, just as time is an order between existences that are not together' (Gerhardt, 3.622).

This order of time and space is an order of *continuity*. The continuum, Leibniz defines, is not real; and in it the whole precedes the parts (3.622). On one level, this is Leibniz's answer to the ontological difficulties raised by the infinite divisibility of the continuum (abstractly conceived, the parts are not real; though any real thing will situate itself in the continuum). In our context, the notion that time and space are an *unreal frame* in which everything is situated is the principal point.

In many respects, Husserl takes over this scheme fairly directly. In the *Ideas*, he expresses it in terms of his distinction between immanence and transcendence (*Id*, 76f). Ideal objects, we may say, 'exist', and, moreover, they can be 'perceived' *immanently*. Husserl here calls them 'Erlebnisse', which means 'experiences', but distinguishes them from empirical experience, 'Erfahrung'. Empirical experience is the experience of things – typically, says Husserl, of *things we see*. And they are perceived only against the visual coordinates of space – in perspective, in other words.

> We perceive a thing by means of the fact that it 'shades' ['sich abschatten' – i.e. presentation perspectivally] in accord with all the determinants that 'really' and properly 'fall' into perception. *An 'Erlebnis'* [i.e. an immanent or ideal perception] *does not shade.*

This kind of perspectival perception, meanwhile, is associated with perception by an I. Perspective, obviously (as Leibniz says) is relative to the standpoint of an observer. For Leibniz, this inessential differentiation is one of the characteristics of merely human, 'confused' knowledge. It is also worth noting that Kant's description of time and space as *subjective* forms of 'our' sensuality follows the same theme (*Gesammelte Schriften* VIII 391n.). For Kant, indeed, space could not even be treated as a form of display appropriate to lower minds; as he argued throughout the critical enterprise, it was not reducible to the 'logical' in any respect. The whole force of his argument on, for example, the 'orientation' question, was devoted to establishing the irreducible independence of space as a kind of subjective a priori; I cannot orientate myself without a *feeling* of right and left relative only to *my own subject* (VIII 134). We considered this earlier in relation to Heidegger.[43]

For Husserl, by contrast, perspectival I-relatedness, orientation, and so on, are at bottom *essential*:

> it is an essential necessity, and to be grasped as such in apodeictic insight, that spatial being in general for an I (for every possible I) is only perceivable in the indicated manner of giving. (*Id*, 77f)

The point would seem to be this. Perception is (for both Leibniz and Husserl) unification of the manifold. The things that can be perceived intuitively are (unless you are God) a very small proportion of the whole. The rest are displayed spatio-temporally. For Leibniz this is a contingency, an aspect of our weakness as created beings. For Husserl, however, the spatio-temporal, and its centredness on an I, are essential to 'the world'. There are no possible worlds without time and space. The standpoint of Leibniz's God is not available even as a speculation.[44]

> It is not a fortuitous idiosyncrasy of the thing, or a contingency of 'our human constitution', that 'our' perception can only get at things through mere shadows [Abschattungen] of them.

The 'I', in fact, or at least the 'phenomenologically reduced I', forms a 'unitary totality of contents' (*LU*, IIi 354). In a secular monadology, there is no transcendent divine spirit which unifies and guarantees. There is only the phenomenological ego, and that embraces in itself both the direct intuitions of 'immanent' perception and also the perspectival ones of 'things'. It cannot dispense with either; and in that sense the perspectival is essential for Husserl in a way that it is not for Leibniz. In Husserl's exposition, indeed, the centred and ordering time of the phenomenological I is itself *immanent* (*LU*, IIi 259). Time, in other words, need not breach the methodological rigour of the epoché.

With this enhanced status, however, the spatio-temporal plays much the same role for Husserl as it did for Leibniz. It forms a frame which, by being continuously divisible, can accommodate the infinity of possible things in one united structure. Husserl's term for this frame is *horizon* (*LU*, IIi 358). And, appropriating Leibniz's terminology, he talks of the 'order of coexistence', the 'order of succession', and the general principle of 'compossibility' (*LU*, IIi 260; *CM*, 76). Within these orders of possibility, the structures of measure and prediction extend not only across space (coexistence), but also across time (succession). 'Necessary coexistence' (for which Husserl uses the generalising term 'notwendiges Zusammenbestehen') is not restricted, synchronically, to space; if it happens diachronically, it is 'coexis-

---

43 See also *German Philosophy* on 'incongruent counterparts'.
44 See *Id*, 315: perspective and orientation are inescapable not only for human beings, but for God as well!

tence in extended time' (*LU*, IIi 259). In Husserl's formalisation:

> . . . a content α which contains the time determination t_0 can require [fordern] the being of another content ß with the time determination $t_1=t_0+\delta$ and, in that respect, be dependent [i.e. part of a continuing determination].

Less pompously: it is an 'essential law' that the 'conscious present makes continuing requirements of the conscious future'. Or, to put it in the famous Leibnizian formula:

> . . . each present state of a simple substance [i.e. a monad; in Husserl's terms, immanent consciousness] is naturally a consequence of its previous state, such that *the present is great with the future*. (*Monadology*, §22; my emphasis)

27. Positionality

Despite Husserl's 'idealism', the role of *matter* in his system is central. This is, perhaps, an aspect of his need to *include* contingency within the mechanism of the possible world. Possible worlds always already include space and time; they are not merely degenerate consequences of the incarnation; and consequently God, too, sees 'perspectively':

> Anything spatio-temporal is only visible [anschaubar] by means of appearances, in which it is given – must be given – 'perspectively', changing in manifold but determinate ways and thereby in changing 'orientations'. This is the case not merely for us human beings, but also for God (considered as the ideal representative of absolute cognition). (*Id*, 315)

Let us briefly follow the ramifications of this. Traditionally, we recall, time and space are 'matter'. Matter individuates the generalities of the understanding. However much I may specify, in terms of the categories of the understanding, matter is ultimately always required for the final transition into the real. For example, I may proceed from the genus 'animal' to the species 'cat', and by further specifications 'black', 'non-pedigree', and so on, to an utterly specific (or fully described, in Russellian terms) entity whose specificities are satisfied only by one creature – my cat.

So far, so good. But what happens next? This question is one of the great talking points of metaphysics. Does specification individuate? Or is there always a further, distinct step to be taken at the end? What is the status of the implied or express conclusion, 'and this, here, is my cat'? Is it merely a redundant exclamation, or is it the indispensable anchor-point of 'truth'? Kant, in one of the classical expositions of this problem (his refutation of the ontological proof), argues that it is not redundant. 'Existence' is never included in the concept of an object; existence always requires, finally, the attribution of 'position' (i.e. spatial and temporal location), and that is *out-*

side the concept.[45]

Husserl does not tackle this question directly. But the force of his argument is quite clear: the material individuation of the *thing*, as distinct from its specification, is *included* in the structure of the possible world. It is not, in other words, a window open to contingency. The monad, despite now being *essentially* spatio-temporal (which it was not in Leibniz), is still pre-established.

Husserl develops the notion of 'position', accordingly, as a structural aspect of possible worlds. It is clear that 'positioning' something, in the first instance, is indeed a transcendent act; it believes in some kind of external reality. It is, in related terms, *thetic*, or '*setzend*'. ('Setzen', which is usually rendered 'posit' in philosophical contexts, also means to 'place'. Husserl deliberately exploits the connotations setzen-posit-position.) Like all transcendence, however, positional consciousness can be 'modified' or 'neutralised', and retrieved, by epoché, into the possible world (*Id*, 242). Positionality in general, then,

> does not indicate the presence or performance of a real position; it only expresses a certain potentiality for the performance of actually positing doxic acts [i.e. acts of belief]. (*Id*, 235)

Positionality, in other words, is part of the world of *possible* being; it is not confined to the actual (*Id*, 243).

Positionality's role is not to individuate, but to structure in terms of *horizon*. Space and time, as we saw, are the dimensions of compossibility. Positionality situates and unifies the consciousness of the I. Its achievement is

> to give life [allererst lebendig machen] to the connection which all perceptions of an I, whether present or past, have by reason of their being constituted in a consciousness of time. . . (*EuU*, 208).

In that sense, particularly in Husserl's later work, time and space achieve an important primordiality over the operations of pure understanding. They supply the setting, the horizon; and only thereafter can the 'life' of experience emerge.

28. History

In effect, Husserl sees 'existence' as a possible world, systemically cohesive, and displayed against the coordinates of time and space. In this vision, nothing is finally transcendent. Transcendence is what we imagine our-

45 B 626ff. See *German Philosophy*, 46f.

selves to be dealing with in the moment of practice; but there is nothing in practice that cannot, ultimately, be 'reduced' to immanence. With that first insight, philosophy can set about a disciplined and scientific description of *everything*. And phenomenology, which has that insight, will emerge as the new 'basic science [Grundwissenschaft] of philosophy' (*Id*, 1), concerned with the establishment of 'sciences of essence' which are 'indispensable for the progress of . . . the empirical sciences' (*Id*, 34). In particular, phenomenology is the 'essential eidetic foundation of psychology and of the human sciences'.

Depending on which human science one looks at, Husserl's proposals are liable to seem extravagant. On the face of it, the notion that the empirical sciences should be able, even only potentially, to determine everything, in all dimensions of space and time, seems far-fetched. It may also seem rather unattractive. What seems worthwhile for the geometer or engineer may seem more like a nightmare to someone discussing the nature of human freedom.

It was also, indeed, rather out of line with his own contemporaries' thinking. This is most obviously the case with history. The notion that a properly disciplined and philosophically founded science of history would be able, for example, to trace the sense in which the present is great with the future is not a view that recommended itself to many at the beginning of the twentieth century. Wilhelm Dilthey, with his notion of hermeneutics as the fundamental discipline of the human sciences, or Heinrich Rickert (Husserl's predecessor at Freiburg) with his distinction between 'idiographic' and 'nomothetic' sciences, had for some time been arguing against any rule-guided determinism in history.

Husserl, clearly, was aware of this. The question was, however: how could the claims of phenomenology be weakened sufficiently to retain its credibility in areas like history, while maintaining its structure overall? The simplest answer, perhaps, would be to redraw the boundary between the immanent and the transcendent, and to give the transcendent some greater ontological dignity. But it is hard to see how this could be done without upsetting the whole project.

A better answer, perhaps, is to concentrate on the question of *foundations*. 'Truth' is founded in intuitive certainties. But are these certainties universally necessary? Could they, perhaps, be *relatively* necessary? Could we, in other words, account for contingency and discontinuity by accepting the principle of homogeneous and determined possible worlds, but regarding them as *plural*, with *different* sets of foundational intuitions?

This is the question which, in Husserl's later work, introduces the theme of *history*. As we shall see, the later work represents a very substantial derogation from the claims of the early work, and throws into sharp question the viability of the whole scheme of possibility and foundation.

29. Induction

Husserl's 'historical' approach keeps to the same theoretical structures as his earlier work. That, in the first instance, means the structures of possibility, or, more specifically, the notion of the 'horizon'.

In the later work, we find this articulated around the principle of *induction*. Husserl uses the term in its technical sense. Induction (or perfect induction, or primitive recursion) is a way of defining the notion: *proof* that some sentence is a *theorem* of some formalised system. Induction says that if something is true of the first member in a series (i.e. an enumerable set), and that if it is true of any member it is also true of that member's successor, then it is true of all members of the set. If we are talking of the set of natural numbers (non-negative integers), and wish to establish that some function is true of all of them, then we need to establish that it is true of 0 (the first member of the set of non-negative integers), and that if it is true of any member n it is also true of that member's successor $n+1$. For example, any natural number a multiplied by the sum of any two others b and c is equal to the sum of the two products ab and ac.[46] That is inductively established by showing that it is true of 0, and true of any $n+1$ if it is true of n. On the other hand, it is not true that the square of any natural number is equal to half its cube (which would be true of 2, but could not be demonstrated for 0, so we need not worry about its truth for any member's successor).

In other words, if we have strictly enumerable entities, we can use the principle of induction to establish properties that must be true of all of them. In particular, we can *anticipate* entities, into the furthest reaches of infinity. Induction says: once thus, always thus. This represents intoxicating power, even though it only works for mathematical objects of a precisely determinable kind such as numbers, geometrical figures, and so on. (It may be the case that if something is true of one cucumber, it is true of all of them; but this is not what is envisaged in 'perfect' induction.) Mathematical objects, despite their abstraction, dazzle by sheer universality. Geometry works on the moon as well as it does on the earth; and as well aeons hence as it does today. A mathematically guided technology throws its embrace around the entire universe. And the abstractness of these objects is no bar to their detailed and immediate applicability. Even music, as Husserl himself pointed out, is reducible to geometrical wave forms (*Krisis*, 38) – or, now, to the final logicality of digital code.

The notion of induction guides Husserl's later formulations of the prin-

---

46 I.e. distributivity: $a(b+c)=(a\times b)+(a\times c)$.

ciple of possibility, though it is implicit in his early work as well. It has two components: the notion of foundation, and the notion of regular inferential construction. Inductive procedures, in his view, are entirely general. 'All life rests on induction' (Kr, 55). If one thing is the case, then its successor events are also given, in a 'continuity and explicative linkage of individual experiences' (EuU, 27). And this inductive structure implicitly leads back to an 'original and foundational [original und ursprünglich] anticipation' (EuU, 28). At the same time, what is 'original' is always already an anticipation, i.e. it is always already bound into the structure it anticipates. In this respect experience is never absolutely primitive; a 'horizon' of inductive linkages already surrounds it.

> World is already such that cognition has done its work in a variety of ways; so, undoubtedly, there can be no experience in the primary-simple [erstlich-schlicht] sense of a thing experience that grasps this thing for the first time and takes cognisance of it without already 'knowing' more of it than emerges, cognitively, in the process. (EuU, 26f)

The 'work' that always precedes experience is the primordial apophantic judgement.

Experiences never come naked; they are always clothed with cognitive products.[47] And in that respect, too, they appear on a stage that is already set for their arrival. This is the 'horizon of prior validity'. The experiences step onto it as a platform that is 'still empty and devoid of determinate content' (EuU, 30); but they depend on the horizon as a reservoir of possible meanings, as a coordinate grid of logical identities. 'The horizons,' says Husserl, 'are prefigured potentialities' (CM, 47).

These horizons are not to be understood only as bare mathematical coordinates. Induction is essential to 'life' itself; and because of that the practical life of each individual is structured by it as well.

> All possibilities of the kind 'I can or could' initiate this or that series of experiences [Erlebnisreihe] – including: I can look forwards or backwards, can penetrate revealingly into the horizon of my temporal being – obviously belong with essential authenticity to my self. (CM, 105)

'Inductive' stretching out to my horizons, looking to my future and my past, seems to be the basic procedure by which I come to myself. In less technical terminology, Husserl equates induction with 'foresight' ('Voraussicht' – Krisis, 54). And it is this practical 'induction', more than its exact counterpart in mathematics, that constitutes the horizons of my real experienced world. 'Seeing and perceiving are essentially a having-myself [Selbst-haben] together with having-a-purpose [vor-haben] or having-a-

---

47 Husserl speaks, critically, of the 'ideal garments' which the exact sciences tailor for the world – Kr, 55. But the metaphor applies just as well at a level he feels more positively about.

previous-opinion [vor-meinen]' (*Kr*, 55).[48]

30. Self-pondering

The appearance of a 'self' as part of perception or truth should give us pause for thought. In terms of the original phenomenological project, the notion that there might be a practical element to the world, or that the individual agent might somehow be responsible for objective events, is sheer psychologism. Objectivity, in the original project, is part of the timeless order of logic, and has nothing to do with the acts and sensibilities of subjects.

In fact, Husserl's project *does* take a substantive turn in his later work (i.e. from the Twenties onwards); and it is only in terms of that change that Husserl's celebrated later concern with 'history' and the 'life-world' make sense.

The underlying scheme remains that of foundation and possibility. A well-formed 'world', so to speak, is one that is derived from foundational intuitions through an 'inductive' chain. In the original phenomenological project, this process was strictly formal: in other words, the inductive derivation was not important as an event in time, but only as a consistent structure. In the later work, this strict formalism is abandoned. Instead, Husserl comes to be interested in what he calls the 'genetic' question: how, by what sequence of events, did rationality take on the forms in which it presents itself. *Experience and Judgement*, for example, is offered as part of a 'genealogy of logic' (*EuU*, 1) – a preposterous phrase from the viewpoint of Husserl's early work.

There occurs, in other words, a massive devaluation of the formal methods that Husserl had originally hoped to extend from logic throughout the human sciences. Such formalism, instead of being a model, becomes itself an object of study, an objective event. Implicitly, at least, this represents a complete reversal of Husserl's earlier insistence that logic and pure consciousness are totally non-empirical. Here, the very processes of logic are, in an almost psychologistic manner, being made available as objects.

It is hard not to regard this as a retreat from the early aims. Indeed, it is more than a retreat: it is a rout, for there is virtually nothing left of the early principles except a caricature which Husserl then uses as a target for his own reproaches against the evils of the age.

Now, the reason for the devaluation of the purely conceptual, and its recasting in practice ('logical reason too is practical' – *CM*, 80), is that Huss-

48 This is clearly congruent with Heideggerian notions like 'Um-sicht', 'besorgen', and so on. The notion of the 'inductively' unified 'horizon' is imported more or less entire into *Being and Time*.

erl wishes to shift his emphasis from the structure to the foundations. As a general schema, what we now have is this. The primitive intuitions are not merely basic logical identities, they are early in time and primitive in concept. They represent, in some sense, childlike activities (Husserl uses concrete genetic examples from developmental psychology – *CM*, 80, 81, etc.). These, however, become taken up and overlaid by a process of education and training; and it is only at this second stage that the 'ideal' and the 'irreal' structures of the understanding start to appear (*CM*, 80). What the original phenomenological project took as primary, in other words, is now seen as secondary; and, by contrast, the philosopher's task becomes historical in the sense of trying to uncover the *essential primordial forms* which lie at the *beginning* of reasoning (*CM*, 82). What is more, these become recoverable through what Husserl calls 'recollection' ('Wiedererinnerung' – *CM*, 104f), an almost Platonistic anamnesis of the primitive.

What is the primitive? It is the opposite of the ideal and the objective. It is no longer the exact construction of reason, but the foundational appearance of the first intuitions. And just as reason lies in the domain of constancy and public controllability, the 'objective', so its foundations lie in *subjectivity*. Accordingly, the task of the new philosopher is not to spread the gospel of mathematical exactitude, but to tread the road back to a pristine subjectivity. This, says Husserl, is 'self-pondering' ('Selbstbesinnung'), a recovery of the Delphic γνῶθι σεαυτόν (*CM*, 161) which the new phenomenology is eminently suited to achieve:

> Every attempt to move from the historically developed sciences to a better foundation, to a better understanding of oneself in terms of sense and achievement, is a piece of self-pondering by the scientist. But there is only one radical self-pondering, and that is the phenomenological. (*CM*, 157)

At this point, then, phenomenological reflection has been applied to itself. It started by suspending any account of science as pragmatic; and now the whole notion of science, as a self-founding realm, has itself been suspended. Phenomenological reflection ends with the anamnestic recovery of a pure subjectivity behind even itself (cf. *CM*, 156). And its banner now is not the brittle ideality of scientific possibility, but – in truculent paradox – 'transcendental subjectivity' (*Kr*, 111).

31. Subjectivity

The fundamental declaration of Husserl's later work is what he calls the 'suspension of the presupposition of objectivity' in pursuit of an even more fundamental phenomenological epoché. At this stage, the whole realm of the 'ideal', the 'scientific', and the 'exact', which in the earlier work had

provided the paradigm and foundation for Husserl's whole project, are
now to be relative to the individual, pondering 'me'.

> In this abstractive restriction of experience to the realm of what is only for the
> pondering, valid me [nur für mich, den sich Besinnenden, Geltenden], lies
> already the suspension of all the idealisations, the suspension of objectivity, of
> the validity of our judgements 'for everyone', which traditional logic, orien-
> tated towards the ideal of exact determination in the sense of scientific finality,
> always tacitly presupposed as belonging to the essence of judgement. (*EuU*,
> 57)

The relativisation of 'objectivity', however, does not involve a flight
from idealism. In the strict sense, idealism means the notion that 'ideas' are
the foundational elements of reality, either as Platonic 'forms', or as mathematical or logical structures. This, as we saw, was one of the central elements of Husserl's original project. From it, probably, he now moves
away. But he retains an idealism that suspends belief in an 'external' world
as somehow prior, and, correlatively, any belief in the fundamental nature
of the mind-world distinction. In this context, the 'ego' of his later work is
beyond such distinctions.[49]

The basic distinction, now, is between subject and phenomenon. Phenomenon is everything that is knowable; subject is what knows everything,
but is never itself known. The knower recedes eternally from what he
knows.

> I, the I that performs the epoché, am not included in [the world's] objective
> arena; on the contrary, so long as I perform it with real radicality and uni-
> versality, I am excluded in principle. (*Kr*, 85)

The ego, in Husserl's terminology, may never be a 'theme' *within* the
world (*Kr*, 90). Failure to observe this principle led to the difficulties with
Descartes' original epoché, in which the ego, understood as 'soul', became
thematically available as something *in* the world (*Kr*, 88). In that respect,
Husserl regarded Descartes as a precursor of the psychologism he had so
ardently combated from the beginning. If these misunderstandings could
be cleared up, however, and if what inevitably resulted from them – the
misleading notion that the ego was, primordially, confronted with an 'outside' – was corrected, then the view of the ego as the greatest of all riddles
could be discarded (*Kr*, 89).

The properly construed ego, though, purified of any externality, was

49 Although Husserl criticises Kant for retaining 'things in themselves', if only as a 'limiting
concept' (*CM*, 88), the epoché back to a point prior to knower-known distinctions is entirely
consistent with Kant's project. It is perhaps worth noting here that the whole debate in Anglo-
American Kant commentary over the 'subjectivity' of space is based on a misunderstanding.
'Subject' and 'object' are not, either in Kant or, here, in Husserl, equivalent to 'knower' and
'known'.

still of fundamental interest to phenomenology. It is at this point that Husserl's change of position *vis-à-vis* the early work becomes visible. Irreflexivity, as we noted, was always present. The puzzles that result from a strictly irreflexive doctrine of possible worlds are, however, now resolved by an addendum: the ego is not 'thematisable' *in* the world; but it can be situated as a pure practice *outside* the world. This, straightforwardly enough, is achieved by appealing to the agent supposedly necessary for any epoché to take place. Epoché is an act; therefore there must be an actor to perform it. And in the indubitability of this epochal actor lies something utterly necessary and certain:

> I am necessary as the performer [of the epoché]. Precisely in this I find the apodeictic ground that I have been seeking, which absolutely excludes every possible doubt. However far I may take the doubt, and try to imagine that everything is doubtful or even, in truth, non-existent, it is absolutely evident that *I* must still be, as the doubter, as the one who negates everything. (*Kr*, 85)

This reasoning looks weak in the light of Husserl's own earlier objections to a literal understanding of intentional 'acts'. The obvious problem is what exactly 'I' am if I am not part of a knower-known opposition. What constitutive role does the 'ego' actually play for Husserl? We shall consider this in a moment.

But the more fundamental problem is the one afflicting all 'possible world' standpoints in metaphysics. It is one thing to devise internally consistent 'worlds' on a level of possibility; it is quite another to say anything sensible about the *actual* world of change and discontinuity. Husserl, like Wittgenstein and indeed like Heidegger, can only conceive of situating his discontinuity *outside* the formal world system. Or, to put it in terms of his 'know thyself' programme, what puts us in one system or another is the ego, and that is something that, being absolutely outside, is also absolutely irrecoverable in terms of any descriptive system. I can know that there must be something there, exercising the limitless power of its epochal negativity; but it only has that power as long as it remains undescribable. The ego is eternally elusive; and there, for Husserl, lies its positivity and its virtue. Beside this transcendental escape, the world is revealed in all its shabby phenomenality.

> In my situation of epoché over all of them – I may no longer join in. So my entire life of acts, with its experiencing, thinking, valuing and so on, remains with me, and indeed it continues, except that the thing that stood before me in it as 'the' world, as the one that existed and had value for me, has become a mere '*phenomenon*' . . . (*Kr*, 85)

But this triumph over the world is, of course, a deceptive thing. In Husserl's earlier work, logic, though visible in the world, still had a degree of foundational certainty about it. The radicalism of the final position – that anything visible, including logic and mathematics, is merely phenomenal and non-foundational – takes foundations entirely out of the realm of the rationally reviewable. There is something very abrupt about Husserl's entry into the realms of practical philosophy at this point.

32. 'Life-world'

The ego, as we saw, is not to be conceived as an empirical entity, ready situated in a world. Nonetheless, it is in some way an actor – it *must* be, for Husserl, if only because of its capacity limitlessly to suspend the phenomenal world.

But that is not, it would seem, its only active capacity. Henceforth we are to conceive of the world as, in its foundations, engendered by active subjectivity. 'Objectivity', in the guise of 'science', is something that supervenes only later. This entails a strong shift of emphasis in Husserl's attitude towards the logical.

As we noted, Husserl's original position envisaged the objective world arising in a coeval unity of form and content. In this respect, mathematical objects like numbers were not ontologically distinct from any other object arising in fundamental intuition. Within the discipline of the epoché, the world displayed itself as a perspicuous realm of direct intuitability, closed under logical rules. No modal ranking disturbed this; there was no conflict between the necessary and the possible, the real and the fantastic; all were included in the universe of possibility 'objectified' by epoché.

In the later work, formal logic loses its paradigmatic status; and the 'material'-founding intuitions become the only ones that ultimately matter. Furthermore, as we noted, Husserl moves away from the whole notion of the ideal and the objective, and thereby, also, from the notion of a subsistent world of general, public truths independent of individual minds. So, later, the founding intuitions become precisely what they were construed *not* to be previously – i.e. practical *acts* by *individuals*. This is not psychologism, because Husserl's system still disallows the empirical object 'mind' as a basis for explanation. But it is pragmatic and, ultimately, relativist in a way that is inconsistent with the earlier project.

Subject, to put it formulaically, now precedes object. Whatever it is that constitutes subjective experience is there before objectivity, and is its only true foundation. The characteristics of subjective experience are *practice* and *spatio-temporality*; and these, accordingly, become the foundational components of the world.

In the original project, the 'scientific' universe emerged from a general modification into possibility. In other words, you could only do science and philosophy properly once distracting questions about real existence had been 'bracketed'. The entities and intuitions dealt with by science were simply 'sedimentations' ('Niederschläge' – see above) of real acts whose actuality was suspended.

In the later project, the process of sedimentation remains, but is now regarded far less favourably. Husserl is now critical of the ministrations of science and its insistence on converting everything into 'objectivity'. There should, he argues, be a 'return to concealed subjectivity', the active subjectivity now encrusted by sedimentations of science (*EuU*, 47). What is concealed is the 'achievement' or 'effort' ('das Leisten') of subjectivity, the force which lies behind the 'sedimentations of sense' that we assume lie before us ready and complete. What lies sedimented is a truly cosmogonic force; it is

> that subjectivity through whose achievements of sense [Sinnesleistungen] the world as we find it, *our* world, has become that which it is for us. (*EuU*, 47)

And the revelation of that subjectivity is characterised as *history* – precisely that discipline which is concerned not with the necessities of logical connection, but with the contingencies of free human action. At this point, then, Husserl moves *outside* the structure of the possible world ('history' is a meaningless concept within the strictly ordered horizon of possibility), to a foundational contingency of the *practical deed*. The world now arises not only, or even primarily, in the sign of logic, but in that of emotion, desire, practicality.

> The logical achievements of sense are only a part of the contribution to the building of our world of experience. Also involved are the experiences of practice and emotion, the experience of desiring, of valuing and of hands-on doing [handanlegendes Tun], which themselves create their horizon of familiarities of practical commerce, valuation and so on. (*EuU*, 49)

Sensibility, the spatio-temporal, which is merely bundled into Husserl's monadic system in the earlier project, later reaches a fuller emphasis of its own. In the *Krisis*, for example, Husserl discusses the notion (which he attributes to Galileo) that the things of sense are 'merely' subjective. Husserl's argument is not with the classification as such, but with the pejorative adverb. Such an attitude blinds us to the truths of what he now calls 'pre- and extra-scientific life':

> If the intuitive world of our life is merely subjective, then all the truths of our pre- and extra-scientific life that relate to its actual being are devalued. (*Kr*, 58)[50]

---

50 Husserl's phrase 'actual being' ('tatsächliches Sein') is a further indication of his abandonment of the possible; though he takes care not to use the term 'real', which would be burdened with his previous criticisms.

This attitude towards sense is especially evident in 'scientific' attitudes towards time and space. Husserl calls it the 'idealisation of the form of time and space' (*Kr*, 37). It results in disciplines such as geometry, and the reduction of the 'plenitudes' (Füllen) of the sensory world to the arid 'forms' (Gestalten) of mathematics (*Kr*, 36).

Despite the idealised abstractions of mathematical science, the 'prescientific' world remains available to us, did we but know how to look. Nor is it restricted to a mute animality. It is a world of articulate experience in the full sense. There *is* 'nature' (though it is not to be considered as a 'completed object' – *EuU*, 57). There is also 'culture' (*CM*, 88). These things are not dependent on the paradigmatic structures of mathematics; they are self-sufficient 'efforts' by the creative subject.

But how, if at all, does philosophy gain access to the creations of 'subjectivity'? The earlier answer would have been that only 'objective', 'ideal' entities are appropriate to rational enquiry. But this is precisely the route that Husserl has now closed to himself.

The initial answer is that 'self-pondering' happens through meditation on history. But what is history? To what extent can there be such an entity in the purely subjective sphere? A central concept in the later work is what Husserl calls 'transcendental intersubjectivity' (e.g. *CM*, 80). This serves for a preliminary sketch of the nature of 'community' (Gemeinschaft), the entity that has history. The principle of subjectivity is reflected in it in two ways. First, Husserl emphasises that the community engenders a 'cultural world' (kulturelle Umwelt) that is *not* universal. 'Nature', perhaps, is the same for everyone; but even at the most rudimentary level of human co-existence communities appear that are 'relatively or absolutely distinct', and which, to varying degrees, are 'closed to a human being coming into contact with the community from another one' (*CM*, 136). Contact with different cultures is something that can only be accomplished through processes of 'empathic understanding' (Nachverstehen), which are clearly different from the techniques of mathematical science.

The second 'subjective' aspect of culture is that its paradigm is not the ordered inferential structure of mathematics, but the 'subjective' structure of spatio-temporal *orientation* (*CM*, 137).

On 'transcendental intersubjectivity', then, 'intersubjectivity' indicates that there *is* a public, shared world independent of the ideal realm of scientific objectivity. Its constitution is the shared practice of individuals, and its first expression is in culture. 'Transcendental' is a term Husserl is borrowing from Kant. The phenomenological epoché is transcendental in being concerned neither with the transcendent (the world of ready-made empiry) nor with the immanent (the closed world of logical possibility), but with the absolute possibility conditions of anything at all. From this perspective, the first entity we encounter is the single human subject (though, again, not conceived as an empirical mind, but as a kind of absolute abstract agent); and the second is subjectivity in community. Only thereafter emerge more 'immanental' considerations such as those dealt with by mathematics.

33. Science – the questionable tradition

This, then, is the basis for Husserl's celebrated attack, at the end of his life, on scientific culture: *The Crisis of the European Sciences and Transcendental Phenomenology*. This attack, which appeared in various forms from 1935 onwards, is a dismissal of many of the principles Husserl had previously held dear.

The fundamental point, perhaps, is Husserl's explicit abandonment not only of logic as a paradigm, but of logic as a bearer of certainties even in its own realm. The transcendental epoché brackets everything that does not have the primordial certainty of subjectivity. In that respect we are left only with the ego: the *cogito*, as a package of intellectual processes, is suspended. In particular, the mathematical axioms are suspended, and, beyond that, even the 'thinkability of falsehood' – by which Husserl presumably means negation, perhaps the most fundamental element of any logical calculus (*Kr*, 86).

The second part of the attack is Husserl's rejection of his own earlier esteem for the natural sciences. These are now represented as being obsessed with the notion of a single, universal world structure. Modern physics is convinced of

> the unbroken certainty, binding us all together and continuing through all the variability of subjective conceptions, of the one identical world, the reality which exists in itself. (*Kr*, 34)

It seeks to penetrate and colonise this world by the notion of 'universal inductivity' – i.e. in effect, the principle that Husserl himself had prized in connection with monadic possible worlds (*Kr*, 40). Physicists, he now complains, see the world as an infinite but predictable series of events, the machine of perfect induction. As a result it is seen as forming a theory-like unity, one that is limitlessly *controllable* by the techniques of mathematical construction. Geometry's reduction of everything to the abstract quality of form and 'extendedness' is the instrument of this. Seen in this way, the world,

> as a universal configuration of all bodies, has a *total form embracing all forms*, and this is *idealisable* in the manner analysed and *controllable [beherrschbar] through construction*. (*Kr*, 35)

This control expresses itself in the development of exact method, which is always understood as unique and exclusive in 'correctness' (*Kr*, 44); and among its aspirations is the prediction of regularities even in the practical life-world (*Kr*, 46).

The only defence against this tyranny is the radicalism of the transcendental epoché, and the historical meditation of 'self-pondering'. More specifically, it expresses itself in Husserl's late interest in the history of science and of mathematical techniques such as geometry. The origin of geometry as a practical technique in the measurement of land, for example, helps us understand that it too has its foundations in the 'pre-scientific life-world'. The work of Galileo, though immensely estimable, has to be understood as an 'occlusion' ('Verdeckung') as well as a discovery ('Entdeckung' – *Kr*, 56). In general, the progress of science has to be confronted, and freed from its 'unquestioned traditionality' (*Kr*, 50). Science is a derivative scheme that has 'become', historically; it does not have an exclusive claim to determine one hegemonic 'world' for human beings.

34. Lost foundations

Husserl's oeuvre is marked, then, by a striking 'turn' in its concluding moments (*Kr*, XI). It seems that Husserl himself decided that his original 'possible world' project was perhaps unrealisable and certainly undesirable. The notion that there was anything compellingly universal and in that sense 'objective' faded fast, for Husserl and for many others between two world wars, confronted with the high technology of death. By contrast, the delicate blooms of culture, perceived as the most intimate acts of subjectivity, seemed far more worthy of affirmation and defence.

This verdict on the original project seems to have been shared by most of the many thinkers who have been influenced by Husserl. Even in the realm of mathematical logic, the intuitionists picked up from Husserl precisely the move *away* from claims about 'facts', the 'external world' and so on; and the 'value' of mathematics becomes directly comparable with that of art.[51] Elsewhere, Husserl's later change of mind inspired the whole modern development of 'hermeneutics', particularly in the work of Heidegger, and in that of Gadamer (whose major work was precisely on the *disjunction* of 'truth' and 'method'). The other thinker heavily, though inexplicitly, influenced by Husserlian thought is Jürgen Habermas, whose notions of the 'transcendental' (or 'quasi-transcendental'), and of subjectivity, take their cue directly from Husserl's account of the pre-scientific life-world.

51 See Arend Heyting, 'Disputation', 72ff.

As far as we are concerned, however, the overriding conclusion is this. Husserl started by looking at the world as a single, closed formal system – a monad, in Leibnizian terms. He found, however, that the expectation he had of his system – that it should be 'founded' – could not be satisfied. In the later work, accordingly, he abandoned the search for any kind of 'objective' foundation, and took the view that foundations could lie only in the imperspicuous depths of 'subjectivity', practice, and so on. The result, implicitly in Husserl, and increasingly stridently in some of his successors, was a historicist relativism. Systematic formalism still prevailed, but only as the account of something internal to systems founded elsewhere, in rationally irrecoverable subjectivity. Not surprisingly, the formal and systemic aspects could hardly be regarded as very interesting after this move. Or, put another way, breaking them down ('questioning the tradition') became their main use, as a new way of returning to foundations.

Husserl's failure, from our point of view, is his inability to think through the problem of systemic discontinuity as something accessible to reason. It is not true that everything is *either* set in the concrete of scientific regularity, *or* consigned to a human practice seen as absolute contingency. More technically, a system can observe itself without forcing itself into an entirely unrelated system; in Husserl's terms, the absolute invisiblity of the I is not a foregone conclusion. The statement that is undecidable in one system is decidable – in exactly the same form, using the same language – in the observer's meta-system. There is discontinuity; but the first system is not lost. The 'foundation', if that is the right word for it, is in the relation between the systems. This, as I have tried to show in Chapter 1, gives us the elements for a notion of translation which *avoids* the complete relativism of Husserl and so many since.

5

Dialogue and History: Jürgen Habermas and the Erlangen School

1. Introduction

Jürgen Habermas, who was born in 1929, is probably the best known philosopher working in Germany today. Because of his considerable range he also represents a culmination, at least provisionally, of the debates we have considered in this book. Habermas now describes himself as a 'social philosopher', though this is intended polemically rather than defensively: for him, social philosophy is the highest level of generality to which philosophy, as *prima philosophia*, may now legitimately aspire. Within what traditionally counts as 'philosophy', Habermas has concerned himself with most topics other than mathematical logic. This includes aesthetics and the philosophy of history, as well as metaphysics and, centrally, ethics and political philosophy. Habermas's work is systematic, in the sense that it sets out to produce an elaborated body of doctrine *ab initio*; but at the same time its presentation is firmly in the critical-hermeneutic tradition of *Geistesgeschichte* (Dilthey and followers) and dialectical historiography (Benjamin and the Frankfurt school). The effect of this hermeneutic presentation is to reverse what would for many seem the obvious rhetorical priorities; rather than parade his systematic contributions and consign predecessors and opponents to footnotes, Habermas offers his system almost as asides ('Zwischenbetrachtungen', in the *Theory of Communicative Action (TkH)*), in the intervals of critical exegesis. This, combined with the fact that Habermas's exegesis directs itself to an immense range of sources (from Schiller to Searle, one might say), inevitably makes him a rather exotic figure for the purposes of 'analytical' philosophers.[1] But Habermas's

1 'For Anglo-Saxon readers, in particular, it is perplexing to find the history of philosophy written for systematic ends (though on the Continent this mode of thought and presentation has, perhaps to its own disadvantage, not needed explicit justification since Hegel).' *Erkenntnis und Interesse (EuI)*, 368.

method, as we shall see, is anchored in his metaphysics.

Even in German terms, Habermas is by no means a 'typical' philosopher, and his career has reflected this. He wrote his doctoral dissertation on Schelling, working with Erich Rothacker. Rothacker is an interesting thinker, though now little discussed. This is perhaps because of his continuity with the pre-1945 university system, perhaps also because of the comment he is alleged to have made on Benjamin's failure at Frankfurt – 'One cannot habilitate *Geist.*' Rothacker remained an important and largely unacknowledged source for Habermas's subsequent work.

Between 1956 and 1959 Habermas was Adorno's *Assistent* in Frankfurt. Although Habermas is popularly regarded as the heir to the 'Frankfurt School' of critical social philosophy, it is easy to exaggerate the amount that he took over from it. It is not apparent, for example, that Habermas's relations with Adorno himself were personally close (see Dews, 1986, 200), or that Adorno's highly elitist and 'theological' form of social criticism ever appealed much to him. On the other hand, the deep seriousness of Habermas's polemic, together with the convoluted homileticism of his German, at least aspire to the passion of the master (and indeed, at a further remove, to that of Walter Benjamin, whose style continues to revenge itself on would-be imitators!).

Habermas's first major piece of independent work, his 'Habilitationsschrift' on *The Structural Change of the Public Sphere*, was written not for Adorno, but for the Marxist social historian Wolfgang Abendroth, at Marburg. As far as the 'Frankfurt School' were concerned, this text shows if anything the influence of Marcuse rather than Adorno, concentrating as it does on an *empirical* group of people as bearers of revolutionary hope for the future.

Habermas's initial philosophical development reached its conclusion at Heidelberg, where H.-G. Gadamer was teaching. This, probably, represented a confirmation of his origins with Rothacker, a thinker also prized by Gadamer. It also provided a basis for what subsequently became the centre of Habermas's project – the notion of *language* as a universal normative source not so much in epistemology, as in ethics.

After Heidelberg, Habermas was professor of philosophy and sociology at Frankfurt (Horkheimer's chair), from 1964-71. He ran his own branch of the Max Planck Institute in Starnberg from 1971 until 1983, when he returned once more to Frankfurt to teach.

Habermas's basic position is an ethical cognitivism: the doctrine, in this case, that there is a universal rational basis to ethics.[2] Such a doctrine has

---

2 'I defend a cognitivist position. In fact, I am defending an outrageously strong claim in the present context of philosophical discussion: namely, that there is a universal core of moral intuition in all times and in all societies.' Habermas in Dews, 1986, 206. We should, though, dis-

obvious attractions for any German writing after the catastrophes of
National Socialism. Weimar academics had happily produced relativist or
conventionalist ethical theories in which right action was an accommodation to the interests of the *Volk* (Heidegger), or in which political legitimacy followed the leader who asserted himself in the vacuum of the 'state
of emergency' (Carl Schmitt). These two thinkers, indeed, form a more or
less explicit counterpoint to all Habermas's work.

They are not, however, the opponents around whom Habermas's
thought actually develops. They come from elsewhere. There are two of
them: positivism and Hegelian 'identity philosophy'. Habermas's campaign against positivism is designed to reinsert the 'subject', and hence the
source of moral norms, into the human sciences. His campaign against
Hegelianism is directed towards a danger within his own system, namely
the disappearance of any critical 'outside' down the maw of dialectical
totality.

This broad strategy is close to that of Adorno. The attacks on positivism
echo Adorno's repudiation of a simplistically technological 'Enlightenment'.[3] And the replacement of Hegel's 'positive' dialectic by a soteriology
of the 'extra-mundane' (see *TkH* I 394) is also Adornian in inspiration (the
'negative' dialectic). Habermas, though, is basically a more worldly philosopher than Adorno, and his central method, *reflection*, is an attempt to
maintain the 'other' as a guide in this world, a concrete vision of utopia.

2. Positivism and Utopia

Historically, 'positivism' is a doctrine associated with two rather distinct
areas. The first is the positivism of Auguste Comte, which argued for a
rigorously 'scientific' view of the world, cleansed of Gods and other metaphysical entities. In the twentieth century, this reached a more sophisticated articulation in 'logical' positivism, which reconstructed 'science' as
sets of observation statements ordered by laws which were manipulated by
a subject which was itself not amenable to observation.

The second sense of positivism is legal positivism, which (in opposition
to philosophies of natural law) concerns itself with the law as it is actually
propounded and followed in particular societies, rather than with notions
about natural or 'universal' norms. Positivist lawyers take law as, in some

tinguish between strong cognitivism (Habermas's argument for moral intuitions) and weak
cognitivism, which would state that there are formal 'possibility conditions' for rightness or
legitimacy, though not commit itself to specific intuitions of content. In the weak sense, Carl
Schmitt is himself perhaps a cognitivist. Habermas's attachment to strong cognitivism is
something of a liability.
3 See, especially, the *Dialectic of Enlightenment*. See *German Philosophy*, ch. 10.

sense, a fact of natural history, rather than as something that can be 'rationalised' in a deliberate manner.

As Habermas's treatment implies, these two forms of positivism end up with very similar views on ethical matters. His discussion of 'positivism', though, centres around 'scientistic' positivism, and in particular that represented by, for example, Ernst Mach and Karl Popper.

The central principle of positivism, in Habermas's account, is that *facts are essences* (*EuI*, 105). This is a critical position: there are no 'essences' in relation to which facts might be mere 'appearances'. So, for example, there are no Platonic essences, nor any other kind of metaphysical 'substructure' serving as a 'ground' for what we experience. That would include a Kantian subject serving as 'possibility condition' for knowledge (e.g. as a source of transcendental categories).

There seem to be two stages to scientific positivism. The first is the attitude of no nonsense common sense. Habermas characterises it as the 'shirt-sleeved world view' (*Zur Logik der Sozial Wissenschaften (LS)*, 74). The world is the world, and science is just the record of what happens in it. Hence the absolute priority of 'protocol sentences', i.e. reports of observed events, over the derivative or even distortive role of any individual observer's subjectivity (*EuI*, 111). In this context, positivism claims to be the 'veil-less' representation of external facts (*EuI*, 110). And, in this context, everything is 'external' to the extent that it may be represented as a fact. That includes psychological events. Introspection, in other words, does not reveal the existence of a 'subject' in any metaphysical sense (*EuI*, 107f).

The second stage, which is (in Habermas's account) associated with Popper, develops in response to the recognition that *laws* become extremely difficult to explain in a straight positivism. If we say that 'laws' (of causation, say) are real parts of nature, then we run into the difficulty that they are not observable facts, and it is unclear what exactly we are talking about (in a positivist ontology). If we say that they are observable in the sense that they are psychological facts, then we have lost our notion of the universality implicit in 'law'; a fact is not a law. The fact that a particular brain happens to function in a particular way at a particular time is not binding on itself, still less on anyone else.

An associated difficulty is that the distinction between facts and laws itself seems problematic. A 'fact', presumably, is something that 'is the case', and, as such, something we attribute to *statements* of some kind. But if I say, 'this is a book', I am already going beyond a brute protocol of sensuality. I am using the general term 'book', a term laden with prior non-empirical commitments. Knowledge only happens at all because 'I' (or, at least, something prior to the observation statement) contribute something to it myself. In other words, as Popper concedes, there are no brute facts, but only theory-laden observations (*LS*, 49).

However, positivists can still live with this restriction on the absolute primacy of external 'facts'. Theory-loading is converted into an account of the way 'facts' become mapped on to 'statements' (*EuI*, 90f). Statements are themselves a particular kind of fact, so positivism's absolute monism is not lost. The function of science becomes the improvement of the brain's statement-generating mechanisms (its 'conjectures', in a Popperian term); and the polemical stand against 'metaphysics', e.g. in the form of arguments for internal or 'subjective' conditions of knowledge, remains strong.[4]

3. Circularity

Habermas has two main arguments against essentialism of the fact. The first is a version of infinite regress, the second of circularity.

The regress argument is concerned with positivism's difficulties in accounting for truth. Popper, as we saw, abandons reliance on brute facts; external sense does not come ready packaged in laws and interpretations. So 'truth' cannot be a simple 'photographic' mapping of facts into statements; it must somehow be a matter of arranging statement events so that they succeed, in some further-to-be-explored sense, in forming isomorphisms with non-statement events, or events external to the particular observation. (It is probably necessary, in the positivist account, that the statement sets should be disjoint with the sets with which they are isomorphic. That is what the ban on reflection is all about.) The difficulty is: if we only 'know' anything by means of a mapping of statement sets on to event sets, how do we know about the success of the mapping? What event set is being mapped onto what statement set in the case of a predication of 'truth'?

In more practical terms, if we only know things by means of theories, how are we able to compare 'things' with 'theories' at all? I may take a particular view about something, using my theory. Someone else may insist that my view is wrong. To this, though, my answer need only be that his view is just as much based on a theory as mine, so that putting forward 'observations' as a means of choosing between the two amounts to no more than reassertion of the theories. The ground for accepting one theory rather than another, or one contention about reality rather than another, ultimately depends on theories which are themselves no more than asserted.

---

4 This is also neatly expressed in the *Tractatus* (see above, ch. 3), though Habermas does not use this source.

Popper, as is well known, tries to circumvent this problem by the doc-trine of falsification. If positive observations cannot support a theory (in itself, or against a rival), nonetheless (according to Popper) the *failure* of the theory's own observations, or predictions, provides a negative control which is not prejudged by the acceptance of any rival theory, or observa-tions formed through rival theories. In other words, this doctrine preserves access, even if only in negative form, to the raw, non-'subjective' data. It thus saves the correspondence theory of truth (*statements* are true to the extent that they correspond to [i.e. are isomorphic and disjoint with] *things*).

There seem to be two objections to this. The first is that it does, in the end, depend on some kind of positive access to raw data – something which the thesis of theory-ladenness would seem to rule out (*LS*, 49ff.). How, for example, would counter-instances to a theory ever be formulated? How-ever, this objection may not be as substantial as it looks; in principle, at least, there does not seem to be any requirement that counter-instances *should* be formulated. In any event, for Habermas's purposes, the whole idea of falsifiability seems actually to fit quite well with Adorno's notion of negativity in reason.

The more important objection would seem to be this. Falsifiability may give me a 'truth' criterion internal to a theory. But it does not give me any general framework for comparing one theory with another. Introducing a further theory for evaluating 'facts' and their mappings in 'statements' would, first, lead to infinite regress, and, second, threaten the principle that facts have to be rigorously 'external' and disjoint with statements. For this reason, the positivists' truth evaluation stops with the original mapping; and the evaluation is not reflexive (application of another statement-mapping procedure), but pragmatic. I simply *decide*, irreflexively, that a particular theory is, or is not, successful.

4. The Vienna Circle

For important reasons that we shall consider later, Habermas's objections to 'positivism' are not entirely convincing.[5] In particular, his charge that the choice between theories itself takes place in a theory-free realm, irra-tionally (he says 'decisionistically'), is one that the 'positivists' would acknowledge, but not regard as a liability. If we are to reconstruct the later stages of Habermas's own argument, we need a more precise identification of what positivism means.

The source of what Habermas is objecting to is the thought of the Vienna

5 See also Geuss, 1981, 26-31, for a critical appraisal of Habermas's account of 'positivism'.

Circle, as nowadays mediated by Quine. This includes Wittgenstein, in the terms we have already discussed, as well as the work of Carnap.[6] Habermas never discusses Quine; but it will help if we expand our exposition of 'positivism' in these other terms.

The two axiomatic beliefs in 'Viennese' positivism are:

i.) ontologically, facts occupy one single world ('monism'),

ii.) (1) statements are about facts, but (2) not themselves facts ('irreflexivity').

As a corollary of i.) and ii.), we can also say that statements are either true or false, in the sense that facts from the one world can either be mapped into them or not. If no fact can be mapped into it, a statement is simply false.

This can be expanded in various ways. Wittgenstein's system in the *Tractatus* is one. Another, drawing roughly on Carnap and Quine, would be as follows.

a. Statements do not have subjects. Truth and falsehood have nothing to do with any 'subjectivity' uttering the statement. The system of knowledge suffers a 'radical exorcism of the subject' (Vossenkuhl, 1990b, 2). As Quine puts it, the determination of what is said to exist 'applies in the first instance to discourse and not to men' (see Quine, *From a Logical Point of View*, 103).

b. 'Knowledge' is a matter of statements, not of facts. It is coextensive with what we say; but we have no basis for positing any substantial identity between what we say and what 'is'. Thus we regard statements of existence (Quine calls them 'ontological commitments') as the output of systems of statements, but not as somehow 'real'. Statements cannot get outside their own realm. Accordingly, 'I favour treating cognition from within our own evolving theory of a cognised world, not fancying that firmer ground exists somehow outside all that' (*Word and Object*, 235). Pursued radically, this view ends up dismissing not only hypostatised general terms ('redness'), but *any* really existing general entities, including physical objects. 'Physical objects are conceptually imported into the situation as convenient intermediaries – not by definition in terms of experience, but simply as irreducible posits comparable, epistemologically, to the gods of Homer' (*FLPV*, 44f). The dismissed entities, of course, include numbers – 'myths on the same footing with physical objects and gods'. All may be described as 'cultural posits'.

The manipulation and development of knowledge depends on one internal principle, that of 'simplicity', and one external one, namely pragmatic success. Formulaically, 'we adopt ... the simplest conceptual scheme into which the disordered fragments of raw experience can be fitted

6 For a summary of Carnap's position, with important criticisms, see Vossenkuhl, 1990b.

and arranged' (*FLPV*, 16).

The 'raw experience', of course, is not to be understood as data offered in a neutral observation language. Quine, like Popper, is aware of the difficulties that would bring; and his whole thesis of the 'indeterminacy of translation' (translation of individual sentences is *in principle* indeterminate because their referential element is inextricable from the language's prior structural commitments – see *Word and Object*) is an elaboration of this.

So, the languages from within which we 'refer' are based on 'free prior decisions' (*Word and Object*, 74); they emerge as 'cultural posits'. A choice as between languages, or accounts of the world, is (given equal simplicity) a choice of convenience, utility, or just taste. It does not, whatever happens, guarantee a securer ontological foothold. As Habermas protests, knowledge in the positivist universe is characterised by perpetual 'incompleteness and relativity' (*EuI*, 100).

Nonetheless, given that languages and theories *are* all that we have for 'knowledge', it is there that we should devote our attentions. In exchange for giving up claims to determine reality itself, philosophy asserts its supremacy over the realms of method and calculus.[7] Hence the importance, for positivism, of formal logic: methodology is the only place left for reasoning. As Habermas notes, positivism propounds the 'priority of method before matter' (*EuI*, 97); and, indeed, the old philosophical discipline of epistemology is effectively replaced, in the new tradition, by 'theory of science' ('Wissenschaftstheorie' – *EuI*, 89).

    c. 'Truth' depends on facts, not on statements. Though statements are all we have, they still have no *ontological* status. Method is a kind of *via negativa*; it should strive to minimise its own 'ontological commitments' precisely because it is itself hopelessly unreal. If the scientific method is allowed to get out of hand, it will end up obscuring our access to the real facts, not helping it.

In Quine, this deference to the eternally other is enshrined in the insistence that truth is extensional. Extensionality is the principle that truth depends on facts, not on internal features of statements. This is the central concern of all Quine's philosophical work, and cannot be explained in detail here. Its basic force, though, could be rendered in the claim that meaning is vacuous.

Meaning, according to Quine, is a modern successor to the Aristotelian notion of essence. In Aristotelian cosmology, he claims, there is a certain *essential* structure to the world (that human beings are rational, for

---

7 'For the first time a philosophical system would not embrace "reality" or the knowledge of the world. The powerful description of the real world by the natural sciences moderated philosophical pretensions. With structural knowledge philosophy seemed to be on the safe side.' (Vossenkuhl, 1990b, 2)

example), and the way the world happens to be is superimposed on this as basically *accidental* (*FLPV*, 22). This means that one can explore the world in terms of its essential structure without any recourse to empiry. This armchair attitude (Quine implies, following the Whig account of modern learning) was swept aside by the experimental science of the seventeenth century.

It persisted, however, in the doctrine of *meaning* – the notion that words, and in particular names, have a kind of a priori non-empirical content. To the extent that they name 'real entities' – like trees, perhaps, or human beings – they bear a kind of irreducible content, shared in some way with the real object-classes that they name. And that, in turn, means that the irreducible content, 'meaning', can be manipulated as an aprioristic entity, proof against any of the uncertainties of actual existence. 'All bachelors are unmarried men', for example.

Quine's reply is that 'meanings' are as illusory as 'essences', and for the same reason. Meaning is strictly and absolutely contingent on reference. That is to say, sentences only have meaning to the extent that things of which they are true actually present themselves. A sentence, in fact, is never more than a slot held open to catch an object. It may be compared with the games where children have to fit objects with particular shapes through a matrix in which those shapes are cut. The sentence is like the holes in the matrix: for any hole, if there is an object which fits through it, that is the object to which it 'refers', and thanks to which it has (if you insist on using the word) 'meaning'. If no object presents itself, the hole is just a hole, not an entity of any kind. Its only property, if that is how it can be described, is falsehood.

That, more or less, is the basis for Quine's commitment to Russell's theory of descriptions. The theory of descriptions, as Quine uses it, is a way of ridding language even of the most stubborn 'apriorisms', proper names. A proper name seems, at first sight anyway, to be far more than just a schematic hole through which someone may or may not fit. Nonetheless, this is precisely how it can and should be rendered logically. A 'hole' for Sir Walter Scott, in Russell's celebrated example, might be, *inter alia*, 'someone who wrote *Waverley*'. Whatever the rich intuitions which we associate with any named individual, in a logical context this is always eliminable in terms of things that we may predicate of him or her (e.g. the property of having written *Waverley*). So the proper name is not, or at least not 'logically', a repository of a priori meanings we can deploy in a pre-experimental way.[8]

Quine calls this the 'primacy of predicates' (*Mathematical Logic*, 229). It

8 'On Denoting', in Russell, *Essays in Analysis*.

involves what we have already seen about the 'positivist' contention that all observation is theory-laden; we cannot assume of *any* 'knowledge' that it is unmediated by language (predication). But, beyond that, it involves also the complete ontological evacuation of language; language is *nothing* until it catches its object. The fundamental character of language is not to name, for that suggests that it somehow shares in the ontological status of the object it names; it is to predicate, i.e. to offer descriptions which may or may not be 'taken up' by the objects to which they are offered.

The link with reality, Quine insists in accordance with this principle, is not through names but through *pronouns*. Language gets its confirmation by facts by offering sentences of the form 'something that wrote *Waverley* is the same as something called Sir Walter Scott'. Nouns (*nomina*, names) should, from this point of view, be rechristened 'propronouns', i.e. short-hand for descriptions involving 'something that' locutions. 'Pronouns are the basic media of reference,' Quine insists (*FLPV*, 13).

So if all we are talking about is pronouns, there is no scope for the content we intuitively associate with names. Consequently, also, notions such as analyticity (a priori truth) are redundant and misleading. The statement that 'all bachelors are unmarried men' is not (according to Quine) an 'analytical truth' arising purely from the 'meaning' of the nouns involved; it is, at best, an assertion that the two terms are in extensional agreement – i.e. they apply to the same objects (*FLPV*, 13).

Quine's disembowelling of the noun, if we can call it that, is relatively straightforward in itself (though it has led to celebrated controversy, for example with Strawson). The more substantial problem, in our context, is his further implementation of the basic 'positivist' principles of the single world and of the ontological nullity of reason.

Quine believes, in effect, that there is a world in terms of which any statement is either true or false. When we produce a 'description', we can in principle say quite definitely whether there is anything that corresponds to it or not. There may be practical difficulties in finding out, for example, whether there are blackcurrant bushes on Mars; but in principle, at least, there either are blackcurrant bushes there or there aren't.

The second point of belief is the ontological nullity of reason. This states, in effect, that whatever there 'is' is not something put there by 'us'. This is not to deny that subjectivity plays a central role in what we know, or what we *think* there is. Quine is happy to admit that our discourse is laden with ontological preconceptions. And, furthermore, discourses are 'holistic'; what we think there is depends on a whole interlocking structure of linguistic components. But the competition between these theoretical 'wholes' is not an ontological one; it makes no difference to *the real facts*. We never get at the real facts, because of theory-ladenness; but at least (for

Quine, at any rate) we rest secure in the knowledge that there *are* such things, and nothing we do will change them.

Now, both of these articles of faith are open to challenge. In the first place, the notion that everything is either true or false, *tout court*, is a useful way of explaining quantification, as Quine emphasises, but it does involve a kind of secularised platonism (the forms are no longer in heaven; they are in the one truth-determining, though not directly accessible, world of 'reality'). But we do not have to look at reality on the model of a single world viewed from varying perspectives; it could equally well be a variety of worlds, or, better, an unceasing flow in which logic's apparently 'time-less' vistas are merely artificial conceits, like frames in a movie. The latter approach certainly seems to do more justice to the elusive quality of 'reality'; and it also encourages us to move beyond the ontological dogmas still lurking in positivism. Intuitionist logic, which, as Quine (though un-happily) comments, 'infuses logical laws with temporal process' (*FLPV*, 126), is one way of doing this.

Another way is through modal logic, which, in effect, dispenses with the presupposition of one world in which everything is either true or false, and countenances a plurality of worlds in which truth or falsity is relative to the world you are talking about. Quine is notoriously hostile to modal logic (*FLPV*, ch. VIII), and suspicious of intuitionism (e.g. *Philosophy of Logic*, 87-89; *FLPV*, 126). Quine's criticism of modal logic is that it re-imports essentialism or analyticity (*FLPV*, 150, 155), and consequently that it becomes 'referentially opaque' – i.e. it breaks the rule of deference to the one world of truth-functional determination. The modal technique of counterfactuals ('if kangaroos had no tails they would topple over') is sus-pect precisely because it *expressly* suspends reference to the real world of actuality (*FLPV*, 30).

5. Reflection

From a practical point of view, Habermas's objection to metaphysical pos-itivism is that it is 'decisionistic' and irrationalist (*LS*, 32). The adoption of any explanatory framework, however 'scientific', is in the last result grounded in a decision, or an act of faith. Popper's 'critical' tradition, in Habermas's reproach, is in the end no more than a tradition - a convention that depends on sentiment, and can as well be broken as observed (*LS*, 50, 84). And the danger with this, in turn, is that such arbitrariness can be transferred to the political and ethical realm. What there *is* is a completely autonomous given; and my responses to it, as well, are cocooned in an ana-lytically inaccessible 'decision'. The discontinuity between the two results is what Habermas calls a politics of 'the leader with the machine', 'decisionistic self-affirmation in the middle of a rationalised world' (*LS*, 83 – this is a comment on Max Weber). The obvious danger is that science is left without an answer when a demented leader gets control of an overwhelmingly powerful machine. This, one infers from Habermas's reference to Carl Schmitt, is an explanation for National Socialism (*LS*, 85).

As we noted, however, 'decisionism' is not necessarily a characterisation the positivists would object to. Habermas's argument against, or alternative to, the positivist position is grounded in what he calls 'reflection'. It is the thesis of reflection that enables him to mount his charge of circularity (*LS*, 36).

'Reflection', here, is a direct appeal to Kant, and designates a consideration of the subjective conditions of knowledge.

> Reflection [reflexio] does not deal with objects themselves, in order to derive concepts of them, but is the condition of our mind [Gemüt] in which we first set about discovering the subjective conditions under which we can reach concepts. (B 316)

In Kant's critical philosophy, it is argued that knowledge is not purely, or even primarily, conceptual; knowledge involves a concatenation of concept and sensibility. The 'forms' of sensibility, Kant argues in the Transcendental Aesthetic, are time and space. These forms are, furthermore, termed 'subjective' by Kant. This does *not* mean that they are somehow produced by the individual empirical ego (which is a common misinterpretation in the English-speaking world). It means that they are not 'objective' in the sense of being displayed across pure generality. Time and space particularise generality; in *that* sense, they are 'subjective'.[9]

This, too, is the sense in which Habermas appropriates the Kantian 'question as to the subjective conditions of the objectivity of possible knowledge' (*EuI*, 109). Through reflection we see that knowledge is always particular. It is inescapably and intrinsically situated in time and space; it is not simply a *methexis* of timeless forms with a 'matter' that can, ideally, always be discarded. In other words, the 'philosophical' grounding of science – any science – has to include this understanding of particularisation. I have to know, in other words, that my apparently solid 'objective knowledge' grows out of a foundation that is situated in time, and that can, in principle, be different in a different situation. This much is an intuitionistic attack on the Platonic one world; but it does not necessarily imply relativism. One can, for example, prescribe some kind of logic of transition from one 'particular' knowledge to another.

Habermas, however, adopts a stronger extension of this principle,

9 See *German Philosophy*, 13ff., 38ff.

namely that any particular grounding is 'subjective' in the sense that human beings are in some practical respect responsible for it. In other words, I can, so to speak, 'free' myself from the particularity of my particular knowledge by becoming aware of the fact that it is a product of my 'subjectivity'. From this point of view, the tendency towards a 'subjectivism' in the empirical sense becomes more dangerous; and, as we shall see, Habermas has to take a strategic course to avoid this.

In any event, Habermas's criticism of positivism is that it proscribes this kind of reflection. 'Positivism *is* the notion that we should deny reflection.' (*EuI*, 9). It imposes 'an interdict on self-reflection' (*EuI*, 113). Mach's 'shallow materialism' simply bans the 'epistemological' question (i.e. the properly philosophical one), and suspends any reflection beyond the one that *excludes* reflection on the knowing subject (*EuI*, 109).

This is not a difficult charge to make; as we have seen, positivism expressly *insists* on an 'exorcism of subjectivity' from science. The problem, though, is what exactly 'subjectivity' is held to contribute to science. The 'positivists', presumably, would accept that the standards and perhaps even the axiomatic structure of science is the result of a 'decision', and that that is a subjective matter. Thus far, there would be no difference between them and Habermas. Habermas, however, is purporting to go beyond this, to a point where the grounding practice of the subject is itself exposed to rational review. What can this look like?

6. History

Habermas's position changed, at least in emphasis, between the 'early' thought culminating in *Knowledge and Human Interests* (1968), and the theories of communicative action which started to reach their full articulation from the late 1970s. Nonetheless, the basic elements are already in place by 1968. They are distributed between, first, a historicist methodology, and, second, a normative metaphysics.

The historicist methodology is directed against positivism's 'essentialism of the fact'. In Habermas's approach, the subject is not merely a nonempirical 'outside', but is part of the world described by the philosopher. In his early work, at least, Habermas speaks of 'the dialectical concept of the whole' (*LS*, 15), an entity of which the observing subject is itself part. To the extent that philosophy is trying to describe general contexts and conditions, it is itself included in what it describes. 'The investigative process undertaken by subjects is, through the acts of knowing, itself part of the objective system that is to be known' (*LS*, 16). Nonetheless, access to the 'subjective' conditions of objectivity cannot be through empiry.

Empiry, the proceeding of established science, merely observes within the boundaries already set by the subject.

In order to follow the boundaries themselves, and hence the 'sense' of knowledge rather than just its contents, a different discipline is needed, namely *hermeneutics* (*LS*, 18, 36). Hermeneutics is interpretative description, initially of historical texts. The 'sciences', at least in the eyes of positivism, have a basically hypothetico-deductive approach (*LS*, 18); that is, they test hypotheses against the single and universally present world. If, however, we assume that the human 'world' is particular to subjectivities, or that subjectivity is present as the boundary of the 'world', then knowledge of the world cannot be obtained by hypothetico-deductive means. Any hypothesis we form about our world changes the world; if it is related to the boundaries of the world, it changes it substantively. So, rather than manipulate the world by hypothesis and test, we should seek to trace the course of its development. In order to know where we are, we need to find out what route we took to get here. Hermeneutics provides this historical-temporal orientation.

There are two important points to bear in mind here. First, historicism (and its method, hermeneutics) are opposed to positivism's methodological individualism. The metaphor underlying 'positivist' history is that of the observing individual. The individual watches what is going on from a detached position, like the press box at a football match. The resources of observation are autonomously controlled by the observer; there is no interference or interdependence between observer and observed. In hermeneutics, by contrast, observer and observed are both part of the same entity – the social or cultural community. The instruments of historical description, such as truth and falsity or right and wrong, are generated in the reciprocity of community and thinker. There is no absolute normative 'outside' in terms of which historians can describe a world of which they are themselves a part.

In this respect, the locus of history is always in some degree collective; history 'happens' as a collective event. Consequently, Habermas generally accepts the terminology of 'social subject' or of 'species' (*EuI*, 55). Equally, he opposes any model either of history, or of political philosophy, which starts from the 'atomistic' model of 'lonely actors' (*TkH*, I 369). The 'programme of founding [rights] individualistically' is described by Habermas as 'problematic' (*Zur Rekonstruktion des historischen Materialismus (RhM)*, 346).[10]

10 For a more detailed version of this argument, see Gadamer, 1975, e.g. 209-211.

7. Normativity

In its pure form, historicism poses metaphysical difficulties. If everything, including the critic's viewpoint, is relative to a particular point in time, then how is universal (non-relative) normative valuation possible? This question has supplied the agenda for most of the significant debates in German cultural philosophy for the last hundred years.[11] It later becomes Habermas's guiding concern, and already reaches a preliminary outline in the early work.

Provisionally, for the purposes of our exposition of Habermas, we can say that there are two possible answers. First, there is the view popularly associated with the 'historical' school, that all truth and normativity is historical. Habermas's own invocation of 'dialectics', and his early concern with 'totality', seem to flirt with this position. In this view, history is the science that is concerned with human acts. But acts escape concepts; they move in a realm of absolute freedom. History, as Windelband put it in the famous lecture distinguishing between 'nomothetic' and 'idiographic' sciences, deals with *events*; *laws* are the concern of natural science (Windelband, 1894, 167). Or, in the comment Habermas quotes from Fichte, 'What action is can only be known intuitively, and cannot be derived from concepts or communicated in them' (*EuI*, 54 n). So: if all reality is grounded in acts, and if acts are not 'conceptually' recoverable, but only 'intuitively', then the general conditions of truth are not rationally recoverable either. Such a position, of course, would leave the way open for a 'decisionism' of precisely the kind Habermas objects to in straight positivism.

And, indeed, this is the basis of his attack on Hegel's view of politics. In §§13, 14 of *The Structural Transformation of the Public Sphere* Habermas traces the perversion, by Hegel, of a certain Enlightenment ideal of politics. First came the principle 'auctoritas non veritas facit legem' which legitimised the absolute rule of baroque princes; Habermas associates this with Hobbes (1984a, 128). The Enlightenment (here, in the form of Kant) replaces this with a principle of public rationality. This works in analogy with Kant's maxim of practical reason: 'political acts, i.e. those which relate to the rights of others, must themselves correspond with law and morality only to the extent that their maxims can bear, or indeed require, publicity' (1984a, 133). The eventual effect of reasonable coexistence will be to convert 'pathologically constrained consent' into a 'moral whole' (1984a, 140, quoting Kant); or, in other words, politics will be converted into morality (1984a, 133).

This morality, however, rests on (for Habermas) a rather arbitrary con-

---

11 Compare F. Vollhardt's interesting 'Nachwort' in Rickert, 1986.

cept of procedural rationality – that residing in the interests of individual buyers and sellers on the market-place. The progress of bourgeois social forms converts relations of *status* into those of *contract*; and for contracts, which are regulated by the market, the absolute equivalence of all participants is required (all contractual obligations, regardless of whether the parties are kings or paupers, are of equal weight). The model participant, of course, is someone who has something to sell, or the means to buy. Accordingly, *capacity for the market* becomes a model for Kant's political public:

> Only owners of private property are admitted to the public of political discourse [Habermas explains], for their autonomy is rooted in the sphere of commodity exchange and therefore also coincides with their interest in preserving it as a private sphere. (1984a, 135)

However, says Habermas, this 'fiction of a justice that is immanent in the free exchange of commodities' (1984a, 137) is unconvincing, and the morality of bourgeois individualism, far from being a 'natural order', will collapse under the conflicts immanent in capitalism (1984a, 143). Hegel grasped this weakness in Kant's system. In what Habermas interprets as Hegel's extreme historicism, however, the damage is only compounded. For Hegel, reality and objectivity are concentrated on the *state*. The state comes to be regarded as the incarnation of the rational world spirit. For Hegel (according to Habermas) reason is 'realised' in 'the existing state', i.e. in the political relations as they actually are at any moment, not in some abstract model of morality or procedural justice (1984a, 148). The appeal in truth, justice, or any element of normativity lies only to 'the objectivity that *Geist* has given itself in the form of the state' (1984a, 147). Morality, in any event, does not represent a normative resource for politics, which are at a distinct and higher level of 'objectivity' – namely, of 'Sittlichkeit' (ethos). The state, as 'the reality of the ethical [sittlich] idea' supersedes morality (1984a, 148), and disqualifies attempts by a Kantian 'public' to bring rationality into political administration.

According to Habermas, though, the result is a new kind of legal positivism; in its mere *existence*, as the incarnation of reason, the state determines justice. Enlightenment gives way to a 'world-historical existentialism of tribal spirits [Volksgeister]' (1984a, 149). Veritas has once more been supplanted by auctoritas.

Marx remedies this situation somewhat by taking the bourgeois ideal of the reasoning public seriously, and tracing its internal contradictions. The notion of a political authority constituted in the free deliberations of individuals is a good one; what is not good is its restriction to those enfranchised by capitalism. The dissymmetries of power that had perverted political relations on the old feudal basis of 'status' return again in a different guise under capitalist 'freedom of contract'; in particular, they emerge between the owners of capital and the wage labourers (152). But the weapons forged by the bourgeoisie for its own revolution – the press, for example – turn their point against the new masters (154). Eventually (says Habermas, interpreting Marx) the history of oppression will end with the triumph of a universalised 'public':

> Under these circumstances the public sphere will then be able to realise in earnest what it always promised – the rationalisation of political authority as the authority of human beings over human beings. (156)

As a result, political revolutions, which were only the struggles between immediate material interests, will cease, and be replaced by evolutions within a sphere of collective self-administration. Contrary to what Hegel proclaimed, the state will wither away and politics will dwindle into mere administration (156). The norms of *realpolitik* will be displaced by a reasserted morality of the individual, and the *private* will also finally actualise its potential as the sphere which is emancipated from the burden of labour:

> In it, the informal and intimate commerce of human beings with one another will have emancipated itself for the first time as one genuinely 'privated' of the coercion of social labour, which remains as before a 'realm of necessity'. (157)

The freedom of individual citizens in an 'intimate sphere released from economic functions' (e.g. where sexual relations are no longer colonised as economic transactions through marriage, prostitution and so on) will consist, according to Habermas's interpretation of Marx, in a 'new form of derived private autonomy'. Morality – the normative interests of the private individual – will finally, as Kant had hoped, destroy the arrogance of a hypostatised 'politics'.

8. Macro-subjects

Habermas's scheme, then, is twofold. His objection to positivism is that it excludes subjectivity from 'science', and that this results in a decisionistic ethics (because practice is no longer accessible to reason). His objection to historicism (represented by Hegel in Habermas's exposition) is that it too results in a version of positivism. This is because, although subjectivity is not excluded by the outset by the system's premises, any critical individual subjectivity is sooner or later swallowed by the cosmic subjectivity of *Geist*. *Geist*, in this version, is always right, and nobody is in a position to gainsay it. What is needed, in other words, is an account which gives us a real base for criticism. To find this, we must identify some further strands in Habermas's argument.

In the earlier work, Habermas deals with Hegel by means of the re-proach of 'identity philosophy' (e.g. *EuI*, 35). Identity philosophy is, in essence, the idea that thought and being can, or should, become identified in some remorseless logical totality. This is a view of Hegel that owes its provenance to Feuerbach, and it is one that Adorno adopts (for the pur-poses of attack) in his project of 'negative dialectics'.[12]

In the later work, Habermas generalises his reproach in terms of what he calls 'subject-philosophy' – a conception which enables him to include Marx as well as Hegel in his criticism, and to localise his own objections to a particular aspect of modernism (*Der philosophische Diskurs der Moderne (PDM)*, 79f). This is the principle of *praxis*, or of the *self-realising in-dividual*.[13] In this account, the rationality of the purely reflexive subject, which gave us the personal, critical input prized by Kant, is overwhelmed by a metaphor of creativity. The concept of praxis, says Habermas, is 'aes-thetic-expressive', drawing on Romantic notions of artistic genius (*PDM*, 81; *TkH*, II 501). In it, the community becomes a 'macro-subject' (*PDM*, 403) engaged in the 'collective self-realisation of the producers' (*PDM*, 81).

Habermas's judgement of Marx now has two elements. In the first place, Marx is seen to have overcome the affirmatory positivism of Hegel. In other words, the brutal faith in *auctoritas* represented by Hegel's equation of the present political order with rationality is gone.[14] Nonetheless, Marx still remains within the conception of history as enacted by a single macro-subject, engaged in self-realisation (though in ways that are not always clear to itself – hence revolutions and other organic disturbances). In that respect, Habermas comments, Marx failed to 'resist the temptations of Hegel's totality thinking' (*TkH*, II 501; *PDM*, 396). And this is what vitiates Marx's concentration on *labour* as the central category of his eco-nomic and metaphysical thought.

On one level, says Habermas, Marx uses a straightforward metaphor of the self-production of an 'absolute I' (*EuI*, 66). The struggles of history will eventually result in a situation where human subjectivity has overcome

12 See relevant chapters in *German Philosophy*. Habermas's view of Hegel is clearly un-satisfactory as an interpretation. For useful comments on this, see Pippin, 1989, 282.

13 Habermas also appropriates Charles Taylor's interpretation of Hegel as offering an 'ex-pressive' metaphysics (*PDM*, 80, 96).

14 It is not hard to see why Habermas objects to the tenor of Hegel's later, highly con-servative writings. In particular, Hegel expressly disqualifies what he calls the 'vanity of knowing better', i.e. the capacity of an individual to mount the kind of criticism for which Habermas is seeking a grounding. 'It is just as foolish to imagine that any philosophy can go beyond its present world as it is to imagine that an individual can jump over his time, or jump beyond Rhodes. If his theory does indeed go beyond it, then he is building a world *as it should be*; and, indeed, such a world exists, but only in his opinion – a soft element, in which any whim can be imagined.' *Philosophy of Right*, Preface (Hegel VII, 26).

its 'other' – nature – to the extent that 'necessary labour' purely for the purpose of reproducing life is redundant (*EuI*, 66, 79). That, in one view,
would be the end of the matter. Subjectivity and self-consciousness relate
simply to the one subject – society (*EuI*, 75). 'In principle, members of
society all live on the same level of domination over nature, determined at
any point by the available technical knowledge.' So, in that context, we talk
about the self-consciousness of 'the' social subject, a self-consciousness
more or less coextensive with technology and our instrumental control
over nature (*EuI*, 69). Technical history becomes human history, and self-
reflection is reduced to the observation of techniques of natural domination. Critical individuality, in this scheme of things, is lost as surely as it
had been in Hegel.

Nonetheless, says Habermas, there is a 'second dimension' in Marx
(*EuI*, 77). In order to describe the development of social formations, even
under the laws of economics, Marx 'makes use of a conception of . . . social
labour that involves more elements than are declared in the model of a self-
creating species' (*EuI*, 71). The undeclared element, essentially, is the
notion of *interaction*. Labour is not simply a brutish self-instrumental-
isation; it is something that can only develop within a system that is not reducible to the requirements of survival and efficiency. Marx, indeed, had
said that the forces of production were distinct from the relations of production; but his insistence that both were tied to 'production' disabled the
dialectic he tried to construct at this point (*EuI*, 77). Without the relations,
not only would there be no forces, but these relations appealed to an entirely *autonomous* normativity. Habermas glosses them as 'cultural':

> The medium in which these relations of subjects and groups is normatively
> regulated is cultural tradition; this forms the linguistic context of com-
> munication from which the subjects interpret nature and themselves in their
> environment. (*EuI*, 71)

So, alongside *instrumental* action, which is the domination of nature, there
is also another dimension to social development, namely *communicative*
action, which has its own unique role in historical progress and emancipation. 'Synthesis through labour,' says Habermas, is matched by 'synthesis
through struggle' (*EuI*, 77).

Accordingly, the course of history is not just a matter of producing more
and better machines and reducing socially necessary labour time to its
automated minimum. The conflicts and struggles that arise are not simply
technological hiccups, or administrative failures in the organisation of
labour. They represent struggles within the cultural or ethical realm itself.
As Habermas puts it in *Knowledge and Human Interests*,

> The road of social formation [Bildung] is marked not by new technologies,

but by stages of reflexion which dissolve the dogmatism of superseded forms of domination and ideology, sublimate the pressure of the institutional frame, and set free communicative action *as* something communicative. (*EuI*, 76)

The 'communicative' is, so to speak, a distinct world of its own. The 'subject' is not, in this view, simply swallowed by a monolithic self-creating 'society'; it arises also within the sphere of communication, and because of that it is plural, reflexive, and moral. We shall explore this in more detail later.

9. *Ideologiekritik*

The question now is: what will be the status of a critical science of society? How do we realise the moral claims implicit, for example, in Marx, but obscured by the metaphor of 'production'? The answer to this question involves, for Habermas, taking up a particular metaphysical position.

The first element of this is his rejection of 'identity philosophy' on the grounds that it represents a kind of logicism. Habermas's treatment of this is somewhat brisk, but it is an indispensable component of his position. The argument is that all the 'idealist' philosophers who appear in the context of *Knowledge and Human Interests* believe that there is basic logical structure to reality.

> Kant starts from formal logic in order to derive the categories of understanding from the table of judgements; Fichte and Hegel start with transcendental logic, to reconstruct either from pure apperception the deed of the absolute I, or from the antinomies and paralogisms ... the dialectical movement of the absolute concept. (*EuI*, 43)

So the infection of 'logic' enters at the beginning, and (in Habermas's very abrupt account) spreads its contagion throughout the system. It is only halted by Marx's 'materialist' introduction of the category of labour. For the idealists, 'synthesis' happened in the medium of thought; in Marx, life re-enters the arena in all its unpredictable variety, and puts the arid symbolism of logic to flight:

> It is not a law-bound concatenation of symbols but the processes of social life, the material generation and appropriation of products, that provide the material on which reflexion can set to work to bring to consciousness the underlying synthetic achievements. (*EuI*, 44)

The core of Hegel's project, then, was to 'explain the structure of spirit in "logical" terms' (Habermas, 1982b, 224). If that could be done, Habermas implies, the world would indeed be no more than the 'expression' of one monological centre. Existence would be reduced to what could be conceived by the ideal macro-subject. With the world held in the dead hand of logic, philosophy indeed has no role as critical reflection. What will be is predetermined regardless of our attempts at normative intervention. This seems to be the force of Habermas's very formulaic comments about ideal-ism and identity philosophy – comments which probably echo Adorno, but supply little in the way of argument or grounded exposition.[15]

This position is more fully specified in Habermas's comments about the relationship between the natural and human sciences. The poles of Marx's thinking are mankind and nature. In recapitulation of Habermas's exposi-tion of Marx, we could say there are two kinds of 'synthesis'. One is *be-tween* the two poles, and takes the form of labour. The danger of leaving things at that point, however, is that we revert to a Hegelian total subject: mankind appropriates nature (its 'non-I'), and history is completed. The effect of such a view, as we have seen, is indistinguishable from the effects of positivism. All three approaches – positivism, absolute idealism, and 'materialist scientism' – produce one single, monolithic 'universal science' (*EuI*, 86). There is no 'outside' from which the progress of history-nature can be criticised. In practice, all that is left to us is a) to expedite this pro-gress by assisting in the development of technology, and b) 'reflecting' on it by means of a Whiggish triumphalist history. And the science of human-kind itself is, thus, no different from the natural sciences. Usually, it is social engineering – the technical refinement of labour organisation. Beyond that, it is just description: history is proceeding in such-and-such a manner.

To the extent that Marx follows this line, he slides (according to Haber-mas) into a 'positivist' elision of the natural sciences with the human sciences.

> This positivistically coloured demand for a natural science of human beings is astonishing; for the natural sciences are transcendentally conditioned by the system of social labour, whose structural transformations in turn are sup-posed to be reflected by economics, the science of humankind (*EuI*, 63).

In other words, according to Habermas, the natural sciences are basically devoted to the purposes of labour, mankind's instrumental relations with nature. The totality of this process is the 'system of social labour', which 'transcendentally conditions' the ancillary sciences. This system, however, is itself subject to *reflection* from another level, namely the level of human

---

15 Habermas does not attempt to argue this through, so we shall not answer it here either. But it is a fundamental point. Briefly, one could say this. 'Transcendental' logic – the table of cate-gories – does *not* import general logic – the table of judgements – into metaphysics. That might have been the position of Leibniz, but it certainly was not that of Kant or his successors. *Inter alia*, that means that cheap appeals to the contingency of 'real life' are quite beside the point. See chapter 1, above, and *German Philosophy*, chapter 1.

practice within which the 'structural transformations' of history are fought out. And that reflection, we may infer, is the point at which subjectivity becomes conscious of itself as a free participant in history, and not merely as a piece of baggage in the voyage of world spirit. The second synthesis, in other words, is not between mankind and nature, but between human beings themselves, as distinct but interacting subjects.

The crucial metaphysical point here is that humankind and nature *remain* separate. The reason why human history is never subsumed under a total history of man and nature is that nature remains, as Habermas puts it, 'external' (*EuI*, 83); despite all the efforts of technology, nature preserves its 'ineradicable strangeness' (*EuI*, 46).

Now, the force of this is that Habermas can revert, implicitly, to Windelband's distinction between the law-describing natural sciences and the individualistic but value-promoting human sciences. Nature, as Geuss puts it, is 'given away' to the positivist by Habermas (Geuss, 1981, 28). In that way, the overall 'logicality' of the world is preserved. At the same time, however, the human part of the world escapes logical determinism. So we have the human sciences concerned with what 'subjects' do in freedom, and we have the natural sciences concerned with the mechanisms of the real world.

There is a question here as to whether the 'deeds' of subjects – in the arena of class struggle, for example – are to be the objects of causal explanation, in the manner of natural science, or are simply to be described idiographically and treated as undetermined (see Geuss, 1981, 28). Either solution poses difficulties for Habermas. If we can 'causally' describe human actions, then it seems to lose the element of freedom he is trying to preserve. But without such descriptions, his cognitive, and to that extent 'scientific' ethics seem to be in danger.

One solution is to adopt the Kantian distinction between phenomena and noumena. The things that we experience in the world are phenomena, and to them apply all the categories of causation and the like. Human beings however, as free agents, are noumena, so we do not suppose their acts to be subject to categories in the same way. Nonetheless the fruits of their actions are in principle always describable, *ex post facto*, in phenomenal terms.[16] Habermas discusses this model sympathetically in *Structural Transformation of the Public Sphere* (137ff.).

The question, in sum, is this. The sciences would seem to be concerned with the description of reality, the phenomenal world. They are, properly, 'strict sciences of experience' (*EuI*, 85). If, however, we are dealing with something that is not part of experience, i.e. with human agency, then how

16 See *German Philosophy*, 52f.

can we apply a 'science' to it? One answer would seem to be the proceeding that Habermas counterposes to the strict science of experience, namely 'critique'.

Critique we can, presumably, understand as a kind of Adornoesque *via negativa*. It puts forward nothing positive, but, in its own negativity, it destroys the presumptions of the positive. In more specifically Marxist terms, it recognises and destroys the false objectivities (objektiver Schein) produced in the course of class struggle (*EuI*, 85). Each stage in the class struggle produces a false consciousness that serves to obscure the interests of the oppressed, and, by extension, of humanity generally. 'Critique' is the capacity to rise above this, not in terms of scientifically quantifiable efficiency, or the facilitation of synthesis by labour, but in terms of the purely human interests of freedom. Critique marks the 'stages of reflection' in the road of social emancipation.

However, the 'content' of critique is purely retrospective (in this model). There is nothing positive to recognise. It is a matter of seeing that the 'tradition' is its own tradition, and that freedom from the false objectivities of that tradition is in its own hands.

> Knowing consciousness can . . . only discard the traditional form in which it finds itself to the extent that it conceives of the formative process of the species as a movement of class antagonism mediated through processes of production, recognises itself as a result of the history of appearing class consciousness, and thereby frees itself *as* self-consciousness from objective illusion. (*EuI*, 84)

In other words, the result of critique would be reflection, self-consciousness. But that is all. No concrete precepts present themselves for the future road to emancipation. In Kantian terms, the self presented by reflection in 'self-consciousness' is purely noumenal – it is the extensionless point of freedom, and has no phenomenal content.

Accordingly philosophy, or the reflective 'epistemology' (Erkenntniskritik) that had been supplanted by positivist 'theory of science' (Wissenschaftslehre), is resurrected in the negativity of 'critique'. Philosophy that has freed itself from the hubris of 'identity philosophy', absolute knowledge, and the like, no longer has an independent positive content; in that respect, it dissolves itself through critique.[17] But it survives as a kind of restraint, or even methodology, in the activities of the positive sciences. 'Philosophy is preserved in science as critique.' Specifically, this moment of reflection attaches to science in the form of 'Ideologiekritik', 'which

17 'The universal science that had pretended to the role of philosophy falls under the annihilating judgement of critique' (*EuI*, 86). See also *RhM*, 56, where philosophy is allowed as 'the most radical form of self-reflection possible at any time', but banned in the form of any attempt 'to think the unity of the world with means that are not taken from the self-reflection of the sciences'.

itself determines the method of scientific analysis' (*EuI*, 86).

Moreover, a particular dignity attaches to the social sciences in this scheme of things. 'Radical epistemology,' says Habermas, 'is only possible as social theory' (*EuI*, 9). The two are mutually dependent: the subject can only 'reflect' by means of the concrete history in which it has been realised; and the empirical work of the 'strict science of experience' needs philosophy to enable it to complete the object it is describing with *itself*.

> A radicalised epistemology can, in the end, only be carried out in the form of a reconstruction of the history of the species; and, conversely, social theory, taken from the viewpoint of a self-constitution of the species in the medium of social labour and the class struggle, is only possible as self-reflection of the knowing consciousness. (*EuI*, 85f)

10. Quasi-transcendentalism

If this exhausted Habermas's position, however, it would be hard to distinguish it from positivism. If 'reflection', or 'Ideologiekritik' is devoid of content, then how does it differ from the decisionism of positivist 'Ideologiekritik'? The positivists are in just as good a position as Habermas to decry ideologies, 'critically', as mere conventions. The important question goes beyond that: if we are to avoid decisionism, presumably we need to obtain new *positive* norms that are cognitively grounded.[18] To see how Habermas answers this problem, we shall reconstruct his argument.

> Stage 1. Positivism cannot coherently account for itself. The demarcation of the 'scientific' realm – of what can be either true or false – is not itself 'scientific': we have no means of ascertaining whether its demarcation is itself true or false. Thus it rests on a circular argument. (e.g. *EuI*, 96)

> Stage 2. Positivism, like any science, rests on a de facto, rather than an analytical, self-constitution. This is recognised by positivists; but they fail to take the further step of considering whether this self-constitution is not itself rationally recoverable (and not just an irrational 'decision').

> Stage 3. This self-constitution *is* rationally recoverable by means of Kantian 'reflection', which (e.g. in the 'Amphibolies' section of the first *Critique*) reveals the 'subjective' conditions of our 'objective' concepts.

> Stage 4. 'Subjectivity' has a logic. This is because (a) 'knowledge' is linguistic,[19] and (b) language is intersubjective – it is there for the purposes of com-

---

18 'In a way the oddest thing about this whole discussion is the extent to which Habermas is himself infected with the positivism against which he is struggling.' Geuss, 1981, 30.
19 Cf. Gadamer's dictum at page 450 of *Wahrheit und Methode*: 'Sein, das verstanden werden kann, ist Sprache' ('Being that can be understood is language').

munication between a plurality of subjects. I.e. (as a transcendental argument) if you have knowledge at all, you must have intersubjectivity. And this inter-subjectivity is governed by pure categories of reason (basically, my self-understanding depends on my understanding others as 'selves').

At this stage, Habermas's argument is starting to depart from Kant in significant ways, principally because of his contention that the categories of intersubjectivity are concrete and historical. The purpose of Kant's 're-flection' arguments was to demonstrate that pure formal thought was *limited* by factors that it could not itself account for. These, essentially, were time and space, the pure forms of sense. However, reflection only re-veals limits; it does not reveal anything beyond those limits. In other words, the 'subjective conditions' (as Kant calls time and space) are not themselves in any way meaningfully describable. At most, we can only talk about them in a purely formal way.[20] However, Habermas rejects this, partly because of his antipathy towards an ontological logicism (which seems to be the basis of his complaints about 'idealism'), and partly because he endorses Hegel's historicist critique of Kantian moral theory.[21]

Habermas's next step is Husserlian rather than Kantian.

Stage 5. Since Habermas follows Hegel in rejecting pure ethical transcenden-talism as dogmatic, and Marx in rejecting the notion that history is determined by 'reason', he does not believe that the Stage 4 ethical imperatives, as norma-tive content, are timeless or universalisable. The concrete historical entity from which the rules of intersubjectivity proceed is what Habermas calls, in a variety of compound expressions, *life*. Their common root is the Husserlian concept of the 'life-world' – the pre-systematic, pre-rationalised level of exist-ence which Husserl discovered after the failure of his initial monadic enter-prise.

In other words, the purely formal 'maxims' that guide Kantian ethics are 'historicised' by Habermas into 'grammars of world-view and of practice' (*EuI*, 241). This satisfies Hegel's critique of Kant, without falling into the rigid logicism of a hegemonic 'world spirit'. It gives us a 'subject' that is strongly normative, but is nonetheless free from the scientific processes of labour. So it gives content to our ethical prescriptions – content, for example, directed at the specific interests of the oppressed at a specific moment of the class struggle – but in a way that is independent of technolo-gical progress in the appropriation of Nature.

From this perspective, the normative rightness of revolutions is not

20 See above, ch. 1.
21 Kantian transcendentalism, and its development in Hegel, do not have to mean that sub-jectivity is noumenal in a merely negative way, and that it eventually, with Hegel, gets lost in a deterministic logic of phenomenality. The logic of phenomenality ('phenomenology') is not deterministic, as Habermas (perhaps with Adorno) seems to think. However, Habermas does not take this way out.

merely, or even primarily, a matter of technical efficiency, but is a matter of 'the reaction of oppressed life' (*EuI*, 79). 'Life' is something that is characterised precisely by being prior to the dispositions of science and political administration. As Habermas says, echoing Husserl, life is 'pre-scientific' (*LS*, 19). And it is, we might say, the material pathos of this 'life' that resists the formalism of a purely transcendental approach: 'into the place of a transcendental subject' has to step 'a species that is reproducing itself under cultural conditions, i.e. that is *still engaged in constituting itself* in a formative process' (*EuI*, 240).

> Stage 6. This, finally, gives us the methodological distinction between natural and human sciences. The natural sciences are 'nomological', says Habermas in a version of Windelband's 'nomothetic', and they deal with the timeless – what is technically conceivable 'always and everywhere' (*EuI*, 241). The 'hermeneutic' sciences, meanwhile, concern themselves with historical practice, in that they 'direct themselves towards the transcendental construction [Aufbau] of diverse factually existing life forms'. Nomological knowledge is 'technically exploitable'; hermeneutic knowledge is 'practically effective' (*EuI*, 240). The conditions within which the two forms of knowledge operate are described by Habermas as 'quasi-transcendental'.

So, as Habermas puts it, the rules he is able to derive by this device 'have a transcendental status, but emerge from the factual context of life' (*EuI*, 240). The basic framework of human practice is transcendental not in the sense that it is only conceivable in one way, but in the sense that it precedes the scientific and technical dimensions. The norms of human coexistence and interaction are 'quasi-transcendentally' binding; and because they are only *quasi*-transcendental they are neither ahistorical nor merely part of some non-subjective technological progress. They are a world, a 'lifeworld', in themselves. The whole project Habermas describes as a 'transformed transcendental philosophy' (*EuI*, 380).

11. Axiom and construction

Transcendentalism, or even 'quasi-transcendentalism', ceases to be a guiding concept in Habermas's later work. Nonetheless, the structure remains the same. Basically, we are looking for a non-irrationalist (Habermas calls it 'cognitivist') ethics. Ethical and political decisions must be guided by some kind of 'rational' set of norms. In itself, the notion of 'radical reflection' has not made decisive progress in the quest for such norms. Reflection, in principle at least, reinstates practising subjectivity into the position from which positivism expelled it – as an integral part of the object of the human sciences; but it does not of itself indicate what 'rationality' is supposed to look like in this area.

There seem to be two possibilities. In the first place, we could argue purely transcendentally, as in Stage 4 of our reconstruction above: knowledge implies language, language implies intersubjectivity, intersubjectivity implies selves (i.e. individuals with rights derived from some mutual symmetry of recognition).

The second possibility is what introduces the 'quasi' into Habermas's transcendentalism – namely, the introduction of an empirical 'life-world' (cf. Stage 5). This probably accords better with his (basically Husserlian) understanding of 'reflection'. In this argument, the 'subject' expelled by positivism is revealed to be an entity with some kind of content, i.e. something going beyond the merely transcendental or procedural elements of Stage 4.

Now in fact, as we have already indicated, Habermas seems to want both of these sources for rational normativity. The disadvantage with a Stage 4 source alone is that, although it seems fairly 'rational' (in that it is an inference from the structure of knowledge *per se*), it gives us little that could be described as content or as history. This is important to Habermas if only because he is convinced by Hegel's critique of Kant's very formalist ethics.

On the other hand, Stage 5 on its own is unsatisfactory because there seems to be nothing about it that is intrinsically 'rational'. Indeed, in Husserl's vision, the life-world is delimited almost by its distance from rationality, at least in the usual 'scientific' sense. Such an ontological irrationalism is close to the use Heidegger makes of Husserl, but would be quite inappropriate for Habermas's project.

So Habermas wishes to hold to both. In a formula, we could say, the life-world articulates itself according to a priori norms of intersubjective rationality. That preserves both its historicity (in a positive sense) and its rationality.

To see in a little more detail how he does this, we should look at the notion of dialogical reasoning developed by Paul Lorenzen, of Erlangen, and appropriated to a considerable extent by Habermas.[22]

Lorenzen's work in mathematical logic falls around the opposition between *axiomatic* and *constructive* approaches. He adopts a broadly intuitionist position. Intuitionism, for these purposes, is the doctrine that conceptual entities like numbers are 'constructed' by human beings. This means that their genesis can be constructed (or, indeed, reconstructed) from elementary human *acts*. A number is a human instrument, like, say, a

22 Habermas's explicit references to Lorenzen are sparing, though regular. The 'Erlangen School', though (e.g. *EuI*, 370), may be taken to include references to Lorenzen; and Lorenzen terms such as proponent and opponent recur in his work (e.g. *Nachmetaphysisches Denken (NmD*, 80).

hammer. A hammer can be 'constructed' in the sense that it arises through a visible and repeatable sequence of acts – mining, refining, and forging ore for the head, cutting, sawing and shaping wood for the handle. It is, one could say, a 'realisation' of human labour. There is no sense in which the hammer is pre-given; nor is any of its value distinguishable from the human acts that went to make it. It is, through and through, a human construction.

On this basis, intuitionism claims that numbers too are constructions. Its opponent is Platonism, to which is attributed the view that numbers are irreducible givens, 'creatures of God'.[23] In the Platonist account, we can say things about numbers (i.e. and hence do mathematics) because they are, so to speak, always already there. In particular, we can describe numbers with the aid of *axioms*, where axioms are more or less self-evident statements that immediately, or through their logical consequences, encompass the whole field. Because the entities described by axioms are timeless and absolutely general, they have an a priori status; and there is no sense in which a valid axiom is partial or variable.

Constructivism is easier to follow in application than in principle. Lorenzen claims that arithmetic is based not on divine entities, but on human procedures. Its roots, as he puts it, should be interpreted *operatively* rather than *ontologically* (*KW*, 178). These operative procedures, moreover, should be associated with a basic human practice, something that is essentially intimate and pre-reflexive; he speaks of pre-arithmetic practice' and a 'non-logical calculus' (*KW*, 199, 204). The intimacy of this view is that it makes mathematics into something that is accessible to understanding (*verstehen*). 'Constructive mathematics has the additional advantage that the mathematician can *understand* what he is doing (because here, philosophically speaking, he is producing his objects himself)' (1965: see *Theorie der technischen und politischen Vernunft (TtpV)*, 67).

12. Intuitionism

To understand the details of Lorenzen's position, and the way in which it connects Habermas's project with wider concerns, we need to situate it in the general context of logical intuitionism.

23 E.g. Lorenzen, *Konstruktive Wissenschaftstheorie (KW)*, 153. Lorenzen argues here and elsewhere that the opposition between Leibniz, propounding the view that numbers are divine, and Kant, the critic of this position, is fundamental for the modern debate. Lorenzen expresses the constructivist objection to its axiomatic opponents thus: 'The difficulties only begin when we turn to the fundamentals, i.e. when we no longer accept as self-explanatory that entities like the natural or the real numbers, or entities like sets or functions are in some way already *given* to us, that they are in some way already at our disposal: as if they were flowers in a garden to which we only need to give names, and about which we can then start to discover truths' (Ibid., 221).

Intuitionism involves two main metaphysical attitudes. The first is the view that mathematics is an 'activity' (Heyting, 1956: see Benacerraf and Putnam, *Philosophy of Mathematics (PoM)*, 72). Herein resides the evidentiality of mathematics: if you have 'constructed' something in a deliberate way (so you could do it again, for example), the clarity of what you have done (to you) cannot sensibly be challenged. If I divide apples by counting on my fingers, there is no point in arguing that 'really' I am applying the Peano axioms, did I but comprehend properly what I am doing.

The converse – repeatability through clear construction – applies as a requirement upon anything that is to count as 'mathematics':

> A mathematical construction ought to be so immediate to the mind and its result so clear that it needs no foundation whatsoever. One may very well know whether a reasoning is sound without using any logic. . . (Ibid., 70)

In general, then, activity precedes reflection upon it. In the case of mathematics, construction precedes logical formalisation. 'Intuitionism proceeds independently of the formalisation, which can but follow after the mathematical construction' (ibid., 69). So logic (e.g. the Peano axioms) does not provide 'foundations'; it provides retrospective generalisations about abstractions.[24]

The second major intuitionist principle is its abandonment of truth-functional semantics. The classical view supposes that there is one external or 'real' world and that any statement about it is (in principle) decidably true or false. For a full classical view, the real world includes numbers. Even in a modified classicism, such as that of Quine, there is a kind of 'honorary' real world that includes numbers (though relativised by epithets such as 'Platonistic'). Brouwer attacks this as 'formalism':

> Formalism is compelled to mark off, at least temporarily, the domain that it wishes to consider as 'true mathematics' and to lay down for that purpose a definite system of axioms and laws of reasoning, if it does not wish to see its work doomed to sterility. The various ways in which this attempt has actually been made all follow the same leading idea, viz. the presupposition of the existence of a world of mathematical objects, a world independent of the thinking individual, obeying the laws of classical logic. . . (Brouwer, 1913: *PoM*, 81)

This does not mean that intuitionistic mathematics has no relation to the 'real world'. It is (by the principle of 'activity') itself already something in a real world. Its relation to other 'realities' is mediated through construction rather than semantics; and brute requirements of 'correspondence' be-

---

24 Which is one of the strengths it claims over classical logic. Classical logic gets into difficulties over Gödel's 1931 result because it would like axioms to precede the implementation of a system. Intuitionism, in this account, dispenses with any such requirement and hence escapes problems over the incompleteness of arithmetical axiomatisability.

tween static systems (say, of sets of mathematical statements and sets of empirical 'facts') miss the point. 'The characteristic of mathematical thought is, that it does not convey truth about the external world, but is only concerned with mental constructions' (Heyting, 1956: *PoM*, 72f). The objects to which intuitionistic formulae refer do not 'exist', whether as full classical entities or conventionalist 'Platonisms'; they are, so to speak, constructibilities. '"To exist",' Heyting insists, 'must be synonymous with "to be constructed"' (ibid., 67). More generally, we can say that intuitionism puts *provability* above semantic considerations of truth and falsehood.[25]

The third principle of intuitionism follows from the first two. It is that 'objects' about which it makes statements, being 'constructions', are not to be classified as external or internal to something ('mind', perhaps), but as stages or states of some single system. They are, so to speak, reflections on 'where we've got to at this point'.

If we think for a moment about the metaphorical aspect of 'construction', we could look at things this way. Let us think of a hammer, or, better, of two hammers. I may have 'constructed' these hammers (or designed them, if I got someone else to make them) with certain random decisions. For example, one of them, I decided, should have a round face and a flat face, and the other should have a round face and a sharp spike.

Having taken delivery of my hammers, and reflecting on the relationship between the two, I see that their differing heads give them different possible uses. In fact (abbreviating my reflections somewhat), I might come to the view that one was a regular woodworking hammer and one was a geologist's hammer. Now, at this point I have, so to speak, paused in my progress and 'reflexively' determined identities for my new constructions. What initially was a partly random sequence of decisions is transformed, *ex post facto*, into a static object or identity.

Another possibility is that I might decide that the hammer with the spike was dangerous and probably useless. In that case I would throw it away; it would acquire no identity.

In the first case, then, my 'constructions' would become objects, things which I can use for further constructive activity. In the second case, one does become an object, while the other leaves my universe. If we allow with the intuitionists that mathematical objects are practical constructs (like hammers), we can see how the metaphor of 'things in the external world' being opposed to 'mental images' may be replaced by a metaphor of con-

25 This 'internalisation' of logic should be compared with Husserl's prioritisation of *reell* over *real* – see above. The whole project of intuitionism, appealing as it does (a) to an 'intensional' level of intuitive evidence, and (b) to the inclusion of the aesthetic forms, time and space, in the domain of 'logicality', draws strongly, and explicitly, on Husserl's main project.

tinuing construction and reflection. (For this image to work, of course, we have to abandon any expectation that an 'external world' coherently verifies or falsifies my constructs. Coherence comes only from the system's constructive activity; 'externality' has the same semantic status as my random design decisions.)

This notion enters intutionism as the principle of *stages*, which can be compared to moments in the biographical history of an idealised mathematician (van Dalen, 1986, 246).[26] In this history, there are few if any absolute restrictions on what the mathematician does from one moment to the next. His or her starting point at any moment, clearly, will involve the mental activity that got him or her there (since, according to principle three, there is no immediate outside to start from). And it is assumed that the mathematician has perfect memory and never forgets what he or she once knew (and hence, presumably, never acquires knowledge inconsistent which what he or she once knows). But that is the only restriction on the metamorphoses of what Brouwer, puzzlingly and controversially, called the 'creative subject' (ibid., 323f, 326).[27]

The creative subject, perhaps, is what subsists under transformation (there has to be *something* that 'never forgets'). And it is the creative subject's accumulation of knowledge (i.e. of all that is constructedly the case – there are no other 'facts') which provides the ontological counterpart for classical truth and falsehood: at any stage, the creative subject 'knows' or 'doesn't know' ϕ. The difference from the classical view, of course, is that for intuitionists 'doesn't know' only means 'cannot at this stage prove'.[28] Unless and until it can be proved, ϕ is not part of the universe; but that proof *may* yet come about, and from then on something which was not a 'fact' before will become one. That historicality applies, in the intuitionist view, even to mathematical objects – entities that the classicists would tend to regard as the most timeless of all.

13. Mathematics and pre-scientific practice

If we watch how Lorenzen applies these principles, we can see how they provide underpinning for Habermas's project. The question, we recall, is how ethical norms can be given some kind of content (i.e. more than the

26 The 'stages' can be regarded analogously to modal 'possible worlds'. See Kreiser, Gottwald, Stelzner, 1988, 163ff.
27 The creative subject is cognate, probably, with Husserl's notions of internal time consciousness. Perhaps because it is difficult to make sense of intuitionist logic without it, the 'creative subject' does seem to be widely accepted even in very abstract contexts. For example, van Benthem (1990) calls it the 'epistemic agent', and uses it as a central element in his notion of cognition 'growing' through states or worlds.
28 Cf. Kreiser, Gottwald, Stelzner, 1988, 161.

minimal formal 'conditions' of Kantian ethics) without resorting to prescriptions that are no more than empirically grounded (e.g. in monistic historicism). The structure of Habermas's approach is dualistic. On the one side, he wishes to hold to formal transcendental structures; and on the other he insists on the empirical and historical character of the grounding life-world. The same (basically Husserlian) programme is worked out in the Erlangen school's 'logic of dialogue'.

Lorenzen's initial challenge is to what he calls the dictates of 'tradition and the arbitrary decision' (1970: *KW*, 75). Such dictates are visible in mathematics as axioms. Axiom systems are arbitrary because they cannot justify themselves without circularity or infinite regress, and in the last resort have to be installed by fiat. The result is a science bedevilled by a 'plurality of irrational decisions' (1974: *KW*, 226). In the worst case, the 'decision' for a particular axiom system can be harnessed to crudely political interests; Lorenzen mentions the Nazis' concept of 'German mathematics' (1957: *KW*, 156).

A constructivist philosophy of mathematics, by contrast, devotes itself to the possibility of a rational grounding (1974: *KW*, 220). It is able to avoid circularity because its rules and principles are grounded outside, in *practice*. There are (interpreting Lorenzen somewhat) two aspects to this. First, there is the 'practice' of pre-theoretical instrumental activity, i.e. of coming to terms with our environment. This is what Lorenzen calls 'our practical capacity to act subject to conditions' (1962: *KW*, 176). It is associated with '*a practical* language that is to be learned before any theory'. In this respect, theoretical activity is only ever a 'refinement [Hochstilisierung] of what one is always already doing in practical life' (1962: *KW*, 169). Because of that, theoretical norms can be grounded by reference to pre-reflexive practice, and circularity is avoided (1962: *KW*, 180).

The second aspect of theoretical grounding is more formal. It rests on what Lorenzen calls his 'thesis that logic is interlingual' (1970: *KW*, 62). This is, in effect, the notion that 'truth' is something that we attribute not to simple relations between 'thoughts' and 'things', but to processes, or results of processes, between human beings. In that respect, the 'interlinguality' of speech – the fact that more than one person is involved – imposes certain inescapable formal rules. Those rules enable us to ground theory: not in pre-theoretical behaviour, but in a meta-theory of the statement *per se*.

Although Lorenzen does not systematically distinguish between these forms of grounding, regarding them both as somehow related to 'practice', and crediting them indifferently with being a remedy for circularity (*KW*, 62, 180), they guide separate parts of his project. Pre-theoretical grounding, we may say, informs his doctrine of the concept; meta-theoretical grounding is concerned with his doctrine of the proposition.

Lorenzen's theory of the concept consists of what might be called a technological theory of abstraction. Again, much of this echoes Husserl (for example, Husserl's theories about geometry – see above). His basic idea is that the realities of survival produce the basic cognitive equipment for producing mathematical objects and concepts in general. This consists, it would seem, in the capacity to generate abstract identity, or identity in difference. Mathematically, an object is one which, for the purposes of some technical calculus, is treated as being the same as another.

This may be seen in the calculus of counting. For example, the shepherd counts his sheep out in the morning and back at night by means of stones. If, at night, there are more stones than sheep, he knows he has lost one. This is achieved by means of an abstract identity of sheep and stones. The 'rules' for this procedure are completely basic and intuitive. Such 'axioms' as we later formulate about this calculus, e.g. the Peano axioms, are 'constructively true'; in other words, the shepherd could have produced them himself by reflecting on his 'constructions' with the stones (1970B: *KW*, 199). He was not relying, *Meno*-like, on the anamnesis of some divine set of verities. Number concepts are produced by abstractive identification; but axioms which express that come later.

Other mathematical disciplines produce their basic concepts in an analogous manner, each drawing on some 'fundamental technology' (1977: *TtpV*, 91). For example, geometry, says Lorenzen, does not have to be 'axiomatised' in the manner of Euclid. The system of geometry can be derived from the two basic elements of planes and right angles; and they in turn arise from the technical procedure of crafting solids to have surfaces that are everywhere in contact with the surfaces of other similarly crafted solids (for example, with flat sides). Planes are flatness, one might say; flatness is what you have when surfaces touch regularly at all points however you address them to each other; and flatness is a technical issue (for example, in lens grinding).

Chronometry (which, linked to geometry, gives you mechanics) depends on exactly measured and repeatable intervals. However, this is not a matter of recovering the sublime verities of 'absolute time': it is simply a matter of having more than one time-measuring device and devising abstract identities between them. An hour glass and the revolving earth will do; though clocks are necessary for the exact regularities needed by mechanical science. The principle is the same as for geometric planes: a unit is what is identical, by technical 'abstraction', with another. 'How does one tell that the clockwork is running "regularly"? Technically, that is simple: one compares the instrument with a copy of itself' (1977: *TtpV*, 77).

Stochastics (probability), says Lorenzen, is drawn from similar technological presuppositions. Randomness is not pre-given and waiting to be 'discovered', any more than geometry or chronometric intervals in time. In the first instance, randomicity is something we attribute to the results of 'chance machines' designed to observe certain criteria – principally, that they will *repeatably* produce *single* results *symmetrically* (i.e. not in a fore-castable manner). A die is a 'chance machine', though, like the hour glass, insufficiently exact (here, symmetrical) to produce the notion of identity or *equality* (here, of likelihood). Probability in application is the treatment of results as though they came from aggregated and for that reason no longer symmetrical 'chance machines'. But the original conceptual framework for this is given by the machine, which, as Lorenzen says of a roulette wheel, is a technically challenging and usually expensive product (1977: *TtpV*, 74).

There seems to be two sides to Lorenzen's account of the primary practice of science. One we might call the Husserlian side, the other the Kantian.

The Kantian side is the notion of, so to speak, the synthetic a priori. Kant argued that the understanding was not purely a matter of the timeless calculus of combination and judgement (as, in his interpretation, Leibniz had suggested). Rather, thought was only possible because of feeling (or intuition, *Anschauung*). As one example, arithmetic was synthetic because it dealt with the contingencies of time and space, rather than pure analytical verities. I could only conceive of things to add or multiply because I had a general formal intuition of identities in time or space. It was this general intuition that I was manipulating when, for example, I calculated that $7+5=12$. At the same time, of course, such calculations were a priori and, for all the purposes of 'truth' now, unrevisable.

This appeal to Kant, quite consciously, lay behind the terminology of the 'intuitionists' when they argued that mathematics was dealing with real constructions in the mind, and not just with pure formalisms.[29] It also guides Lorenzen's attempt to prove the inseparability of the intuitive from the arithmetical, even in the a priori 'ideal sciences', as he calls geometry and the others. Lorenzen's schematisation of these sciences involving time, space and contingency are a slightly embellished rendering of Kant's 'pure forms of intuition' in the transcendental aesthetic.[30]

29 See, e.g., Brouwer, 1913: *PoM*, 78, 80.
30 Much of this can be read in terms of traditional metaphysical categories. The principle of identity is matter, possibility, δύναμις; the principle of difference is form, μορφή. Matter, as unactualised possibility, remains eternally the same; form gives it reality, plurality, distinctness. Matter – what is perceived by the 'aesthetic' sensibility – gives thingness, here-and-now-ness, to form. Form gives perceivability and distinctness to the *hic et nunc*. In Kantian terminology, 'subject' corresponds to matter, 'object' to form. The intuitionists' 'creative subject' is an echo of this; it should perhaps be read, though, not as an active subject on the analogy of an artist (or even a mathematician), but as the subject within which potentialities

The Husserlian reading is rather different. Kant did not regard the synthetic a priori as in any way historical, or part of a particular empirical practice. Arithmetic may involve intuition, but counting apples or matching
stones to sheep are only illustrations, not grounding events. Lorenzen, by
contrast, argues firmly that 'we proceed from a historical fact' in our
reconstruction of disciplines like probability (1974: *KW*, 229). In terms of
mathematics generally, he claims that the recovery of 'prior opinions'
(*Vormeinungen*) is the initial step in any mathematical philosophy.

> Thus the philosophy of mathematics is assigned the task of bringing to light
> the prior decisions that lie hidden already in the move towards the formation
> of any mathematical theories. It does this by putting them in the larger context
> of the history of our pre-scientific opinions. (1957: *KW*, 156)

The important thing about these 'prior opinions' is that they are *pre-
reflexive*. As Lorenzen puts it in appeal to Dilthey, 'life' 'cannot be gone
behind' (ibid., 156). In other words, there is a world of content, of practices
perhaps, which is not itself subject to scientific or critical reflection. The
'understanding' we have of this pre-scientific life 'does not formulate itself
in sentences that can be components of science'. In Lorenzen's view, of
course, that is why practice can supply a non-circular grounding for
theory.[31]

The force of all this, as Lorenzen emphasises, is not that science and
philosophy should abandon themselves to a relativistic celebration of pre-
cognitive 'life', but that the philosophical discipline appropriate to mathematics as well as to more obviously human questions is 'understanding'
(*verstehen*). Reconstruction, in Lorenzen's interpretation of intuitionism,
is (he strongly implies) the same discipline as hermeneutic understanding.
To trace mathematics back to its practical elements is the same as to trace
back any cultural phenomenon to its roots. Hence Lorenzen's demand that
the mathematician should 'understand' (*verstehen*) the origins of his or her
discipline; and hence also his programmatic linking of logic and hermeneutics as the twin disciplines of the new philosophy:

> The precondition [for a new philosophy] is a logic and hermeneutic that can be
> methodically taught, a synthesis of enlightened and historical consciousness
> as it was first attempted by Hegel, but which could not have been developed –
> to name just two names – before Frege and Dilthey. (1968: *KW*, 21)

are actualised. Heidegger was aware of the richness of these terms, and strongly critical. For
more, see *German Philosophy*, 260f.
31 Lorenzen's term 'Vormeinung' in fact predates Gadamer's use of the equivalent concept
'Vorurteil' in *Truth and Method* (see 255ff.), which was published three years later. Gadamer
does not cite Lorenzen.

14. Logic of dialogue

The second element to Lorenzen's 'practical' grounding of mathematics is more clearly formal. It is the interpretation of 'truth' as something that arises in the practice of reasoning. The practice of reasoning, i.e. the way in which it happens in time, rather than in some imagined divine instant, is conceived to be something that happens dialogically. It happens, that is to say, either between two real disputants where one tries to maintain a thesis against objections, or in the form of one thinker's silent dialogue with himself. The basic formal structure is, first, that the speakers are not omniscient: in particular, the person maintaining the thesis (in Lorenzen's terminology, the 'proponent') does not know in advance what objections his opponent will be able to sustain. Second, the disputants observe a principle of relevance: that is to say, they pursue the theme in a persistent manner, without raising unrelated issues or leaving attacks unanswered. This, roughly, is presupposed by Lorenzen as a kind of pure transcendental structure for any process of reasoning. The development goes as follows.

First, Lorenzen follows the intuitionist tradition in attacking any notion that mathematics is an absolute realm, either because 'God' made it, or because it is a set of formal conventions which we can neither prove nor disprove. The problem is this. If, so to speak, 'God' made mathematics (or, equally, if mathematics is somehow the result of a 'convention' installed by decision), then 'God' (or the convention-decider) should have access to all the answers. If we imagine 'God' as a perfect mind, or as a limitless computer, then this mind or computer should be able, given time, to calculate all the theorems of the system; or, conversely, to decide of any particular formula whether it is a theorem of the system or not. Potentially, at least, the system is there for instantaneous inspection.

In propositional logic, this is the case. It is possible to decide of any formula whether it is valid or invalid, in a finite number of steps. With formulae using quantifiers this may or may not be the case. If I assume that I am quantifying over a finite domain, then the formulae behave as though they contained straight quantifier-free propositions. If I am quantifying over the books on my shelves, for example, any formula

$$\forall x F x$$

– for any x, x is an F – will be decidable in a finite number of steps. If the predicate F here is 'is either a hardback or a paperback, but not both', then the quantifier notation can be eliminated in terms of the conjunction of a set of propositions $p_1, p_2, \ldots p_n$, where p is of the form 'Fx', and n is the number of books on my shelves. Quantification over finite domains, in other words, is a kind of harmless shorthand.

In non-finite domains, however, the situation is less clear. If, for example, I claim that for any natural number x, no x is both odd and perfect (perfect numbers are the sum of their own integer factors, e.g. $6=3\times2\times1=3+2+1$), possible counter-instances, though none are yet known, could be adduced indefinitely (cf. Kamlah and Lorenzen, 1974, 208, 224). Or, as another example, Fermat's conjecture is that there are no four natural numbers x, y, z and n, with $n>2$, for which

$$x^n+y^n=z^n$$

Nobody has yet succeeded in finding any three for which this is the case; but equally, nobody has proved that it cannot be the case. 'If God in heaven made numbers like he made the stars, he ought to know whether there are any such triples,' Lorenzen challenges (1957: *KW*, 157).

If you are a classical logician, in other words, there *must* be an answer one way or the other. In that view, mathematical infinities are 'actual'; they 'exist' in the same way as the books on my shelf exist, only on a grander scale. But, of course, this involves strong assumptions about the ontology of mathematical objects – and, by extension, about the ontology of all objects of reason. Do we stand to such objects as though we were 'God'? – i.e. in such a way that we could, as of now, know all about them if we only had sufficient computational power – in, as Lorenzen puts it, a 'rerun of divine cognition' (1957: *KW*, 159)? Why is it, asks Lorenzen,

> that mathematics regards the totality of its linguistic resources as given in advance, or at all events as unambiguously delimited, independently of us? (1957: *KW*, 161)

The other view is that mathematics does *not* depend on predetermined answers. The insistence on a pre-existing infinite totality is one of mathematical philosophy's 'pre-opinions'. If we abandon it, we no longer need to think of numbers as a bounded structure with a monolithic set of axioms and rules of inference. That is, as Lorenzen points out, just as well, since Gödel's 1931 result demonstrates that no complete axiomatisation of arithmetic is possible anyway. The appropriate response to this is not Quine's conventionalist conclusion that mathematics is 'myth-making' (*FLPV*, 19), but to see that 'arithmetic and analysis do not belong to the type of the axiomatic sciences' (1970a: *KW*, 60). Mathematics, in this contention, is the dynamic and continuing construction of things that are not complete in advance; from that perspective, incompleteness is precisely what one would expect, and attempts at 'total axiomatics' (1957: *KW*, 164) are merely perverse.

From this perspective, we can reread, 'dialogically', the nature of the logical constants. Now, from the classical perspective the logical connectives (&, ¬, →, and so on) can be read as statements about the truth values of the component propositions. This has a kind of pictorial representation in the truth-table method used, for example, by Wittgenstein in the *Tractatus*. In the truth tables the connectives are 'eliminated' in terms of combinations of true and false elementary propositions. For example,

p	q	$p+q$
T	T	T
T	F	T
F	T	T
F	F	F

is a representation of the connective 'v' ('either . . . or . . . or both', understood to apply as long as it is not the case that both component propositions are false). A similar tabular representation of the connective '→' ('if . . . then . . .') would be

T	T	T
T	F	F
F	T	T
F	F	T

Now, the dialogicians' reproach is that this way of eliminating the connectives (i.e. of defining them in such a way that they do not themselves occur in the definition) rests on the ontology of omniscience we have already met. In other words, it defines reasoning in terms of external states of affairs – knowing and combining static givens. Reasoning, in this image, is constantly referring to its 'truth-functional' roots in *facts* – things that are already the case. Nothing is made (or 'constructed') by reasoning; reasoning simply reflects, or fails to reflect, the outside 'reality' of things, numbers or whatever. Truth values are, so to speak, always already there; and reasoning has at least to presuppose the *possibility* of sooner or later establishing those truth values (e.g. that we shall one day know whether there are any perfect odd numbers; cf. *LP*, 157). The kind of truth illustrated by truth tables is 'semantic' truth – i.e. a truth depending on successful reference (*LP*, 214).

The dialogical or constructivist elimination is quite different. It appeals, as we have noted, to the *practice* of reasoning. If we imagine reasoning to be a dialogue, we can understand statements not as combinations of factually-based 'truth values', but as ways of dealing with hypotheses and their reasoned defence. As Lorenzen presents the matter, we can imagine any logical concatenation of elementary statements, say 'p v q', as shorthand not for an inventory of truths and falsehoods, but for a certain course of reasoning (*LP*, 158). If a combination of propositions (the hypothesis) turns out to be defensible in a certain way, in debate, then we can say that the dialogue can be summarised as having established '$p \lor q$' as a thesis. In Lorenzen's notation, we would have:[32]

$$? \ \| \ \begin{array}{l} p \lor q \\ p \end{array}$$

At this point, we could say that the proponent has established $p \lor q$ (if we read alternation as 'at least one of . . .').

For conjunction, the pattern requires the opponent to be selective in her attack; if the proponent fails to establish either part of the conjunction, his hypothesis fails. So an exchange for conjunction might look:

$$R? \ \| \ \begin{array}{l} p \ \& \ q \\ q \end{array}$$

In other words, the proponent resists his opponent's attack on the right-hand side of the hypothesis by defending q.

In Lorenzen's dialogue rules, both of these patterns suffice to defend the hypothesis. In the case of alternation, it is perhaps obvious. It is less so in the case of conjunction; but one has to imagine that the opponent has the choice of which part of the conjunction to attack, and will therefore presumably attack the one that she regards as weaker. If the proponent can defend the weaker part, then, constructively, he can be regarded as winning the conjunction.

On this basis we can also give a single-exchange account of implication. If implication ('$\rightarrow$') means, 'if . . . then you *must* have . . .', we get the exchange:

$$p \ \| \ \begin{array}{l} p \rightarrow q \\ q \end{array}$$

In other words, if the opponent successfully asserts p, the proponent must be able successfully to assert q.

The quantifiers match conjunction and alternation, as one might expect. If an existential quantifier appears in the hypothesis, the proponent is allowed to choose what to defend (anything of which the predicate is true). So,

$$? \ \| \ \begin{array}{l} \exists x \ Fx \\ Fy \end{array}$$

– i.e. the proponent proves that y is F, thus establishing that 'for some . . ., F

---

32 In Lorenzen's notation, the lines are a succession of dialogical exchanges, with the proponent's utterances appearing to the right of the central bar, and the opponent's to the left. The first line of any dialogue contains only one formula: the proponent's statement of the thesis to be defended. The symbol ? indicates an attack on all or part of the interlocutor's last statement ('?R', for example, would mean an attack on the right half of some formula).

is true'. With a universal quantifier, the proponent is claiming that he can demonstrate F for *anything* in the domain of the quantifier. So the opponent may choose some individual to mount an attack over. Hence

$$\begin{array}{c|l} & \forall x\ Fx \\ y? & \ldots \end{array}$$

The proponent, in other words, has to defend his contention of F as a predicate for the y chosen by the opponent.

Obviously these dialogues all take much longer as soon as the logical structure is more complex.

The point of all this is that the logical connectives 'disappear' (1970a: *KW*, 73) – are eliminated, in other words – in terms of the *practical* steps in an imagined dialogue. The basic categories are all given (according to Lorenzen) in terms of *agreement* between *two people*. When a hypothesis is defended, the only operative notions that are needed are 'I attack . . .' and 'I defend . . .', and the two people to perform those actions.

Implicitly, this changes our understanding of what propositions or theses might be. The basic point is that instead of regarding statements as reflections of displays of 'facts' (as the truth-tabular method suggests), we regard them as programmes for interpersonal exchanges. A universal quantifier, for example, is not an ontological assertion about '*every* fact' in some range; it is simply a statement about what the proponent is prepared to defend. Furthermore, the dialogue is not to be imagined as going on ad infinitum, tediously going through every imaginable case to produce a counter-example: it is simply an ascertainment of what the interlocutors are, in their present state of knowledge, prepared to agree on.

This is not a justification for empirical laziness; it is a rendering of the intuitionistic notion that we are not omniscient, and omniscience (a 'God's eye view') is not even potentially available to us. Knowledge – any knowledge, God's included[33] – progresses through construction rather than through discovery. More technically, we could say that, for an intuitionist, propositions come with a tensed modal operator of some kind. p is to be read not as 'the state of affairs p obtains', but as 'I can, now, prove (or "construct") p' (or 'I am in a state of having constructed p'). Assuming p is a compound statement (rather than something atomic like 'this is a book'), dialogues represent a testing of such a claim of provability.

This interpretation also illuminates the intuitionist idea of negation. Notoriously, the intuitionists dispute *tertium non datur*, the law of excluded middle ('for any statement, either it is true or not true': '$p \lor \neg p$'). In intuitionist terms, this is because '$\neg p$' is to be read not as 'p is not true', but

---

33 See above, chapter 4, on this theme. Also Lorenzen, 1957: *KW*, 153 for Husserl's comment on the notion that God is a mathematician.

as 'I can prove that p is absurd (i.e. unconstructable)'. If we reformulate the law of excluded middle in those terms ('for any statement, either I can prove it is true or I can prove it is not true'), we can see why it would be rejected. If I can prove the matter one way or the other, obviously I cannot also prove it the other way (i.e. the law of non-contradiction applies: '$\neg(p$ & $\neg p)$'). But if I have, at present, no proof either way, then I can make no assertions that presuppose I ever shall have a proof. *Tertium non datur* presupposes that the truth values of all propositions are, in principle, always discoverable. Intuitionism rejects this because there may well be plenty of things I never prove at all. In informal or pragmatic reasoning this is probably not a great loss.

The same reservation applies to the intuitionist interpretation of double negation. Classically, '$\neg \neg p$' implies 'p' (and is derivable from 'p v $\neg p$'). Two negatives make a positive, so to speak. Intuitionistically, though, '$\neg \neg p$' is to be interpreted as 'I can prove that it would be absurd to say that p is absurd' (or 'a proof for the unconstructability of p is unconstructable'). That does not amount to saying that p is provable. In terms of practical reasoning, this means that intuitionistic logic does not support argument by *reductio ad absurdum*. Again, *reductio* (winning by a demonstration that the opposite of what you are trying to establish is absurd) is not necessarily as useful as it might seem in informal kinds of reasoning.

Like truth tables, dialogues illuminate the 'ontological commitments' of the logic they are associated with.[34] The distinctions emerge most clearly in the tautologies – the patterns of reasoning that are valid irrespective of the truth or falsity of their component elementary statements. Non-tautological patterns of reasoning are uninteresting in the sense that who wins (dialogically) depends ultimately on whether or not the elementary statements are true or false. They can only, that is to say, be decided by recourse to semantics, to an 'outside' of 'facts'. This is the case with all the single exchanges illustrated above. (E.g. the proponent wins $\forall x(Fx)$ if he chooses an appropriate domain and function.)

The classical tautologies, in Lorenzen's argument, continue to presuppose that the elementary statements have a truth-functional value, even though the validity of the tautology does not depend on them. They are, in his terminology, 'value-definite'. Constructive logical truth, however, does not make this assumption. The elementary statements only need to be what Lorenzen calls 'dialogically definite' – i.e. the disputants must be agreed on what would constitute a good defence if required (*LP*, 211). That,

34 The term, of course, is Quine's. But Quinean ontological commitments – numbers and so on – are at a significantly higher level than those associated with the logical constants. The opposition between dialogue and truth table is, perhaps, an approach to the metaphysical foundations of logic.

as we have seen, does not involve comprehensive catalogues of elementary facts; it simply means that, for example, the opponent must not be able to produce any counter-examples (to a conjunction or universal quantification), or must accept the proponent's assertion (in support of an alternation or an existential quantifier).

'Constructive logical truth', by contrast with the classical tautologies, says nothing about elementary truth values, but confines itself to *argumentative strategies*. The proponent wins not because he can rely on particular constellations of 'facts', but because he has a strategy which always works. The basic principle is not semantic, but argumentative; and its winning moment is not reference to truth values, but to the principle of 'ipse dixisti' – i.e. where the proponent can say to his opponent, 'you've already admitted yourself what you now want me to establish!'[35] As Lorenzen puts it,

> In contrast to the definition of tautological [i.e. classical] truth we do not even need to know that the elementary statements are value-definite. We do not need to talk about truth values, since we are only looking for a strategy that would lead to a situation in which the proponent has to defend an elementary formula already posited by his opponent: no elementary formula need actually be defended. (*LP*, 220)

The 'constructive logical truths' generated by dialogues do not match the tautologies of classical logic at all points. In particular, the rules of *tertium* (p v $\neg p$) and *reductio* ($\neg\neg p{\rightarrow}p$) turn out not to be supportable by 'universal winning strategies'; the defensibility of the statement depends in each case on the defensibility of the component elementary statements (cf. *LP*, 219, 221).

15. Formalist and naturalist foundations

However, the situation is not as plain as Lorenzen would like it to be because it is hard to generate *any* interesting strategies without tinkering with the dialogue rules. The problem is this.

In the case of implication, the proponent really needs to be able to answer two possible challenges. This is because when he asserts '$p{\rightarrow}q$', he either needs to be able to dispute p successfully (without p, he does not need to worry about the consequent), or he needs to be able to defend q. (Or, to put the same thing another way, '$\neg p$ v q', which is equivalent to '$p{\rightarrow}q$'.) In the dialogue scenario, the disputants are assumed not to know in advance their interlocutor's ability to dispute any particular elementary statement. So whereas, intuitively, it may seem acceptable for conjunctions

35 See Felscher, 1986, 356.

or alternations to be settled by exchanges over single elementary statements (we are, so to speak, satisfied that the opponent's failure to impugn
the one statement he has chosen does allow the proponent to carry the
day), the same does not apply in the case of implications.

Let us put this another way. In the basic dialogue model, each player responds strictly only to the statement the other has just made. There is a
simple reasonableness about this which gives it its 'constructive' appeal (cf.
LP, 213). It is, in fact, a rule of *relevance* (cf. Felscher, 1986, 368). If the
dialogue proceeds rigidly according to this rule, however, an implication
can be 'lost' by the proponent because he makes the wrong initial response
to his opponent's challenge. For example, he attacks the precedent only to
find that his opponent can defend it, whereupon he is then unable to assert
the consequent because it is no longer 'relevant' in terms of what his opponent last said. Alternatively, he responds to his opponent's assertion of the
precedent by asserting the consequent, finds himself unable to defend it,
and is then precluded from going back to attack the precedent because of
the relevance rule.

So, in order to allow dialogues to produce patterns comparable to classical logic, Lorenzen has to 'liberalise' the relevance rule. Basically, this now
says that the proponent may attack *any* assertion by the opponent, and
defend himself against the *latest* of the opponent's attacks. In other words,
as far as the proponent is concerned the rule confining relevance to the last
statement has disappeared; and, in fact, the only remaining restriction is
that the proponent may not answer any attack earlier than the last one.
(The opponent's rules do not change: she is limited to strict relevance.)

The difficulty here is that a good deal depends on dialogue rules. In particular, if the rules are 'liberalised' sufficiently, dialogues can be made to produce *all* the classical tautologies, i.e. *tertium non datur* as well (Lorenz,
1961; Felscher, 1986, 352). The question then arises: what is the justification
for adopting one set of 'liberalised' rules rather than another? If the justification is merely pragmatic – because one set happens to correspond with
the intuitionism we prefer anyway – the 'constructive' element of the argument disappears.

In Lorenzen, the formal argument for adopting constructive rather than
classical dialogue rules is weak; it merely consists in saying that the constructive rules can differentiate compositions which, for classical purposes,
are indistinguishable (for example, '$\neg p \lor q$' and '$\neg(p \ \& \ \neg q)$'; *LP*, 217).
This is a different claim from saying that the dialogue rules 'reconstruct
what we "always already" do' (Kamlah's expression in *LP*, 162). The fact
that Lorenzen is apparently willing to countenance the uncertain status of
his rules in strictly 'constructive' terms, however, is probably a reflection
of the 'Lebenspraxis' justification we considered above.

The point is, there is an ambiguity in Lorenzen's work between the 'practical' founding of logical norms in terms of *reconstruction* (formally), and in terms of *verstehen* (of pre-scientific practice). When in doubt, Lorenzen resorts to a *verstehen* account. Or, to put it in his polarity, he seems to see the main pillar of recent philosophy in Dilthey rather than in Frege. Another way of putting it might be to say that reflexion, in Lorenzen's account, is directed more towards the life-world concerns of the later Husserl than towards the formal interests of his early work.

The apparent advantage of this approach is that we have a 'praxis' in which logical matters can be grounded (thus avoiding circularity), and which, furthermore, helps to bridge the gulf between historical and natural-scientific understanding of the world. 'Insight into life's irreducibility [Unhintergehbarkeit],' says Lorenzen, gives philosophy a 'new immediacy' (1962: *KW*, 170).

The common source both of the norms of *reasoning* and of *moral behaviour* is what he calls the 'principle of transsubjectivity' (1970a: *KW*, 93). It is a *principle* because it *comes before* all normativity ('principium' is technical Latin for Greek αρχή, 'origin'). Practice, in this sense, is absolute aprioricity. It takes the form of 'collective, immediate life practice [Lebenspraxis]' (1970a: *KW*, 96). Its irreducible, pre-reflexive standing is similar to that of Wittgenstein's 'language games', suggests Lorenzen (1962: *KW*, 175). The life-world's rules are not available as explicit prescriptions: they only emerge in the course of a practice that is always already rule-guided.

The difficulty is: how does this approach escape naturalism? What a priori norms can 'Lebenspraxis' contribute other than anthropological or biological ones? On that level, it would be hard to distinguish Lorenzen's approach from the relativism of 'German mathematics' he attacks. Naturalism is not an answer to positivism; it merely seeks to hold a fig-leaf before the nakedness conceded by positivism. Rather than, as with positivism, speak of 'conventions' or 'traditions', naturalism speaks of the 'life-world'. But the positive precepts of the life-world, to the extent that they are merely fragments of anthropology entrenched in 'pre-reflexivity', are not obviously different from conventions.

Before we move on to consider Habermas's appropriation of the dialogue model, it is important to point out that the problem of producing dialogue rules in a fully formal and 'constructive' way is not as intractable as it appears.[36] The problem, we recall, is to allow dialogues that will produce a logic sufficiently strong to do the sorts of things we need it to do (e.g. mathematical philosophy), but which is also 'grounded' by intuitionistic constructions. The procedures should be operative rather than ont-

36 See, in particular, Felscher, 1986, on this.

ological. Truth tables are ontological in their basic metaphor, and excessively strong in some of their interpretations, e.g. of negation and quantification. We need something that is at least as self-evident as the truth table, but is better able to explain logic as part of *reasoning practice*.

Lorenzen's resort to 'rules' is perhaps too abrupt. We need to consider a little longer what a dialogical disputation involves, 'a priori'. It is, first and foremost, the proving of some contention. 'Proof', in this context, needs to be understood in a more forensic sense. It does *not* indicate the deductive demonstration of a mathematical proof. To prove forensically is to affirm without credible resistance. It means to 'try' (*probare*), as in the 'trial' in court. A trial is a proof procedure. By means of it certain contentions are tested; persons making them are 'examined'. At the end, something stands proven, not mathematically, but 'on the balance of probabilities' (for example).

In a forensic procedure, in other words, we do not (in English law, at least) start with the assumption that there are 'facts' to be discovered. What is 'proved' is not a fact, but the decision itself. To use Lorenzen's terminology, a trial is 'irreducible' (unhintergehbar) in the sense that what is constituted is a decision, not an 'account' of something. That is the reason why findings of fact are usually not reviewable. Reviewability (the availability of appeal procedures, and so on) is generally confined to issues of *procedure*. The foundation of forensic proof, in other words, is propriety in the disputation of contentions (the plaintiff's claims, the prosecution's charges, and so on), rather than the searching out of facts in some inquisitorial, 'scientific' way.[37]

As is well known, this can raise difficulties in the area of criminal law, where the popular view is that courts *are* there to establish 'the facts'. For example, it can seem odd that the defendant is not obliged to testify (examining the prosecution evidence is quite enough, formally). Moreover, once a conviction has been found on appeal to be procedurally sound, even 'fresh evidence' will often not suffice to get the case back into court. A procedurally proper court has discharged its function; the justice of 'facts' (assuming such things exist!) has to be administered by the prerogative of mercy which is, by its very nature, a non-procedural individual decision.

The intuitionistic reasoning produced by dialogues is comparable to forensic proof. The general criterion of intuitionistic truth – 'provable in the present stage of knowledge' – is analogous to that for discharging the burden of proof in a trial.

37 There are of course differences between common law and civil law traditions on this. My comments apply principally to the common law tradition. But even within civil law traditions, the 'principle of investigation' (truth-discovering) can be seen as a derogation from the 'principle of negotiation' (decision-constructing). See Thomas-Putzo, Introduction I1.

Beyond this, Felscher (1986) has produced an account of dialogues which 'reconstructs' Lorenzen's apparently arbitrary rules much more satisfactorily. It can be summarised as follows. First, simply asserting 'dialogue rules' is clearly no advance on relying on 'axioms'.

Second, the rules about who may attack what statement and when reflects the fact that the two participants, proponent and opponent, are playing formally distinct roles. Everything flows from the basic formal notion: the proponent is defending his contention. Because we are dealing with reasoning strategies (logical validity of argument forms), not with empirical issues, winning or losing are easy to define. The proponent wins if he can relevantly assert an atomic proposition already asserted by the opponent, or if the opponent can say nothing that is not absurd. The crucial issue is that of *relevance*. Is relevance merely a contingent matter of content, or can it be seen as a way of describing part of the structure of the dialogue? Felscher has tried to argue the latter.

Informally, the point is this. The proponent makes a contention: 'I say such-and-such.' His opponent has to try to undermine this contention by producing hypothetical situations: 'Well, what if such-and-such?' The dialogue proceeds by the disputants narrowing themselves down from long composite contentions to elementary propositions. If, at that point, we merely have a truth-functional stand-off ('you say p, I say not-p'), then clearly the proponent has not won. If, on the other hand, the proponent ends up needing to assert an elementary proposition that the opponent has already conceded, hypothetically, as part of her attack, then the proponent has clearly won: *ipse dixisti*, 'you just said that yourself!' Or, to put it another way, if the opponent has already said 'well, what if p?' (as a way of forcing the proponent to defend something, say the consequent of p) earlier in the dialogue, then the proponent's ability later on to say 'yes, p, but that is something you already posited as part of our argument' represents a win for him.

We can illustrate this with two formalised dialogues. First, we shall look at the formula '$p \rightarrow \neg \neg p$' ('from p's constructibility follows that the construction of the unconstructibility of p is absurd').

O		$p \rightarrow \neg \neg p$
1	p	$\neg \neg p$
2	$\neg p$	p

The proponent wins this because he is able relevantly to assert a proposition already asserted by his opponent. In words, we could render the exchange as:

O   Proponent: '$p \rightarrow \neg \neg p$'

1   Opponent asserts the antecedent ('Well, what if p?'); proponent asserts the

consequent ('In that case I'd say $\neg\neg p$').

2　Opponent attacks proponent's answer ('To which I'd reply $\neg p$'); where-upon proponent answers attack, and wins exchange, by asserting what opponent has already asserted ('$\neg p$ can't be right – you've just said p yourself!')

In a second dialogue we reverse antecedent and consequent: '$\neg\neg p{\rightarrow}p$'. This, of course, is the *reductio* which intuitionism does not support. Keeping to the usual rule of relevance, we might get:

O　　　　　‖ $\neg\neg p{\rightarrow}p$
1　　$\neg\neg p$ ‖ p
(O asserts ante; P defends)
2　　...　‖ ...

Here, the proponent has not produced an *ipse dixisti*, and has therefore failed to defend his assertion. We could render this exchange as: Proponent: '$\neg\neg p{\rightarrow}p$'; Opponent: (attacks by asserting antecedent) 'Well, what do you say to $\neg\neg p$?'; Proponent: 'I'd say p'. End of dialogue. In other words, the proponent needs to attack his opponent in order to keep the dialogue going.[38]

If he does so, we would have:

O　　　　　‖ $\neg\neg p{\rightarrow}p$
1　　$\neg\neg p$ ‖ $\neg p$
(O asserts ante; P attacks)
2　　p　‖
(O attacks P's line 1 attack)

At this point, however, the proponent is still stuck, despite having attacked the antecedent rather than affirming the consequent. The opponent has attacked his $\neg p$ in line 1 by asserting p. In response, the proponent could repeat the $\neg p$ he's already said; but in that case we simply have a stand-off over the truth of an elementary proposition.[39] So there are no further steps the proponent can take on the level of strict reasoning.

There *would* be, however, if he were following the liberalised, 'classical' dialogue rules. Using them, he would be allowed to leave his opponent's last attack (at line 2) open and tackle the attack in line 1 again, this time by

38　The opponent is not obliged to attack P's defence 'p' in line 1, because p is non-composite (*LP*, 221; Felscher, 1986, rule D01).
39　Though in fact this would be technically against the rules anyway. Lorenzen states the argument form for negation as 1) '$\neg p$' (assertion), 2) 'p' (attack), 3) no answer possible (*LP*, 210). Felscher expands this by saying that '$\neg p$' should be understood as '$p{\rightarrow}!!$', where !! is a constant indicating absurdity. No disputant may assert absurdity without immediately losing (by a rule of *ex absurdo quodlibet*: anything follows from absurdity). So, no stage 3 is possible after 1) '$p{\rightarrow}!!$' and 2) 'p' because affirming the consequent would be to assert absurdity, and the antecedent cannot be attacked because it is not composite (Felscher, 1986, 353f; see also Lorenzen, *Logik und Agon*, 6).

affirming the consequent, 'p'. Since this has only just been affirmed by the opponent, we have an *ipse dixisti*, and the proponent wins. Classically, then, the proponent has a strategy for always winning this formula: when the opponent attacks with the antecedent, counterattack the antecedent first to elicit a 'p', and then ignore the opponent by taking a second, now defensive, bite at the antecedent. This does, however, depend on leaving an issue unresolved; and that is why such a proceeding does, from a constructive point of view, offend against the basic structure of the dialogue.[40]

In this context, then, the complex and at first sight arbitrary 'rules' make more sense. In particular, the formal-argumentative reason why we should not admit the 'classical' liberalisation – that the proponent should be allowed to respond to or attack anything said by his opponent, at any time and as many times as he wants – becomes more clear. The point is that the opponent's statements are only hypotheses produced in direct response to the particular contention that the proponent has just made. To allow the proponent to attack these hypotheses as though they were contentions in their own right, aspects of the opponent's 'position', would be to confuse the issue. In the forensic examination of a witness, the examiner has no 'position'; the barrister is, so to speak, merely a catalyst, an irritant. To treat a hypothetical objection as though it constituted a material contention would introduce absurd distortions.

For example, the witness is claiming to have gone out without a coat. Question: what if it had rained? Answer: I knew I had an umbrella in the car. And so on. On another, unrelated point, for example, if the witness is claiming not to have sat on the veranda, he cannot then say: 'but you said it might rain!' The point, in other words, is not for the proponent (the witness) to 'undermine' the opponent (the barrister), but for him to show consistency in his own responses.

The 'rules' of disputation, in other words, seem to emerge from the basic formal preconditions governing the *defence* of a *contention*. It is entirely plausible that dialogue reasoning is a kind of practical a priori, not because it is rooted in the 'life-world', human transsubjectivity or any other 'pre-scientific' condition, but simply because the disputation of a contention has to follow certain patterns in order for a decision to be reached. If it is possible to establish such a pattern, or a set of equivalent patterns, then this would have a strong claim to self-evident formal normativity.

The central notion would seem to be that of *winnability* (rather, say, than that of 'discoverability', the metaphor underlying semantic truth).

---

40 Leaving an attack hanging is acceptable *if the attacker agrees*, e.g. by continuing the dialogue anyway. But if the dialogue is to be settled by answering an attack, then the answer must direct itself to the *latest* attack (see Felscher, 1986, rule D11). Presumably the procedural rule by which amendments are voted on before the main motion has a similar justification.

The 'rules' governing dialogues may be reconstructed intuitively in terms
of their ability to produce a winning position. Winning, itself, involves two
things. First, it involves an opponent. I only win if I dispute. There is no
absolute pre-existent 'answer' to which I may individually turn (as there
might be in the ontology of semantic truth); there is only a stage which I
may win if my contentions and my opponent's attacks fall out a certain
way. This is the principle of 'non-omniscience'. The second component of
winning is that it must produce certainty. I must win an issue. I, the proponent, do not want to discredit my opponent, or prove something she says
wrong. I want to prove that what I claimed is right by successfully defending it against her. When I have done that, perhaps we can change roles and
go on to another topic. But the topic itself must be won and resolved. That
is the basic character of the logical dialogue: the issue remains live until its
specific defence has been completed. Attacks on the opponent, or winning
on other issues, are immaterial. All the 'rules', including those which exclude the 'classical' liberalisations, may be reconstructed along that intuition.

We can now revert to our commentary on Habermas's project.

16. Rationalisation

In the later work, Habermas rejects what he calls 'historical philosophy'
(*Geschichtsphilosophie*: e.g. *LS*, 8, *TkH*, II 583). This may be understood as
a term for Hegelian totalising 'expressivism', for the elements of that in
Marx, and indeed also for Habermas's own early reliance on notions like
class struggle. In another sense, however, history remains fundamental to
his project. There is, it seems, a process in history, a process whereby
things change in a rationally recoverable way. It is not the coming-to-itself
of a historical subject, as it might be in *Geschichtsphilosophie*,[41] but what
Habermas calls *rationalisation*.

Rationalisation invokes a version of Aristotelian teleology, a tradition in
which Hegel also stands. The idea, if we can put it in a 'metaphysical' terminology Habermas himself would probably not favour, is that the world
steadily emerges from a dull unconsciousness into the daylight of intellect
and spirit. Moreover, this is a good thing; we could even say that the nature
of goodness lies precisely in the 'perfecting' of each thing towards its
telos.[42]

There are three elements to Habermas's later metaphysics. The first two

41 Habermas's view of Marx, and to some extent of Hegel, seem to be heavily coloured by the
Lukács of *History and Class Consciousness*. This, presumably, is attributable to his pupillage
with Adorno. But this kind of historicism is idiosyncratic, to say the least. See *Introduction*,
chapter 8.
42 Heidegger, of course, took a dim view of such conceptions. See *Introduction*, 259.

follow the lines of classical German idealism. Its elements are, first, that there is no logic of Being, but there is one of change. Second, change is teleological and perfecting. Up to this point Habermas is close to Hegel, and to the Marxism of the early Lukács.

The difficulty that critical theorists like Adorno had with a straight Hegelianism, however, was its supposition that perfection could be a concrete reality; or, that the 'perfection' wrought by rational 'enlightenment' was a desirable one. For Adorno (perhaps following Husserl), the intellect represented a violation of body and nature. Enlightenment was a trap, and to free ourselves we had to turn reason against itself, in the 'negative dialectic'. Metaphysically: body and nature are real though not reasonable; and indeed reason can only reach them indirectly, by allusion and by its own deliberate self-destruction.[43] In particular, reason must remain aware of its inability to encompass the realities of body and nature; reality is never identical with what reason says about it (this is the hubris of 'identity philosophy'). The end of history, in this respect, is the self-immolation of reason and the freeing of the body. But that, of course, is not something that can happen in our world.

Habermas's appropriation of this is more optimistic. A duality of the critical theorists' kind remains. For Habermas, it is the duality between a pre-conceptual life-world and the operations of reason. But in this account, the process of rationalisation is, in general, a good one, and produces good things on earth. The life-world is subjected to rationalisation; but that is a good thing. In order to avoid the incipient Hegelianism of this position, however (the 'spiritualisation' of the life-world in history, for example), Habermas breaks up the identity at the level of the life-world itself. In other words, while traditional critical theory had resisted identity thinking by simply insisting on a fundamental dichotomy between nature and reason, Habermas avoids monolothic Lukácsian subjects of history by breaking up the 'subject' at the outset. So the entity that is rationalised, the life-world, becomes in Habermas's account a *plurality*. It is no longer a life-world, so much as a collection of life-worlds, each with its own procedures of rationalisation and its own historical progress. To put the whole thing another way: the life-world, although pre-scientific, is not pre-distinct. It has a 'content' of its own, independently of the differentiating procedures of reason. What subsequently emerges in those procedures is not, in other words, merely a product of reason, but has a differentiated content of its own.

There are congruent positions in the history of thought. We have already noted that of Lorenzen: mathematics is 'practical' not only in the sense that

43 See *Introduction*, chapter 10. Allusion was achieved by Adorno's notion of the 'constellation'.

it grows from a reconstructable sequence of purely formal operations, but in the further sense that it is rooted in the praxis of the pre-scientific life-world. In the early work, as we noted, Habermas appealed to Hegel and Marx as an overcoming of the pure formalism of Kant. In general, though, positions of this kind evoke the *anti*-Hegelian stream of German nineteenth-century thought, notably perhaps Schelling's doctrine of 'unprethinkable' Being (i.e. Being that precedes concept), and Feuerbach's 'return to Nature'.[44]

Habermas's basic development of his position has three elements: the notions of the life-world, of 'linguification', and of intersubjective symmetry.

17. Life-world

The life-world, roughly, is the world humanity finds itself in before deliberate manipulation takes place. This 'before' is to be understood both chronologically and as a metaphysical priority. It is, perhaps, an αρχή that can be seen both as origin in time – archaeology – and as a trans-historical principle or cause.[45] The simplest way of identifying it is indeed historical; and Habermas enlists the anthropology of primitive tribes to explain life-world from this aspect. But life-world is also the deep structure of our own collective existence; and as such it echoes the quasi-transcendentalism of Habermas's first project (Habermas now uses the term 'half-transcendence' for language and culture, the 'constitutive' elements of the life-world: *TkH*, II 190). In other words, human beings were in a life-world before historical development brought them to the deliberate manipulation of themselves and nature. And they are always already in a life-world: one that is no longer primitive, but still continues as background and foundation for all their thoughts and utterances.

More intuitively, we could say that a contemporary northern-hemisphere life-world involves things like the family, social and ritual ties, and the subjective aspects of being in employment. These are situations we find ourselves in without thinking about it, just as the world of things surrounds us without our making a conscious deliberate effort. Because the life-world clearly has distinct historical features (rather than just abstract or formal ones), Habermas refers to its 'institutions' (*TkH*, II 537) or

---

44 See *Introduction*, chapters 3 and 5. The Hegelian (and, in our view at least, Kantian) position would not be that conceptuality is 'prior' any more than its opposite. The two are coeval (assuming the chronological metaphor has any meaning here).
45 On arché, see *Introduction* 150n., etc.

'structures'.[46] The 'structural components' of the life-world, specifically, are listed by Habermas as culture, society and personality (*TkH*, II 209). We shall consider the central aspect of this triad shortly; for now, we can say that the three components enable human beings to share an understanding of 'the world', to experience solidarity with others, and to find a personal identity for themselves.

Now, because the life-world is a universal context it is something we cannot reduce to conceptuality (or 'thematise', in Husserlian terminology). We are in the life-world before we start thinking about it; and as part of that we cannot, at least of our own unaided efforts, reflect conceptually upon it. As Habermas puts it, the life-world is an object of certainty (*Gewißheit*) but not of knowledge (*Wissen* – *TkH*, II 589). It is 'pre-reflexive' (*TkH*, I 449, 451). The intuitions it supports are 'pre-theoretical' (*TkH*, I 386), and, as such, not recoverable in or revisable by a general explicit theory (*TkH*, II 201). The commonality (*Gemeinsamkeit*) of the life-world 'lies beyond any possible dissent; it cannot become controversial like intersubjectively shared knowledge, it can at most *disintegrate*' (*TkH*, II 200).

This axiom, or argument, would seem to need amplification. There appear to be two implicit sources of authority for the approach. One is Husserl; and, indeed, Habermas repeatedly uses the metaphor of the 'horizon' in this context. We are, he says, '*locked* in the horizons of a life-world' (*TkH*, II 199; cf. also 188). Another authority is Wittgenstein, who seems to be evoked in the comment that 'the boundaries of the life-world cannot be transcended' (*TkH*, II 201). Perhaps the most important one is Freud, whose distinction between the conscious intentions conceived by the analysand and the unconscious structures that her utterances reveal to the analyst is echoed in a comment by Habermas on Searle's speech-act theory:

> With it he directs our gaze to a continent that remains hidden so long as the theorist analyses the speech act from the perspective of the speaker, who relates herself in her utterance to something in the objective, social and subjective world. (*TkH*, I 452)

In summary, we could say with Habermas that 'knowledge' within the life-world is *implicit* (in that it cannot be completely stated), *holistic* (in that each element is related to the whole), and *unavailable* (in that we cannot give a critical account of it; *TkH*, I 451).

We shall return later to the argumentative basis for Habermas's version of 'unprethinkable Being'. For the moment, the life-world can be illustrated in the mythic and ritualistic world-views studied by anthropology.

---

46 'Institutions' of the life-world are distinct from functional 'systems'. Habermas probably gets this use of the term from Arnold Gehlen. Cf. Apel, *Transformation*, I 197.

In Habermas's interpretation of Lévi-Strauss, Godelier and others, the mythic world view is characterised first by its tendency towards *totalisation*, and second by its *inconsistency*.

The mythic world-view is totalising in that, first, it does not have an adequate distinction between nature and culture at its disposal. The result is that nature is anthropomorphised, and on the other side human affairs become a naturalised battleground where the anonymous necessities of fate and malediction struggle (*TkH*, I 78). Mythic culture is 'egocentric' in that it imagines all events to be concentrated around its own immediate experiences (cf. *TkH*, I 111n); and the characteristic *narrative* character of the myth is an articulation of this form of primitive explanation – the world is an epic unfolding around a single consciousness, and over it consciousness exercises a direct magical control (*TkH*, I 79). This is mirrored also in myth's view of the relation between speech and objects: names, in particular, are 'totalised' into a magical identity with the objects they name (*TkH*, I 81); and the objective world becomes integrated into a purely semiotic tissue of analogies, resemblances and correspondences (*TkH*, I 77).

The result of all this is that myth does not allow space for subjectivity (*TkH*, I 83). There is no space for individual choices, or rational evaluations, in a cosmos crowded with natural forces and the necessities of an overarching narrative. Personal identity bleeds away into the homogenised collective. Myth, Habermas says, can neither *differentiate* (between the outer and the inner, between the world and our choices in it), and it cannot *reflect* (i.e. see itself as the active projector of choices, values, institutions: *TkH*, I 85).

Myth does not support rationality (*TkH*, I 73). The mechanism which might allow rationality, but which is blocked, is the procedure of assertion and criticism. Myth is irrational because explanations and accounts are not put forward as criticisable claims, but as narrated dogma unavailable for critique – 'it *is*, it *happened*' (*TkH*, I 83). Primitive tribes are not irrational in the sense that they cannot observe the law of non-contradiction, or believe it to be invalid. They simply refuse to apply it to their world interpretations, and as a result they have a high tolerance of inconsistencies in such areas.

What Habermas calls the 'idealism' of a pure hermeneutic position might treat this as a perfectly legitimate form of 'rationality'. In Habermas's argument, though, it is important to consider whether 'willingness to learn and openness to criticism' are not in fact something rather more than just 'idiosyncratic features of our own culture' (*TkH*, I 97). Is there not a universalisable rationality which would ban such tolerance of inconsistency? (*TkH*, I 95). The search for norms of this kind guides his theory of language.

18. Reflection and language

The notion that language is all that philosophy can sensibly be 'about' is, of course, a commonplace of twentieth-century philosophy in all traditions. Various celebrated metaphors have set the course of this conviction, of which Wittgenstein's 'The boundaries of my language indicate the boundaries of my world' (*Tractatus* 5.6), Neurath's ship (language is a ship we cannot get off; we rebuild it as we go), and Heidegger's 'Language is the house of Being' are only the best known. Results can be seen in programmes such as analytical philosophy's 'linguistic turn', and the hermeneutic project encapsulated in Gadamer's 'Being that can be understood is language'. In Habermas's immediate context, it may be his close associate Karl-Otto Apel's notion of the 'communicative *Gemeinschaft*' that accords most closely (Apel, 1976; *TkH*, I 34).[47]

One account would be this. The twentieth-century turn towards language may be seen, so far, to have gone through three stages (*NmD*, 79f). First we had straight truth semantics, which say that 1) speech is all we have, and 2) speech is only interesting to the extent that it is decidably true or false about objects. This is echoed in the austere postivist refusal to talk about things 'outside' speech (as in proposition 7 of the *Tractatus*). Second there is an 'epistemic' turn which argues that the 'validity' of an utterance cannot be separated from wider concerns outside pure truth-functionality (this, in Habermas's account, is typified by Austin and Searle). Finally, we have a 'pragmatist' turn (tentatively associated with Dummett) in which truth-functionality is subordinated to a wider concept of validity, namely, what makes *any* utterance *acceptable*.

It is simpler, however, to disentangle Habermas from his well-meaning engagements with analytical philosophy and to present his theory of communication in more sympathetic theoretical surroundings. This goes against the grain of much of Habermas's own rhetoric. But analytical philosophy does not always have the resources to cope here; and Habermas's maieutic attempts to coax something directly out of the English-speaking tradition, at least along this route, probably cause more trouble than it is worth.

The central concept behind Habermas's account of the life-world and its 'rationalisation' in language is *reflection*; and this invokes a set of arguments that may be found most readily in Schelling, on whom Habermas wrote his doctoral dissertation.[48] The figure of thought here is this. First, we have an absolute primal Being. Or, less luridly, we could say that we

---

47 Habermas regards the 'turn' carried out by recent philosophy not as linguistic but, more generally, as 'communication-theoretic' (*TkH*, I 531).
48 See *Introduction* 125ff. on this.

start with an unarticulated aggregation of stuff – Nature, perhaps, and human beings living in primitive naturalness. This primal Being then *reflects*: i.e. in idealist terms, it becomes aware of itself, or 'posits itself'. The basic character of this positing is differentiation, or negation. By becoming aware of itself it 'negates' itself in the sense that it posits itself as an *object*, and takes itself out of the immediacy of being just the knowing subject. So a splitting or reduplication occurs: it still is there as a subject, even though it has posited itself as an object.

The derivative character of this reflection is self-knowledge. By negating its own immediacy, consciousness comes to know itself as others know it. It loses its primitive egocentricity, and sees itself as one subjectivity among others.

Habermas ties this down to his account of the development of the life-world in language. The primitive life-world, as we saw, vegetates in monological immediacy. Everything is reduced to a dream-like narrative, the myths with which an undifferentiated collective ego surrounds itself. Habermas speaks of the 'collectively shared homogeneous life-world' where 'the collectively available interpretations of any situation are stored identically by all interaction participants and can be called up at need as narrative' (*TkH*, II 234).[49]

This immediacy is broken by language, which 'unlocks' or 'opens' (*erschließen*) the world (*NmD*, 81). The totalising monologue of ritual and sacrament is 'broken up' by 'linguification' (*Versprachlichung*: *TkH*, II 218, 287). Language opens the possibility of saying 'no': it changes the holistic narrative of myth into an array of 'yes/no' decisions (*TkH*, I 65, 411 etc.). What was ego-centred narrative becomes 'decentred' (*TkH*, I 106); the world becomes 'differentiated' (*TkH*, I 85), 'split up' (*TkH*, II 584), and made 'fluid' (*TkH*, I 109; II 427). Overall, language has the potential simultaneously for *negation* and for *innovation* (*TkH*, II 237).[50]

A *social* differentiation proceeds concurrently with language's 'breaking' of mythic totalities. The totalising ritual dogma which pervaded all areas of the primitive life-world is thrown open to critique. Traditions and the 'basic religious consensus' are 'reflexively broken' and become 'fluid' in the medium of 'communication' (*TkH*, II 427, 507); they lose their blind hegemonic authority, and, now opened to critique, they become transformed into potential elements of identity and fulfilment. This break-up of

49 Habermas's image of the 'total institution' which 'reproduces itself as a whole in every individual interaction' (*TkH*, II 234f) seems also to be an implied dig at Marxist or Hegelian notions of the 'dialectic', at least as seen from Habermas's preferred 'expressivist' interpretation.

50 This almost ontological capacity – language creates new identities by determining them, i.e. by drawing boundaries – matches the idealists' appropriation of *omnis determinatio est negatio*. See *Introduction*, 130.

wholes applies not only to pre-historical changes, but also to contemporary societies' escape from *ideological* domination (*TkH*, II 520).

As a result of this process the 'structural components' of the life-world are able to develop their own distinct identities. Habermas makes the 'rationalisation' of the life-world conditional on the 'differentiating out of its symbolic structures' (*TkH*, II 469, 502). With the dispelling of the sacred 'aura' from art works, culture becomes an area of free critical inter-action,[51] and as religion is forced back, social norms become abstracted and generalised. The global 'Sittlichkeit' (conventional duty) of traditional societies opens up into its component parts of *morality* and *legality*, thus allowing new freedoms of individuality and of discursively constituted association (*TkH*, II 427f). Potentially, then, modernity offers precisely that transformation of both the private and the public spheres to which Habermas had always looked forward (cf. *TkH*, II 471).

19. Symmetry

Much of this is empirical or homiletical. The question remains: to what extent can Habermas's diagnosis of ethical normativity in the modern world claim a 'transcendental' status? Here, everything depends on the formal aspects of his view of reflection. Habermas is presupposing that, in some 'half-transcendental' way or other, there is a collectively constituted life-world that differentiates itself in language. The contention is that the human collectivity is an absolute a priori underlying logic as well as ethics, and that the two share the same degree of normativity.[52] To make this point interesting, of course, it is necessary to show that the ethical dimension has a 'content' (like the principle of non-contradiction in logic, which gives us the basic structure of the propositional calculus). Without an elementary content of some kind, the ethical project has nothing to develop, and fails even if it is a priori in some way.

The first point for Habermas is that 'rationality' cannot be treated on the model of traditional truth-functional semantics. In particular, the distinction between statements about objects (which are amenable to true/false determinations) and all other statements is unacceptable.[53] The basic move in rational discourse is the making of a *validity claim*. These are assertions by, so to speak, a Lorenzen proponent – i.e. anything that can be

---

51 Habermas takes his theory of the aura from Benjamin (though he leaves behind its sophistication and much of its real power). See my *Walter Benjamin*, 178f, etc.

52 For more on the question of whether, and to what extent, logic and ethics presuppose one another see Apel, *Transformation der Philosophie* II 401ff.

53 To a provisional extent, Habermas develops this position in 'Wahrheitstheorien' (1972: now in *Vorstudien und Ergänzungen*, 127-183).

contested by an opponent. No semantic content is presupposed; only openness to an *argument form* of some kind. Accordingly, as Habermas argues, it is necessary to break with the 'narrow ontological presuppositions of truth semantics' (*TkH*, I 375). Rationality is not co-extensive with 'having a cognition' (*TkH*, I 25); instead, at the most fundamental level, it is an observance of the procedural rules of communication.

Accordingly, the basic character of rationality does not depend on semantic truth, or 'correspondence' ('Wahrheitstheorien', 133), or somehow reporting on a static cosmos of 'facts'. It consists in actions (*Handlungen*) which result in agreement (*Verständigung*). And the full process of rationality consists in knowing that what is happening is happening between commensurate partners: it is self-aware, or reflexive. The full formula is that rationality emerges from *actions* (speech utterances) directed to *agreement* with *others* (cf., e.g., *TkH*, I 48).

The empiricists' truth-functional metaphysics reduced logical reasoning to a monologue; and in so doing it promoted an ethics of the 'lonely actor' (*TkH*, I 369).[54] 'It conceives of actions under the ontological presupposition of exactly one world of existing states of affairs, and neglects those actor-world relations that are essential to social interaction.' Specifically, the world and everybody in it appear from the perspective of a single actor, and the theory of action becomes a probabilistic calculus for the manipulation of objects by that one actor.

Habermas's concept of rationality, by contrast, requires real actors, in the plural, taking one another into account as an essential part of any cognitive operation. Those real actors have attributes. In particular, they are (to the extent that they are rational) *cooperative* (*TkH*, I 60, 149). They see the other as essentially identifiable with themselves. And this vision is not merely formal, but consists in the reciprocal attribution of an interest in the 'search for truth' (*TkH*, I 48). Rational actors *must* presuppose the 'perspective of the other' (*TkH*, I 106). And this is because the *telos* of *Verständigung* is inherent in language (*TkH*, I 387). Speech loses its purpose if it is not, ultimately, directed towards communication with others whom we presuppose to be equal to us.

How does Habermas make good this claim?

The central notion is that of *symmetry*. Habermas's argument is that

---

54 At this point Habermas allows himself a rare moment of exasperation at his Anglo-Saxon colleagues: 'In the realm of analytical theory of action empiricism is fighting age-old battles again; once again we get the relation between mind and body (idealism vs. materialism), ground and cause (free will vs. determinism), behaviour and action (objectivist vs. non-objectivist description of action) . . . Not to put too fine a point on it, the analytical theory of action is dealing with the venerable problems of pre-Kantian philosophy of consciousness without breaking through to the basic questions of a sociological theory of action.' (*TkH*, I 370)

'rationality' is impossible without presupposing a symmetry between actor and the human object of action. Rational action presupposes the capacity of other actors to respond back in the same way, 'symmetrically'. This may be seen as a widening of the formal structure of argumentation put forward by Lorenzen: in order to establish his contention, the proponent has to defend it against an opponent with the same rational powers as himself. Without this defence – without the participation of an equal other – the contention is altogether irrational, even in some private ('monological') world of the proponent. The function of a general theory of practical reason, i.e. one that subsumes the particular structures of 'objective' disputation in the manner of Lorenzen, is to 'reconstruct the general conditions of symmetry that every competent speaker, insofar as he understands himself to be engaging in argumentation, has to presuppose as adequately satisfied' (*TkH*, I 47).

The details of Habermas's 'reconstruction' need not concern us. The basic point, however, is that the 'world' is not a simple array of reportable facts; it is a life-world that articulates itself around us in a variety of ways. Habermas speaks of a plurality of 'worlds', of which the 'objective' world, target of the natural sciences, is only one. The differing worlds are a function of differing human orientations or practices, and these differing practices relate to the life-world with different expectations and 'validity claims'. One practice, that of 'teleological action', mobilises criteria of *truth* and *efficacy* (*TkH*, I 130). Another considers events according to their *legitimacy*, or consistency with social norms (*TkH*, I 134). A third practice, which Habermas calls 'dramaturgical', involves appeals to issues of sincerity and *authenticity* (*TkH*, I 139).

The epiphany of the life-world in these various classes of practice, however, is only the first, pre-reflexive stage. The 'worlds' are present as a basic material; but the stage which makes possible the elaboration of general norms only comes in the next stage, that of *language*. In this context, the reflexive power of language resides not so much in its capacity for determination and differentiation, as in its status as a medium of *self-identification*. In particular, the level of what Habermas calls 'communicative action' can be seen to involve the taking of responsibility. The rational actor, at this point, deliberately puts a contention into play with other actors viewed as equal partners and contestants. She is no longer egocentrically following a goal, nor blindly observing a social norm, nor narcissistically displaying her sincerity. She is *starting* with the supposition that she, along with the others involved, is moving in an arena of more or less successfully observed facts, shared standards, and achieved honesty. And she anticipates a conclusion which will determine the space of her rationality in a way that binds her as much as it binds the other contestants. This shared framework hap-

pens in language. And just as language, so to speak, determines the mark-
ings on the court, it also governs the course of play. The rational speaker
submits herself (reflexively, as one among others) to the rules of a game
which will end in ascertainable winning or losing.

> The speakers integrate the three formal world concepts, which appear in other
> models of action individually or in pairs, into one system, and presuppose this
> in common as a framework for interpretation within which they can achieve
> *Verständigung*. They no longer *directly* relate to something in the objective,
> social or subjective world, but they relativise their utterance to the possibility
> that its validity will be disputed by other actors. (*TkH*, I 148)[55]

20. Pathology and colonisation

The normative force of Habermas's 'rationalised life-world' is, roughly, as
follows. First, our world is inherently linguistic, and 'reality', at least for
the social sciences, is constituted by what can be established in language.
The form taken by this establishment is a dialogue procedure, which, we
could say, involves a) non-omniscience (nothing is valid except to the extent that it is subjected to the uncertainties of dialogical proof), and b) some
degree of 'symmetry' between proponent and opponent. Within this, there
are three basic kinds of claim that may offer themselves for testing: claims
about 'facts' (truth), claims about normative rightness (legitimacy), and
claims about sincerity and authenticity. These are all termed 'worlds' by
Habermas to underline the extent to which *rationality* is not bound to any
particular kind of validity claim.

From this basic schema, Habermas purports to extract universal norms
that are formal and yet substantive. In particular, his argument is directed
towards showing that the three kinds of validity claims (about 'worlds') are
equal before the tribunal of reason. His recurrent term here is 'without
constraint' (*zwanglos*: e.g. *TkH*, I 525, II 432, II 487). The three worlds are
ontologically, or at least practically, coeval; and in that respect their en-
titlement to a hearing before dialogical reason, and to the enforcability of
any resulting decision, is equal.

Habermas's strongest, and thus most contentious, claim is probably that
the subjectivity displayed in 'dramaturgical practice' has the status of a
'world'. From one perspective, it provides a satisfying complement to the
other two worlds, and obviously echoes the aesthetics of Kant's third critique, coming after the scientific and ethical concerns, respectively, of the

---

55 What 'reflection' involves in the context of language probably needs a more careful
formalisation than this. To some extent, this is supplied in Apel's discussion of the distinction
between 'calculus language' and reflexive language in *Transformation*, II 318f.

first two. From another perspective, however, the assertion of an aprioristic human sensibility seems to be rather arbitrary, and invites the sort of objection levelled by Engels and Marx at Feuerbach.[56] In particular, the 'symmetry' of partners in formalised Lorenzen dialogues does not seem to go anywhere near far enough to support Habermas's attribution of an intention to cooperate. Disputation need not involve the unconstrained mutual recognition on which Habermas builds his pathos of the subjective and reflexive life-world.

However, Habermas's diagnosis of the ills of modernity will clarify the problem. Essentially, it revolves around a notion of alienation and its overcoming. I shall express this in terms which emphasise the metaphysics of the theory. Although this is largely concealed in Habermas's own exposition, he seems to be applying the basically Schellingian notion that we start with a primary Being, are alienated from it because of conceptuality, but are eventually restored to our true nature once we learn to use conceptuality properly.[57]

At an elementary level, then, there are three 'worlds'. They become distinct and capable of historical development once they are bathed in language, and brought into the reflexive self-consciousness of 'communication'. Through the determinative and reduplicative effect of language a process of 'rationalisation' sets in, releasing the *potential* latent in the basic structure of determinate Being (*TkH*, II 232).

Now, because the three worlds are distinct, this process of release is variable and contingent. In particular, the purposive behaviour by means of which we relate to the world of objects (the 'first' world) seems to become rationalised more quickly than the others. Indeed, control over nature and over ourselves increases much faster than our ability to make sense of the process in terms of the other components of rationality. The result is that the human world is objectified and turned into quasi-natural 'systems', to be suppressed and exploited like all the other non-human resources around us. The non-teleological reason of *ethics* and *culture*, and with it the universe of human sensibility, is forced aside.

> The rationalisation of the life-world makes possible an increase in system complexity so hypertrophic that the systemic imperatives thereby released burst the capacity of the life-world . . . (*TkH*, II 232)

Conventional critiques of modernity (says Habermas) stop at this point. This is the inadequacy, in his view, of analyses like that of Weber on rationalisation or of Horkheimer and Adorno on 'enlightenment'. They all end up with more or less pessimistic views of where modernity can take us:

56 'The human essence is no abstraction inherent in the single individual. In its actuality it is the ensemble of social relations' (6th of the *Theses on Feuerbach*). See *Introduction*, 192.
57 See, for example, *Introduction* 158ff.

history is about rational systems, systems have failed us, and there is no alternative (except, perhaps, for 'post-modern' ideologies of irrationality and fragmentation – cf. *TkH*, II 521).

This melancholic conclusion, however, is only necessary because such approaches still hold at one level or another to the old totalising view of Marx or Hegel – namely, that purposive reason is primary, and that rationality and history have to be seen in its terms alone (*TkH*, II 498 etc.). Once 'systems' are perceived as rationalisations of one part only of the life-world, however, then the other parts can be reinstalled in their rightful place. Teleological reason may, for the moment, have got out of control; but 'reason' contains more than that, and its other elements supply the normative certainties to correct the excesses of its first project. In particular, the disorders of modernity can be seen as symbolic pathologies, imbalances between the components of our symbolic-communicative economy. This basically Freudian metaphor gives Habermas his account of the 'therapeutic' function of philosophy and critical social theory.

In summary, it runs as follows. As part of its hypertrophic development, the 'systematised' world of purposive action starts to 'colonise' the other worlds. Areas which are the province of moral or aesthetic rationality get taken over by systems. For example, legislation encroaches on family life. This is not necessarily a bad thing, from many perspectives; but the danger is that it alienates members of the family from the kind of rationality which alone makes sense of such an institution. Another example might be the intrusion of the market into art: art is alienated from its symbolic role and becomes subjected to the imperatives of commodity exchange. 'Experts and specialists' appear everywhere. Healing and caring get taken over by a 'therapeutocracy' (*TkH*, II 533). Culture is 'professionalised' (*TkH*, II 482). Attempts to break down subject boundaries in the world of science (Habermas particularly mentions philosophy) run up against the determination of an 'exclusive, stubbornly idiosyncratic culture of the expert' to keep them (*TkH*, II 521).

The result is that the dismantling of mythic dogma has gone too far, and brought wide areas that should be in the discretion of individuals into a realm devoid of normative rationality. Extensive parts of the human lifeworld are assimilated to the systemic media of money and administrative power (*TkH*, II 461). They become 'norm-free', suspended 'beyond the horizon of the life-world' (*TkH*, II 483). Elements of communicative rationality are converted into operational media and, in a reversal of the basic character of rationalisation, '*de*-linguified' (entsprachlicht – *TkH*, II 269). The result is a 'de-moralised regulation by constraint', and a 'legitimation delay': systemic bureaucracies dispense with attempts to legitimisetheir actions – the administrative goal is everything.

This perspective, however, enables Habermas to be relatively sanguine about the future of modernity. In the first place, there is nothing intrinsically bad about systems. The fact that we are not ontologically bound to them means both that we can take a distanced view and, furthermore, that we are not condemned to the (Marxist) revolutionary lurches of economic crises. In his later work, Habermas is reconciled to the capacity of capitalism to deal with its own less savoury by-products. Indeed, one of the advantages of 'systems' is that they can extract from the life-world conflicts which are better dealt with free of normative intensity and moral concern. The class struggle, Habermas now notes with approval, has been 'institutionalised', and social class structures have been converted into a system (*TkH*, II 512). With rising living standards, wage labour no longer involves 'ill-making' proletarianisation (*TkH*, II 514). Certainly there are still conflicts, but nowadays these arise more as communicative pathologies, when 'functions of the symbolic reproduction of the life-world are affected' (*TkH*, II 516).

21. History and the metaphysics of unconstraint

Habermas's theory invites objections on two levels – empirical and formal. The empirical objection is obvious. Whatever has happened to the class struggle on our doorsteps, western Europe's economic interests and economic crises continue to make people extremely 'ill' in other parts of the world; and this reflects a form of colonisation far more real and dangerous than the rather mild discomforts envisaged by Habermas.

On the formal level, Habermas's theory is more convincing. His contention that rationality exceeds the objectivism of truth-functional semantics must be correct. His critique of the shallow individualism of Anglo-Saxon ethical thinking has to stand.

The weakness of his argument, however, lies in his treatment of the life-world. Part of this is the problem of the Schellingian 'unprethinkable'. For Habermas, despite all the power of language, reflection, and rationalisation, there is still a level which is absolutely and irrecoverably pre-reflexive. That includes, in particular, the ethical and aesthetic sensibilities of the individual. There is, perhaps, a possibility of confronting and changing these sensibilities, but it does not lie in the hands of reflexive reason itself. It seems, somehow, to be a product of the inscrutable forces of history.

> The phenomenologist, no more than any other social scientist, does not have at his disposal the totality of the background knowledge constitutive for the construction of the life-world – unless some *objective challenge* arises in view

of which *the life-world as a whole becomes problematic.* That is the reason why a theory that wishes to ascertain general structures of the life-world cannot start transcendentally; it can only hope to match the *ratio essendi* of its objects if there is reason for the assumption that the objective life context in which the theorist finds himself will result in the *ratio cognoscendi* opening itself to him. (*TkH*, II 590)

In other words, the knowledge that grasps the totality (the *ratio cognoscendi*) may emerge spontaneously at some point in objective historical development, but it is not accessible to individually initiated reflection. Reconstructive rationality, in other words, may well reach its limits quite quickly.

The correlative of this, in Habermas's account, is the reliance on some utopian intuition to guide us through the night:

> In the measure that ... culture, society and personality distinguish themselves, and that the validity basis of action oriented towards *Verständigung* replaces the sacral foundations of social integration, there will emerge, intimated by the structures of the life-world, as though transcendentally [gleichsam transzendental], a *pre-illumination (Vorschein) of post-traditional communication for daily life.* This would stand on its own feet, would set limits to the autonomous dynamics of independent systems, would burst open the encapsulated expert cultures, and thus avoid the combined dangers of reification and disillusion [Verödung]. (*TkH*, II 486)

We hope, in other words, that we will eventually live in an integrated (and in that sense 'total') world which accords with the needs of a complex rationality, and in which the life-world is no longer racked by symbolic pathologies. The more worrying point is that the normative resources of Habermas's life-world, whether preflexive or otherwise, seem relatively slender. He concentrates his hopes on the notion of unconstrained human association; but his model of this seems to be small-group conviviality which excludes the dynamics of larger groups such as nations or, indeed, classes. Is the struggle at such levels to be dismissed merely as an aberration of alienated systems? Or would it not, in fact, be better to develop the logic of disputation to include group conflict, and to constitute politics as an integral but distinct part of the life-world? Habermas's retreat from politics, at least on the theoretical level, speaks for a dangerous complacency.

6

Conclusion

1. The Good, the true and the beautiful

At one time, the primary concern of philosophy was right conduct – the Good. The Good formed the central pillar in the idealists' triad of truth, goodness and beauty. This arrangement expressed the tenor of 'Aristotelian' philosophy in general, from the *Nicomachean Ethics* to its far echo in Hegel's *Philosophy of Right*. Questions about the True ('logic'), however interesting, were ultimately auxiliary; their role was to explain how the good could be grounded in reason. The question of the Beautiful ('aesthetics') is modern, but crucial because it represents the first attempt to deal with the historicity of norms (ethical or otherwise).[1]

Grandly systematic philosophy is now believed to have reached an 'end' somewhere around the middle of the nineteenth century. More than anything, this came with the growing consensus that valuative norms are not like concepts, and can never be instruments of cognition, but only – at best – its objects. Comtean positivism and Engels's 'scientific materialism' were among the first assertions of this view.[2] Nietzsche remains its most celebrated advocate (most explicitly, perhaps, in his affirmation of the mechanical sciences and 'physics': see Nietzsche, 1887b, Section 335). But it was Rudolf Carnap, doyen of the 'analytical' generation, who had the greatest influence on modern professional philosophy. In Carnap's well-known view, the judgement of *meaninglessness*

   must be passed on all *philosophy of norms*, or *philosophy of value*, on any eth-

1 See Roberts, 1988, ch. 1; Roberts, 1979.
2 In the case of Engels, with the formulation that ideas are part of the ideological superstructure, and hence empirical and epiphenomenal. His essay, *Ludwig Feuerbach and the End of Classical German Philosophy* is the originatory text, albeit secret and unacknowledged, of a whole tradition.

ics or aesthetics as a normative discipline. For the objective validity of a value
or norm is . . . not empirically verifiable nor deducible from empirical statements; hence it cannot be asserted (in a meaningful statement) at all. . . . It is
altogether impossible to make a statement that expresses a value judgment.
(Carnap 1932, p. 77)

Most of this tradition shared an intense hostility to Christianity. Chris-
tian norms were the instruments of oppression and conservative self-
interest (the 'scales on the dragon', in Nietzsche's phrase); and the philosophy of norms and values amounted to a disguised Christianity. This re-
vulsion still serves to unite the most otherwise widely disparate intellectual
traditions, from hard-headed analysts at one extreme to the various in-
heritors of Francophone anticlericalism at the other.

Our position in this book is that one and a half centuries of positivism
have left us wide open to the charlatanry and bogus theology they hoped to
supplant. The declaration that norms *cannot* be rational opens the door to
purveyors of values who are more than happy to dispense with the stric-
tures of rationality.

The most telling reproach is probably Nietzsche's own, at the beginning
of *Daybreak*. There he argues that Kant's technique was to make the intellect recognise its own limits, and, beyond those limits, 'to posit an unprovable world, a logical "beyond"'. The result was the dark Lutheran pes-
simism of the *credo quia absurdum est*: idealism uses paradox and dialectic
to consign us to a universe where *only* faith remains (Nietzsche, 1887a, 13-
15).

But that, of course, is precisely the position occupied, implicitly or explicitly, by most of idealism's *opponents*. Among those we have discussed
in this book, for example, Wittgenstein argues strenuously for it in the
Tractatus. For him, as we saw, norms are not ruled out, they are merely
placed in an extra-rational ('non-meaningful') universe.

Our concern, in following the *logic* of reflection, is to recover the sense
in which norms *are* rational, or at least contestable before a rational tribunal. And in doing so, we have been using the Kantian initiative as our guide
– to distinguish, in other words, between rationality in the narrow sense
(understanding, *Verstand*, 'computability'), and in the wider sense (Kant's
Vernunft). Reflection seeks to recover the rationality of *Vernunft*. In this
conclusion we shall review the arguments.

2. Reflection: the pattern of argument

Reflection is not an assertion about 'the world', or 'truth', or the 'laws of
thought': it is a pattern of argument. In the first instance, it is neither an in-

strument nor a prescription. It is an interpretation that emerges from a sequence of what might be called meta-argumentative experiences.

The reflective argument, typically, takes the following course. It starts with something akin to common-sense realism: there is a world and knowledge is an account of that world.

At this point, the experience supervenes that the notion of a 'description' can be elusive and puzzling. This is because, under certain circumstances, a particular description seems *intrinsically* unable to 'describe' what, on some level at least, we actually know to be the case. This is not just a matter of the contingent limitations of human knowledge (the 'weather forecasting problem'); it is something that seems to afflict description as an activity.

Thanks to the advances in logic during the last hundred years, we can formulate these difficulties in precise terms. They seem to have two aspects. On the one hand, there is what might be called the 'underdetermination' problem: what we 'know' is underdetermined by our capacity conceptually to describe it. The problems illuminated by the work of Skolem and of Gödel seem to be examples of this. In the case of Skolem, the 'intention' of a non-denumerable set is, so to speak, sabotaged by the fact that any particular formal theory we devise to capture it is also satisfiable in a denumerable model. We think we know something; but it turns out that our 'description' of it (the formal theory) in fact underdetermines the thing we imagine ourselves to know. So do we know it or not? Or, if we do, what is the sense of this 'knowledge'?[3]

Gödel's incompleteness theorem poses a similar difficulty of underdetermination. The Gödelian formula '17 Gen *r*' is undecidable within the system, and yet is true. *Within* any particular system, the formula that says of itself that it is not provable within the system can be proved *as well as its negation*; so if we want the system to be consistent (without contradictions), we must rule the formula out as undecidable for the purposes of that system. Moreover, this formula can be constructed within any system, however much it is extended. So what, exactly, is 'true' to mean here? For it to mean anything, there must be something that is system-like (in allowing us to produce a true description), though is not, and can never be, presently formalised into our current system of description. So it is not merely that description, our instrument of knowledge, is contingently limited; it seems to be inherently unable to extend itself to the frontiers of what we actually 'know'.[4]

3 See above, ch. 1; Putnam 1980, 422ff.
4 Much of the apparent paradox exploited by interpretations of Gödel falls away if we keep this distinction in mind: there is systematically demonstrable truth, and there is truth generally. The term 'proof' is best restricted to the first area. Nagel and Newman (1958), for example, do not observe this restriction (86). The result is that the mind becomes a super-machine, endowed with contradiction-crunching properties and mysterious 'powers of

The other aspect of these difficulties matches the first. If underdetermination shows that we cannot conceptually construct (by 'description') the
full extent of what we 'know', then the other difficulties show us that
attempts to cognise over that full extent produce contradictions within our
descriptive apparatus. These are the paradoxes of the 'excessively large'
class.

The most obvious problem of excessive size is self-inclusion. Does
'everything that is the case' include itself? To put it ontologically: is our
description of the world itself a part of the world, or not? The fact that it
cannot be, at least not for formal set-theoretic purposes, is revealed by
paradoxes like the liar and Russell's paradox.

This throws up difficulties of philosophical interpretation. Removing
the description entirely from the world it describes is an obvious initial
answer. A Platonistic mathematics, in Frege's manner, would be an
example of this. But the trouble is that such a mathematics, even apart from
the question of where it came from (God? the structure of the mind? – but
in the latter case surely it *is* 'in the world'?), still seems to be subject to dis-
turbingly arbitrary restrictions – the theory of types, or the set-theoretic
axioms, for example.

The odd point is this: a description, one would think, is either correct or
not, true or false. But the disturbances, or paradoxes, constructed in
modern logic do not seem to allow for this interpretation. Gödel's formula,
for example, is neither true nor false, but, so to speak, *not yet true*. So what,
if it is a description, is it talking about? Equally, in Skolem's case, we seem
to have intuitions we cannot rigorously capture in description.[5]

The next move in the argument is the one characteristic of reflection. The
mind's experience of itself, so to speak, seems to urge the conclusion that
formal theoretic rationality moves within a sphere over which it does not
fully extend. The formally described is only a subset of what, in some respect or another, 'is'. Moreover, description is not the same as the activity
of describing; completed descriptions (perfective aspect) are in the 'world'
in a way that description-as-process (imperfective aspect) is not. The
simple ascription of 'reality' to 'world' fails to apprehend the manner in
which description and world interact as parts of the same process.

There are various ways in which this can be represented. A direct set-

creative reason' (102). The better answer, as we have argued above, is to say that rationality can
never be adequately interpreted in terms of a Platonistic universe: we must, in Husserl's terminology, abandon the metaphors of the 'natural attitude'.
5 The puzzles of modern logic are useful in their precision, but not unique or unprecedented.
Zeno's attempts to demonstrate that *motion* cannot be 'thought', and indeed all the long-
standing problems over the continuum, can be compared with Skolem's 'paradox', and are of
course much more ancient. Kant's cosmological antinomies are another argument along the
same lines, though they are perhaps less conclusive.

theoretic analogue is the axiom of comprehension: 'classes' of unlimited size are certainly thinkable, in some respect or other, but only more pared-down entities can be manipulated, as sets, by concept and calculus.

In Kantian terms, as we saw, 'reflection' ascertains the conditions under which we attain to concepts. These conditions are associated by Kant with what he calls the 'aesthetic' – the forms of material particularity, time and space. We could say, then, that the conceptually constructed world ('concept') is conditioned by material particularity.

This does not mean that we only have knowledge of material particulars: that would be the empiricism from which we started. The argument (with Kant) is that knowledge is itself a material particular; or, better, that it emerges from a process of material particularisation.

We have various ways to think of this. First, we can think of truth modally, rather than as a static relation between description and one simple world. Truth *tout court* is provable truth in 'this' world; possibility and necessity characterise relations of truth with *other* worlds.

The plurality of worlds, in turn, can be interpreted 'aesthetically', in terms of time and space. Time gives us the 'progress of knowledge': there may be future truths that are not true now, not for want of being 'discovered', but in a more absolute sense. (Perhaps also there are past truths no longer true today; though this is a more puzzling idea, and has an unattractively relativistic savour.)

Space, correspondingly, gives us the 'location' of truths – in minds, or bodies of knowledge, or wherever. Truths evolve within axiomatic systems.[6]

This aesthetic understanding also suggests a more appropriate way of representing the mind's 'other'. Common-sense realism takes the 'other' of description to be the 'world'. If we see 'worlds' as situated systems, however, the world's 'otherness' becomes not an inert external state of affairs, but the otherness of *another system*. Empiry, from that perspective, is not interaction of mind with world, but of mind with other minds. The mechanical formulation of particular truths within an existing system is mere involution, distinct from the genuine *evolution* of learning interaction.

Taken together, these elements point to the dialogical interpretation of logic. Particular knowledges are things done, or constructed. They have a primary location, in other words, in *practice*; they do not hover in a depersonalised realm based on pure description. Moreover, the logical calcu-

---

6 The 'aesthetic', here, has to be considered as something entirely pre-conceptual, not as Newtonian absolute space or time. Knowledge is not 'in' any measurable time or space: the whole point of the 'transcendental aesthetic' is that the aesthetic location is not determinable by measurement and concept. Heidegger (1976) is useful on this.

lus comes to be seen not as a means of ordering states of affairs (Wittgenstein, at least in the *Tractatus*), but of moving to conclusions via confrontations with other bodies of knowledge (Lorenzen).

3. Reflection and its implications

Logic: beyond monologue

In common-sense realism, the 'interest' of mind is to account for the 'outside world'. The acquisition of knowledge consists in perfecting one's description of what is.

Viewed dialogically, however, this interest appears less as a monological accumulation of statements about an outside, and more as a dialogical interaction. Genetically, one could say, the baby does not simply 'explore' and 'discover' the world lying inertly about it; the baby interacts with its human environment, and only thus acquires a system of knowledge within which particular bits of the world become present. 'Normal', non-interactive acquisition of knowledge is, so to speak, confirming what you already know. Dialogical acquisition, which any acquisition must be at least initially,[7] is a matter of determining what you may thenceforth possibly know. Knowledge 'grows' in discontinuity and dialogical confrontation with the unfamiliar. Monologically, it merely consolidates itself. (Done properly, i.e. with history, philosophy is a paradigm for the discontinuous and ruptured growth of knowledges. Institutional philosophy – Kuhn's 'normal science' – is of course constantly under pressure to abandon this in favour of continuity, self-confirmation, and 'progress'.)

In this respect, the 'interest' of knowledge, viewed dialogically, lies in the dialogue with other worlds. And the satisfaction of science is, so to speak, in transition, not in accumulation.

If this is so, what knowledge 'needs' is not an inert other, but a refractory, resistant one that plays its part in the dialogue. 'I' need to know whether 'you' know things that can destroy my universal generalisations, or disrupt my implications. For this, I need you as a source to whose interventions I can attribute truthfulness; and I need you to recognise me as a truthful source. Only in this way can my 'interest' in knowledge be satisfied. In a monological world, or one in which I have no dialogue partners whom I can take seriously, or who take me seriously, my interest in knowledge is entirely frustrated.

7 As Schleiermacher puts it, the beginning of knowledge is not knowledge, but (in his term) 'dialectic' (Schleiermacher, 1988). This is the essence of the constructivist position, too: insights do not pre-exist our construction of them.

In this interpretation, then, logic is conditioned by a prior interest in the mutual recognition of dialogue partners. This plays the same role as the 'interest in correct description' implicit in the model of common-sense realism. We could say, it is the *interest in apprehending other as self, and being oneself apprehended as other*. More generally, we could say that any interest in 'truth' *presupposes interaction between a plurality of knowledge-bearers*. The first task of a philosophy of reflection is to explore this interpretation of formal logic.[8]

Ethics: beyond atomism

For a considerable time, ethical and political theorists have simplified their starting point by ruling out norms that are anything more than conventions or biological dispositions. 'Absolute' norms, from this point of view, are no more than a residual theology. This defect, for example, is commonly associated with Kantian ethics, which are criticised for their content (arbitrary quasi-Christian 'duties') and, most of all, for their disregard of context.

On the other side, it has long been clear that a hard-headed insistence that all we have are benefit-maximising individuals, and that 'ethics' is essentially a matter of providing a calculus of interaction for them, soon runs into difficulties. Partly, that is because almost any 'philosophical' approach (as opposed to one that is really a descriptive anthropology) is more or less forced to invoke norms, even if only such abstract ones as the notion that survival, at least by some person or community, is a good thing. Beyond that, however, the difficulty is that simple benefit maximisation, on the utilitarian model, cannot in any event provide a model for social choices. There seems to be no means of correlating the individual motive of benefit maximisation with a stable, non-implosive distribution of social goods; pure atomistic self-interest, in other words, can never be enlightened to the extent of sustaining a community.[9]

The result is that ethical philosophers are forced to fall back, if not on duties, then at least on concepts such as 'moral adhesive'. But the status of these is obscure, not least from a positivistic point of view. If the only permissible 'norms' must be grounded in atomic individuals, then such notions can, at best, only be associated with some kind of natural function

8 Gentzen's formulation of 'natural deduction' provided the first elements in this. It has been extended by the Husserlian approaches of the Erlangen school, among others. There are, of course, important technical issues of whether an intuitionistic calculus, without the law of excluded middle, is sufficient for arithmetic. But behind them stand philosophical and interpretative questions. What, for example, is 'natural' about 'natural deduction'.
9 This would be one interpretation of Arrow's theorem. Individualism, it seems, cannot satisfy the requirement that it should function without recourse to dictators. See McLean, 1987, 165.

(the 'altruistic gene', and suchlike). Like worker bees, it seems, human
beings are supposed to be endowed with some self-sacrificing reflex. Such
statements are no more than speculative anthropology.

However, the reflective notion that interaction in some sense *precedes*
'truth' – that it emerges in dialogue, for example, rather than in monologue
– provides an equally good model for ethics. The analogy, or indeed corre-
lation, between truth in language and morality in practice has been put per-
suasively in recent work (see, for example, O'Neill, 1989; Vossenkuhl,
1982, 1991). In this respect, the basic given of human practice is not individual profit maximisation, for that is ultimately incoherent. Rather, the
basic given is interaction, from which individual identity is derived. It is, so
to speak, 'eliminable' in terms of interaction in the same way that logic is
eliminable in terms of argumentative contests (in Lorenzen's project: see
above, ch. 5). The notion of self is constructed, derived from possibilities of
practice that are, indeed, directed to individual profit maximisation, but
also, and perhaps primarily, to social recognisability. 'We have a rational
[vernünftig] interest in our moral credibility, in a positively identifiable
continuity on the basis of our moral actions' (Vossenkuhl, 1991, 186). This
account, in other words, invokes the Kantian notion of a general practical
rationality ('Vernunft'). Only this can set the terms within which the calculus of atomistic interests (corresponding to 'Verstand') takes effect.

Specifically, perhaps, I have to be recognisable as an other before I can be
recognisable as a self. More generally, the proper and indispensable concern of ethics is, as Aristotle said, with *political* morality, or, in recent terminology, with *public* choice.[10] Hume's reliance on the notion of *taste*, by
contrast, and his characteristic argument that his 'honest and opulent'
friend is no more likely to steal his silver than his house is suddenly to collapse, underlines the individualism of the competing approach.[11]

Aesthetics: beyond beauty

Aesthetics has become the Cinderella of modern institutional philosophy.
Here above all, the arbitrary nature of norm and prescription seems to be
evident. It may be said, however, that modernistic positivism has done as
much damage here as elsewhere – not so much in the built environment, for
that is, to a degree, replaceable, but principally in the natural and social environment, which has been subjected to a truly Hobbesian war of the
strong against the weak.

10 Specifically: politics is the 'master art' (*architektoniké* – *The Nicomachean Ethics*,
1094a27). 'Since politics uses the rest of the sciences, and since, again, it legislates as to what we
are to do and what we are to abstain from, the end of this science must include those of the
others, so that this end must be the good for man.'
11 See Hume, 1975, 91, 294; also Roberts, 1988, 55.

The notion that, as the eighteenth century put it, aesthetics is the 'science of the beautiful', is clearly discredited; but then Kant by 1790 no longer regarded it as a science in the limited sense either. In Kant's critical project, 'aesthetics' enter the argument not in connection with beauty, but in connection with logic, at the very beginning of the first critique. The aesthetic indeed, as we have seen (chapter 1, above), is precisely what 'reflection' is initially directed towards. The transcendental aesthetic is the particularity – in space and time – that conditions understanding. So it appears at the beginning of the critiques; and it appears again at the end, in the *Critique of Judgement*. Its role there strictly complements its role at the beginning; for while the transcendental aesthetic argues that conceptual understanding is always conditioned by particularity, the critique of aesthetic judgement demonstrates the wider sense in which developed social reason continues, also, to be historically conditioned. The judgement of taste invokes assent, despite the fact that it is essentially undetermined. The structures of style and art are free and self-imposed, but at the same time social. They are, in other words, new (and hence historical), but also general, at least in aspiration. This apparent paradox, of free generality, is what Schiller characterised as 'play'.[12]

Aesthetics in the looser sense ('what makes things beautiful?') is important not as a rather inconsequential branch of psychology or sociology, but as part of the understanding of the historical context of intersubjectivity. We have an interactive community, as the sense-giving medium both of logic and of ethics; but this community, the polis, is itself a historical, freely self-disposing entity. In this respect, as Schiller insisted, 'art' is itself a political force; the free 'play' of the community is the vehicle of its utopian aspirations, and of its rational self-determination. Furthermore, precisely because it does not simplistically prioritise the community's profit maximisation, this approach can encompass social and environmental issues before which the calculus of individualism fails.

The resources of philosophical aesthetics have been overlooked; a systematic approach to these issues is overdue.[13]

12 See Roberts. 1988, 63ff. on Kant and the relationship between general and individual in aesthetic judgement.
13 Useful work has been appearing in the form of methodologies of the cultural sciences. But such an aim is probably too limited. For a more robust, though historical, approach, see Bowie, 1990. See also Bernstein, 1992.

Bibliography

Aicher O., Greindl G., Vossenkuhl W., 1986, *Wilhelm von Ockham. Das Risiko modern zu denken* (Munich, Callwey)

Anscombe, G.E.M., 1959, *An Introduction to Wittgenstein's Tractatus* (London, Hutchinson)

Aristotle, 1973, *Categories. On Interpretation. Prior Analytics* trans. H.P. Cooke, H. Tredennick (Loeb Classical Library; London, Heinemann)

Aristotle, 1980, *The Nicomachean Ethics*, trans. D. Ross (Oxford, World's Classics)

Apel, Karl-Otto, 1976, *Transformation der Philosophie* 2 vols. (Frankfurt/M, Suhrkamp)

Ayer, A.J. (ed.), 1959, *Logical Positivism* (Glencoe, The Free Press)

B: see Kant

Baldwin, Thomas, 1984, 'Moore's rejection of idealism', in Rorty, Schneewind and Skinner

Barwise, Jon and Etchemendy, John, 1987, *The Liar. An Essay on Truth and Circularity* (New York, Oxford U.P.)

Becker, Oskar, 1975, *Grundlagen der Mathematik in geschichtlicher Entwicklung* (Frankfurt/M, Suhrkamp; photographic reprint of Freiburg, Alber, 1964)

Bell, David, 1990, *Husserl* (London, Routledge)

Bell, David and Vossenkuhl, Wilhelm (eds.), 1992, *Wissenschaft und Subjektivität* (Berlin, Akademie-Verlag)

Benacerraf, Paul and Putnam, Hilary, 1983 *Philosophy of Mathematics. Selected readings* (Cambridge, C.U.P.) (*PoM*)

Benjamin, Andrew, 1990. *Translation and the Nature of Philosophy* (London, RKP).

Bernet, Rudolf, with Iso Kern and Eduard Marbach, 1989, *Eduard Husserl. Darstellung seines Denkens* (Hamburg, Felix Meiner)

Boolos, George and Jeffrey, Richard, 1980, *Computability and Logic* 2nd ed. (Cambridge, C.U.P)

Bowie, Andrew, 1990, *Aesthetics and Subjectivity* (Manchester, Manchester University Press)

Bradley, James, 1979, 'Hegel in Britain: A Brief History of British Commentary and Attitudes'. *The Heythrop Journal*, vol xx, nos 1 & 2.

Brouwer, L.E.J., 1913, 'Intuitionism and formalism', in Benacerraf and Putnam

Brouwer, L.E.J., 1949, 'Consciousness, philosophy, and mathematics', in Benacerraf and Putnam

Bubner, Rüdiger, 1984, *Geschichtsprozesse und Handlungsnormen* (Frankfurt/M, Suhrkamp)

Bubner, Rüdiger, 1989, *Ästhetische Erfahrung* (Frankfurt/M, Suhrkamp)

Cantor, Georg, 1899, 'Letter to Dedekind', in van Heijenoort

Carnap, Rudolf, 1932, 'The elimination of metaphysics through logical analysis of language', in Ayer, 1959

Cohen, Hermann, 1896, 'Introduction' to F.A. Lange's *History of Materialism*; repr. in *Neukantianismus*. Text ed. Ollig (Stuttgart, Reclam, 1982)

Davidson, Donald, 1984, *Truth and Interpretation* (Oxford, O.U.P.)

Deleuze, Gilles, 1988, *Le Pli* (Paris, P.U.F.)

Dews, Peter (ed.), 1986, *Autonomy and Solidarity. Interviews with Habermas* (London, Verso)

Dews, Peter, 1987, *Logics of Disintegration. Post-Structuralist Thought and the Claims of Critical Theory* (London, Verso)

Dummett, Michael, 1973, *Frege. Philosophy of Language* (London, Duckworth)

Dummett, Michael, 1975, 'The philosophical basis of intuitionistic logic', in Benacerraf and Putnam

Dunn, John, 1968, 'The identity of the history of ideas', reprinted in *Political Obligation in its Historical Context* (Cambridge, Cambridge University Press, 1980)

Eisler, Rudolf, 1930, *Kant-Lexikon* (repr. 1989: Hildesheim, Georg Olms)

Eley, Lothar, 1985, *Philosophie der Logik* (Darmstadt, Wissenschaftliche Buchgesellschaft)

Engels, Friedrich, 1894, *Herrn Eugen Dührings Umwälzung der Wissenschaft*, in Marx and Engels, 1978, vol. 20

Engels, Friedrich, 1946, *Ludwig Feuerbach and the End of Classical German Philosophy* (Moscow, Progress Publishers)

Felscher, Walter, 1986, 'Dialogues as a Foundation for Intuitionistic Logic', in Gabbay and Guenther (eds.), 1986

Fichte, Johann Gottlieb, 1969, *Ueber den Begriff der Wissenschaftslehre*

(1794). Grundlage der Gesammten Wissenschaftslehre (1794/95) Stu-
dientextausgabe (pagination and text = vol. I,2 of Fichte Gesamtaus-
gabe, ed. R. Lauth and H. Jacob) (Stuttgart-Bad Cannstatt, Frommann)

Förster, Eckart (ed.), 1989, *Kant's Transcendental Deductions* (Stanford,
Stanford U.P.)

Frege, Gottlob, 1879, *Begriffsschrift, eine der arithmetischen nachgebildete
Formelsprache des reinen Denkens* (Halle, 1879) (*BegrS*)

Frege, Gottlob, 1893, *Grundgesetze der Arithmetik*, vol I. (Jena, Pohle)
(*GGA*)

Frege, Gottlob, 1918, 'Der Gedanke. Eine logische Untersuchung' *Beiträge
zur Philosophie des deutschen Idealismus* 1 (1918/19), 58-77 (repr. Frege,
1976) (*Ged*)

Frege, Gottlob, 1892a, 'Über Sinn und Bedeutung', *Zeitschrift für Philosophie und philosophische Kritik*, N.F. 100 (1892), 25-50 (repr. Frege,
1962) (*SuB*)

Frege, Gottlob, 1892b, 'Über Begriff und Gegenstand', *Vierteljahrsschrift
für wissenschaftliche Philosophie* 16 (1892), 192-205 (repr. Frege, 1962)
(*BuG*)

Frege, Gottlob, 1891, *Funktion und Begriff*, Jena (repr. Frege, 1962)(*FuB*)

Frege, Gottlob, 1987, *Die Grundlagen der Arithmetik* (Stuttgart, Reclam)(*GA*)

Frege, Gottlob, 1976, *Logische Untersuchungen* ed. G. Patzig (Göttingen,
Vandenhoeck & Ruprecht)

Frege, Gottlob, 1980, *Philosophical and Mathematical Correspondence* ed.
G. Gabriel, H. Hermes, F. Kambartel, C. Thiel, A. Veraart; abr. B.
McGuinness, trans. H. Kaal (Chicago, University of Chicago Press)

Frege, Gottlob 1962, *Funktion, Begriff, Bedeutung* ed. G. Patzig (Göttingen, Vandenhoeck & Ruprecht)

Gabbay, G. and Guenther, F. (eds.), 1986, *Handbook of philosophical logic*
vol. 3 (Dordrecht, Reidel)

Gadamer, Hans-Georg, 1975, *Wahrheit und Methode. Grundzüge einer
philosophischen Hermeneutik* (Tübingen, J.C.B. Mohr)

Gasché, Rodolphe, 1986, *The Tain in the Mirror: Derrida and the Philosophy of Reflection* (Cambridge, Mass., Harvard University Press)

Geach, P.T., 1972, *Logic Matters* (Berkeley, University of California Press)

Gentzen, Gerhard, 1934, 'Untersuchungen über das logische Schließen', in
Mathematische Zeitschrift 39 (1934-35) pp. 176-210

Gerhardt: see Leibniz

German Philosophy: see Roberts

Geuss, Raymond, 1981, *The Idea of a Critical Theory. Habermas and the
Frankfurt School* (Cambridge, C.U.P.)

Gödel, Kurt, 1931, 'On formally undecidable propositions of *Principia*

Mathematica and related systems I', in van Heijenoort

Grayling, A.C., 1982, *An Introduction to Philosophical Logic* (Brighton, Harvester)

Haack, Susan, 1978, *Philosophy of Logics* (Cambridge, Cambridge University Press)

Habermas, Jürgen, 1969, *Protestbewegung und Hochschulreform* (Frankfurt/M, Suhrkamp)

Habermas, Jürgen, 1972, 'Wahrheitstheorien', in Habermas, 1984b

Habermas, Jürgen, 1973, *Erkenntnis und Interesse* (Frankfurt/M, Suhrkamp)(*EuI*)

Habermas, Jürgen, 1976, *Zur Rekonstruktion des historischen Materialismus* (Frankfurt/M, Suhrkamp)(*RhM*)

Habermas, Jürgen, 1981a, *Philosophisch-politische Profile* (Frankfurt/M, Suhrkamp)

Habermas, Jürgen, 1981b, *Theorie des kommunikativen Handelns* 2 vols (Frankfurt/M, Suhrkamp)(*TkH*)

Habermas, Jürgen, 1982a, *Zur Logik der Sozialwissenschaften* (Frankfurt/M, Suhrkamp)(*LS*)

Habermas, Jürgen, 1982b, 'A reply to my critics', in Thompson and Held

Habermas, Jurgen, 1984a, *Strukturwandel der Öffentlichkeit* (Darmstadt, Luchterhand)

Habermas, Jürgen, 1984b, *Vorstudien und Ergänzungen zur Theorie des kommunikativen Handelns* (Frankfurt/M, Suhrkamp)

Habermas, Jürgen, 1986, *Autonomy and Solidarity. Interviews with Jürgen Habermas* ed. P. Dews (London, Verso)

Habermas, Jürgen, 1988a, *Der philosophische Diskurs der Moderne* (Frankfurt/M, Suhrkamp)

Habermas, Jürgen, 1988b, *Nachmetaphysisches Denken* (Frankfurt/M, Suhrkamp)(*NmD*)

Hegel, G.W.F., 1971, *Werke in 20 Bänden* ed. E. Moldenhauer, K.M. Michel (Frankfurt/M, Suhrkamp)

Heidegger, Martin, 1976, *Sein und Zeit* (Tübingen, Niemeyer)(*SuZ*)

Henrich, Dieter, 1967, *Hegel im Kontext* (Frankfurt/M, Suhrkamp)

Henrich, Dieter, 1989, 'Kant's Notion of a Deduction and the Methodological Background of the First *Critique*', in Förster, 1989

Heyting, Arend, 1931, 'The intuitionist foundations of mathematics', in Benacerraf and Putnam

Heyting, Arend, 1956, 'Disputation', in Benacerraf and Putnam

Hilbert, David, 1904, 'On the foundations of logic and arithmetic', in van Heijenoort

Hilbert, David, 1925, 'On the infinite', in van Heijenoort

Hofstadter, Douglas, 1979, *Gödel, Escher, Bach* (London, Penguin)

Hollis, Martin, 1991, *Rationalität und soziales Verstehen* (Frankfurt/M, Suhrkamp)

Hollis, M. and Vossenkuhl, Wilhelm (eds.), 1992 *Moralische Entscheidung und rationale Wahl* (Munich, Oldenbourg)

Hollis, Martin, 1978, ['Say it with flowers'] in Tully and Skinner, 1988

Honderich, Ted, 1988, *A Theory of Determinism* (Oxford, Oxford University Press)

Hookway, Christopher, 1988, *Quine. Language, Experience and Reality* (Cambridge, Polity Press)

Hughes G.E. and Cresswell M.J., 1972, *An Introduction to Modal Logic* (London, Routledge)

Hume, David, 1975, *Enquiries concerning human understanding and concerning the principles of morals*, ed L.A. Selby-Bigge and P.H. Nidditch (Oxford, Clarendon)

Husserl, Edmund, 1922, *Ideen zu einer reinen Phänomenologie und phänomenologischen Philosophie* (Tübingen, Niemeyer)

Husserl, Edmund, 1931, *Ideas. General Introduction to Pure Phenomenology* (= *Ideen*) trans. W.R. Boyce Gibson (London, George Allen & Unwin)

Husserl, Edmund, 1980, *Logische Untersuchungen* vols. I, II/1, II/2 (Tübingen, Niemeyer)(*LU*)

Husserl, Edmund, 1982, *Die Krisis der europäischen Wissenschaften und die transzendentale Phänomenologie*, ed. E. Ströker (Hamburg, Meiner)

Husserl, Edmund, 1985, *Erfahrung und Urteil. Untersuchungen zur Genealogie der Logik*, ed. L. Landgrebe, L. Eley (Hamburg, Meiner)(*EuU*)

Husserl, Edmund, 1987, *Cartesianische Meditationen. Eine Einleitung in die Phänomenologie*, ed. E. Ströker (Hamburg, Meiner)(*CM*)

Hylton, Peter, 1984, 'The nature of the proposition and the revolt against idealism', in Rorty, Schneewind and Skinner, 1984

Hylton, Peter, 1990, *Russell, Idealism, and the Emergence of Analytical Philosophy* (Oxford, Clarendon)

Ingram, David, 1987, *Habermas and the Dialectic of Reason* (New Haven, Yale University Press)

Introduction: see Roberts

Kamlah, W. and Lorenzen, P., 1973, *Logische Propädeutik* (Mannheim, Bibliographisches Institut)

Kant, Immanuel *Gesammelte Schriften. Herausgegeben von der Königlich Preußischen Akademie der Wissenschaften* (= 'Akademieausgabe'; first nine vols repr. Berlin, 1968, de Gruyter). Kant citations to 'B' are, as standard in all editions and translations, to the second edition of the *Kritik der reinen Vernunft*.

Kneale W. and Kneale M., 1984, *The Development of Logic* (Oxford, Clarendon)

Koch, Anton Friedrich, 1990, *Subjektivität in Raum und Zeit* (Frankfurt/M, Klostermann)

Kreiser, L., Gottwald, S., Stelzner, W., 1988, *Nichtklassische Logik. Eine Einführung* (Berlin, Akademie-Verlag)

Kripke, S. 1975, 'Outline of a theory of truth', in Martin, 1984

Lange, F.A., 1974, *Geschichte des Materialismus und Kritik seiner Bedeutung in der Gegenwart* (Frankfurt/M, Suhrkamp)

Lawson, Hilary, 1985, *Reflexivity: the Post-Modern Predicament* (London, Hutchinson)

Leibniz, G.W., *Die philosophischen Schriften*, ed. C.J. Gerhardt, 7 vols, reprint of Berlin 1875 edition (Hildesheim & New York, Georg Olms Verlag)

Lemmon, E.J., 1965, *Beginning Logic* (Wokingham, Van Nostrand Reinhold)

Lessing, G.E., *Die Erziehung des Menschengeschlechts*, ed. Thielicke (Stuttgart, Reclam 1975)

Lewis, Charles, 1985, 'Kant and E.T.A. Hoffman: The Sandman', *Ideas and Production* 3

Lewis, D.K. 1973, *Counterfactuals* (Oxford, Blackwell)

Lorenzen, Paul, 1975, 'Logik', in *Konstruktive Logik, Ethik und Wissenschaftstheorie*, ed. Lorenzen P. and Schwemmer, O. (Mannheim, Bibliographisches Institut)

Lorenzen, Paul, 1978, *Theorie der technischen und politischen Vernunft* (Stuttgart, Reclam)(*TtpV*)

Lorenzen, Paul, 1960, 'Logik und Agon', in Lorenzen and Lorenz, 1978

Lorenzen, Paul, 1968, *Methodisches Denken* (Frankfurt/M, Suhrkamp)

Lorenzen, Paul and Lorenz, Kuno, 1978, *Dialogische Logik* (Darmstadt, Wissenschaftliche Buchgesellschaft)

Lorenzen, Paul, 1974, *Konstruktive Wissenschaftstheorie* (Frankfurt/M, Suhrkamp)(*KW*)

Lukács, Georg, 1973, *Die Zerstörung der Vernunft* (Darmstadt, Luchterhand)

McCarthy, T., Bohman, J., Baynes, K., 1987, *After Philosophy. End or Transformation?* (Cambridge, Mass., MIT Press)

McLean, Iain, 1987, *Public Choice. An Introduction* (Oxford, Blackwell)

McKeon, Richard, 1930, (editor and translator) *Selections from medieval philosophers*, 2 vols. (New York, Charles Scribner)

Martin, Robert L. (ed.), 1984, *Recent Essays on Truth and the Liar Paradox* (Oxford, Oxford University Press)

Marx, Karl and Engels, Friedrich, 1978, *Werke* (Berlin, Dietz) (= MEW)

Marx, Karl and Engels, Friedrich, 1846, *Die deutsche Ideologie*, in MEW, vol. 3

Mellor, D.H., 1984, *Real Time* (Cambridge, C.U.P.)

Meschkowski, Herbert, 1971, *Einführung in die moderne Mathematik* (Mannheim, Bibliographisches Institut)

Metschl, Ulrich, 1989a, *Über einige verwandte Möglichkeiten der Behandlung des Wahrheitsbegriffes* (Würzburg, Königshausen & Neumann)

Metschl, Ulrich, 1989b, 'Eine kleine Überraschung für Gehirne im Tank', *Zeitschrift für philosophische Forschung*, Band 43, 519-527

Nagel, Ernest and Newman, James R., 1958, *Gödel's Proof* (repr. 1989, London, Routledge)

Nietzsche, Friedrich, 1988, *Kritische Studienausgabe* in 15 vols. ed. Giorgio Colli and Mazzino Montinari (Berlin & Munich, de Gruyter & dtv)

Nietzsche, Friedrich, 1887a, *Morgenröthe*, in Nietzsche, 1988

Nietzsche, Friedrich, 1887b, *Die fröhliche Wissenschaft* in Nietzsche, 1988

Ollig, H.-L. (ed.), 1982, *Neukantianismus. Texte* (Stuttgart, Reclam)

O'Neill, Onora, 1989, *Constructions of Reason* (Cambridge, C.U.P)

Pippin, Robert B., 1989, *Hegel's Idealism. The Satisfactions of Self-Consciousness* (Cambridge, C.U.P.)

Putnam, Hilary 1980, 'Models and reality', in Benacerraf and Putnam

Quine, W.V., 1936, 'On the axiom of reducibility', *Mind*, vol. 45, pp. 498-500.

Quine, W.V., 1960, *Word and Object* (Cambridge, Mass., M.I.T. Press)

Quine, W.V., 1969, *Set Theory and its Logic* (Cambridge & London, Harvard U.P.)

Quine, W.V., 1973, *Mengenlehre und ihre Logik* (*Set Theory and its Logic*, trans. Anneliese Oberschelp) (Frankfurt, Ullstein)

Quine, W.V., 1974, *Methods of Logic* (London, RKP)

Quine, W.V., 1980, *From a Logical Point of View* (Cambridge Mass., Harvard U.P.)(*FLPV*)

Quine, W.V., 1981, *Mathematical Logic* (Cambridge Mass., Harvard U.P.)

Quine, W.V., 1986, *Philosophy of Logic* (Cambridge Mass., Harvard U.P.)

Reinhardt, Fritz and Soeder, Heinrich, 1974, *dtv-Atlas zur Mathematik* (München, dtv)

Reuter, Peter 1989, *Kants Theorie der Reflexionsbegriffe. Eine Untersuchung zum Amphiboliekapitel der Kritik der reinen Vernunft* (Würzburg, Königshausen & Neumann)

Rickert, Heinrich, 1928, *Der Gegenstand der Erkenntnis. Einführung in die Transzentalphilosophie* (Tübingen, J.C.B. Mohr)

Rickert, Heinrich, 1986, *Kulturwissenschaft und Naturwissenschaft*, ed. F. Vollhardt (Stuttgart, Reclam)

Roberts, Julian, 1979, 'German cultural criticism 1755-70 and its theoretical presuppositions' (PhD Diss, Cambridge University)

Roberts, Julian, 1982, *Walter Benjamin* (London, Macmillan)

Roberts, Julian, 1988, *German Philosophy. An Introduction* (Cambridge, Polity)

Rorty, Richard, 1980, *Philosophy and the Mirror of Nature* (Oxford, Blackwell)

Rorty R., Schneewind J.B., Skinner Q., 1984, *Philosophy in History. Essays on the historiography of philosophy* (Cambridge, C.U.P.)

Rosen, Michael, 1990, 'Modernism and the two traditions in philosophy', in Bell and Vossenkuhl, 1992

Russell, Bertrand, 1905, 'On Denoting', *Mind*, vol. 14, pp. 479-493

Russell, Bertrand, 1908, 'Mathematical logic as based on the theory of types', in van Heijenoort

Russell, Bertrand, 1973, *Essays in Analysis*, ed. D. Lackey (London, Allen & Unwin)

Russell, Bertrand, 1985, *The Principles of Mathematics* (London, George Allen & Unwin)

Schleiermacher, Friedrich, 1988, *Dialektik* ed. Rudolf Odebrecht (Darmstadt, Wissenschaftliche Buchgesellschaft)

Schmidt, Alfred, 1974, 'Einleitung' (Introduction) to Lange, 1974

Schulte, J., 1989, *Wittgenstein. Eine Einführung* (Stuttgart, Reclam)

Skolem, Thoralf, 1922, 'Some remarks on axiomatised set theory', in van Heijenoort

Sluga, Hans, 1984, 'Frege: the early years', in Rorty, Schneewind and Skinner, 1984

Stegmüller, Wolfgang, 1975, *Hauptströmungen der Gegenwartsphilosophie*, 2 vols., 5th ed. (Stuttgart, Kröner)

Strawson, P.F., 1950, 'On Referring', *Mind* n.s. vol. 59, 320-344.

Strawson, P.F., 1966, *The Bounds of Sense* (London, Methuen)

Strawson, P.F., 1974, *Subject and Predicate in Logic and Grammar* (London, Methuen)

Strawson, P.F., 1982, 'Logical Form and Logical Constants', *Jadavpur Studies in Philosophy* 4

Tennant, N.W., 1990, *Natural Logic* (Edinburgh, Edinburgh University Press)

Thomas-Putzo, 1990, *Zivilprozeßordnung* (Munich, C.H. Beck)

Thompson, John B., 1981 *Critical Hermeneutics: A Study in the Thought of Paul Ricoeur and Jürgen Habermas* (Cambridge, C.U.P)

Thompson, John B. and Held, David (eds.), 1982, *Habermas. Critical Debates* (London, Macmillan)

Tully, James and Skinner, Quentin, 1988, *Meaning and Context: Quentin Skinner and his Critics* (Cambridge, Polity)

Van Benthem, Johan, 1988, *A Manual of Intensional Logic* (Stanford, CSLI)

Van Benthem, Johan, 1990, 'General Dynamics' (to appear in *Theoretical Linguistics*, P.A. Luelsdorff (ed.), special issue on 'Complexity in Natural Language')

Van Dalen, Dirk, 1986, 'Intuitionistic Logic', in Gabbay and Guenther (eds.), 1986

Van Heijenoort, Jean, 1967, *From Frege to Gödel. A Source Book in Mathematical Logic, 1879-1931* (Cambridge Mass., Harvard U.P.)

Von Neumann, John, 1925, 'An axiomatisation of set theory', in van Heijenoort

Vossenkuhl, Wilhelm, 1982, *Anatomie des Sprachgebrauchs* (Stuttgart, Klett-Cotta)

Vossenkuhl, Wilhelm, 1986, 'Wilhelm von Ockham: Theologie und Philosophie', in Aicher, Greindl, Vossenkuhl, 1986

Vossenkuhl, Wilhelm, 1987, 'Rationale Überzeugungen', *Ratio*, vol. 29, no. 2

Vossenkuhl, Wilhelm, 1988, 'The Paradox in Kant's Rational Religion', *Proceedings of the Aristotelian Society* New Series, vol. 88

Vossenkuhl, Wilhelm, 1990a, 'Carnap's Penultimate System: The Aufbauprogram' in Bell and Vossenkuhl, 1992

Vossenkuhl, Wilhelm, 1990b, 'Schönheit als Symbol der Sittlichkeit. Über die gemeinsame Wurzel von Ethik und Ästhetik bei Kant', *Philosophisches Jahrbuch* 1992, I. Halbband

Vossenkuhl, Wilhelm, 1991, 'Vernünftige Wahl, rationale Dilemmas und moralische Konflikte', in Hollis und Vossenkuhl, 1992

Vossenkuhl, Wilhelm and Eva Schaper (eds.), 1989, *Reading Kant* (Oxford, Blackwell)

Walker, R.C.S., 1978, *Kant* (London, RKP)

Wellmer, Albrecht, 1986, *Ethik und Dialog. Elemente des moralischen Urteils bei Kant und in der Diskursethik* (Frankfurt/M, Suhrkamp)

Whitehead, A.N. and Russell, Bertrand, 1962, *Principia Mathematica* (Abridged paperback edition, to *56) (Cambridge, C.U.P.) (*PM*)

Windelband, Wilhelm, 1894, 'Geschichte und Naturwissenschaft', in Ollig

Wittgenstein, Ludwig, 1963, *Tractatus logico-philosophicus* (Frankfurt/M, Suhrkamp)

Wittgenstein, Ludwig, 1984, *Werkausgabe in 8 Bänden* (Frankfurt/M, Suhrkamp)

Wittgenstein, Ludwig *Über Gewißheit*, in Wittgenstein, 1984, vol. 8 (*ÜG*)

Wittgenstein, Ludwig, *Bemerkungen über die Grundlagen der Mathematik*, in Wittgenstein, 1984, vol. 6 (*BGM*)

Wittgenstein, Ludwig, *Wittgenstein und der Wiener Kreis. Gespräche, auf-*

gezeichnet von Friedrich Waismann, in Wittgenstein, 1984, vol. 3 (*WWK*)

Wittgenstein, Ludwig, *Philosophische Untersuchungen*, in Wittgenstein, 1984, vol.1 (*PU*)

Wittgenstein, Ludwig, 1972, *The Blue and Brown Books. Preliminary Studies for the 'Philosophical Investigations'* (Oxford, Blackwell)

Zermelo, Ernst, 1908, 'Investigations in the foundations of set theory I', in van Heijenoort

Index